I0114210

Forensic Neuropsychopathology

Clinical and Medical Insights into Brain-Behavior, Mental Disorders, and the Legal System

Understanding Neuropsychology, Neurophysiology, Neuroscience, Psychology, Psychiatry, and Law

Vol. 3

Monique M. Chouraeshkenazi, PhD, PsyD, MSCP
U.S. Air Force Combat Veteran

Contents

Foreword

By Dr. Judy Ho, PhD, ABPP, ABPdN
Triple-Board Certified Clinical & Forensic Neuropsychologist

Forensic Neuropsychopathology by scientist and scholar, Dr. Chouraeshkenazi, represents an ambitious and groundbreaking contribution to the intersection of neuroscience, psychology, and law. Across three volumes, she constructs a comprehensive framework for understanding how brain function, neurodevelopment, and psychopathology intersect with questions of criminal behavior, competency, and justice.

Volume 1 lays the theoretical foundation—introducing the field's origins, distinctions from traditional forensic psychology and neuropsychology, and its central mission to bridge neuroscience with legal decision-making. Volume 2 moves deeply into the application of neuropsychological evidence to legal questions of competency, responsibility, and the insanity defense, offering detailed analyses of landmark cases and the neurocognitive science that informs them. Volume 3 integrates ethical, legal, and professional practice issues—addressing the absence of formalized guidelines for this emerging specialty while articulating the standards, licensure pathways, and professional competencies needed to shape it as a recognized subdiscipline.

Dr. Chouraeshkenazi's voice is scholarly yet accessible, drawing from decades of military, clinical, and academic experience. Her synthesis of neurobiological science, psychological theory, and jurisprudence provides an invaluable resource for clinicians, forensic experts, attorneys, and policymakers seeking to navigate the complexities of brain-behavior relationships in the justice system.

Chapter 9:
Ethical and Legal Issues in Forensic Neuropsychopathology

Since there are currently no specific guidelines for forensic neuropsychopathology from the American Psychological Association or the American Psychiatric Association, professionals in this field should adhere to the established specialty guidelines for forensic psychology. Additionally, the *American Psychological Association Handbook of Forensic Neuropsychology* can serve as a guideline for forensic neuropsychopathology (Bush et al., 2017). The goal is for forensic neuropsychopathology to be recognized as a distinct clinical subdiscipline by both the American Psychiatric Association and the American Psychological Association. Therefore (and as mentioned in Chapter 1), all individuals working in or interested in this specialized area, particularly forensic neuropsychology and neuropsychopathology, will be referred to as "forensic professionals;" however, when directly concerned with the emerging field of forensic neuropsychopathology, those who want to pursue the emerging role will be referred to as "forensic neuropsychologist," ensuring consistency in practice while navigating the ethical and legal complexities of integrating neuropsychopathological evidence in the legal system.

The junction of neuropsychology and law has become an increasingly vital area of focus, particularly in forensic psychology. Understanding the brain and its impact on human behavior as it continues to expand, forensic professionals are playing an increasingly central role in legal cases that involve mental health, cognitive dysfunction, and neurological impairments.

Neuropsychopathological evidence can shed light on a range of issues within the legal system, such as an individual's competency to stand trial, criminal responsibility, the assessment of damages in civil cases, and the evaluation of mental health conditions in both criminal and civil contexts. Insights provided by neuropsychologists are invaluable for ensuring that decisions are based on accurate, scientifically grounded information, ultimately contributing to a fairer and more equitable legal process.

However, using neuropsychopathological evidence in the courtroom is not without challenges. Applying scientific principles within the legal system involves complex ethical, legal, and practical issues. These challenges are exacerbated by the adversarial nature of legal proceedings, where expert testimony is frequently scrutinized and contested by opposing parties. Forensic professionals must navigate this complex landscape, ensuring that assessments and testimony are scientifically sound and legally admissible. Adherence to stringent standards for the admissibility of evidence, which vary by jurisdiction, is necessary, as is maintaining objectivity, transparency, and impartiality in evaluations and testimony.

Licensure and certification are critical components of a forensic neuropsychopathologist's professional journey, and these requirements will be discussed in detail throughout this chapter. Aspiring professionals must undergo extensive education and training, including completing internships, postdoctoral programs, or residency programs, particularly in the field of clinical neuropsychology. Additionally, board certification through bodies such as the American Board of

Professional Psychology (ABPP), the American Board of Forensic Psychology (ABFP), and the American Board of Clinical Neuropsychology (ABCN) is a key milestone for those seeking to practice as forensic neuropsychologists (and emerging forensic neuropsychopathologists).

These certification processes ensure that professionals meet the highest standards of competence in both the neuropsychological and legal realms, preparing them for the challenges of providing expert testimony and making critical decisions in legal proceedings. Further discussion of these licensure and certification requirements will provide a comprehensive overview of the requirements for practicing in this specialized field.

This chapter examines the multifaceted role of forensic neuropsychopathologists within the legal system, with a focus on the ethical, legal, and practical challenges they face when providing expert testimony. Key standards that govern the admissibility of neuropsychopathological evidence are examined, along with strategies for navigating these frameworks to ensure that testimony is scientifically valid and legally relevant. Ethical considerations, including impartiality, transparency, and adherence to professional standards, are also emphasized. The legal ramifications of neuropsychological testimony, particularly in criminal cases, and the potential consequences for defendants and plaintiffs are discussed.

The chapter also explores the growing role of emerging technologies and diagnostic tools in neuropsychological assessments, as well as the evolving understanding of brain function and its relationship to behavior. Balancing cutting-edge scientific discoveries with the legal principles that govern the courtroom becomes increasingly essential as neuroscience advances. Integrating science and law requires neuropsychologists to remain flexible and adaptable, ensuring that the most accurate and reliable testimony is provided while maintaining ethical standards. This provides the necessary supervised training and experience to develop expertise in both the scientific and clinical aspects of neuropsychological assessment and intervention.

Ultimately, this chapter serves as a comprehensive guide for understanding the complexities of neuropsychological evidence in legal proceedings. It provides theoretical and practical insights into the role of forensic neuropsychologists, along with strategies for navigating the legal system, maintaining scientific rigor, and addressing the ethical considerations inherent in the work. By the end of this chapter, readers will gain a deeper understanding of the critical role neuropsychologists play in shaping legal outcomes and the importance of maintaining the integrity of neuropsychopathological evidence in the courtroom.

Integrating neuropsychopathological evidence into legal proceedings is not solely a matter of scientific accuracy and legal admissibility; it also involves a critical ethical dimension. Ethical considerations play a fundamental role in shaping the responsibilities of forensic neuropsychologists, particularly when their findings and testimony can significantly influence legal outcomes. The tension between scientific objectivity and the advocacy-driven nature of legal proceedings necessitates a careful balance of impartiality, transparency, and integrity. As expert witnesses, they provide scientifically valid assessments and ensure that their work upholds the profession's ethical standards. The following section examines the ethical challenges that arise when neuropsychologists interact with the legal system, including the principles and guidelines that govern their conduct, the potential for conflicts of interest, and their responsibility to ensure that their testimony serves the interests of justice rather than any particular party.

Purview of Ethics

No matter their interest or subdiscipline in psychology, any licensed or mental health professional, including graduate students, externs, interns, and residents who engage in clinical work and provide services, is bound by ethical standards and policies. As subdisciplines, forensic neuropsychology and forensic psychology require practitioners to uphold legal responsibilities and adhere to the ethical guidelines established by the American Psychological Association. This will be no different for forensic neuropsychopathology. These guidelines ensure that assessments, diagnoses, and expert testimony are conducted with integrity and scientific rigor. Also, practitioners must remain aware of potential biases and maintain objectivity when providing evaluations or opinions in legal settings.

While laws and regulations vary by state, the American Psychological Association's Ethical Principles of Psychologists and Code of Conduct provide a consistent framework for ethical practice. This Code includes an Introduction, Preamble, General Principles, and specific Ethical Standards. The Introduction outlines the Code's purpose, scope of application, and procedural considerations. The Preamble and General Principles serve as aspirational goals, encouraging psychologists to pursue the highest ethical standards. Though these principles are not enforceable, they are intended to guide psychologists in making sound ethical decisions.

To prevent confusion between the American Psychological Association and the American Psychiatric Association (by abbreviating to APA for this section), this section will refer to the organization's Ethical Principles of Psychologists and Code of Conduct as the "Code." Unlike the General Principles, the Code contains enforceable ethical standards that regulate the conduct of psychologists across various subdisciplines. These standards are intentionally broad to account for psychologists' diverse roles. Consequently, the interpretation and application of the standards may differ based on the psychologist's role. Notably, the standards are not exhaustive; situations not explicitly addressed in the Code may arise, but this absence does not inherently imply that such behavior is either ethical or unethical.

The Code applies to professionals who provide psychological services, conduct research, and assume other professional roles. Additionally, unlicensed individuals, including psychology students, postgraduates, and members of the American Psychological Association, must adhere to the Code and its associated enforcement policies. All psychologists and members must be familiar with these ethical standards, as ignorance or misunderstanding is not a defense for unethical conduct. Ethical competence requires continuous education and self-awareness to navigate complex situations. Violations of the Code can result in disciplinary actions, including sanctions, loss of licensure, or expulsion from professional organizations.

This section will provide a brief overview of the American Psychological Association's ethical principles, emphasizing the collective responsibility of professional psychologists and the organization's members to uphold these standards. While the General Principles offer broad ethical guidance, this discussion will primarily focus on the specialty guidelines specific to forensic psychology. Forensic professionals in psychology working within legal contexts must navigate the American Psychological Association's ethical standards and applicable legal regulations. By adhering to these principles and guidelines, psychologists can ensure ethical integrity and maintain public trust while contributing responsibly to the legal system.

Preamble

The Preamble of the Code affirms psychologists' commitment to advancing scientific and professional knowledge of behavior and improving the well-being of individuals, organizations, and society. It emphasizes the importance of respecting human rights and supporting the freedom of inquiry. While the Preamble is not enforceable, it serves as a foundational statement that reflects the APA's vision for ethical practice ("Ethical Principles of Psychologists and Code of Conduct," 2003). The primary purpose of the Code of Conduct is to offer specific standards that address the ethical challenges psychologists may encounter in their professional roles. Ultimately, these standards prioritize the protection and welfare of individuals and groups with whom psychologists work.

General Principles

The American Psychological Association's General Principles are aspirational goals that inspire psychologists to uphold the highest standards of ethical conduct. Although these principles are not enforceable and cannot serve as a basis for disciplinary actions, they offer valuable guidance for psychologists when making ethical decisions. The five General Principles include:

- **Principle A: Beneficence and Nonmaleficence**—Psychologists are encouraged to strive for the well-being of those they serve while taking deliberate care to avoid causing harm. This involves being aware of potential conflicts of interest, minimizing risks, and ensuring that their actions promote the welfare of both clients and research participants.
- **Principle B: Fidelity and Responsibility**—Psychologists must foster trust in their professional relationships. They should uphold ethical standards, accept responsibility for their behavior, and promote ethical conduct within the field. Additionally, they are encouraged to contribute to society through mentorship, community service, and peer collaboration.
- **Principle C: Integrity**—This principle requires psychologists to maintain honesty, transparency, and accuracy in all aspects of their work, including research, teaching, and clinical practice. While deception may be justified in certain research contexts, it must adhere to established ethical guidelines and be carefully managed to minimize potential harm.
- **Principle D: Justice**—Justice mandates fairness and equality in psychology. Psychologists must ensure their decisions, actions, and professional competencies do not result in unfair treatment or discrimination. They are responsible for recognizing and addressing biases that could impact their professional judgments.

- **Principle E: Respect for People's Rights and Dignity**— Psychologists must respect all individuals' rights, dignity, and autonomy. This includes maintaining confidentiality, obtaining informed consent, and recognizing the importance of cultural, individual, and role differences. Promoting a respectful and inclusive environment is fundamental to upholding this principle ("Ethical Principles of Psychologists and Code of Conduct," 2003).

The Code establishes enforceable standards that govern the behavior of psychologists. While the General Principles offer aspirational guidance, the specific standards are designed to be applied directly to professional conduct. These standards address various aspects of psychological practice, including confidentiality, informed consent, competence, and the appropriate use of assessment tools. By adhering to these standards, psychologists ensure that they engage in responsible and ethical practices, prioritizing the welfare and rights of those they serve.

Building upon ethical principles, psychologists in specialized fields are also expected to adhere to discipline-specific guidelines. Forensic psychology, which involves applying psychological expertise within legal settings, presents unique ethical and legal challenges. Recognizing these complexities, the American Psychological Association has established *Specialty Guidelines for Forensic Psychology* to provide further direction for practitioners. These guidelines address issues such as maintaining impartiality, managing dual relationships, and ensuring the accuracy and integrity of assessments. By adhering to these standards, forensic psychologists contribute to the fair administration of justice while upholding the profession's reputation and integrity.

The specialty guidelines outline the distinct responsibilities of forensic psychologists, including conducting psychological evaluations, providing expert testimony, and offering consultation in legal contexts. They emphasize maintaining impartiality, providing accurate and objective assessments, and understanding the potential impact of their work on legal outcomes. Forensic psychologists must also remain informed about jurisdictional laws while upholding the APA's ethical principles and professional standards. Additionally, they are encouraged to engage in ongoing education and training to stay current with advancements in the field and evolving legal standards.

The following section will explore the *Specialty Guidelines for Forensic Psychology* in greater detail, highlighting their role in ensuring ethical conduct, promoting fairness, and supporting the integrity of the legal system. By adhering to these guidelines, forensic psychologists contribute to the responsible application of psychological knowledge within legal and judicial processes. These standards also provide a framework for addressing ethical dilemmas that may arise in complex legal cases. Furthermore, they protect the rights of all parties by promoting transparency, accountability, and professional integrity.

Specialty Guidelines for Forensic Psychology

The specialty guidelines for forensic psychology are designed to ensure the provision of high-quality forensic services, foster the methodical development of the discipline, and encourage professionals to uphold excellence in their practice while respecting the rights of those they serve in the field. These guidelines serve as a resource for psychologists engaged in forensic practice, providing expectations and principles that will be further discussed in this section. By adhering to these guidelines, forensic psychologists can maintain professional integrity, minimize potential biases, and ensure that their work upholds ethical standards in complex legal settings. Furthermore, the guidelines help bridge the gap between psychological expertise and the legal system, ensuring that psychological assessments and testimony are reliable, relevant, and scientifically sound.

According to the American Psychological Association's Specialty Guidelines for Forensic Psychology (2011), the field encompasses the professional practice of any psychologist applying psychological principles to legal contexts. This applies across various sub-disciplines, including but not limited to clinical, developmental, social, and cognitive psychology. Forensic psychology involves the application of scientific, technical, or specialized psychological knowledge to legal, contractual, or administrative cases. These guidelines are not determined solely by a psychologist's area of expertise but rather by the nature of the service being provided within the legal system.

It is essential to clarify that psychological practice is not classified solely as forensic because responsibilities occur within an administrative, judicial, legislative, or tribunal forum. For instance, if an adult is court-ordered to undergo psychological treatment with a licensed psychologist, this treatment does not automatically constitute forensic practice. Additionally, testimony provided by a psychologist who provided the individual with the court-ordered treatment is based exclusively on the delivery of psychotherapy without offering psycho-legal opinions and is not typically considered forensic. Forensic practice explicitly involves the application of psychological expertise to legal matters, such as competency evaluations, risk assessments, and providing expert testimony on legal issues.

The Code serves as a foundational reference for these guidelines. While guidelines suggest or recommend specific professional behaviors and best practices, they differ from standards, which are mandatory and may carry enforceable consequences. Unlike standards, guidelines are aspirational, akin to the American Psychological Association's Preamble and General Principles. They are intended to support the ongoing professional development of forensic psychologists and promote a consistently high level of practice. However, they are not exhaustive and may not apply to every situation. Psychologists are encouraged to apply their professional judgment in determining how to interpret and implement these guidelines within their specific roles and responsibilities.

Background on the Specialty Guidelines for Forensic Psychology

The guidelines cover various ethical and professional considerations that forensic psychologists must navigate. These guidelines aim to ensure the competent, fair, and ethical application of psychological knowledge in legal contexts ("Specialty Guidelines for Forensic Psychology," 2011). They emphasize the importance of maintaining impartiality and objectivity when evaluating and providing testimony. Additionally, the guidelines emphasize the importance of forensic psychologists staying informed about the evolving legal landscape and advancements in psychological research. Ultimately, these guidelines help safeguard the integrity of the legal process while promoting the responsible use of psychological expertise.

- **Scope of Competence:** Forensic psychologists must practice within the boundaries of their expertise. Competence is established through appropriate education, training, supervised experience, and continued professional development.
- **Multiple Relationships:** Psychologists must avoid multiple relationships that could impair objectivity or create conflicts of interest. Engaging in dual roles, such as providing treatment and evaluation to the same individual (should be determined on a case-by-case basis), is generally discouraged in forensic practice. However, another example would be a psychologist accepting a student as a client for psychotherapy.
- **Therapeutic-Forensic Role Conflicts:** Practitioners should exercise caution when navigating between therapeutic and forensic roles. Providing forensic evaluations while maintaining a therapeutic relationship can introduce bias and compromise objectivity. As a result, if a psychologist is ordered to provide concurrent or sequential forensic and therapeutic services, there should be an acknowledgment of the potential harm or risks and reasonable efforts to give referrals.
- **Provision of Emergency Mental Health Services to Forensic Examinees:** In situations where a forensic examinee requires emergency mental health intervention, psychologists should act

appropriately to ensure the individual's safety, even if the psychologist's primary role is forensic evaluation.

- **Fees and Fee Arrangements:** Psychologists must establish transparent and fair fee arrangements. Financial matters should be addressed in writing, and psychologists should avoid contingency fees or any other agreements that could influence the objectivity of their evaluations.
- **Informed Consent, Notification, and Assent:** Psychologists must provide forensic examinees with clear and comprehensive information about the nature and purpose of evaluations, potential uses of information, and the limits of confidentiality.
- **Communication with Forensic Examinees:** Effective and transparent communication is essential. Forensic psychologists should ensure that examinees understand their rights, the evaluation process, and any potential consequences of their participation in the evaluation.
- **Persons Not Ordered or Mandated to Undergo Examination:** When an individual voluntarily participates in forensic evaluations, psychologists must ensure informed consent is obtained without coercion. However, if the individual declines to proceed with the examination once notified of its nature and purpose, the psychologist can choose to postpone, advise them to speak to their counsel, and inform the retaining party (e.g., the court) about the individual's refusal to proceed.

- **Persons Ordered or Mandated to Undergo Examination or Treatment:** If a court orders an individual to participate, the psychologist can examine their denial and consent. Therefore, if the individual declines to participate after being notified of the nature and purpose of the examination, the psychologist can postpone the examination, advise the individual to contact their attorney, and notify the retaining party of the refusal to participate. The psychologist should remain mindful of the ethical and legal distinctions between individuals who are court-ordered to participate and those who do so voluntarily.
- **Persons Lacking Capacity to Provide Informed Consent:** In cases where an individual is unable to provide informed consent, psychologists should take appropriate steps to obtain assent from the individual and consent from legally authorized representatives.
- **Privacy, Confidentiality, and Privilege:** Forensic psychologists must protect the privacy and confidentiality of information obtained during evaluations. They must also navigate legal and ethical considerations when courts or other parties request information.
- **Release of Information:** Psychologists must obtain proper authorization before releasing forensic information. They should comply with applicable laws and ethical standards regarding the disclosure of sensitive information.
- **Use of Case Materials in Teaching, Continuing Education, and Other Scholarly Activities:** Psychologists must safeguard individuals' privacy

by appropriately disguising identifying information when using case materials for educational purposes.

- **Assessment and Focus on Legally Relevant Factors:** Forensic evaluations must be conducted using empirically supported methods directly relevant to the legal questions. Psychologists should ensure their assessments are objective and avoid extraneous or prejudicial information.
- **Recordkeeping:** Accurate and thorough recordkeeping is essential in forensic practice. Psychologists are responsible for maintaining detailed and organized records in accordance with legal and ethical standards.
- **Professional and Other Public Communications:** Forensic psychologists must ensure that their public statements, including written reports and testimony, are truthful, accurate, and objective. Misrepresentation or misleading statements are strictly prohibited.
- **Out-of-Court Statements and Commenting on Legal Proceedings:** Psychologists must exercise caution when making public statements regarding ongoing legal proceedings. Commentary should remain objective and respectful of the judicial process ("Specialty Guidelines for Psychology," 2011).

These guidelines serve as a vital resource for maintaining the integrity and professionalism of forensic practice. By adhering to them, psychologists can ensure that their evaluations, testimony, and consultations remain objective, ethical, and legally sound. The principles foster accountability, protect the rights of individuals involved in legal processes, and support the administration of justice. Additionally, the guidelines emphasize the importance of continuous education and the application of evidence-based practices.

Forensic psychologists are encouraged to remain current with legal and psychological advancements, ensuring that their work reflects the field's highest standards. Ongoing supervision, peer consultation, and adherence to the Code and relevant legal standards further enhance ethical decision-making. Ultimately, the guidelines serve as a foundation for responsible forensic practice, striking a balance between the demands of the legal system and the ethical obligations of psychology. As the field evolves, forensic psychologists must remain vigilant in upholding these principles, demonstrating professional competence and a commitment to the fair and just application of psychological knowledge.

The guidelines play a critical role in maintaining the ethical integrity of the field. By adhering to these guidelines, forensic psychologists ensure their work is grounded in professional competence, impartiality, and respect for legal and ethical standards. These guidelines provide a comprehensive framework for navigating the complex interactions between psychology and the legal system. Through their commitment to these principles, forensic psychologists contribute to the responsible application of psychological knowledge in legal contexts, ultimately promoting justice and fairness. Continuous professional development and ethical vigilance are crucial for maintaining high standards in forensic practice, fostering public confidence in the profession, and ensuring the fair administration of justice.

Building upon the foundational principles outlined in the *Specialty Guidelines for Forensic Psychology*, it is important to consider the more specific ethical and legal challenges encountered within forensic neuropsychopathology. As this subspecialty involves assessing and evaluating cognitive and psychological functioning in legal contexts, practitioners must navigate intricate issues related to confidentiality, consent, and the complexities of their dual roles. Further, they must carefully balance their responsibility to provide accurate assessments while maintaining ethical boundaries in situations where their findings may significantly impact legal decisions. Practical communication skills are also crucial, as practitioners must present their evaluations clearly and understandably to legal professionals and courts.

Additionally, building on the core principles outlined in the Specialty Guidelines for Forensic Psychology, it is essential to address the ethical and legal challenges that forensic neuropsychopathologists face. This subspecialty, which involves assessing cognitive and psychological functioning in legal settings, requires practitioners to carefully navigate issues such as confidentiality, consent, and the complexities of their dual roles. Forensic neuropsychopathologists must strike a balance between providing accurate assessments and maintaining ethical boundaries, especially when their findings may significantly influence legal decisions.

Strong communication skills are also essential, as they must present their evaluations clearly and comprehensively to legal professionals and courts. Alongside these ethical considerations, licensure and certification requirements are essential in ensuring that practitioners possess the necessary qualifications and expertise to provide reliable, legally admissible neuropsychological evaluations. The following section will examine the licensure, certification, and professional development pathways required to practice forensic neuropsychopathology, emphasizing the importance of adhering to these standards to maintain both ethical and legal integrity.

Licensure and Certification

Becoming a licensed forensic psychologist, forensic neuropsychologist, or forensic neuropsychopathologist involves meeting various educational and professional requirements, which may vary by state. Both types of professionals can work in a wide range of settings, including academic institutions, criminal trials (e.g., competency to stand trial and insanity defense), government agencies, hospitals, independent/private practice, insurance companies, jails/prisons, laboratories, law enforcement agencies (e.g., fitness for duty evaluations), law offices (in areas such as criminal defense, medical malpractice, personal injury, product liability, and workers' compensation), mental health clinics, and research institutions. In addition, however, forensic neuropsychopathologists specialize in areas such as clinical psychopharmacology, medical psychology, neuropsychology, neuroscience, and research, which requires further expertise in these disciplines.

The educational path to becoming a forensic neuropsychopathologist begins with obtaining an undergraduate degree, ideally in criminal justice, psychology, or a closely related field. Some academic institutions offer specialized bachelor's programs in forensic psychology, providing foundational knowledge in clinical forensic neuropsychology. Core topics in these programs typically cover clinical neuropsychology, forensic assessment, criminal law frameworks, criminal profiling, ethics in forensic psychology, neuropsychopathological evaluation and assessment, investigative psychology, police psychology, and the legal system, among others. This curriculum prepares students for graduate education and practical experience in forensic neuropsychology.

After completing an undergraduate degree, aspiring forensic neuropsychopathologists must pursue graduate education, which typically involves two programs: a master's degree in forensic psychology or a related field, followed by a doctoral program (Chouraeshkenazi, 2024b). The doctoral program is necessary for licensure and independent practice and can be obtained through either a Doctor of Philosophy (PhD) or Doctor of Psychology (PsyD) degree. The PhD program strongly emphasizes research and scientific inquiry, whereas the PsyD degree focuses on clinical practice and experiential training (Chouraeshkenazi, 2024b). Both degrees prepare students for licensure but differ in their educational approaches. Prospects should review their state's specific requirements to ensure their chosen program aligns with licensure criteria.

However, forensic neuropsychopathology differs from forensic psychology, as it requires components of neuropsychology and a background in neuroscience, psychopathology, neuroanatomy, and some aspects of medicine. An individual who wants to practice independently in neuropsychology or neuropsychopathology must complete a neuropsychology-focused internship, postdoctoral program, or residency program. Most postdoctoral and residency programs must be at least two years in duration to ensure the individual is effectively trained to practice in the field and claim the title of "neuropsychologist." However, this is based on various requirements by states, psychological organizations, and board certifications for licensure requirements. This specialized training is essential for individuals aiming to work in neuropsychology or neuropsychopathology, as it provides the in-depth expertise necessary to work with "neurodisorders" within the context of the legal system.

In addition to the educational and clinical requirements, emerging forensic neuropsychopathologists may also choose to pursue board certification. Suppose an individual wants to become board-certified in both forensic and neuropsychology (or neuropsychopathology). In that case, they must obtain certification through both the American Board of Forensic Psychology (ABFP) and the American Board of Clinical Neuropsychology. As a result, an individual may be double-board-certified or even triple-certified if they also choose to pursue board certification in clinical psychology (with the American Board of Clinical Psychology). This advanced credentialing demonstrates the clinician's specialized expertise in multiple areas, enhancing their qualifications in the field.

Furthermore, in addition to academic qualifications, aspiring forensic psychologists and neuropsychopathologists must meet other professional requirements, such as completing clinical hours under supervision, passing the Examination for Professional Practice in Psychology (EPPP), and, in some cases, taking additional exams related to state ethics or jurisprudence (Chouraeshkenazi, 2024b). In certain states, there are extra steps beyond completing one or more degrees and obtaining licensure. For example, some states require prospective forensic neuropsychopathologists to pass a jurisprudence or state ethics examination. Therefore, it is essential to consult the respective state's requirements where you plan to practice.

Any clinical professional in psychology must periodically renew their licensure to remain in good standing with their respective states. This process also typically involves completing continuing education (CE) credits, with CE and renewal requirements varying by state (Chouraeshkenazi, 2024b). Interestingly, many states have reciprocity agreements, offering opportunities for mobility. According to the American Board of Professional Psychology (ABPP), 26 states have agreements in place that allow licensed psychologists to practice in multiple jurisdictions without obtaining new credentials (Clay, 2021). However, becoming a forensic psychologist and later relocating to a state that does not recognize your existing license is possible. In such cases, you would need to apply for licensure in the new state, which may involve additional coursework, supervised clinical hours, and/or training to meet the new state's requirements.

The path to becoming a licensed forensic psychologist, forensic neuropsychologist, or forensic neuropsychologist involves rigorous academic and clinical training, adherence to state-specific licensure requirements, and, in some cases, obtaining board certification to practice independently. Both professionals have diverse career opportunities in settings ranging from criminal trials to research institutions, and they specialize in areas that require advanced knowledge of neuropsychology, neuroscience, and the legal system. Moreover, licensed forensic psychologists must maintain their credentials by completing periodic renewals and continuing education, with mobility across states facilitated by reciprocity agreements in many jurisdictions. However, relocating to a state that does not recognize one's license may require additional steps to obtain licensure in the new state. Aspiring forensic neuropsychopathologists must also complete specialized training in neuropsychology and may pursue double or triple board certifications to enhance their professional qualifications.

Ethical and Legal Issues in Forensic Neuropsychopathology

Emerging practitioners in forensic neuropsychopathology are tasked with evaluating cognitive and psychological functions to offer objective, evidence-based findings that can inform judicial decisions. The role is complex, requiring them to adhere to stringent ethical standards and legal requirements to ensure that their evaluations are accurate and fair. One of the primary ethical considerations in forensic neuropsychopathology is confidentiality. While confidentiality is a cornerstone of psychological practice, it becomes more nuanced in forensic settings, where the results of evaluations may be shared with third parties, such as lawyers or courts.

Forensic professionals must clearly explain the limits of confidentiality to individuals being evaluated and inform them that their findings may be disclosed in legal proceedings. Another crucial ethical issue is obtaining informed consent. In forensic contexts, individuals may be coerced or feel pressured to undergo evaluations, which can complicate the process of ensuring that consent is fully informed and voluntary. Practitioners must ensure that individuals understand the purpose, nature, and potential consequences of the evaluation, especially when it is court-ordered. Additionally, clinical professionals in forensic settings often serve as expert witnesses, with the responsibility of providing objective and impartial testimony. They must base their findings on scientifically supported neuropsychological principles and avoid bias or advocacy for the party that hired them.

The dual roles that forensic neuropsychologists sometimes face (and forensic neuropsychopathologists will face)—being both evaluators and therapists—can create ethical conflicts of interest. When neuropsychologists are asked to evaluate and treat an individual, it may undermine the neutrality of the evaluation, especially if the individual perceives the evaluation as part of a therapeutic relationship. To avoid such conflicts, they must communicate the scope and purpose of their role and, when necessary, refer individuals to other professionals to maintain objectivity. Transparent communication is essential, and individuals should understand that an evaluation for legal purposes is distinct from any therapeutic intervention.

The broader legal landscape in which forensic professionals operate is also critical to their practice. Legal standards for the admissibility of expert testimony, such as the Frye and Daubert tests (which will be discussed later in the chapter), require that the methods used by forensic professionals be scientifically valid and widely accepted within the relevant scientific community. They must ensure that their evaluations adhere to these standards and that their findings are accepted in court. Forensic professionals may assess defendants for competency to stand trial, criminal responsibility, or the impact of brain injury on behavior in criminal cases. In civil cases, their evaluations may inform decisions on personal injury, disability claims, or custody disputes. Regardless of the type of case, neuropsychologists must remain impartial, providing clear and concise testimony that is free from bias toward any party involved in the case.

Forensic professionals must be aware of their legal liabilities and ethical responsibilities. Failure to conduct thorough, unbiased evaluations or accurately report findings can lead to malpractice claims or legal consequences. They are ethically obligated to report any findings that suggest abuse, neglect, or other illegal activities, even if these findings are not favorable to the parties involved. To protect themselves, neuropsychologists should maintain detailed records of all assessments and consultations and seek legal counsel when faced with ethical or legal dilemmas.

Forensic neuropsychopathology requires practitioners to navigate a complex landscape of ethical and legal challenges. By upholding rigorous standards of confidentiality, informed consent, impartiality, and professional responsibility, forensic professionals can make meaningful contributions to the legal system, ensuring that scientifically valid and unbiased evaluations inform judicial decisions. This commitment not only provides the fairness and integrity of legal proceedings but also enhances the credibility of neuropsychological assessments in the eyes of the court. Furthermore, it fosters trust between neuropsychologists and the legal system, reinforcing the critical role that objective psychological evaluations play in achieving justice. By adhering to these ethical and professional standards, neuropsychologists can safeguard the integrity of their practice and the individuals they evaluate.

As forensic professionals navigate the complex relationship between psychology and law, it is critical to know and comprehend the ethical principles that guide their practice. The integrity of neuropsychopathological evaluations depends not only on the accuracy of the assessments but also on the ethical framework within which they are conducted. Adhering to ethical standards, such as confidentiality, informed consent, and impartiality, ensures that evaluations are both scientifically sound and ethically responsible. In this context, understanding the ethics of neuropsychopathological evaluation is crucial, as it directly influences the quality and fairness of the findings presented in legal cases. This next section will delve deeper into the ethical considerations that shape neuropsychological evaluations, highlighting their importance in both clinical and forensic settings.

Ethics in the Neuropsychopathology Evaluation

Neuropsychopathological evaluations are central to forensic neuropsychology, where integrating psychological and neurological insights is crucial in legal decision-making. Ethical considerations in these evaluations are fundamental to ensuring the process remains scientifically rigorous and professionally responsible. These evaluations must be conducted with a keen awareness of confidentiality, informed consent, and the responsibilities tied to the role of an expert witness. The delicate balance of maintaining objectivity and managing dual roles further complicates the ethical landscape, requiring neuropsychologists to carefully navigate these challenges to preserve the integrity of their assessments and the legal process.

Confidentiality, Informed Consent, and the Role of the Expert Witness

Confidentiality is a cornerstone of neuropsychology and is essential to building a trusting relationship between the practitioner and the client. Confidentiality ensures that sensitive personal information is protected in clinical settings, thereby fostering a safe environment in which individuals can share their concerns. However, in forensic settings, confidentiality becomes more complex due to the legal nature of the evaluation. Forensic professionals must clearly explain the limits of confidentiality from the outset of the evaluation. Clients must be informed that the assessment results may be shared with third parties, such as attorneys, courts, or judges, as required by law or as necessary for the assessment.

Sometimes, information that is typically protected may be disclosed to assist in legal proceedings. This is particularly important when the evaluation is court-ordered, as the information may directly affect the legal outcomes, such as sentencing, competency evaluations, or custody decisions. Clear communication of these limitations ensures that clients fully understand the implications of their participation, including the potential consequences, such as the possibility that their evaluation results may be used in court. Neuropsychologists should document the disclosure of confidentiality limits to avoid misunderstandings and ensure ethical transparency.

Informed consent is another foundational ethical principle, particularly in forensic neuropsychology (and psychology), where the evaluation's purpose and procedures must be communicated clearly to the client. Before conducting an evaluation, forensic professionals must clearly explain the scope of the evaluation, the specific tests and assessments to be administered, and how the results will be utilized, particularly within the context of the law. Clients must understand that, while they may have some rights to withdraw from a typical clinical evaluation, the court often requires participation in a forensic evaluation, and refusal may have legal consequences. This distinction is crucial because individuals involved in legal cases may feel compelled to undergo the evaluation, even if they do not fully understand the purpose or consequences.

Ensuring informed consent safeguards the client's autonomy and protects the integrity of the evaluation. The consent process should be documented, with the client explicitly acknowledging that they understand their rights, including the potential use of their information in the legal system. Forensic professionals should also assess whether the individual can give informed consent, particularly when mental illness or other cognitive impairments may interfere with their decision-making capacity. In cases where cognitive impairments or mental illness are present, neuropsychologists must carefully evaluate the individual's capacity to understand the information provided and make decisions about their participation in the evaluation. Suppose there is doubt regarding the individual's ability to give informed consent. In that case, the neuropsychologist should involve a legal guardian, advocate, or other appropriate third party to ensure the individual's rights are upheld.

The role of the expert witness introduces an additional layer of complexity in forensic neuropsychology, where practitioners must shift from a therapeutic mindset to one of impartiality and objectivity. Forensic professionals often serve as expert witnesses, providing specialized knowledge to the court and helping legal professionals understand complex psychological and neurological issues. When acting in this capacity, neuropsychologists must maintain strict objectivity. Their primary responsibility is not to advocate for the party that hired them but to provide scientifically grounded, unbiased testimony that assists the court in making informed decisions. This commitment to impartiality ensures that the neuropsychologist's evaluations and testimony are seen as credible and reliable, contributing to a fair legal process.

Forensic professionals must ensure that their testimony is based on well-established, evidence-based neuropsychological methods and that their conclusions are rooted in data obtained through comprehensive evaluations. The role of the expert witness is not to offer personal opinions or engage in speculation but to convey the facts in a clear and accessible manner. Neuropsychologists should be transparent about their methods, discussing the tests administered, the rationale behind their selection, and the limitations of their findings. Additionally, they must avoid overstating their conclusions, recognizing the inherent uncertainty and variability in neuropsychological assessments. This transparency enables the court to evaluate the validity and reliability of the testimony, ensuring that legal decisions are based on credible, scientifically sound information.

While serving as an expert witness, forensic professionals must also navigate the potential for conflicting interests. The legal system often requires neuropsychologists to present their findings in adversarial settings, where opposing parties may interpret the same evidence differently. In such situations, forensic professionals should strive to uphold ethical standards by focusing solely on the facts of the case and the integrity of their professional opinions. They must resist any temptation to align their testimony with the interests of the party that retained them, as doing so could undermine the fairness and accuracy of the judicial process. In this context, the role of the expert witness is to contribute to the legal process by offering objective, scientifically validated assessments that can guide decision-making in a fair and informed manner. Neuropsychologists must also be prepared to face cross-examination, where their methods' objectivity and reliability will be scrutinized. This highlights the importance of thorough documentation, adherence to ethical guidelines, and a clear commitment to providing the most accurate and unbiased testimony possible.

The Challenge of Dual Roles (Evaluator vs. Treatment Provider)

The potential for dual roles in forensic neuropsychopathology (or neuropsychology)—where the same practitioner serves as both an evaluator and a treatment provider—poses one of the most significant ethical challenges in the field. These dual roles can create inherent conflicts of interest, undermining the objectivity and impartiality necessary for valid forensic evaluations. Forensic professionals must remain neutral, providing assessments based on scientifically validated methods and objective data without any influence from therapeutic relationships or personal biases. This ensures that their findings remain impartial and solely focused on the legal questions.

However, when a forensic professional serves as the treating clinician for the same individual, it becomes more challenging to maintain that neutrality. Clients may perceive the evaluation as influenced by the prior treatment experience or believe the findings will be skewed in favor of the treatment goals rather than the legal inquiry. This can not only jeopardize the integrity of the evaluation but also raise ethical questions about the fairness and validity of the assessment in legal contexts, potentially undermining the credibility of the forensic professional's testimony and the overall legal process.

In addition to the risk of bias, dual roles can confuse the client, particularly in legal cases where the evaluation may have direct implications for sentencing, custody, or other significant outcomes. When individuals undergo treatment, they often expect the forensic professional to act in their best interests, providing care, guidance, and support. In contrast, the role of the evaluator is distinctly different—focused on providing an objective, evidence-based analysis without regard to the client's personal welfare or therapeutic goals. This tension can create ethical and emotional challenges for both the neuropsychologist and the client, as the individual may struggle to understand the purpose of the evaluation within the context of their ongoing treatment.

Forensic professionals must clearly define their roles from the outset to address these concerns. This includes informing the client that the evaluation is separate from any therapeutic work and that its primary purpose is to provide the court with objective insights. Clear communication about the evaluation's scope, limits, and nature helps ensure the client understands the distinction between treatment and forensic evaluation. This transparency is critical to establishing trust and preventing misunderstandings. Forensic professionals should also consider the timing and setting of the evaluation, ensuring that the client is not undergoing an evaluation while simultaneously receiving treatment from the same clinician. If a forensic professional has treated a client and then is asked to conduct a forensic evaluation, referring the client to another professional is often the best practice to avoid any conflict of interest.

When dual roles are unavoidable, forensic professionals should ensure proper safeguards are in place to maintain the integrity of the therapeutic and evaluative processes. One such safeguard is referring clients to independent professionals for either treatment or evaluation, as this separation helps preserve the objectivity of the evaluation and prevents potential bias. For example, if a forensic professional is already providing treatment to an individual, they should not conduct the forensic evaluation related to that same case. Similarly, if an evaluation is necessary, the forensic professional should refrain from providing treatment unless explicitly warranted by the situation and should have in place appropriate safeguards to ensure an unbiased evaluation. Referring to another professional helps prevent ethical dilemmas and maintains the credibility of the evaluation.

Additionally, neuropsychologists should establish clear professional boundaries in all interactions with clients and other professionals involved in the case. This includes establishing written agreements that outline specific roles and expectations, as well as discussing any potential conflicts of interest upfront. By setting these boundaries, neuropsychologists minimize the risk of ethical concerns and ensure that their work is transparent and unbiased, thereby fostering trust among all parties involved and maintaining the integrity of the evaluation process.

Forensic professionals should seek supervision or consultation in particularly challenging cases where dual roles may create conflicts. Peer consultation offers a valuable opportunity to discuss complex situations and receive guidance from colleagues who have experience managing dual roles in forensic contexts. This ensures that forensic professionals make ethically sound decisions and adhere to best practices. Supervisors and experienced colleagues can offer insight into handling dual role situations, whether by recommending referrals, suggesting alternative approaches, or helping to identify potential ethical pitfalls. Regular supervision is essential for maintaining high professional standards and can serve as an ethical safeguard when navigating challenging cases.

Managing dual roles in forensic neuropsychopathology requires vigilance, transparency, and an unwavering commitment to ethical standards. By maintaining clear boundaries, seeking supervision, and making appropriate referrals, neuropsychologists can navigate the complex ethical terrain of dual roles and protect the integrity of the therapeutic and evaluative processes. Such practices help ensure the validity of their evaluations and safeguard the trust placed in them by clients, the legal system, and the broader community. They also minimize the risk of conflicts of interest that could compromise the objectivity of their assessments.

As forensic professionals navigate the complex ethical and professional landscape of forensic evaluations, the next crucial step is understanding how their findings are utilized within the legal system. Using neuropsychopathological evidence in court requires a thorough and objective evaluation and a deep understanding of how these evaluations are interpreted and weighed in legal proceedings. Neuropsychopathological evaluations and assessments can provide invaluable insights into cognitive functioning, mental health, and behavior, offering critical information that can impact legal outcomes such as sentencing, competency, or criminal responsibility. However, accepting such evidence in court involves meeting rigorous standards of scientific validity, ensuring that forensic professionals' findings are relevant but also credible and reliable in the eyes of the law. This section will examine how neuropsychological evidence is presented in court, the admissibility standards, and the responsibilities of neuropsychologists in ensuring that their testimony contributes meaningfully to the judicial process.

The Use of Neuropsychopathological Evidence in Court

Neuropsychopathological evidence has become increasingly important in the courtroom, especially in cases where cognitive functioning, neurological impairments, or mental health issues are central to the legal matters at hand. This evidence can profoundly influence judicial decisions, impacting critical legal issues such as criminal responsibility, competency to stand trial, sentencing, custody, and personal injury claims. For neuropsychologists, however, providing such evidence is not a straightforward process. Strict legal and scientific criteria govern the admission of neuropsychological testimony in court to ensure that it is both relevant and reliable.

Forensic professionals must meet these criteria when serving as expert witnesses, presenting their findings in a manner that is both scientifically grounded and legally admissible. The standards for the admissibility of neuropsychological testimony are primarily shaped by the Daubert Standard and the Frye Test, and neuropsychologists must navigate these frameworks carefully to ensure their testimony holds up in the legal context. Additionally, neuropsychologists are expected to maintain a critical role as expert witnesses, ensuring their evaluations are objective, transparent, and comprehensible to the court.

Admissibility of Neuropsychopathological Testimony

For neuropsychopathological testimony to be admitted in court, it must meet specific criteria that ensure the evidence is scientifically valid and legally relevant. In the United States, courts typically rely on two standards for determining the admissibility of scientific testimony: the Daubert Standard and the Frye Test. These standards provide different approaches to evaluating the reliability and relevance of expert testimony, and neuropsychologists must be familiar with both to ensure that their testimony is considered valid and credible. Additionally, understanding the specific legal requirements of the jurisdiction where the case is being heard is crucial, as different courts may apply these standards in varying ways.

The Daubert Standard is the most widely used standard for determining the admissibility of expert testimony in federal courts and many state courts. The U.S. Supreme Court established the Daubert Standard in the 1993 case *Daubert v. Merrell Dow Pharmaceuticals, Inc.*, which held that the trial judge serves as a "gatekeeper" to determine whether the scientific evidence presented is relevant and reliable ("Rule 702. Testimony by Expert Witness," n.d.). The judge must evaluate the scientific basis of the expert's testimony, ensuring that it is grounded in scientifically valid methodologies and relevant to the issues at hand.

The Daubert decision established five primary factors that judges should consider when assessing the admissibility of scientific testimony:

1. **Testability**: The scientific theory or technique used must be capable of being tested and falsified. For neuropsychologists (or neuropsychopathologists), the evaluation methods, such as cognitive tests or neuroimaging tools, must effectively measure what they are intended to assess. These tests must have undergone empirical validation, demonstrating their ability to produce consistent and reliable results when applied to individuals with similar characteristics.

2. **Peer Review and Publication**: The methods and tools used in neuropsychopathological evaluations must have undergone peer review and be published in reputable scientific journals. This factor emphasizes the importance of using well-established, empirically validated neuropsychological tools, such as the WAIS (i.e., Wechsler Adult Intelligence Scale) or the Bender Visual Motor Gestalt Test, which have been extensively studied and critiqued by experts in the field.

3. **Error Rate**: The neuropsychologist (or neuropsychopathologist) must provide information about the error rate associated with the assessment tools. The expert must explain the potential margin of error in their findings and how these limitations

may affect the interpretation of the results. For example, cognitive testing may have a specific error rate, particularly when the individual being evaluated has severe neurological impairments or comorbid mental health conditions.

4. **General Acceptance**: Although the general acceptance of a method is not a strict requirement under Daubert, it remains a key consideration in evaluating scientific validity. The methods used in the neuropsychological evaluation should be widely accepted within the scientific community. Tools like the WAIS and the MMPI (Minnesota Multiphasic Personality Inventory) are examples of neuropsychological assessments that are widely used and accepted by professionals in the field.
5. **Reliability**: The technique or method used must produce consistent and reliable results. Neuropsychological tests must be stable and reliable, yielding consistent results across different evaluators and contexts. This reliability ensures that the conclusions drawn from the assessment are trustworthy and reproducible ("Rule 702. Testimony by Expert Witness," n.d.). Without such reliability, the validity of the assessment would be compromised, potentially leading to misdiagnoses or inaccurate conclusions about an individual's cognitive functioning.

By meeting these criteria, forensic professionals can increase the likelihood that their testimony will be admitted under the Daubert Standard. However, they must also be prepared to demonstrate that their methods and conclusions are scientifically valid and based on well-established research. This includes providing evidence of the reliability and validity of the assessment tools used and articulating how these methods have been peer-reviewed and accepted within the scientific community. Additionally, neuropsychologists should be ready to defend their findings and methodologies against potential challenges from opposing counsel, ensuring that their testimony remains credible and objective throughout the legal proceedings.

The Frye Test predates the Daubert decision and is still used in some jurisdictions, particularly in older legal cases. In *Frye v. United States* (1923), the U.S. Court of Appeals held that scientific evidence is admissible only if the methods or techniques used are "generally accepted" by the relevant scientific community ("Frye Standard," n.d.). The Frye standard does not require that the methods be peer-reviewed or tested for error rates; instead, it focuses on whether experts in the field widely accept the techniques employed. This means that even if a process is not extensively tested or published, it may still be admissible in court if it is generally recognized and endorsed by professionals within the relevant discipline.

Under the Frye Test, forensic professionals must demonstrate that a broad consensus of neuropsychology professionals accepts the tools and techniques used in their evaluations. For example, suppose forensic professionals use a relatively new cognitive test or a novel neuroimaging technique. In that case, they may face challenges in demonstrating that the scientific community accepts these methods as valid. In contrast, established tests and techniques, such as the Wechsler scales, are generally accepted and widely used, which makes them more likely to meet the Frye standard. While the Frye Test remains relevant in certain jurisdictions, its use is less common than the Daubert Standard, which is more detailed in evaluating scientific methods.

The Role of Neuropsychologists as Expert Witnesses

When forensic professionals serve as expert witnesses, their role differs from their clinical work. Instead of providing treatment or therapy, their primary function is to assist the court by offering expert knowledge regarding the psychological and cognitive functioning of the individual involved in the case. Forensic professionals are tasked with providing clear, objective, and scientifically grounded opinions based on their evaluations. They must also be prepared to explain complex neuropsychopathological concepts in a way that is accessible to judges, juries, and attorneys. Additionally, their testimony should be impartial and evidence-based, ensuring that it accurately represents the findings of their assessments without bias or advocacy for either side.

A forensic professional's primary ethical responsibility as an expert witness is to remain impartial. Unlike in clinical settings, the former's goal is to help the individual, while the latter must offer an unbiased opinion based solely on the scientific evidence obtained during the evaluation. The forensic professional must not advocate for any party involved in the case, as their role is to assist the court, not to support one side over the other. This requires maintaining professional detachment and ensuring their conclusions are transparent and well-supported by objective data. By adhering to these principles, neuropsychologists contribute to the integrity of the legal process, providing courts with reliable information to make informed decisions.

To maintain objectivity, the forensic professional must avoid becoming emotionally involved in the case and refrain from making statements that could favor one party over another. Their testimony should focus solely on the facts, objectively analyzing the individual's cognitive and psychological state rather than speculating on their motivations, character, legal guilt, or innocence. Additionally, forensic professionals should clearly distinguish between their opinions and assessment limitations, acknowledging areas where data may be inconclusive. By doing so, they uphold the ethical standards of their role and ensure that their contributions remain a credible and impartial resource for the court.

Another critical skill for expert witnesses is communicating complex neuropsychological and pathological concepts to non-expert audiences. Judges, jurors, and attorneys may not have a thorough understanding of neuropsychology or neuropsychopathology; therefore, forensic professionals must explain their methods, results, and conclusions in simple, understandable terms. They must be able to break down the findings from complex cognitive tests and neuroimaging data into accessible language while maintaining the scientific integrity of their conclusions. Additionally, forensic professionals should anticipate questions and challenges to their testimony and provide clear, evidence-based explanations that withstand scrutiny. Effective communication enhances the court's understanding and strengthens the credibility of the expert's findings.

For instance, if a forensic professional is called to testify about an individual's competency to stand trial, they must explain how their cognitive deficits affect their ability to understand the charges, participate in their defense, or comprehend the legal process. This requires the forensic professional to translate complex data into clear explanations without oversimplifying or distorting the findings. In such cases, they may describe how specific memory, reasoning, or executive functioning impairments directly impact the individual's legal competence. By providing a balanced and objective analysis, the forensic professional ensures that the court thoroughly understands the psychological factors influencing the case.

Ethical Considerations

Ethics are pivotal in the responsibilities of forensic neuropsychologists (and emerging forensic neuropsychopathologists) as expert witnesses. They must be transparent about their methods and results, acknowledging any limitations in their evaluations. They should not make over-generalized claims or offer opinions that fall outside their area of expertise. Additionally, forensic professionals must be aware of the potential consequences of their testimony. In criminal cases, for example, their findings may directly influence sentencing or decisions about criminal responsibility. In contrast, their evaluations may significantly impact child welfare and custody arrangements in custody cases.

Forensic professionals are also expected to maintain professional integrity throughout the process. This includes ensuring that their evaluations are conducted with the highest scientific rigor, that their testimony is based solely on objective data, and that they remain unbiased in their assessment of the individual being evaluated. Ethical principles also dictate that forensic professionals refrain from conflicts of interest or undue influence from parties involved in the case, ensuring that their testimony remains impartial and focused on serving the interests of justice.

The use of neuropsychopathological evidence in court plays an integral role in helping the legal system make informed decisions, particularly in cases involving mental health, cognitive function, and neurological impairments. For forensic professionals, providing testimony in a legal context requires careful adherence to legal standards, including the Daubert Standard and the Frye Test, to ensure that their methods and conclusions are scientifically valid and accepted within the professional community. Additionally, as expert witnesses, forensic professionals must remain impartial, communicate effectively, and adhere to high ethical standards in their evaluations and testimony. By meeting these rigorous requirements, forensic professionals can make meaningful contributions to the judicial process, ensuring that legal decisions are based on objective, scientifically sound evidence.

Balancing Science and Law: The Role of Forensic Neuropsychopathologists

The relationship between science and law presents intricate challenges that demand careful navigation by forensic neuropsychologists. Unlike the controlled and objective environments of scientific research, legal settings introduce adversarial dynamics that influence how evidence is presented and interpreted. Emerging forensic neuropsychopathologists serve as critical intermediaries, ensuring that complex scientific findings are accurately conveyed within a legal framework. Successfully balancing the objective nature of neuropsychological assessments with the contentious nature of courtroom proceedings requires practitioners to uphold the highest standards of scientific integrity, ethical conduct, and clear communication. By maintaining impartiality and ensuring the accuracy of their evaluations, neuropsychologists play a pivotal role in promoting the fair administration of justice.

Applying neuroscience, neuropsychology, neurophysiology, and neurology in addition to psychology and psychiatry in the courtroom necessitates careful consideration to ensure accuracy and fairness. Forensic neuropsychopathologists must rely on reliable, validated assessment tools and adhere to standardized procedures to derive objective findings. Comprehensive evaluations that consider cognitive, emotional, and behavioral factors are crucial for drawing informed and defensible conclusions. Peer-reviewed research established clinical guidelines and evidence-based practices that underpin credible neuropsychopathological testimony. Comprehensive evaluations that consider cognitive, emotional, and behavioral factors are crucial for drawing informed and defensible conclusions. Peer-reviewed research established clinical guidelines and evidence-based practices underpin credible neuropsychopathological testimony, ensuring the findings are reliable and scientifically grounded.

To maintain accuracy, forensic neuropsychopathologists must recognize the limitations of their assessments. No single neuropsychopathological test can thoroughly explain an individual's cognitive or psychological state. Instead, practitioners integrate data from multiple sources, including clinical interviews, medical records, collateral reports, and standardized assessments. This multi-method approach supports well-rounded and objective conclusions. Transparent reporting of methods and results enables courts to assess the validity of the evidence and evaluate its significance in legal decisions, thereby ensuring the application of sound and credible neuropsychological evidence in legal proceedings.

Moreover, forensic neuropsychopathologists must guard against overstating the certainty of their conclusions. In adversarial legal settings, attorneys may selectively emphasize evidence to support their arguments, increasing the risk of misrepresentation. Practitioners counteract this by clearly communicating the nuances of their evaluations, including alternative explanations and the inherent limitations of the data. Balanced testimony helps courts receive objective, evidence-based perspectives, enhancing the fairness of judicial proceedings by ensuring that the full scope of the evaluation is considered in the decision-making process.

Ethical considerations further underscore the importance of impartiality and scientific rigor. Forensic neuropsychopathologists must conduct their evaluations independently, free from external pressures or bias. Adhering to professional standards established by organizations such as the American Psychological Association (and the National Academy of Neuropsychology) ensures the integrity of their practice. Practitioners must also disclose potential conflicts of interest and take appropriate measures to mitigate them, thereby maintaining the credibility and impartiality of their evaluations. By following these guidelines, neuropsychologists uphold ethical standards and foster trust with the legal system and the individuals they assess.

The Potential for Neuropsychopathological Evidence to Influence Legal Outcomes

Neuropsychopathological evidence can significantly influence legal outcomes in both criminal and civil cases. In criminal proceedings, forensic neuropsychopathologists often evaluate a defendant's competency to stand trial, criminal responsibility, or cognitive functioning during the offense. Their findings can determine whether a defendant possessed the mental capacity to understand their actions or conform their conduct to the law. Testimony regarding diminished capacity, insanity, or incompetency to stand trial may lead to reduced sentences, diversion to mental health treatment, or other legal outcomes.

Sentencing hearings also frequently involve neuropsychopathological testimony. Evaluations may provide mitigating factors that influence sentencing decisions, particularly in cases involving brain injuries, mental illness, or developmental disorders. Additionally, risk assessments conducted by forensic neuropsychopathologists can inform decisions regarding parole, rehabilitation, or continued incarceration. These evaluations enable the court to assess the potential for rehabilitation, ensuring that individuals receive the appropriate treatment or accommodations tailored to their needs. Neuropsychopathological findings also guide the development of tailored interventions, which can reduce the likelihood of recidivism and improve long-term outcomes for individuals involved in the criminal justice system.

In civil litigation, neuropsychopathological evidence is central to determining damages and liability. Plaintiffs may present evidence of cognitive impairments resulting from traumatic brain injuries, medical malpractice, or exposure to toxic substances. Accurate assessments are crucial for determining the extent of impairment and supporting claims for compensation related to lost wages, medical expenses, and a diminished quality of life. Conversely, defendants may introduce neuropsychological evidence to challenge the validity or severity of alleged impairments.

The persuasive nature of neuropsychopathological evidence underscores the need for courts to evaluate expert testimony critically. Judges and jurors must assess the credibility of expert witnesses, considering their qualifications, the validity of the assessment tools used, and the transparency of their methods. Effective cross-examination further tests the reliability of expert opinions, encouraging clarity and accountability. Additionally, the expert's ability to clearly and understandably explain complex concepts is crucial in helping the court make informed decisions based on the evidence presented.

Forensic neuropsychopathologists are also responsible for educating legal professionals about the proper interpretation and limitations of their findings. Courts may lack the specialized knowledge necessary to understand complex neuropsychological data. Clear, accessible explanations from expert witnesses enable legal professionals to make informed decisions while minimizing the risk of misinterpretation. By providing context for the scientific findings and explaining their relevance to the case, neuropsychologists help bridge the gap between specialized knowledge and the legal framework.

Ethical and Legal Challenges in the Use of Neuropsychological Evidence

Introducing neuropsychopathological evidence in court brings ethical and legal challenges, particularly when conflicting expert opinions arise. Courts must navigate these disagreements by scrutinizing the qualifications, methodologies, and scientific basis of competing testimonies. Forensic neuropsychopathologists can enhance the credibility of their contributions by remaining transparent about the limitations of their assessments, adhering to evidence-based practices, and maintaining professional objectivity.

Additionally, the potential for bias presents a significant ethical concern. Forensic neuropsychopathologists must remain vigilant in recognizing and mitigating bias in their evaluations. Engaging in ongoing professional development, peer consultation, and interdisciplinary collaboration supports unbiased and scientifically sound assessments. These practices help forensic neuropsychopathologists stay current with the latest research, diagnostic techniques, and ethical standards. Collaboration with legal professionals and other experts ensures that neuropsychological evaluations are appropriately contextualized within the broader legal framework.

Furthermore, advancements in neuroscience continually introduce new technologies and diagnostic tools. While emerging research offers valuable insights, applying novel findings in legal settings requires careful consideration. Courts rely on forensic professionals to accurately interpret evolving scientific evidence, ensuring that speculative or unvalidated claims do not unduly influence legal outcomes. By grounding their testimony in established research and validated methodologies, forensic neuropsychopathologists help maintain the integrity of the legal process. This responsibility also requires them to distinguish between well-supported scientific facts and emerging hypotheses that may not yet be fully substantiated.

Balancing science and law require forensic professionals to uphold scientific integrity, ethical conduct, and clear communication. Their assessments offer courts valuable insights into cognitive and psychological functioning, thereby contributing to informed and fair legal decisions. They play a crucial role in the relationship between neuroscience and the legal system by maintaining objectivity, accurately conveying findings, and acknowledging the limitations of their evaluations. As neuroscience advances, ongoing professional development and interdisciplinary engagement will remain essential for ensuring the responsible application of neuropsychological evidence in the courtroom.

Conclusion

The role of neuropsychological evidence in legal proceedings is a critical relationship between science, law, and ethics. Forensic professionals provide indispensable insight into mental health and cognitive functioning, helping the court assess issues such as competency, criminal responsibility, and damages in civil cases. However, the integration of neuropsychopathological evidence into legal decisions is not without challenges. Forensic professionals must meet stringent legal standards to ensure the reliability and relevance of their testimony. These legal frameworks serve to evaluate whether the expert testimony meets accepted scientific and methodological criteria, and forensic neuropsychologists must be well-versed in both.

The application of forensic neuropsychopathology in the courtroom requires meticulous adherence to these standards to guarantee that the evidence presented is scientifically valid and legally sound. Forensic professionals must also navigate the complexities of providing testimony in an adversarial environment, where opposing parties often scrutinize their findings. To maintain credibility and ensure that their testimony is understood by non-expert audiences, such as judges and juries, forensic professionals must present their evaluations in an impartial, clear, and transparent manner. This reinforces their responsibility to contribute to the court's understanding of the case without bias or ambiguity.

Ethical considerations are at the heart of forensic neuropsychopathology, guiding professionals to uphold the integrity of both the scientific process and the judicial system. Forensic professionals must remain vigilant about potential conflicts of interest and the risks of bias, which could compromise the fairness of their assessments. The evolving nature of neuropsychopathological science necessitates ongoing professional development to ensure that practitioners stay current with advancements in the field while maintaining the highest ethical standards. Additionally, forensic professionals must acknowledge the limitations of their assessments, ensuring that their testimony is not overstated or misinterpreted in court.

Ultimately, integrating neuropsychopathological evidence into legal proceedings is crucial for enabling the court to make informed and just decisions. By adhering to legal standards, maintaining ethical integrity, and ensuring that their evaluations are scientifically grounded, forensic neuropsychologists make meaningful contributions to the judicial process. As neuroscience continues to evolve, the role of forensic professionals in the legal system will become increasingly important. This growing responsibility demands ongoing reflection, professional growth, and unwavering commitment to the principles of justice. By fulfilling these obligations, forensic professionals will continue to ensure that their work promotes fair, evidence-based legal outcomes that respect both the complexities of human cognition and the legal rights of individuals involved in the judicial process. Through these efforts, neuropsychologists uphold the integrity of their practice while contributing to the fair administration of justice.

Chapter 9: End-of-Chapter Questions

Comprehension and Reflection

1. **What is the central role of neuropsychological evidence in legal proceedings, and how does it help the court make informed decisions?**

➢ Explain how neuropsychologists bridge the gap between scientific findings and legal standards in courtrooms.

2. **How does the Daubert Standard influence the use of neuropsychological evidence in legal cases?**

➢ Discuss how the Daubert Standard ensures expert testimony is based on scientifically valid principles.

3. **What challenges arise when neuropsychologists present their findings in court, and how can they be addressed?**

➢ Reflect on the difficulties of communicating complex neuropsychological concepts to a non-expert audience.

4. **What is the significance of maintaining objectivity in neuropsychological evaluations for legal cases?**

➢ Discuss why impartiality is essential in the evaluation process, particularly in the adversarial legal environment.

5. **How do ethical considerations guide the practice of forensic neuropsychologists?**

➢ Explain how neuropsychologists ensure their evaluations remain ethical and scientifically sound in legal settings.

6. **How do potential biases impact neuropsychological assessments in the courtroom, and what steps can be taken to minimize these biases?**

➢ Analyze how awareness of bias is critical to ensuring the integrity of neuropsychological evaluations.

7. **What is the role of peer consultation and professional development in reducing bias in neuropsychological assessments?**

➢ Discuss how ongoing professional development and interdisciplinary collaboration help neuropsychologists stay unbiased and up to date with research.

8. **How do emerging technologies and advancements in neuroscience affect the use of neuropsychological evidence in the legal system?**

➢ Explore how new neuropsychological tools and technologies must be cautiously applied to avoid influencing legal outcomes based on unproven claims.

9. **What is the relationship between scientific integrity and the responsibility of neuropsychologists in the courtroom?**

➢ Explain why neuropsychologists must uphold scientific integrity, ensuring their testimony aligns with established research and methodologies.

10. **How does the legal system rely on neuropsychologists to interpret complex scientific data in a manner accessible to judges and juries?**

➢ Reflect on the challenges faced by neuropsychologists when simplifying complex scientific data for legal professionals.

➢ ***Critical Thinking and Application***

11. **What are the ethical implications of presenting speculative or unvalidated neuropsychological findings in court?**

- Discuss why neuropsychologists must avoid speculative conclusions and focus on well-supported evidence when testifying.

12. How does the legal system ensure that neuropsychological evidence is appropriately scrutinized in court?

- Explain how courts evaluate the credibility and relevance of neuropsychological evidence.

13. In what ways can neuropsychologists help the legal system understand the limitations of their assessments?

- Explore the importance of transparency in neuropsychological evaluations and how it helps courts make informed decisions.

14. What challenges do neuropsychologists face in maintaining objectivity during adversarial legal proceedings?

- Reflect on the difficulties when competing expert testimonies are presented and how neuropsychologists can maintain objectivity.

15. How can interdisciplinary collaboration improve the accuracy and relevance of neuropsychological evidence in legal proceedings?

- Discuss how collaboration with other experts, such as legal professionals, can enhance the validity and clarity of neuropsychological evaluations.

Application to Legal and Ethical Framework

16. What ethical dilemmas arise when a neuropsychologist is hired by one side in a legal case, and how can these dilemmas be addressed?

- Explain how neuropsychologists can avoid conflicts of interest and maintain impartiality even when hired by one party.

17. How does the evolving nature of neuroscience affect the ethical responsibilities of neuropsychologists in legal cases?

- Reflect on the challenges neuropsychologists face in applying new scientific findings to legal proceedings and how they must manage these advancements ethically.

18. What is the importance of neuropsychologists acknowledging the limitations of their assessments in court?

- Discuss how transparency about the limitations of neuropsychological evaluations contributes to ethical and credible legal testimony.

19. How can neuropsychologists ensure their testimony remains scientifically valid as new research and techniques emerge?

- Explore neuropsychologists' ongoing responsibilities to stay current with scientific advancements to provide reliable expert testimony.

20. What role does scientific research play in maintaining the integrity of neuropsychological evidence presented in court?

- Analyze how ongoing scientific research ensures that neuropsychological evaluations remain grounded in current, credible evidence when presented in legal settings.

Chapter 9: High Profile Cases that Influence Ethical Practices in Forensic Neuropsychopathology

Dr. George Rekers

The case of Dr. George Rekers is a high-profile example of a forensic psychologist whose ethical practices and professional conduct have been widely scrutinized and criticized. Rekers was a proponent of conversion therapy, which aimed to change individuals' sexual orientation from homosexual to heterosexual. His controversial views and therapeutic interventions have been the subject of significant academic and public debate. Other scholars have heavily criticized Rekers' work for reinforcing sex-role stereotypes and relying on dubious rationales for therapeutic intervention, such as parents' worries that their children might become homosexual. His academic work was also critiqued for its intense polemical stance and its attempt to strengthen societal norms related to gender and sexuality, using what some described as conservative political reasoning rather than scientific evidence.

Rekers' 1982 book *Growing Up Straight* provided parents with guidelines on how to prevent their children from becoming homosexual. The book has been criticized for its harmful approach, reinforcing negative stereotypes about non-conforming gender behavior, and was even described as a "horror show" by some scholars (Schiavi, 2001). His other work, *Shaping Your Child's Sexual Identity*, similarly encouraged parents to take drastic actions to prevent their children from developing homosexual tendencies. Rekers' position on homosexuality as a disorder and his use of aversion therapy to "correct" behaviors deemed non-conforming have been rejected by most of the psychological community, including the American Psychological

Association, which considers such therapies unethical and harmful.

Rekers' career as a forensic expert witness brought his controversial views into legal settings. He was involved in several high-profile court cases, including the 1998 Boy Scouts of America hearing and cases involving gay adoption in Arkansas and Florida. In these cases, Rekers testified that placing children in same-sex households would be detrimental, offering his testimony based on his personal beliefs rather than empirical evidence. Judges and legal experts frequently criticized his testimony for lacking scientific credibility and being motivated by his ideological and theological convictions. In the 2004 Arkansas gay adoption case, Judge Timothy Fox condemned Rekers' testimony as "extremely suspect" and stated that Rekers was primarily promoting his ideology rather than providing an unbiased, scientific perspective ("Howard v. Arkansas Decision," 2015; Egelko, 2005).

Rekers' reputation suffered further damage in 2010 when it was revealed that he had hired a male escort for a trip to Europe, despite his vocal stance against homosexuality. The scandal, widely covered by the media, raised questions about Rekers' credibility as an expert witness. His explanation—that the escort was hired as a "travel assistant"—was widely ridiculed, and the incident added to the growing perception that his professional opinions were deeply influenced by personal biases rather than scientific evidence (Baily, 2010). The controversy led to his resignation from several professional organizations, including the National Association for Research and Therapy of Homosexuality (NARTH).

Perhaps one of the most alarming aspects of Rekers' career was his involvement in experimental treatments for gender-variant children. In collaboration with Ole Ivar Lovaas, Rekers conducted several controversial studies that sought to "correct" gender-nonconforming behaviors in children. One subject of these studies, a young boy who was later found to be homosexual, committed suicide as an adult, with his family attributing the tragedy to the harmful treatment he had undergone (Szalavitz, 2011; Rekers & Lovaas, 1974). This further compounded concerns about the ethical implications of Rekers' therapeutic interventions and professional conduct.

Dr. George Rekers faced significant ethical and professional backlash due to his involvement in promoting conversion therapy and his public scandal. While there is no record of his professional license being formally revoked or suspended due to his advocacy of conversion therapy, his credibility as a psychologist was severely damaged by the controversy surrounding his personal life and his professional practices. Rekers' promotion of conversion therapy was widely criticized by mental health organizations, including the American Psychological Association, which explicitly discredited the practice. Though Rekers continued to advocate for conversion therapy, his scandal further undermined his professional integrity.

Rekers was involved in various legal cases as an expert witness. While his work was not explicitly deemed unethical in a legal context, his credibility as an expert witness became questionable. The fallout from his actions, combined with the scientific discrediting of conversion therapy, led to a tarnished reputation within the psychological and broader professional communities. In short, while Rekers may not have faced direct legal consequences in terms of license revocation, his involvement in controversial therapy practices, along with his scandal, severely affected his professional standing and the acceptance of his work.

Dr. George Rekers' career serves as a cautionary tale of how personal biases, controversial beliefs, and unethical practices can erode the integrity of the field of forensic psychology. His work has had significant negative consequences on individuals and communities, particularly in reinforcing harmful stereotypes and promoting scientifically unsupported practices. This case underscores the importance of adhering to ethical standards, maintaining scientific rigor, and upholding impartiality in forensic psychological assessments, particularly when such assessments have significant legal implications.

Dr. George Rekers, a psychologist and Baptist minister, is a controversial figure known for his advocacy of conversion therapy. This discredited practice aimed to change individuals' sexual orientation from homosexual to heterosexual. His involvement in promoting harmful psychological practices and his public scandal had significant effects on the field of forensic neuropsychopathology. While Rekers' work primarily targeted sexual orientation and gender identity rather than criminal behavior, the ethical and psychological ramifications of his actions provide critical lessons for forensic practitioners.

Dr. Rekers' promotion of conversion therapy, including his involvement in harmful behavioral interventions, has been widely condemned by the psychological and medical communities. One of the most infamous cases associated with Rekers was his involvement in the "Sissy Boy Experiment" conducted at

UCLA in the 1970s. In this study, young boys displaying gender non-conforming behavior were subjected to aversive conditioning, which involved positive reinforcement for "masculine" behaviors and punishment for "feminine" behaviors. One of the participants, Kirk Murphy, experienced severe psychological trauma, and he tragically died by suicide as an adult.

This case exposed the devastating effects of unethical psychological interventions. In forensic neuropsychopathology, professionals are tasked with evaluating psychological harm, particularly in cases involving abuse, coercion, or unethical medical practices. The Rekers case serves as a reminder of the need for practitioners to adhere to strict ethical guidelines and ensure that interventions are evidence-based, prioritizing the patient's well-being. The psychological damage caused by conversion therapy has been well-documented, including increased rates of depression, anxiety, PTSD, and suicidal ideation. Forensic professionals frequently assess individuals who have experienced trauma and its neurological effects. Conversion therapy, like that promoted by Rekers, can lead to severe emotional and cognitive disturbances. Understanding the neurobiological impact of prolonged psychological abuse is crucial in forensic evaluations, particularly when victims are involved in legal cases related to mental health claims, personal injury lawsuits, or criminal defense.

Dr. Rekers' reputation as an expert witness also brought attention to the role of credibility in forensic testimony. Despite his controversial views and the lack of scientific evidence supporting conversion therapy, Rekers was hired as an expert witness in several court cases, including those involving LGBTQ+ rights and custody disputes. His testimony often promoted harmful, pseudoscientific beliefs, leading to decisions that adversely affected the lives of individuals. In forensic neuropsychopathology, maintaining credibility and objectivity as an expert witness is essential. Courts rely on expert testimony to make informed decisions, and presenting biased or scientifically unsupported opinions can result in miscarriages of justice. The Rekers case highlights the importance of ensuring that expert testimony is grounded in empirical research and adheres to ethical standards.

The exposure of Rekers' unethical practices and his scandal— including his hiring of a male escort despite his anti-LGBTQ+ rhetoric—further discredited his standing as a psychological authority. His case contributed to the growing rejection of conversion therapy within both medical and legal frameworks. Today, many states and countries have implemented bans on conversion therapy, recognizing it as a harmful and unethical practice. Forensic professionals are often involved in policy advocacy and expert consultation in legal matters. The Rekers case underscores the importance of utilizing evidence-based research to inform legal decisions and safeguard vulnerable populations. It also highlights the necessity of challenging pseudoscientific practices and ensuring that legal rulings reflect contemporary psychological knowledge.

Rekers' views were rooted in personal biases rather than objective scientific understanding. Forensic professionals must remain vigilant in recognizing and addressing biases that may influence their assessments and testimony. Implicit bias can lead to unfair treatment of marginalized individuals, particularly in legal settings.

Developing cultural competence, maintaining scientific integrity, and prioritizing patient welfare are essential components of responsible forensic practice. The case of Dr. George Rekers has had a lasting impact on forensic neuropsychopathology by highlighting the dangers of unethical psychological practices and the misuse of expert testimony. It serves as a powerful reminder of the need for adherence to ethical standards, the importance of evidence-based practice, and the responsibility forensic professionals have in protecting vulnerable populations. By learning from such cases, the field continues to evolve towards more compassionate, science-driven care and legal advocacy.

Dr. John Money

Dr. John Money was a psychologist and sexologist best known for his controversial work in the field of gender identity and sexuality. He made significant contributions to the early understanding of gender and sexual development. Still, his involvement in the tragic case of David Reimer has led to widespread ethical criticism of his work. He was a prominent figure in the study of gender identity from the 1950s to the 1970s, particularly in the examination of how children develop a sense of their gender. He was one of the earliest proponents of the idea that gender identity is primarily learned and influenced by social and environmental factors rather than being strictly biological. Money believed that gender could be shaped by upbringing and that a child's gender identity could be malleable through appropriate socialization and parenting. His work on gender identity disorder (now referred to as gender dysphoria) and his ideas about the role of biology versus socialization in the development of gender became highly influential at the time. He coined the term "gender role" to describe the expectations and behaviors associated with being male or female in each society.

However, one of the most controversial aspects of his career emerged when he became involved in the David Reimer case. This tragedy raised serious ethical and professional concerns about his approach to gender identity and his experimental theories. In 1966, David Reimer, who was born male, became the subject of a controversial and ultimately tragic experiment conducted by Dr. John Money. When David was 8 months old, he suffered a botched circumcision during a routine medical procedure (Woo, 2004). The circumcision accident left his penis severely damaged, and doctors advised his parents to have him undergo gender reassignment surgery to become a girl, as they believed that raising David as a girl would be a more socially viable solution than trying to reconstruct his penis. His parents, desperate and unsure, agreed to this suggestion, and David was renamed Brenda.

Dr. Money was enlisted as a key figure in the case. He believed that because David was so young, he could be socialized and raised as a girl, which would result in a stable and healthy gender identity. Dr. Money provided guidance to the Reimer family, insisting that the child could adapt to a female gender identity if raised as such and that the surgery and subsequent socialization would help Brenda develop as a girl. For several years, Dr. Money and his colleagues continued to monitor David/Brenda's development and the Reimer family's adherence to his advice. However, this experiment was deeply flawed, and its consequences were tragic.

As David grew older, it became increasingly apparent that he was struggling with his assigned gender role. He exhibited a strong preference for typically male behaviors and rejected the female gender identity that had been imposed on him. Despite the Reimers' efforts to conform to Dr. Money's instructions, David's distress continued to grow. By the time he was a teenager, David had become very aware of the mismatch between his biological sex and his gender identity. In his adolescence, David revealed the truth to his parents. After years of emotional turmoil and psychological distress, he chose to stop living as a girl and transitioned back to being male (Woo, 2004). David changed his name to David again and began living as a male. Unfortunately, the psychological scars of the ordeal were deep, and David continued to experience significant struggles with his mental health.

The trauma David endured was further compounded by the loss of his twin brother, Brian Reimer. Brian had also experienced significant mental health issues throughout his life, struggling with depression and schizophrenia. In 2002, Brian tragically died from an overdose, which was believed to be suicide. The loss of his brother deeply affected David, further amplifying his emotional suffering. In 2004, after years of battling depression, financial hardship, and the lingering effects of the psychological trauma he endured, David Reimer died by suicide at the age of 38. His death highlighted the devastating long-term consequences of the unethical experiment he had been subjected to and emphasized the need for greater accountability and ethical considerations in the field of psychology.

David Reimer's story became widely known in the media, especially when it was revealed that Dr. Money had insisted on continuing the gender reassignment experiment despite the clear signs of distress in the child. Dr. Money's refusal to acknowledge the failure of his hypothesis and the harm caused to David raised serious ethical questions about his approach to human subjects and his willingness to push forward with an experimental treatment that violated the rights and well-being of the Reimer family. The David Reimer case has been widely criticized for several reasons. First, Dr. Money failed to consider the psychological harm being caused by the gender reassignment.

Despite mounting signs that David was suffering due to the imposed gender role, Dr. Money continued to advocate for the treatment. Second, the case lacked proper informed consent. David's parents were not fully aware of the potential risks involved in the procedure, and David, as a young child, could not consent to the treatment. Third, Dr. Money's approach was unscientific. His hypothesis—that gender identity is entirely shaped by socialization—was not supported by solid scientific evidence. Finally, Dr. Money's insistence on defending the experiment even after its failure and the family's suffering further undermined his credibility in the field.

In the aftermath, the field of gender studies and psychology has evolved significantly. There is now a much greater emphasis on respecting individuals' self-identified gender and an understanding that gender identity is influenced by a combination of biological, social, and environmental factors rather than being solely shaped by socialization. Dr. Money's legacy is primarily defined by the tragic outcome of the Reimer case, and his work is often cited as a cautionary tale about the dangers of experimental treatments that lack scientific validation and ethical oversight.

The case of David Reimer and the unethical practices of Dr. John Money have significant implications for forensic neuropsychopathology. This field focuses on understanding the relationship between brain function, psychological behavior, and criminal or problematic behavior within a legal context. While the case itself is not directly tied to criminal behavior, it offers critical lessons regarding the ethical responsibilities of psychologists and the psychological impact of unethical interventions. Here's how it influences forensic neuropsychopathology:

Forensic neuropsychopathology emphasizes the importance of adhering to ethical guidelines, especially when dealing with vulnerable populations. Dr. Money's decisions in the Reimer case demonstrated a blatant disregard for the patient's well-being. Instead of prioritizing the child's mental health, he pursued his theoretical beliefs without sufficient evidence. Forensic neuropsychologists are often called upon as expert witnesses, and this case serves as a reminder of how unethical conduct can have devastating consequences. It highlights the importance of conducting evidence-based evaluations and maintaining objectivity in legal settings.

David Reimer's experience highlights the long-term psychological consequences of unethical psychological interventions. Being subjected to unwanted gender reassignment and coerced into an identity that did not align with his psychological experience resulted in severe trauma, depression, and eventually suicide. Forensic professionals often assess individuals who have experienced trauma, especially in cases of abuse, neglect, or malpractice. Understanding the profound effects of psychological trauma is crucial for accurately diagnosing conditions like PTSD, depression, and anxiety.

The case also sheds light on how early psychological interventions can shape brain development and mental health. Research in neuropsychopathology suggests that traumatic experiences during childhood can lead to structural and functional changes in the brain, particularly in areas related to emotion regulation and decision-making. David's experience of forced gender identity and the associated psychological stress may have contributed to long-term neurological and psychological damage. This case serves as a reminder to forensic professionals to assess the developmental history of individuals when evaluating mental health and behavioral issues.

Dr. Money frequently served as an expert witness in gender-related cases, influencing legal decisions based on his controversial theories. Forensic professionals are often tasked with providing expert testimony in court, and this case exemplifies the ethical responsibility that comes with such a role. Testimonies must be grounded in reliable, peer-reviewed scientific evidence rather than personal biases or untested theories. Misleading or unethical testimony can contribute to harmful legal outcomes, particularly in cases involving children or individuals with cognitive or psychological vulnerabilities.

The absence of informed consent in the Reimer case is another critical concern for forensic neuropsychopathology. David's parents were not adequately informed about the risks and uncertainties of the experimental treatment, and David himself had no say in the decisions made about his body and identity. In forensic settings, psychologists are often responsible for evaluating whether individuals can provide informed consent in legal and medical matters. This case highlights the importance of ensuring that individuals, particularly minors and vulnerable populations, are given a voice in decisions that affect their lives.

The eventual suicides of both David and his twin brother, Brian, reflect the profound psychological toll of the traumatic experiences they endured. Forensic professionals are often involved in assessing suicide risk and understanding the neurological, neuropsychological, and psychological factors contributing to suicidal behavior. The Reimer case serves as a case study in the importance of early intervention, comprehensive mental health care, and ongoing psychological support for individuals exposed to severe trauma and identity-related distress.

The case of David Reimer remains a pivotal example of unethical psychological experimentation and its devastating consequences. For forensic professionals, it serves as a reminder of the importance of ethical responsibility, evidence-based practice, and prioritizing patient well-being. It also emphasizes the need for rigorous assessments of psychological trauma, informed consent, and the consideration of long-term mental health impacts in legal and medical decision-making. Ultimately, the lessons from this case contribute to a more substantial commitment to ethical conduct and compassionate care in forensic psychology and neuropsychopathology.

Dr. Jason Grigson

Dr. James Grigson, often referred to as "Dr. Death," was a controversial forensic psychiatrist who played a significant role in capital punishment cases in the United States, particularly in Texas. He became infamous for his testimony in support of the death penalty, often testifying with absolute certainty that defendants would be a future danger to society, which was a critical factor in securing death sentences. His unethical practices in forensic psychology had a profound impact on both the legal system and the mental health field.

Dr. Grigson was a licensed psychiatrist with a specialization in forensic psychiatry. Throughout his career, he became a frequent expert witness in capital murder trials, often serving as an expert for the prosecution. His testimony was pivotal in the sentencing phase of many death penalty cases, where he would assert that the defendant posed a future risk of violence or danger to society. This type of testimony, predicting future dangerousness, became an important factor in securing death sentences in Texas. This state had one of the highest rates of capital punishment in the United States.

Dr. Grigson's assessments of the mental health and risk of future violence of criminal defendants were highly influential, but they were also deeply controversial. He was known for making definitive predictions of future violence without conducting thorough evaluations, sometimes without even meeting the defendant in person. His testimony was often based on hypothetical scenarios or the defendant's past behavior without sufficient evidence or a comprehensive understanding of the individual's psychological state. This lack of scientific rigor raised serious ethical and professional concerns.

Several key ethical violations marked Dr. Grigson's practices as an expert witness:

1. **Certainty in Predicting Future Violence:** Dr. Grigson was known for his unequivocal assertions that a defendant would continue to engage in violent behavior in the future, regardless of the evidence or the circumstances. He often stated with confidence that the defendant was "100% certain"

to commit further acts of violence (Dow, 2005; Bell, 1995). This kind of certainty in predicting future behavior was, and still is, highly problematic within the field of forensic psychiatry, as predicting future violence is notoriously unreliable and fraught with uncertainty. There is *no definitive* way to predict with certainty whether an individual will engage in violent behavior in the future. However, forensic professionals can provide comprehensive testimony based on an individual's history, patterns, recidivism, and other supporting and evaluative information to discuss the likelihood.

2. **Substandard Evaluations:** In many cases, Dr. Grigson conducted minimal evaluations or, in some instances, did not personally evaluate the defendant at all (Dow, 2005). He relied on second-hand information, such as police reports and court records, and based his testimony on this incomplete data (Dow, 2005). Forensic professionals are expected to conduct thorough and objective evaluations, including interviews with the individual, before providing expert testimony. Dr. Grigson's failure to adhere to these standards raised questions about the integrity of his work.

3. **Bias and Advocacy:** Dr. Grigson often aligned himself with the prosecution, advocating for the death penalty and presenting himself as an expert who could reliably determine the likelihood of future dangerousness. This advocacy role undermined his objectivity as a forensic expert. Forensic professionals are expected to maintain impartiality in their evaluations and testimony,

which is crucial for the fair application of justice. Grigson's approach was seen as highly biased, as he consistently supported the prosecution's case for death, regardless of the specific facts of each case.

4. **Failure to Adhere to Ethical Guidelines:** Dr. Grigson's testimony violated key ethical principles outlined by professional organizations, such as the American Psychiatric Association, which emphasize the importance of objectivity, evidence-based practice, and the need for forensic experts to base their opinions on thorough, individualized assessments rather than hypothetical or speculative conclusions.

The consequences of Dr. Grigson's unethical practices became evident over time. In 1995, the American Psychiatric Association expelled him from its membership due to his unethical conduct (Death Penalty Information Center, 2018; La Fontaine, 2002). The American Academy of Psychiatry and the Law (AAPL) also revoked his membership (Dreisbach, 2015). These professional sanctions were a significant blow to his career. They reflected widespread disapproval of his methods, signaling a broader movement within the mental health community to hold forensic professionals accountable for ethical misconduct.

Dr. Grigson's testimony had far-reaching consequences, as it was influential in securing death sentences for numerous individuals. However, over time, the flaws in his assessments became apparent, especially as courts and legal professionals began to recognize the lack of scientific validity in his testimony. His practices were part of a broader conversation about the role of expert testimony in capital punishment cases and the ethical standards required of forensic professionals, prompting reforms aimed at ensuring that expert witnesses provide scientifically valid and impartial testimony.

In some cases, the individuals sentenced to death based on Grigson's testimony had their sentences later commuted or overturned as courts began to question the reliability of his evaluations. Grigson's involvement in these cases further highlighted the dangers of relying on unscientific and unethical expert testimony in the criminal justice system. As a result, legal professionals and advocates pushed for stricter standards in the use of expert testimony, particularly in cases with life-or-death consequences. This shift prompted more rigorous scrutiny of expert witnesses and the methodologies they used in high-stakes legal proceedings.

One of the primary concerns in forensic neuropsychopathology is the assessment of an individual's risk for future violence or dangerousness. Grigson's testimony, where he frequently claimed with certainty that a defendant would be a future danger to society, underlined the importance of using scientifically valid methods for predicting risk. Grigson's methods were often criticized for their lack of empirical support, as he made sweeping statements about future violence without conducting thorough, evidence-based evaluations. His approach undermined the credibility of forensic psychiatric assessments, raising concerns about the integrity of expert testimony in the judicial system.

Forensic neuropsychopathologists assess cognitive functioning and behavior to understand how a defendant's mental state might contribute to criminal behavior. The Grigson case emphasized that predictions of future violence based on incomplete or speculative information can be highly unreliable. Following Grigson's practices, the field of forensic neuropsychopathology began to place more emphasis on using validated, structured risk assessment tools (such as the Violence Risk Appraisal Guide or the Hare Psychopathy Checklist) rather than relying on unsupported predictions of future behavior.

Grigson's involvement in the capital punishment system, where he regularly testified in favor of the death penalty and predicted future dangerousness without a complete evaluation, brought ethical issues to the forefront of forensic psychology and neuropsychology. Forensic neuropsychopathologists, like all forensic experts, are held to a high standard of professional conduct. Their testimony must be based on objective, scientifically grounded evaluations of an individual's mental state, cognitive abilities, and potential for rehabilitation or harm. Grigson's approach violated this standard, demonstrating how biased, unsubstantiated expert testimony can lead to unfair legal outcomes, including the imposition of the death penalty.

In forensic neuropsychopathology, professionals are tasked with providing unbiased, accurate assessments of mental functioning, and they must avoid advocacy or the presentation of conclusions that are not supported by scientific data. Grigson's case served as a reminder that forensic professionals must adhere to ethical guidelines and that expert testimony should always prioritize the well-being of the individual being assessed, especially in life-and-death decisions. It also reinforced the critical need for forensic experts to base their opinions on objective, scientifically sound assessments rather than personal biases or external pressures.

Grigson's practice of testifying without conducting thorough, individualized evaluations also highlighted a key principle in forensic neuropsychopathology: the necessity of comprehensive assessments. Neuropsychologists are required to conduct detailed evaluations, including clinical interviews, psychological testing, and consideration of medical and historical records, to form accurate conclusions about an individual's cognitive functioning and psychological state. This comprehensive approach ensures that their assessments are based on reliable data, allowing them to provide informed, objective, and clinically valid testimony in legal settings.

Grigson often relied on second-hand information, such as police reports and court documents, to form his opinions. This practice highlighted a lack of due diligence in forensic assessments. It contributed to the broader awareness that comprehensive, direct evaluations are essential for making accurate psychological assessments, particularly when they are used in legal settings to inform decisions with potentially serious consequences. As a result, the case stressed the importance of forensic professionals adhering to rigorous standards of care and accountability when providing expert testimony that can directly impact a person's fate.

Grigson's testimony often resulted in death sentences, and the growing criticism of his methods helped foster a greater level of scrutiny around the use of expert testimony in legal proceedings. In the wake of Grigson's unethical practices, there was an increasing demand for forensic neuropsychologists to demonstrate that their assessments were based on reliable and valid scientific methods. This shift emphasized the need for greater transparency in the evaluation process. It reinforced the importance of adhering to established guidelines and evidence-based practices in the field of forensic neuropsychopathology.

The case helped drive legal reforms, including a stricter adherence to the Daubert Standard, which requires expert testimony to be based on scientifically valid principles and methodologies. The Daubert Standard is a legal precedent that ensures that expert testimony meets the criteria of being relevant and reliable. As a result of Grigson's practices, courts became more cautious when evaluating the qualifications and methods of forensic psychologists and neuropsychologists, ensuring that their testimony was grounded in evidence-based practices.

The scandal surrounding Grigson contributed to increased awareness within the professional community about the need for specialized training in forensic neuropsychology and a commitment to ethical guidelines. It highlighted the importance of forensic neuropsychologists understanding the boundaries of their role, the need to maintain impartiality, and the dangers of aligning too closely with one side in a legal case. This cautionary lesson stressed the responsibility of forensic experts to serve the court by providing unbiased, scientifically grounded assessments rather than advocating for one party over another.

Forensic neuropsychologists were reminded of the importance of continuing education, peer review, and accountability to ensure that their practices align with evolving ethical standards. Professional organizations, such as the AAFN and the ABCN, place significant emphasis on the ethics and standards of practice for neuropsychologists in legal settings. Grigson's case emphasized the need for these organizations to actively promote ethical training and hold forensic neuropsychologists accountable for their conduct in the courtroom. This case also highlighted the potential consequences of unethical testimony, both for the individuals involved and for the credibility of the forensic psychology profession.

The role of forensic neuropsychologists in death penalty cases became more scrutinized after Dr. Grigson's impact on these trials. As Grigson was often used to support the prosecution in capital punishment cases, his practices served as a cautionary example of how mental health professionals could potentially misuse their authority in life-or-death cases. His involvement in such high-profile cases contributed to growing calls for greater oversight and regulation of forensic professionals in death penalty cases, especially regarding the assessment of an individual's mental state and potential for future harm.

Forensic neuropsychologists are often called upon in such cases to assess whether a defendant has the cognitive capacity to understand the charges against them, whether they are intellectually disabled, or whether they pose a risk of future violence. Grigson's unethical conduct in this area prompted a more critical review of how neuropsychologists evaluate such factors and the necessity of conducting objective, scientifically valid assessments in high-stakes legal contexts. It also led to increased advocacy for stricter oversight and accountability measures to ensure that forensic neuropsychologists adhere to the highest ethical and professional standards when their evaluations influence life-altering legal decisions.

Dr. James Grigson's controversial career and unethical practices had a significant impact on forensic neuropsychopathology. His lack of scientific rigor, failure to conduct thorough evaluations, and biased testimony revealed the need for forensic neuropsychologists to uphold strict ethical standards and adhere to evidence-based practices. The fallout from Grigson's actions led to increased scrutiny of expert testimony in legal proceedings, especially in death penalty cases. It contributed to reforms in how forensic neuropsychologists are trained and held accountable. The Grigson case serves as a stark reminder of the potential consequences when forensic professionals fail to maintain ethical conduct and scientific integrity in their work.

Dr. Elizabeth Loftus

Dr. Elizabeth Loftus is a renowned and highly regarded cognitive psychologist recognized for her groundbreaking research on human memory, particularly its malleability and susceptibility to distortion. Her work on eyewitness testimony, false memories, and the misinformation effect has significantly influenced the legal system, shaping how courts assess the reliability of memory. Loftus has served as an expert witness in numerous high-profile cases, including those of Ted Bundy, O.J. Simpson, and Harvey Weinstein, where her testimony challenged the credibility of eyewitness accounts. Her research has contributed to a deeper understanding of how memories can be influenced, altered, or even entirely fabricated under suggestive questioning or external influence.

However, Loftus' work has also been subject to ethical controversies. A significant point of contention arose from her involvement in the Jane Doe case, where she publicly challenged a woman's recovered memory of childhood sexual abuse (Costandi, 2013; Corwin & Olafson, 1997).

Critics accused Loftus of violating ethical research standards by disclosing personal details without consent, which led to legal battles over privacy and defamation. Additionally, many argue that her research has been used in courtrooms to discredit genuine survivors of abuse, effectively assisting defense attorneys in casting doubt on victim testimonies. Ethical concerns have also been raised about her false memory implantation studies, which some believe lacked adequate safeguards to protect participants from psychological harm.

Despite these controversies, Loftus has not lost her professional license or faced formal disciplinary action from psychological institutions. However, she has experienced professional backlash, with some psychologists and survivor advocacy groups condemning her work as harmful to victims of trauma. In 2002, the University of Washington launched an ethics investigation into her research practices, leading to tensions that contributed to her departure from the institution (Constandi, 2013; Ambrasky, 2004). She later joined the University of California, Irvine, where she continued her research and academic contributions. Additionally, Loftus has faced legal challenges, including lawsuits for defamation and invasion of privacy (Constandi, 2013), but has defended her work on the grounds of academic freedom and the pursuit of scientific inquiry.

Loftus' research has had a profound impact on forensic neuropsychopathology, particularly in the areas of eyewitness testimony, memory reliability, and legal decision-making. Her findings have led courts to become more skeptical of eyewitness accounts, recognizing the potential for memory distortion and suggestibility. Moreover, her work has fueled ongoing debates about trauma and repressed memory recall, challenging traditional views on how traumatic experiences are processed and remembered. In criminal trials, defense teams frequently use her research to question the credibility of witness statements, which has played a role in preventing wrongful convictions. However, this influence has also raised ethical concerns, as it can sometimes result in the dismissal of legitimate victim testimonies. Ultimately, Loftus' contributions to forensic psychology remain both groundbreaking and controversial, highlighting the delicate balance between scientific exploration and ethical responsibility in legal contexts.

Chapter 10:
Special Topics in Forensic Neuropsychopathology

The rapid advancement of technology has fundamentally transformed many fields, and forensic neuropsychopathology is no exception. Over the last few decades, the integration of sophisticated technologies, including neuroimaging, brain-computer interfaces (BCIs), and artificial intelligence (AI), has revolutionized the study of the brain across multiple disciplines. These technologies offer powerful tools that enable neuropsychologists and forensic professionals to examine cognitive and emotional functioning in ways once unimaginable. In forensic neuropsychopathology, these tools promise greater accuracy, precision, and objectivity, which are crucial in high-stakes legal settings such as custody arrangements, criminal assessments, and other legal evaluations where the outcomes can profoundly affect individuals' lives.

As mentioned in Chapter 8, neuroimaging technologies offer in-depth insights into brain activity, enabling experts to visualize patterns of cognitive and emotional processing. BCIs, on the other hand, offer the potential for real-time data on brain activity and direct communication between the brain and external devices, thereby opening up new avenues for evaluating cognitive states in real-time. Moreover, AI systems—through machine learning algorithms—can process vast amounts of data and identify patterns that might be difficult for human experts to detect. These could inform legal decisions, including evaluations of parenting ability, criminal responsibility, or mental fitness.

However, the connection between emerging technologies and forensic neuropsychopathology presents unique ethical, legal, and practical challenges. While these tools offer the potential to enhance objectivity and scientific rigor, they also introduce significant concerns regarding fairness, bias, privacy, and informed consent. One of the most pressing issues is the potential for AI systems and machine learning algorithms to perpetuate societal biases present in historical data, such as gender, racial, or socioeconomic disparities. In the legal context, where decisions made in the courtroom can have lifelong implications for individuals and families, there is a critical need to ensure that these technologies do not inadvertently reinforce existing inequalities or lead to unjust outcomes.

Similarly, as neuroimaging and BCIs provide deeper insights into an individual's cognitive and emotional states, questions arise regarding the privacy and ethical implications of accessing and utilizing such intimate data. How much of a person's inner mental life can be accurately captured by technology, and to what extent can this data be used without violating their autonomy and dignity? Furthermore, these technologies pose the challenge of over-reliance, where legal decisions may be unduly influenced by data-driven insights at the expense of a more holistic, human-centered evaluation of an individual's circumstances. Forensic evaluations must strike a balance between the strengths of technological innovation and a nuanced understanding of human behavior, experience, and context.

At the heart of these discussions lies the crucial role of forensic professionals and other experts in ensuring that these technologies are utilized responsibly and ethically. Forensic neuropsychopathologists will be tasked with interpreting data generated by neuroimaging, BCIs, and AI systems, ensuring that their interpretations align with the broader context of the individual being evaluated. They must consider the complex relationship between cognitive function, emotional regulation, personal history, and environmental factors that these technologies cannot fully capture. Also, forensic neuropsychopathologists must advocate for the ethical use of these tools, ensuring that their application remains grounded in a commitment to fairness, transparency, and the protection of individual rights and dignity.

This chapter explores the ethical and practical challenges of utilizing emerging technologies in forensic neuropsychology. The potential benefits and risks associated with neuroimaging, BCIs, and AI will be explored, particularly in legal contexts where decisions can have profound and lasting consequences for individuals' lives. Ethical concerns, including ensuring informed consent, protecting privacy, addressing bias, and minimizing over-reliance on technological tools, are examined in depth. Additionally, this chapter highlights the importance of maintaining a human-centered approach in neuropsychopathological assessments, ensuring that technological advances supplement, rather than replace, the expertise and judgment of trained professionals.

One of the central themes of this chapter is the need for transparency and accountability in the development and application of these technologies. As AI systems become increasingly integral to legal decision-making, ensuring that algorithms are transparent, explainable, and free from bias is critical to upholding the principles of justice. Furthermore, with the increasing use of neuroimaging and BCIs, it is vital to address the ethical implications of collecting and utilizing data that may reveal deeply personal aspects of an individual's brain function. The challenge lies in using these technologies ethically and ensuring that they do not inadvertently exacerbate existing biases or lead to unfair legal outcomes.

Another critical issue explored is the potential over-reliance on technology in high-stakes forensic evaluations. While these tools undoubtedly offer valuable insights into brain function, neuropsychologists must avoid the temptation to view them as the sole determinants in legal decision-making. Various factors, including personal experiences, social context, and environmental influences, deeply influence human cognition, behavior, and emotional regulation. These nuances cannot be fully captured by technology alone, and over-reliance on data-driven tools could lead to oversimplified or reductionist conclusions about an individual's fitness for parenting, criminal responsibility, or other legal evaluations.

Ultimately, this chapter emphasizes the responsibility of neuropsychologists to promote the ethical application of these technologies and ensure that they are used in a manner that safeguards the rights and well-being of individuals involved in legal proceedings. As these technologies evolve, forensic neuropsychopathologists must remain vigilant in striking a balance between innovation and ethical considerations. This requires staying current with the latest technological advancements, understanding their limitations, and collaborating with legal professionals, ethicists, and technologists to ensure that these tools are fair, transparent, and just.

While integrating neuroimaging, BCIs, and AI into forensic neuropsychology holds great promise for enhancing the accuracy and fairness of legal evaluations, it also presents a range of ethical, legal, and practical challenges. This chapter seeks to comprehensively explore these issues, offering insights into how these technologies can be used responsibly and ethically in forensic settings. By examining the potential risks and benefits, as well as the crucial role of forensic neuropsychopathologists in navigating these challenges, the objective is to contribute to the ongoing dialogue on how best to integrate technology into neuropsychological practice while ensuring that the dignity, autonomy, and rights of individuals remain protected in legal contexts.

As forensic neuropsychopathology continues to evolve with the integration of technologies such as neuroimaging, BCIs, and AI, the field faces a critical responsibility to ensure that these tools are applied with ethical integrity and contextual sensitivity. While these innovations have advanced the precision and fairness of legal evaluations, their practical use demands a nuanced understanding of the populations being assessed, particularly when those individuals are developmentally distinct, such as juveniles. The complexity of adolescent neurodevelopment introduces unique variables that challenge traditional assessment methods and legal judgment. Failing to consider these developmental differences risks applying adult standards to youth, which can potentially lead to unjust outcomes and missed opportunities for effective rehabilitation.

One area where these considerations become especially significant is in the evaluation and adjudication of juvenile offenders. The relationship between neuropsychopathological science and juvenile justice presents a compelling case for how emerging knowledge of brain development can reshape legal responses to young people. As attention shifts from tools to context, neurodevelopmental research informs our understanding of culpability, rehabilitation, and justice for adolescents, and these issues must be examined. This shift encourages legal systems to adopt more developmentally appropriate approaches that recognize the plasticity and potential for growth inherent in adolescence. Ultimately, integrating neurodevelopmental insights into juvenile justice supports a more humane, evidence-based framework that prioritizes both accountability and the opportunity for meaningful change.

The following section explores how insights from adolescent brain science and forensic neuropsychopathology are transforming legal perspectives on juvenile delinquency. By understanding the neurobiological underpinnings of behavior during adolescence, legal systems can adopt more developmentally appropriate and ethically sound approaches that prioritize rehabilitation over retribution. This includes reevaluating traditional notions of culpability and adjusting sentencing practices to account for the unique cognitive and emotional profiles of youth. Through this lens, the justice system can better support positive developmental trajectories while safeguarding public safety.

Juvenile delinquency has been a central issue in the field of criminal justice, often entangled with questions about maturity, responsibility, and the capacity for change. Understanding young people's developmental trajectories and underlying neurobiological processes is crucial for developing appropriate legal responses to juvenile offenders. Recent research has significantly advanced our understanding of adolescent brain development, highlighting notable differences between adolescents and adults in decision-making, impulse control, and emotional regulation. This has profound implications for the treatment and sentencing of juvenile offenders. It is essential to consider the role of neurodevelopment in shaping behavior and how this should influence both legal approaches to juvenile justice and the ethical standards for rehabilitation.

The adolescent brain undergoes critical changes between childhood and adulthood. These neurobiological developments contribute to heightened risk-taking, impulsivity, and emotional reactivity that are often exhibited in juvenile delinquency. As the legal system seeks to hold young offenders accountable, understanding the underlying neurodevelopmental factors becomes necessary for assessing culpability and determining appropriate sentences. The growing body of research in forensic neuropsychopathology has shifted perspectives in juvenile justice, emphasizing the potential for rehabilitation over punitive measures, particularly in cases where neurodevelopmental factors play a critical role.

These evolving insights highlighted the importance of grounding legal interpretations of juvenile behavior in a robust understanding of brain maturation. As neuroscience continues to illuminate the complex relationship between structural brain changes and behavioral outcomes during adolescence, forensic neuropsychopathology is uniquely positioned to inform more just and developmentally sensitive legal frameworks. The following section delves deeper into how specific patterns of neural development contribute to the behavioral characteristics often associated with delinquent acts and why these patterns must be central to discussions of culpability, accountability, and reform in juvenile justice. Understanding these developmental trajectories enhances the fairness of legal responses and supports the creation of rehabilitative strategies that align with adolescents' cognitive and emotional capacities. Ultimately, this perspective promotes a justice system that recognizes the potential for growth, change, and reintegration of young offenders.

Brain Maturation and Juvenile Delinquency

Brain development during adolescence plays a crucial role in juvenile delinquency. **Brain maturation** is a prolonged process, with different brain regions reaching full development at different times. As mentioned throughout the text, the prefrontal cortex, which governs executive functions such as decision-making, impulse control, risk assessment, and planning, is one of the last areas of the brain to mature. This area does not fully reach adult-level functionality until the mid-20s. As a result, adolescents often struggle with impulse control and short-term decision-making, which can contribute to impulsive and risky behaviors that lead to delinquency.

Instead, the limbic system, which regulates emotions and reward-seeking behaviors, matures earlier than the prefrontal cortex. The limbic system is highly susceptible to reward, and its premature development can lead adolescents to seek immediate gratification without considering the long-term consequences. This mismatch between the limbic system and the prefrontal cortex can explain why adolescents are more prone to engaging in risky behaviors, such as substance abuse, violent behavior, or even criminal acts. The heightened dopamine activity in the brain further increases adolescents' sensitivity to rewards and encourages them to engage in risk-taking behaviors.

Research purports that adolescents are biologically predisposed to make impulsive decisions, and this developmental stage leads to difficulties in regulating emotions and controlling impulses. These neurobiological factors provide insight into the reasons behind the elevated rates of juvenile delinquency and suggest that juveniles may not have the same cognitive capacity to understand the consequences of their actions as adults do. Furthermore, the adolescent brain's heightened sensitivity to rewards can drive them to engage in risky behaviors without fully appreciating the potential long-term harm. As a result, interventions that target impulse control and decision-making skills are crucial for reducing delinquent behaviors during this vulnerable developmental period.

Neuroimaging has become a crucial tool for enhancing our understanding of the adolescent brain and its connection to delinquent behavior. By using neuroimaging techniques, researchers can observe structural and functional differences in the brains of adolescents compared to adults. These technologies enable scientists to pinpoint which regions are active during decision-making, emotional regulation, or impulse control tasks—areas that are often impaired in delinquent youth. For instance, neuroimaging studies have consistently shown underdevelopment or hypoactivity in the prefrontal cortex among juveniles involved in delinquent behavior, supporting the theory that executive functioning deficits contribute significantly to poor judgment and increased impulsivity.

The utility of neuroimaging extends beyond simply identifying underdeveloped brain regions; it also helps illustrate the imbalance between the prefrontal cortex and the limbic system during adolescence. While the limbic system matures earlier and drives emotional and reward-seeking behaviors, the prefrontal cortex, which governs impulse control and long-term planning, lags. Neuroimaging helps visualize this developmental mismatch by revealing heightened activity in reward-related areas, such as the nucleus accumbens, during exposure to risk or reward-based tasks. At the same time, the prefrontal cortex shows delayed or reduced engagement. These insights are crucial for understanding why adolescents are more susceptible to engaging in high-risk or delinquent behaviors, particularly in emotionally charged or peer-influenced situations.

Importantly, neuroimaging also has the potential to influence how the legal system views culpability and sentencing for juvenile offenders. By presenting empirical evidence of developmental immaturity, neuroimaging data can be used in courtrooms to argue that adolescents lack the full cognitive and emotional capacity to be held to the same standards of responsibility as adults. This scientific evidence supports policies and legal decisions that favor rehabilitation over punishment, particularly in cases where neurodevelopmental immaturity is evident. Courts in several jurisdictions have already acknowledged the relevance of brain development in mitigating sentences, and as neuroimaging data becomes more sophisticated, its legal influence is expected to grow.

Moreover, neuroimaging can guide the development of more effective intervention and rehabilitation strategies tailored to the neurodevelopmental profiles of delinquent youth. For instance, if imaging reveals specific deficits in brain regions associated with impulse control or emotional regulation, therapeutic interventions can be targeted to those areas. This precision in treatment planning could increase the success of rehabilitation programs, reduce recidivism, and support the long-term developmental needs of juvenile offenders. As a result, neuroimaging not only aids in diagnosis and explanation but also contributes to the formulation of personalized, developmentally appropriate interventions.

Neuroimaging's role in the study of juvenile delinquency exemplifies how interdisciplinary collaboration between neuropsychology, psychology, and the legal system can lead to more just and effective outcomes. By grounding legal decisions in empirical evidence about adolescent brain development, society can better align its justice system with principles of fairness and developmental appropriateness. As research continues to evolve, integrating neuroimaging into forensic neuropsychopathology will be essential for ensuring that juvenile justice not only holds youth accountable but also supports their capacity for growth, change, and reintegration.

BCIs and AI represent a new frontier in studying adolescent brain development and juvenile delinquency, offering novel methods to gather, analyze, and interpret neural data in real time. BCIs allow direct communication between the brain and external devices, enabling researchers to monitor brain activity with exceptional temporal precision. In the context of forensic neuropsychopathology, BCIs can be used to track adolescents' cognitive and emotional responses during decision-making tasks, providing insight into how developing brains process risk, emotion, and impulse. These real-time assessments can help identify specific patterns of neural activity associated with impulsive or maladaptive behaviors, particularly in delinquent youth.

AI enhances this process by enabling the analysis of massive datasets generated by neuroimaging and BCI recordings. The human capacity to detect subtle patterns often limits the effectiveness of traditional methods in interpreting brain data. Still, machine learning algorithms can identify complex correlations between brain structure, function, and behavioral outcomes. For example, AI can be trained to recognize neural signatures of impaired impulse control or heightened reward sensitivity, enabling more accurate predictions of delinquency risk in adolescents. These predictive models can be refined over time with additional data, improving the ability to detect early warning signs of behavioral issues before they manifest into criminal acts.

Besides, AI-driven models can help map developmental trajectories across various adolescent populations, identifying how brain maturation differs based on environmental, genetic, or psychosocial factors. This is especially important in understanding why some youths are more vulnerable to engaging in delinquent behaviors than others. By analyzing longitudinal data, AI systems can detect delayed or atypical development in critical brain regions, such as the prefrontal cortex or amygdala, which are often implicated in emotional regulation and executive functioning. These insights can inform personalized intervention strategies sensitive to everyone's unique neurodevelopmental needs.

BCIs also offer potential for therapeutic intervention, particularly when combined with neurofeedback techniques. Juveniles can learn to modulate their brain activity by receiving real-time feedback from BCIs during cognitive training exercises. For instance, if a youth struggles with regulating emotional responses, a BCI can guide them through exercises designed to strengthen prefrontal cortex engagement or dampen excessive limbic activity. Over time, this neurofeedback training can help foster greater cognitive control and reduce susceptibility to impulsive and delinquent behaviors. Integrating BCIs into treatment programs offers a direct and adaptive approach to rehabilitation that aligns with the brain's plasticity during adolescence.

The combination of BCIs and AI promises to transform the juvenile justice system by supporting more equitable and informed legal decisions. These technologies can provide objective data that highlight the neurodevelopmental limitations of adolescent offenders, reinforcing the argument that young people should not be held to the same standards of culpability as adults. Furthermore, AI-enhanced BCI assessments can be used to track rehabilitation progress, helping courts determine when a juvenile has made sufficient cognitive and emotional improvements to reintegrate into society. As these tools become more refined, they may serve as essential components of the legal framework that emphasizes accountability alongside developmental support and individualized care.

Neurocognitive Aspects of Juvenile Delinquency

Juvenile delinquency is often closely linked to the neurocognitive development of adolescents, particularly in areas related to executive functioning and emotional regulation. Adolescence is a period of significant brain development, during which many cognitive functions are still maturing, especially those associated with the prefrontal cortex (PFC), which is central to higher-level thinking processes such as impulse control, attention, problem-solving, and the ability to consider long-term consequences. These executive functions are crucial for making rational decisions and controlling behavior, and impairments in these areas are commonly observed in juvenile offenders.

During adolescence, the PFC continues to develop, which can lead to deficits in several key cognitive abilities. These include difficulties with impulse control, attention, and focus, which can impair the ability to plan, problem-solve, and think critically about actions. Adolescents may struggle to maintain attention or focus on tasks, leading to hasty decision-making and impulsive behaviors. Additionally, they often struggle to apply logical reasoning to complex situations, leading to choices that prioritize immediate rewards over long-term consequences.

One of adolescents' most significant executive function deficits is the inability to assess future consequences accurately. This lack of mature decision-making can lead them to prioritize short-term rewards or relief, disregarding potential long-term adverse effects. These cognitive challenges make it more difficult for adolescents to make sound decisions or anticipate the outcomes of their actions. This tendency to act without fully considering consequences is a key factor in the higher rates of juvenile delinquency. As a result, many legal systems recognize diminished culpability in youth, emphasizing rehabilitation over punishment.

In addition to impairments in executive functioning, adolescent brains are more vulnerable to emotional dysregulation, which significantly impacts decision-making. The limbic system, which governs emotions and reward-seeking behavior, matures earlier than the prefrontal cortex, resulting in emotions having a strong influence on adolescents' actions. Adolescents often experience emotions more intensely, and these emotional responses can override rational thought. Emotional dysregulation leads to impulsive actions driven by anger, frustration, or the need for immediate gratification. This can manifest in aggressive behavior, such as fighting, or other risky behaviors, such as substance abuse or theft.

The combination of emotional dysregulation and underdeveloped cognitive control systems often leads to behaviors that escalate into delinquent acts. Adolescents may struggle to manage stress and negative emotions, resorting to maladaptive coping strategies that can result in legal consequences. The neurocognitive vulnerabilities inherent in adolescence suggest that juveniles may not fully possess the cognitive maturity necessary to make informed decisions about their actions. As a result, they may act impulsively or without considering the full impact of their behavior, which can lead to criminal actions. These developmental challenges illustrate the need for a legal system that takes into account adolescents' unique cognitive and emotional characteristics. Juveniles may not have the same cognitive capacity as adults to understand the consequences of their actions, and their behaviors may be driven more by emotional responses or impulsivity than by an intentional disregard for the law.

Given these neurocognitive factors, interventions targeting executive function improvement and emotional regulation are crucial in reducing juvenile delinquency. Programs that help adolescents develop better impulse control, emotional management, and decision-making skills can effectively mitigate delinquent behavior. CBT, mindfulness training, and emotional intelligence programs are examples of approaches that can help adolescents enhance their critical thinking skills, manage stress effectively, and regulate their emotions. When implemented early and consistently, these interventions can support healthier developmental trajectories and reduce the likelihood of future criminal behavior.

Providing support during this critical period of brain development can reduce the likelihood of delinquent behavior and the risk of recidivism. The neurocognitive aspects of juvenile delinquency highlight the significant role of brain development in shaping adolescent behavior. The underdeveloped executive functions and heightened emotional responses characteristic of adolescence contribute to impulsive and risky behaviors, which can lead to legal consequences. Understanding these developmental challenges is crucial for creating effective interventions and a legal system that considers adolescents' unique cognitive and emotional characteristics.

Neuroimaging plays a pivotal role in illuminating the underlying neurobiological factors contributing to juvenile delinquency, particularly through its ability to visualize brain structure and function during adolescence. The fMRI and structural MRI provide compelling evidence of the developmental trajectory of key brain regions involved in decision-making and emotional regulation. These tools allow researchers and clinicians to observe the PFC's gradual maturation and the limbic system's earlier development, offering a window into the adolescent brain's heightened vulnerability to impulsivity and emotionally driven behavior. By mapping these developmental patterns, neuroimaging helps establish a scientific foundation for understanding the cognitive and emotional deficits frequently seen in juvenile offenders.

Neuroimaging plays a crucial role in identifying underdeveloped brain regions and highlighting the functional disconnect between cognitive control systems and emotion-generating systems in adolescents. Studies using fMRI, for instance, have shown that adolescents exhibit reduced activation in the PFC when completing tasks that require inhibition, delayed gratification, or risk evaluation—skills directly related to criminal behavior. In contrast, increased activity is observed in the amygdala and ventral striatum, areas linked to emotional reactivity and reward sensitivity. This imbalance explains why many adolescents are more inclined toward impulsive, emotionally charged actions that may lead to delinquent outcomes, especially in high-stress or peer-influenced situations.

Another significant contribution of neuroimaging is its ability to correlate specific structural or functional abnormalities with behavioral patterns in delinquent youth. For example, DTI has been used to assess the integrity of white matter tracts that connect various brain regions involved in executive functioning. Reduced white matter connectivity, particularly between the PFC and limbic regions, has been associated with impaired self-regulation and an increased risk of taking risks. These findings support the hypothesis that structural immaturity or neurodevelopmental delays in these neural pathways contribute directly to the behavioral issues observed in many juveniles involved in the justice system.

Neuroimaging also offers valuable insights into the timing and trajectory of brain maturation, highlighting adolescence as a critical period for targeted interventions.

The visualization of ongoing neural development highlights the plasticity of the adolescent brain, indicating that it remains malleable and responsive to environmental influences, including therapeutic interventions. This is particularly important for designing early prevention and rehabilitation strategies. Suppose imaging reveals that certain executive functions are underdeveloped. In that case, interventions can be timed and tailored to support those areas as they mature, ultimately aiding in reducing delinquent behavior and supporting more favorable developmental outcomes.

In the context of forensic evaluations, neuroimaging can serve as an empirical tool to inform more just legal decision-making. Neuroimaging data can be used to argue for diminished culpability or the need for rehabilitative rather than punitive responses by providing evidence that juveniles' brains are structurally and functionally immature in areas critical for responsible behavior. Legal decisions increasingly rely on neuroscientific evidence to support the idea that adolescents are neurologically distinct from adults, warranting alternative sentencing structures that prioritize education, therapy, and reintegration over incarceration. This has significant implications for ensuring that legal responses align with developmental science and do not disproportionately penalize youth for behaviors rooted in neurobiological immaturity.

Furthermore, neuroimaging enables researchers to assess the effectiveness of rehabilitation programs by tracking changes in brain function and structure over time. For instance, adolescents who undergo CBT or emotional regulation training can be re-imaged to determine whether there are corresponding improvements in PFC activation or connectivity. These findings can validate specific therapeutic approaches and inform policy decisions related to juvenile justice reform. Objective evidence of neurological improvement can also be instrumental in parole hearings or sentencing reviews, offering a data-driven approach to assessing rehabilitation progress and readiness for reintegration.

Another promising neuroimaging application is identifying risk factors for delinquent behavior before it escalates into criminal activity. Longitudinal studies that monitor brain development from early adolescence into adulthood can help detect atypical development patterns associated with poor impulse control or emotional instability. These insights could be used to develop early intervention programs for at-risk youth, providing support before behavioral problems escalate into legal issues. Neuroimaging can thus be part of a preventative framework that integrates neuroscience, education, and mental health services to address juvenile delinquency proactively.

Neuroimaging provides a critical bridge between developmental neuroscience and juvenile justice, offering scientific insight and practical applications. Visualizing the immature and often imbalanced development of the adolescent brain helps explain the cognitive and emotional vulnerabilities that contribute to juvenile delinquency. These insights support a shift toward a more rehabilitative and developmentally informed justice system grounded in evidence rather than punishment. As technology advances and understanding deepens, neuroimaging will remain essential in shaping ethical, effective, and equitable approaches to juvenile delinquency.

BCIs and AI represent transformative technologies in studying neurocognitive aspects of juvenile delinquency, offering new methods for real-time brain analysis and behavioral prediction. BCIs allow researchers to directly monitor and interact with brain activity, providing immediate data on how adolescents process emotional and cognitive stimuli. This can help juveniles identify specific neural responses associated with impulse control, emotional dysregulation, and decision-making. This real-time brain monitoring capability is especially valuable when studying executive function deficiencies, providing insight into how the underdeveloped prefrontal cortex and overactive limbic system contribute to delinquent behavior.

AI plays a complementary role by managing and analyzing the large datasets produced through BCI recordings and neuroimaging. Machine learning algorithms can detect subtle and complex patterns in brain activity that might be missed through traditional statistical approaches. For example, AI can analyze cognitive responses across thousands of juvenile subjects to detect neural markers that predict behavioral tendencies such as aggression, risk-taking, or poor impulse control. These predictive models can be refined over time and used to identify at-risk youth before they engage in criminal behavior, allowing for preemptive interventions tailored to their neurocognitive profile.

BCIs also open new possibilities for neurofeedback-based interventions in delinquent youth. BCIs can improve self-regulation, attention, and emotional control by training adolescents to modulate their brain activity. During neurofeedback sessions, individuals receive visual or auditory cues in response to their brain signals, helping them to recognize and manage maladaptive neural patterns. For instance, a juvenile struggling with emotional outbursts might learn to calm hyperactivity in the amygdala, fostering greater behavioral control over time. AI can optimize these interventions by personalizing training protocols based on each adolescent's unique brain responses.

In forensic and legal settings, BCIs and AI could significantly improve the accuracy and fairness of neuropsychological assessments. Rather than relying solely on behavioral observations or self-reported data, evaluators can use BCI-generated information to make more objective, evidence-based judgments about a juvenile's cognitive capacity and emotional regulation abilities. AI can assist in interpreting these data about normative developmental trajectories, highlighting when an adolescent's brain activity deviates from expected patterns. This can help establish whether a youth's behavior reflects typical developmental immaturity or more severe neurocognitive impairments, thereby informing sentencing, rehabilitation recommendations, or eligibility for diversion programs.

Integrating BCIs and AI into the study of juvenile delinquency highlights the growing intersection between neuroscience, technology, and justice reform. These tools enhance our understanding of the adolescent brain and offer practical applications for early intervention, personalized treatment, and equitable legal evaluations. As technology becomes more accessible and refined, it holds the potential to revolutionize juvenile justice by promoting a system that recognizes the biological foundations of behavior and seeks rehabilitation over punishment. In doing so, BCIs and AI can help bridge the gap between scientific insight and social justice, ensuring that responses to juvenile delinquency are compassionate and informed by the latest advancements in neurotechnology.

Neurodevelopmental Factors in Juvenile Delinquency

As discussed in previous chapters, juvenile delinquency cannot be fully understood without considering the complex interaction between biological, psychological, and environmental factors. While earlier sections have highlighted the role of brain maturation and cognitive development in adolescent behavior, it is crucial to delve deeper into the neurodevelopmental influences, especially how untreated and undiagnosed juvenile issues can significantly impact brain functioning and cognitive performance, leading to severe consequences that may persist into adulthood. The implications of these developmental disruptions are far-reaching, not only affecting immediate behavioral outcomes but also setting the stage for chronic mental health challenges, academic underachievement, social instability, and involvement in the criminal justice system well into adult life.

Adverse childhood experiences (ACEs) have a profound and lasting impact on the developing brain. Chronic exposure to such stressors disrupts the neurodevelopmental processes, particularly in brain regions responsible for emotional regulation, impulse control, and cognitive flexibility. For example, the hippocampus—crucial for memory formation and emotional regulation—often shows reduced volume in individuals exposed to sustained trauma. Similarly, the amygdala, which governs fear and aggression, becomes hyperactive, leading to heightened emotional reactivity and an increased risk of aggressive behaviors. The prefrontal cortex, which orchestrates decision-making and behavioral inhibition, also exhibits impaired functioning, leading to poor judgment and impulsivity.

Empirical data support the correlation between ACEs and increased rates of juvenile delinquency. According to the CDC, individuals with four or more ACEs are five times more likely to engage in violent behavior. They are significantly more prone to substance abuse and mental health disorders. These early experiences compromise a child's ability to develop self-regulation, establish secure attachments, and navigate social situations—all foundational skills that, when underdeveloped, heighten vulnerability to delinquent behavior. The neurobiological consequences of ACEs not only manifest in childhood and adolescence but often persist into adulthood, increasing the risk of chronic psychiatric disorders, unemployment, relationship instability, and ongoing interactions with the criminal justice system.

Environmental and socioeconomic factors also play a critical role in shaping neurodevelopmental and behavioral outcomes in youth. Children growing up in low-income neighborhoods often face a multitude of risk factors, including food insecurity, substandard housing, under-resourced schools, and high levels of community violence. These conditions contribute to chronic stress, which interferes with the development of critical brain regions, including the prefrontal cortex and limbic system. Research from the National Scientific Council on the Developing Child emphasizes that prolonged exposure to stress hormones, such as cortisol, during early life can impair synaptic connections in these areas, leading to deficits in executive functioning and emotional control.

Moreover, children in disadvantaged environments are more likely to witness or be involved in criminal activity, normalizing antisocial behaviors and reducing internal inhibitions against lawbreaking. The absence of positive role models, coupled with the presence of social disorganization, fosters environments where survival often depends on aggression, mistrust, and risk-taking. These contextual factors reinforce maladaptive behavior patterns that become ingrained over time, making intervention increasingly tricky. The plasticity of the adolescent brain means these influences can become biologically embedded, altering neural pathways and reinforcing behavioral tendencies that contribute to delinquency and future criminality.

While environmental and social factors are significant, genetic predispositions also contribute to the likelihood of juvenile delinquency. Studies have identified specific gene variants—such as those affecting the MAOA enzyme—that are linked to increased impulsivity, aggression, and a predisposition to antisocial behavior. However, it is critical to note that genetics alone does not determine outcomes; somewhat, their expression is shaped by environmental factors through mechanisms such as epigenetics. Epigenetic modifications refer to chemical changes to DNA that affect gene expression without altering the DNA sequence. These changes can be triggered by early-life stress, trauma, or environmental toxins and can have lasting effects on brain structure and function.

For example, research has shown that children exposed to chronic adversity may experience epigenetic alterations in genes associated with the stress response system, such as those regulating cortisol. These changes can heighten emotional reactivity and impair stress regulation, making adolescents more prone to impulsive and aggressive behaviors. Notably, such epigenetic changes can be passed down across generations, meaning that the effects of trauma and adversity can become biologically inherited, further perpetuating cycles of poverty, violence, and criminal behavior. This relationship between biology and environment highlights the importance of early identification and intervention for at-risk youth, not only to prevent immediate harm but to break intergenerational cycles of trauma and dysfunction.

Neurodevelopmental factors—including adverse childhood experiences, environmental stressors, and genetic and epigenetic influences—play a pivotal role in shaping juveniles' cognitive and emotional development. When left untreated or undiagnosed, these issues can compromise brain functioning, impair cognitive performance, and create behavioral patterns that persist into adulthood, often with severe implications for mental health, social integration, and legal outcomes. Recognizing the long-term impact of these developmental challenges is essential for developing effective prevention, intervention, and rehabilitation strategies tailored to the unique needs of vulnerable youth populations.

BCIs and AI are pivotal in advancing our understanding of the neurodevelopmental factors that influence juvenile delinquency. BCIs facilitate direct communication between the brain and external devices, enabling real-time monitoring of neural activity. When integrated with AI, these systems can decode complex neural patterns, offering insights into cognitive and emotional processes. This synergy enables researchers to observe how adolescents' brains respond to various stimuli, shedding light on the mechanisms underlying decision-making and impulse control. Such a detailed analysis is essential for identifying neural correlates of delinquent behaviors.

AI enhances the efficacy of BCIs by processing vast amounts of neural data and identifying subtle patterns that may elude traditional analytical methods. Machine learning algorithms can predict behavioral outcomes based on neural activity, providing a deeper understanding of the cognitive processes underpinning delinquency. This predictive capability is crucial for early intervention strategies, allowing personalized approaches tailored to individual neural profiles. By analyzing how adolescents' brains respond to various scenarios, AI-driven BCIs can identify vulnerabilities to risky behaviors. This information is vital for developing targeted prevention and rehabilitation programs.

The integration of AI and BCIs also holds promise in assessing the impact of environmental and socioeconomic factors on brain development. By monitoring neural responses to various environmental stimuli, researchers can assess how stressors, such as community violence or socioeconomic instability, impact brain regions responsible for emotional regulation and decision-making. This approach provides empirical data on the environmental influences contributing to delinquent behavior. Understanding these neural responses is essential for designing interventions that address individual and contextual factors. Such insights can inform policies aimed at mitigating the adverse effects of detrimental environments on youth development.

Furthermore, AI and BCIs can elucidate the role of genetic and epigenetic factors in juvenile delinquency. Researchers can identify biomarkers associated with impulsivity, aggression, and susceptibility to environmental influences by analyzing neural data in conjunction with genetic information. This holistic approach enhances our understanding of the relationship between genetics, environment, and brain development. Identifying specific neural signatures linked to delinquent behavior can lead to the development of personalized interventions. These interventions could be tailored to an individual's genetic predispositions and environmental exposures, optimizing their effectiveness.

These technologies also offer a non-invasive and dynamic method for tracking changes in brain function over time. Unlike traditional assessments that rely on self-report or behavioral observation, BCIs can offer objective measurements of neurocognitive development. AI can then be used to identify patterns that correlate with successful intervention outcomes or relapse into delinquent behavior. This allows for real-time feedback and adjustment of therapeutic strategies based on brain activity. Such adaptive methods are crucial in treating adolescents whose brains are still undergoing critical stages of development.

In the context of clinical interventions, BCIs combined with AI can enhance cognitive training programs. For example, AI analysis can monitor and optimize neurofeedback sessions that target executive function deficits. By identifying how a juvenile's brain responds to these sessions, therapists can refine and personalize treatment plans. This contributes to more efficient rehabilitation strategies tailored to everyone's unique neural development. Moreover, these approaches promote engagement and self-awareness, which are crucial for achieving lasting behavioral change.

AI-powered analysis of BCI data can also help classify different subtypes of delinquent behavior, which may correspond to varying neurodevelopmental profiles. For instance, some juveniles may show heightened emotional reactivity, while others may struggle primarily with attention and planning. By categorizing these profiles, professionals can allocate resources more effectively and select the most appropriate interventions. This segmentation approach ensures that treatment is both efficient and impactful. It also contributes to a deeper theoretical understanding of the diversity within juvenile delinquent populations.

Ethical considerations are paramount in applying AI and BCIs in this context. The collection and analysis of neural data raise concerns about privacy, consent, and potential misuse of information. Establishing robust ethical guidelines is essential to protecting individuals' rights and ensuring that these technologies are used responsibly. Transparent policies governing data usage and robust security measures are essential for maintaining public trust. As these technologies evolve, continuous ethical reviews will be necessary to address emerging challenges and ensure that advancements serve the best interests of society.

Neurodevelopmental research using AI and BCIs can inform legal perspectives on juvenile justice. Empirical evidence showing immaturity in key brain areas may support calls for rehabilitative rather than punitive sentencing. This aligns legal practices more closely with scientific knowledge about adolescent brain development. AI-assisted neuroimaging data can also be introduced during forensic evaluations to better understand the defendant's capacity for judgment and self-control. This helps ensure fairer outcomes that consider developmental science alongside legal standards.

The convergence of BCIs and AI offers transformative tools for studying the neurodevelopmental aspects of juvenile delinquency. These technologies enable the detailed monitoring and analysis of neural activity, providing insights into the cognitive and emotional factors that contribute to delinquent behavior. By integrating neural data with genetic and environmental information, researchers can develop personalized interventions addressing the unique needs of each adolescent. However, it is crucial to navigate the ethical landscape carefully, ensuring that these powerful tools are used responsibly and with respect for individual rights. Continued research and ethical discourse will be crucial in harnessing the full potential of AI and BCIs in promoting positive youth development and reducing delinquency.

Legal and Ethical Implications for Sentencing Juvenile Offenders

One of the most significant legal implications of juvenile neurodevelopment is the question of culpability. Research has shown that adolescents possess underdeveloped executive functioning, particularly in areas such as impulse control, risk assessment, and decision-making abilities, primarily governed by the prefrontal cortex, which does not reach full maturity until the mid-20s. These neurodevelopmental findings challenge traditional notions of legal responsibility by demonstrating that juveniles lack the same capacity for moral reasoning, long-term planning, and emotional regulation as adults.

Landmark U.S. Supreme Court decisions—*Roper v. Simmons* (2005), *Graham v. Florida* (2010), and *Miller v. Alabama* (2012)—reflect a shift in legal thinking influenced by neuroscience. In Roper, the Court held that it was unconstitutional to impose the death penalty on juveniles. In Graham, it prohibited life without parole for non-homicide offenses. In Miller, it banned mandatory life without parole even for homicide cases, mandating individualized sentencing that considers the juvenile's circumstances and potential for change. These rulings acknowledge the developmental differences between adolescents and adults, recognizing that juveniles are less culpable due to their ongoing cognitive, emotional, and psychosocial development. As a result, the justice system is increasingly adopting a rehabilitative approach rather than a punitive one toward juvenile offenders.

These rulings are rooted in scientific evidence that adolescents are less culpable than adults due to their immaturity, susceptibility to peer pressure, and greater capacity for rehabilitation. The American Psychological Association and other expert bodies have submitted amicus briefs in support of these conclusions, highlighting studies that show juveniles are more likely than adults to reform and that their brains are structurally and functionally immature in ways that mitigate their moral and legal responsibility. Additionally, longitudinal studies from institutions like the MacArthur Foundation Research Network on Adolescent Development and Juvenile Justice demonstrate that many juvenile offenders "age out" of delinquency, especially when given access to rehabilitative services rather than harsh punishment.

The distinction between juvenile and adult offenders has become more prominent in the legal system as science has provided a clearer understanding of adolescent development. The age of legal responsibility has been re-examined in many jurisdictions, with an increasing focus on cognitive and emotional maturity rather than chronological age. For example, as of 2024, 28 U.S. states have raised the age of criminal responsibility to at least 18, and several others are considering similar reforms. This movement reflects a growing awareness that punitive systems are often ineffective for youth and may exacerbate recidivism. Juvenile offenders, especially those exposed to trauma or adverse childhood experiences, often lack the neurodevelopmental capacity to foresee the full consequences of their actions. As such, the justice system has begun to shift toward models that prioritize rehabilitation, treatment, and educational interventions over incarceration.

In this context, neuropsychopathological evaluations are increasingly used to inform judicial decisions. Courts may rely on expert testimony regarding an adolescent's cognitive development, emotional maturity, trauma history, or mental health conditions to better understand the psychological underpinnings of their behavior. These evaluations can help illuminate whether a youth acted impulsively or with forethought, thereby distinguishing between developmentally driven behavior and true criminal intent. Such assessments can be especially crucial in cases involving serious offenses, where the court must balance public safety with the potential for growth and reform in the adolescent offender.

There is a profound ethical dilemma in sentencing juvenile offenders, particularly regarding how the justice system should weigh public protection against the rights and developmental needs of youth. On one hand, society must protect its members from harm, especially in cases of violent or repeated offending. On the other hand, ethical principles of justice demand that punishment be proportionate to the offense and the offender's moral and cognitive development. Given that juveniles are in a formative phase of life with considerable capacity for change, many ethicists and legal scholars argue that sentencing practices should reflect this potential for growth and development.

Moreover, emerging data suggest that harsh sentencing measures such as long-term incarceration, solitary confinement, and life without parole do not reduce juvenile crime rates and often lead to worse outcomes. Youth who are incarcerated for extended periods are more likely to suffer from mental health issues, fall behind educationally, and re-offend upon release. According to the Annie E. Casey Foundation, youth in juvenile detention are 39% more likely to be rearrested than those in community-based programs. This supports the ethical and practical case for investing in restorative justice, community-based alternatives, trauma-informed care, and education-focused interventions. These rehabilitative approaches respect the developmental science of adolescence and align with public safety goals by reducing recidivism and supporting reintegration.

The legal and ethical implications of juvenile sentencing must be understood through the lens of developmental neuroscience and the context of justice reform. Adolescents are fundamentally different from adults in their cognitive, emotional, and moral capacities, and the justice system must evolve to reflect these differences. The growing consensus among neuroscientists, psychologists, and legal experts is that a rehabilitative, individualized approach—grounded in science and guided by ethical principles—is both more humane and more effective in addressing juvenile delinquency.

Juvenile Rehabilitation and Treatment Programs

The neurodevelopmental stages of the adolescent brain must inform rehabilitation strategies for juvenile offenders. Because the prefrontal cortex, responsible for executive functions, such as reasoning, planning, and impulse control, continues to mature throughout adolescence, interventions that support the development of these functions are crucial. CBT remains a cornerstone of such interventions. CBT aims to restructure maladaptive cognitive schemas and behavioral patterns by teaching adolescents to recognize distorted thinking, control impulses, and develop alternative problem-solving strategies. Research has consistently shown that CBT significantly reduces recidivism when combined with individualized treatment plans tailored to developmental capacity and psychological needs.

In addition to CBT, neurofeedback—a form of biofeedback that trains individuals to regulate brainwave activity—has shown promise in improving self-regulation among juveniles with histories of trauma or conduct disorders. Neurofeedback enables participants to gain conscious control over neural processes associated with attention, impulse control, and emotional reactivity. Studies have reported improvements in emotional stability, behavioral inhibition, and attention span, particularly in adolescents with ADHD or PTSD, which frequently co-occur in juvenile justice populations. As a non-invasive, individualized intervention, neurofeedback offers an alternative or complementary treatment modality that addresses the neurological underpinnings of dysregulated behavior, enhancing outcomes for at-risk youth within rehabilitative settings.

Cognitive training programs, such as those focused on enhancing working memory and attention control, are also emerging as practical tools for improving neurodevelopmental functioning. These programs focus on strengthening the neural circuits involved in executive function, using repetitive and adaptive cognitive tasks to promote neuroplasticity. Applying these methods in forensic settings has been associated with increased frustration tolerance, improved decision-making, and reduced aggressive behavior. Moreover, research has demonstrated that consistent participation in cognitive training can result in measurable improvements in brain connectivity and functional activation in regions associated with self-regulation and impulse control.

Importantly, trauma-informed care frameworks have gained traction in juvenile rehabilitation. These models recognize the high prevalence of early trauma among justice-involved youth and incorporate strategies designed to avoid traumatization, enhance resilience, and support emotion regulation. Integrating neuroscience-informed practices into rehabilitation ensures that interventions align with the adolescent brain's developmental readiness and its capacity for change. By prioritizing safety, trust-building, and empowerment, trauma-informed approaches foster environments where youth feel supported rather than punished, which is essential for meaningful behavioral transformation. Evidence-based interventions grounded in these frameworks have been associated with reductions in recidivism, enhanced emotional regulation, and increased engagement in educational and therapeutic services.

Educational and vocational programs are foundational to juvenile rehabilitation, providing cognitive enrichment and skills that promote future-oriented social reintegration. From a neurodevelopmental standpoint, educational engagement contributes to cortical development, especially in regions associated with executive functioning and language. Structured learning environments can counteract the developmental delays caused by early neglect, trauma, or environmental deprivation commonly found in justice-involved youth. Moreover, access to education increases self-efficacy and fosters a sense of purpose, both of which are critical for reducing antisocial behavior. Studies have shown that youth participating in education and job training while in detention are significantly less likely to re-offend upon release, underscoring the long-term benefits of academic and vocational investment.

High-quality academic programs within juvenile detention centers can significantly improve cognitive and behavioral outcomes. Research has shown that when juvenile offenders have access to specialized instruction—particularly in literacy, mathematics, and critical thinking—they are more likely to achieve educational milestones and exhibit prosocial behaviors. Furthermore, structured education fosters a sense of competence and personal agency, countering the learned helplessness and low self-esteem often accompanying juvenile offending. These educational gains support cognitive development and serve as protective factors against recidivism by opening pathways to employment and community reintegration. Consistent academic engagement has also been linked to improved emotional regulation and increased adherence to institutional rules, emphasizing its rehabilitative impact.

Vocational training programs enhance rehabilitation by preparing juveniles for future employment and independence. These programs typically include training in trades such as carpentry, culinary arts, automotive repair, information technology, and cosmetology. Vocational training satisfies several developmental needs: It offers a constructive outlet for energy, builds tangible skills, and fosters identity development. For adolescents—whose neural systems are attuned to feedback and reward—earning certifications and receiving praise for skill development may stimulate motivational centers in the brain, reinforcing prosocial behavior.

Integrating academic and vocational programming with therapeutic support maximizes the impact of rehabilitation. When juveniles see clear pathways to legitimate success, their risk of reoffending decreases, and their engagement in self-destructive behavior diminishes. Additionally, these programs provide structure and purpose, which are essential for adolescents who lack stable role models or positive reinforcement. By combining skill-building with emotional and psychological support, these integrated approaches help youth build resilience, develop healthier coping mechanisms, and foster a sense of accomplishment that reinforces their commitment to positive change.

The role of family in juvenile rehabilitation cannot be overstated. Adolescents are developmentally primed for relational learning, and the quality of familial interactions has a significant impact on emotional and neural development. Family-based interventions aim to strengthen the family unit, enhance parenting practices, and mitigate environmental stressors that contribute to delinquency. Functional family therapy (FFT), multisystemic therapy (MST), and parent management training (PMT) are among the most evidence-based approaches in this area.

Multisystemic therapy, for instance, targets multiple areas of the juvenile's life—family, school, peers, and community—to address the systemic contributors to antisocial behavior. MST is rooted in ecological systems theory and emphasizes collaboration between the juvenile, caregivers, and clinicians to reduce negative influences and increase protective factors. This approach has shown long-term success in reducing recidivism, enhancing family cohesion, and improving school attendance and performance. Furthermore, MST's focus on individualized interventions tailored to each juvenile's unique circumstances increases the likelihood of sustained behavioral change and successful reintegration into society.

PMT educates caregivers on effective discipline strategies, emotion regulation, and communication techniques. The goal is to shift the family dynamic from one of conflict and coercion to one of structure, support, and positive reinforcement. Neurodevelopmentally, this type of intervention promotes emotional safety and regulation, which are critical for the maturation of limbic-prefrontal connectivity. By fostering a supportive environment, PMT helps juveniles develop self-control, resilience, and emotional intelligence. This, in turn, improves their ability to regulate impulses, manage stress, and make more thoughtful decisions, all of which contribute to reduced antisocial behavior and lower rates of recidivism.

Family therapy also addresses transgenerational trauma, substance abuse, mental health issues, and unresolved conflicts that may be contributing to the juvenile's behavior. By fostering healthier attachment relationships and modeling effective coping strategies, family interventions lay the foundation for long-term behavioral change. These therapeutic approaches help families break cycles of dysfunction and create a stable, nurturing environment for the adolescent to thrive. Additionally, family therapy promotes the development of prosocial behaviors and emotional intelligence, which are essential for the juvenile's successful reintegration into society.

Rehabilitative efforts must extend beyond institutional walls to include community and peer-based initiatives that support reintegration. During adolescence, adolescents are particularly susceptible to peer influence due to the heightened activity of reward-related brain structures, such as the nucleus accumbens. While negative peer influence can lead to delinquency, prosocial peer environments promote rehabilitation. Positive peer relationships offer emotional support, reinforce healthy behaviors, and foster a sense of belonging that helps mitigate the influence of antisocial peers. Community programs facilitating connections with prosocial peers and mentors can offer accountability and encouragement, which are essential for long-term behavioral change. These environments also help adolescents practice and reinforce the skills they have learned in rehabilitation, thereby increasing their chances of successful reintegration into society.

Restorative justice programs are compelling in this regard. These initiatives bring together offenders, victims, and community members in facilitated dialogues that emphasize accountability, empathy, and reparation. Restorative justice has been associated with lower recidivism rates and improved psychosocial outcomes, especially when combined with other rehabilitative supports. These programs help youth understand the social consequences of their behavior and create opportunities for meaningful reconciliation and community healing. By fostering a sense of responsibility and providing a platform for offenders to make amends, restorative justice encourages personal growth and strengthens adolescents' connections to their community.

Mentorship programs also provide significant support. Mentors can model adaptive behavior, offer emotional support, and guide juveniles toward achieving their educational and career goals. Peer mentorship—where formerly incarcerated youth mentor current offenders—can be incredibly effective, as it combines relatability with a sense of hope for change. These programs create a powerful connection and demonstrate that change is possible, even for those facing similar challenges. By fostering positive relationships, mentorship also helps build resilience and encourages the development of prosocial skills essential for successful reintegration into society.

Finally, aftercare and reentry programs ensure continuity of support for juveniles once they leave detention facilities. These programs include case management, housing assistance, mental health support, and employment placement services. Community-based support mitigates the risk of reoffending by creating a stable, resource-rich environment that encourages long-term behavioral change. Furthermore, these programs help juveniles navigate the challenges of reintegration, including reconnecting with their families and managing relationships with peers. By providing ongoing guidance and practical resources, aftercare programs increase the likelihood of successful reintegration and reduce the chances of recidivism.

The future of juvenile justice lies in the relationship between neuroscience, psychology, and law. Advances in neuroimaging are transforming our understanding of adolescent brain development. These tools enable researchers to observe how brain connectivity and activation patterns differ in juvenile offenders, particularly in areas such as moral reasoning, emotional regulation, and impulse control. This growing body of knowledge enables more precise, individualized assessments of juveniles, which can lead to tailored interventions that address the specific neurodevelopmental needs of at-risk youth. As our understanding of the adolescent brain continues to evolve, it will provide the foundation for more effective, developmentally appropriate approaches to rehabilitation and justice.

For example, fMRI studies have shown that justice-involved youth often exhibit reduced activity in the dorsolateral prefrontal cortex (associated with self-control) and increased activity in the amygdala (linked to emotional reactivity). Understanding these neural signatures could improve individualized risk assessments, treatment needs, and rehabilitation potential. By identifying these neural patterns, clinicians can design interventions that target specific areas of dysfunction, such as enhancing impulse control and emotional regulation.

This neurobiological insight could also inform decisions on sentencing, rehabilitation strategies, and post-release support, ultimately leading to more effective outcomes for juvenile offenders.

Emerging research in forensic psychology is also exploring how trauma, neurodiversity (e.g., autism spectrum disorder or learning disabilities), and psychopathology intersect with juvenile offending. A growing body of evidence supports the development of screening tools that integrate neurodevelopmental assessments with behavioral and social evaluations. These tools may help clinicians and legal professionals make more informed decisions about diversion, sentencing, and intervention. By identifying underlying neurodevelopmental or psychological factors, these assessments can ensure that juveniles receive the most appropriate treatment and avoid punitive measures that may be ineffective or harmful. Ultimately, these advancements will foster a more nuanced and empathetic approach to juvenile justice, where rehabilitation precedes retribution.

Artificial intelligence and machine learning are also beginning to play a role in risk assessment and rehabilitation planning. By analyzing large datasets of neuropsychological, environmental, and behavioral variables, these systems can help predict which interventions are most likely to succeed for a given youth, potentially reducing bias and improving outcomes. These technologies can also track progress over time, allowing for real-time adjustments to treatment plans based on the juvenile's evolving needs. As AI systems become more refined, they could enhance the accuracy of risk assessments and ensure that interventions are tailored to maximize each juvenile's chances of rehabilitation and reintegration.

Integrating neuroscience into legal policy could reshape how juvenile justice systems assess culpability and define rehabilitation. Future legal reforms may codify the adolescent brain's malleability, leading to more individualized and developmentally informed sentencing practices. As science advances, ethical considerations will remain paramount, ensuring that new technologies and findings are used to support—not punish—vulnerable youth. This integration may also promote the expansion of restorative justice models, focusing on healing and growth rather than retribution. Ultimately, these shifts could result in a more compassionate, effective, and just system that recognizes the potential for change in all young individuals.

The integration of neuroscience, psychology, and law into juvenile justice holds the potential to transform the way we understand, assess, and rehabilitate young offenders. As research continues to illuminate the developmental nuances of the adolescent brain, it becomes increasingly clear that juvenile offenders are not fully culpable in the same way as adults, given their ongoing cognitive and emotional maturation. By embracing this scientific understanding, the legal system can adopt more individualized and developmentally appropriate approaches to sentencing and rehabilitation. Moreover, incorporating neurodevelopmental and trauma-informed strategies into juvenile justice practices can foster more effective interventions that prioritize rehabilitation over punishment. As we progress, ethical considerations must guide these advances, ensuring that vulnerable youth are supported in their journey toward positive change and reintegration into society.

The Role of Neuropsychopathology in Civil Forensic Cases

Neuropsychopathology plays a crucial role in civil forensic cases, providing essential assessments of cognitive functioning and brain injuries that inform legal decisions. Civil forensic cases often involve determining the impact of neurological conditions or brain injuries on an individual's ability to perform daily activities, engage in employment, or maintain relationships. Forensic professionals apply their expertise to assess cognitive impairments, emotional regulation, and behavior in individuals involved in legal disputes. Their evaluations are crucial in determining causality, extent of damage, and potential for recovery, all of which influence legal outcomes.

Personal Injury Cases

Personal injury cases are among the most common civil cases where neuropsychological (and neuropsychopathological) assessments are required. When an individual sustains a TBI or other neurological damage because of an accident, neuropsychological evaluations help quantify the cognitive, emotional, and functional consequences of the injury. These assessments determine the extent of impairment and provide objective data to support legal claims related to damages, compensation, and future carc needs.

In personal injury cases, the clinical expert's role is to determine whether the injury has caused a significant and lasting impact on the individual's cognitive abilities, such as memory, attention, executive function, or language. For instance, a person who suffers a concussion may report symptoms such as forgetfulness, mood swings, or difficulties concentrating. A neuropsychologist will use standardized tests to assess these symptoms in detail, comparing the individual's cognitive functioning to normative data and pre-injury baselines (when available). This process provides the court with objective evidence regarding the extent of cognitive deficits and their relevance to the individual's ability to return to work or perform other daily functions.

Neuropsychopathological testing in personal injury cases can also help to clarify whether cognitive complaints are consistent with the alleged injury or if other factors (such as pre-existing conditions or psychological factors) might be contributing to the symptoms. This can be especially important in cases where there is a discrepancy between the reported symptoms and the medical findings, such as when the individual presents with emotional distress but lacks objective evidence of neurological impairment. In such cases, the neuropsychologist's assessment can validate the claims or provide insight into other contributing factors that may influence the case outcome.

Workplace Accidents

Workplace accidents often involve significant injuries that can result in long-term disability or cognitive impairment, making neuropsychological evaluations essential for determining the impact of the injury on the individual's ability to return to work or perform routine tasks. Workplace accidents may lead to traumatic brain injuries, repetitive stress injuries, or conditions related to workplace stressors, and neuropsychologists are called upon to assess the cognitive and emotional consequences of such incidents. These evaluations help identify not only the severity of impairments but also guide rehabilitation planning and workplace accommodations to support recovery and reintegration.

In these cases, the clinical expert conducts a detailed assessment to understand how the injury affects the individual's cognitive functioning, emotional regulation, and overall quality of life. For example, a worker who has suffered a TBI in a construction accident may experience difficulties with memory, attention, or executive function, all of which can hinder their ability to perform tasks at work. Neuropsychopathological evaluations provide empirical data that help determine whether these deficits are permanent or whether there is potential for improvement with rehabilitation. These findings are crucial for calculating appropriate compensation, determining the need for retraining or accommodations, and assessing whether the individual can return to their previous role or should be considered for a different position.

In addition to cognitive assessments, clinical experts also evaluate the emotional consequences of workplace accidents, such as depression, anxiety, or PTSD, which are often seen in individuals recovering from such incidents. Their report can provide the court with a holistic view of the individual's recovery trajectory, guiding decisions on the scope of compensation, the need for ongoing treatment, and long-term employment prospects. These evaluations are critical in determining the extent to which emotional and psychological impairments affect daily functioning and occupational capabilities. By documenting both the neurological and emotional impact of the injury, neuropsychologists help ensure that individuals receive fair and comprehensive legal and medical consideration.

Disability Evaluations

Disability evaluations are another key area where neuropsychopathological assessments play a crucial role. When individuals apply for disability benefits through programs such as Social Security Disability Insurance (SSDI) or Supplemental Security Income (SSI), neuropsychologists evaluate the impact of their cognitive or psychological impairments on their ability to function in daily life and engage in gainful employment. These evaluations assess how neurological impairments, such as those resulting from brain injuries, neurological diseases (e.g., Alzheimer's disease, multiple sclerosis), or psychiatric conditions (e.g., severe depression, schizophrenia), impact the individual's ability to perform work-related activities or manage daily tasks independently.

Neuropsychologists (and neuropsychopathologists) use standardized tests to assess cognitive functioning in various domains, including memory, executive function, motor skills, attention, and social cognition. These tests help determine whether the individual's cognitive deficits meet the criteria for disability under the law. Additionally, they assess how these deficits impact an individual's ability to sustain work or manage household tasks, which is crucial in determining eligibility for disability benefits. Their evaluations often include both objective testing results and clinical observations, providing a comprehensive understanding of how neurological impairments translate into real-world limitations.

In disability evaluations, the neuropsychologist's role extends beyond assessing cognitive deficits. They also offer insights into the individual's potential for rehabilitation or improvement, which is important for decisions regarding ongoing eligibility. By integrating clinical findings with functional assessments, neuropsychologists help stakeholders understand not only the existing impairments but also how these may evolve. For example, if a worker who has suffered a brain injury is evaluated and found to have moderate cognitive deficits but shows signs of recovery with proper rehabilitation, the neuropsychologist's findings may suggest a prognosis of gradual improvement and inform decisions about the need for continued benefits.

Neuropsychopathological Evaluations in Custody and Divorce Cases

Neuropsychopathological evaluations are increasingly being used in family law cases, particularly in custody disputes and divorce proceedings, where one party may claim that the other is incapable of parenting due to cognitive or psychological impairments. In these situations, the forensic expert's role is to assess the mental and cognitive functioning of the parents involved to determine whether they are fit to care for their children. This includes assessing the parents' ability to provide for the child's emotional, developmental, and physical needs. The findings can play a pivotal role in legal decisions, helping courts ensure that custody arrangements are made in the best interest of the child.

In custody cases, forensic experts assess factors such as cognitive stability, emotional regulation, and the ability to make appropriate decisions. For example, suppose a parent has a history of severe depression, cognitive impairments from a brain injury, or personality disorders. In that case, they will assess whether these conditions interfere with the parents' ability to fulfill their parenting responsibilities. Evaluations in these cases can include interviews, standardized tests, and behavioral observations. Also, the expert will often interview collateral sources (such as teachers or caregivers) to gather additional information about the parent's behavior and functioning. These comprehensive assessments help courts determine what custody arrangement is in the child's best interest, ensuring their safety and developmental needs are met.

In divorce cases, neuropsychopathological assessments may also be used to evaluate the emotional and cognitive impacts of the divorce on the individuals involved, particularly if one party claims that the other has suffered from emotional instability or a decline in mental functioning. These assessments can be critical in informing custody decisions, especially when mental health concerns may affect parenting capacity or the stability of the home environment. For instance, in cases where one spouse is accused of being emotionally abusive or neglectful due to mental health issues, the expert's evaluation can provide clarity regarding the severity of the alleged psychological impairments and whether they are significant enough to impact the overall well-being of the children or the ability to co-parent effectively.

The expert's evaluation in these cases can help the court understand the individual's cognitive functioning in family dynamics and determine whether any special considerations are needed to ensure the child's best interests. The goal is to provide the court with objective, scientifically grounded information that supports fair and informed decisions about custody arrangements and the division of responsibilities between parents. By evaluating the parents' emotional regulation, cognitive capabilities, and ability to provide a stable environment, the expert helps ensure that the child's emotional and developmental needs are prioritized. This thorough and unbiased assessment can ultimately assist in creating a custody plan that is in the child's long-term welfare.

Neuropsychopathology is an essential field in civil forensic cases. It offers crucial insights into how neurological impairments and psychological conditions affect individuals' daily functioning, employment, and ability to care for their families. In personal injury, workplace accidents, disability evaluations, and custody disputes, neuropsychologists play a crucial role in providing evidence-based assessments that inform legal decisions. Their expertise in assessing cognitive and emotional functioning, combined with their understanding of neurodevelopment and neuropsychological assessment techniques, helps ensure that individuals receive appropriate compensation, rehabilitation, and care while also ensuring that decisions regarding custody or divorce are made with the child's well-being as the primary focus.

As the field of neuropsychopathology continues to evolve, the integration of cutting-edge neuroimaging techniques, advancements in cognitive rehabilitation, and increased understanding of the brain's role in behavior and decision-making will continue to enhance neuropsychopathologists' contributions to civil forensic cases. These advances further strengthen the role of neuropsychology in the justice system, enabling more informed, fair, and scientifically grounded legal decisions. By providing a clearer understanding of the neurological underpinnings of cognitive and emotional functioning, neuropsychologists can offer valuable insights into the complexities of individual behavior, further refining legal outcomes and ensuring that justice is served. As technology progresses, neuropsychologists will likely play an even more pivotal role in assessing mental health and cognitive impairments in legal contexts.

Neuropsychopathological evaluations play a pivotal role in the decision-making process of custody and divorce cases, particularly when one party raises concerns about the cognitive or emotional fitness of the other to parent effectively. As these evaluations are based on a combination of objective data and clinical insights, they provide the court with a comprehensive understanding of the psychological and cognitive functioning of the parents involved. These evaluations are increasingly viewed as essential for ensuring that decisions are grounded in science and fairness.

The process involves testing cognitive capacities and considers emotional regulation, impulse control, and decision-making abilities integral to successful parenting. Neuropsychopathological evaluations also help identify underlying conditions that may not be immediately apparent, such as subtle cognitive impairments or emotional dysregulation, which can significantly affect parenting abilities. By providing detailed, evidence-based assessments, these evaluations ensure that custody decisions are made with a clear understanding of each parent's strengths and limitations, ultimately prioritizing the child's best interests.

One of the key aspects of neuropsychological evaluations in custody cases is assessing the parent's cognitive stability. For instance, parents who have experienced traumatic brain injuries, strokes, or neurodegenerative diseases may show impairments in memory, executive functioning, or attention. These cognitive domains are essential in parenting, where day-to-day tasks demand planning, organization, and the ability to respond quickly and appropriately to a child's needs. Neuropsychologists use standardized tests and assessments, including measures of intelligence, memory, executive functions, and attention span, to determine if a parent's cognitive limitations could impact their ability to provide adequate care for their child.

In addition to assessing cognitive abilities, neuropsychopathologists also evaluate emotional regulation, which refers to the parent's ability to manage their emotions to support healthy family dynamics. Parents who struggle with emotional regulation—such as those with severe mood disorders, anxiety, or anger issues—may face difficulties in interacting with their children in a consistent and supportive manner. This can significantly impact the child's emotional development, as children often mimic their caregivers' behaviors and emotional responses. Through interviews, behavioral observations, and collateral interviews with other significant individuals in the child's life, neuropsychologists can gain a better understanding of whether emotional instability may impact a parent's ability to provide a stable and nurturing environment.

A crucial component of neuropsychopathological evaluations in custody cases is assessing the parent's decision-making capacity. Parenting requires a continuous decision-making process, from everyday choices such as meal planning to more significant issues like health care or education. The neuropsychopathologist examines whether cognitive impairments, emotional disturbances, or personality disorders affect the parent's ability to make sound, timely decisions that prioritize the child's best interests. The evaluation can show how this might pose a risk to the child's welfare in cases involving parents with a history of impulsive or irrational decision-making. Additionally, the neuropsychologist may assess the parents' ability to recognize and manage their own biases, which can influence their decision-making in emotionally charged situations, such as custody disputes. By evaluating cognitive and emotional factors, the neuropsychologist can provide insight into the parents' overall judgment, helping the court determine whether any potential risks could affect the child's well-being or stability.

Collaboration with collateral sources is also vital to neuropsychological evaluations in custody and divorce cases. Neuropsychopathologists often interview teachers, family members, and other caregivers to obtain a more comprehensive picture of the parent's behavior and functioning. These additional sources of information provide essential context to the evaluation and offer insight into how the parents' cognitive and emotional functioning is observed in different settings. Teachers may provide valuable observations about the parents' interactions with the child. At the same time, family members can shed light on the parents' mental health history or behavior patterns that may not be immediately apparent in a clinical setting. Moreover, these collateral interviews help identify any inconsistencies between the parents' reported behavior and how others perceive them daily. This broader perspective enables the neuropsychologist to understand the parents' ability to consistently function across various environments more accurately, providing the court with a more accurate assessment of their overall parenting capacity.

In divorce cases, neuropsychopathological evaluations focus not only on the parents' fitness but also on the psychological and emotional impact of the divorce itself. Divorce is often a highly stressful and emotionally charged process, and some individuals may experience significant cognitive and emotional changes during this time. The neuropsychopathologist evaluates the effects of the divorce on the parents' mental health, looking for signs of anxiety, depression, or stress that may influence their ability to co-parent effectively. For example, a parent going through a high-conflict divorce may experience significant emotional distress that affects their ability to engage in cooperative parenting or maintain a positive relationship with their children. Neuropsychopathologists use various assessments to gauge emotional functioning, including measures of mood, anxiety, and personality traits that may indicate emotional instability.

The neuropsychopathologist's evaluation can also play a critical role in determining whether a parent's psychological condition or cognitive impairment is temporary or chronic. For example, a parent recovering from a major depressive episode may experience cognitive difficulties such as poor concentration, fatigue, or memory problems. However, suppose the neuropsychopathologist determines that these difficulties are not permanent and will likely improve with treatment. In that case, the court may offer the parent time to recover before making a final custody decision. On the other hand, if the neuropsychologist finds that the impairment is longstanding and significantly impairs the parent's ability to care for the child, this may be considered when determining custody arrangements.

Beyond the immediate concerns of custody and divorce, neuropsychopathologists play an essential role in evaluating the long-term effects of parental mental health and cognitive conditions on children. Children are susceptible to changes in their environment, and growing up with a parent who has a significant cognitive or emotional impairment can have lasting consequences on their psychological development. Neuropsychologists assess the potential risks that a parent's mental health or cognitive impairment may pose to the child's well-being, both in the short and long term. These evaluations may also inform recommendations for therapeutic interventions or parenting support programs that can help mitigate these risks.

The growing integration of neuroimaging and neuropsychological testing in family law cases also enhances the accuracy of these evaluations. Neuroimaging techniques, such as functional MRI and PET scans, provide a more direct view of the brain's structure and activity, offering additional data points that neuropsychologists can use to assess the extent of brain damage or dysfunction. These techniques can be instrumental in cases involving TBI, stroke, or neurodegenerative conditions, where cognitive functioning may be compromised. The use of neuroimaging in custody evaluations is still relatively new. Still, its potential for providing more precise data about brain function is rapidly advancing and becoming a crucial part of the neuropsychological toolkit.

The neuropsychopathologist's role is not limited to providing clinical evaluations; they are also often called upon to testify in court and offer expert testimony based on their findings. In these situations, the neuropsychologist must be able to communicate complex scientific concepts clearly and understandably, ensuring that their findings are presented in a way that is accessible to judges, attorneys, and jurors. Neuropsychopathologists are trained to offer expert testimony that is objective, unbiased, and rooted in scientific evidence. Their ability to present the results of their evaluations in court helps the legal system make more informed decisions based on the latest research and evidence-based practices.

As neuropsychopathology evolves, its contributions to family law cases will grow significantly. With advancements in neuropsychopathological testing, increased knowledge about brain function, and the incorporation of cutting-edge technologies, neuropsychopathologists are better equipped than ever to offer insights into the complex cognitive and emotional issues that arise in custody and divorce cases. These evaluations help ensure that decisions made in family court are fair and grounded in the best available scientific knowledge, ultimately supporting the best interests of the children involved. As new technologies, such as neuroimaging and artificial intelligence, continue to enhance diagnostic accuracy, neuropsychologists can provide even more precise assessments of brain function and its impact on behavior. This progress allows for more individualized recommendations, ensuring that the needs of both parents and children are met with greater specificity and tailored support in custody and divorce proceedings.

Technology and Neuropsychopathology

The relationship between technology and neuropsychopathology has become one of the most exciting and rapidly developing areas in behavioral science. Over the past few decades, technological advances have fundamentally transformed how neuropsychopathologists assess, diagnose, and treat cognitive and emotional impairments. These technological advancements are revolutionizing clinical practice and playing an increasingly prominent role in forensic settings, where high-stakes decisions about individuals' lives, such as those related to custody, divorce, and criminal proceedings, are being made. Integrating emerging technologies, such as neuroimaging, BCIs, and AI, has expanded the possibilities for assessing brain function, offering new insights into complex cognitive processes and providing objective, data-driven approaches to psychological evaluations.

However, as these technologies continue to evolve and become more integrated into the legal system, they raise many ethical and practical challenges that must be carefully navigated. While these tools have the potential to enhance the precision and fairness of legal decision-making, they also introduce new concerns about privacy, informed consent, bias, and over-reliance on technology. This chapter section explores the relationship between technology and neuropsychology, focusing on the emerging technological tools that are shaping the field and the ethical challenges associated with their use in forensic contexts.

Recently, neuropsychopathology has undergone a profound transformation driven by the rapid evolution of technology. The relationship between technology and neuropsychopathology has emerged as one of the most exciting and dynamic areas in the field of behavioral science. What was once a field primarily focused on traditional psychological assessments and clinical observations has now been revolutionized by cutting-edge tools and techniques. Advances in neuroimaging are transforming how neuropsychologists diagnose and treat cognitive and emotional disorders, as well as how they assess and understand human behavior on a neurological level.

These technological innovations have far-reaching implications for clinical practice and forensic settings, where precise and objective evaluations are crucial in high-stakes legal matters, such as custody disputes, divorce proceedings, and criminal investigations. Integrating technologies such as neuroimaging and BCIs into neuropsychopathological assessments enables a more comprehensive understanding of the brain's functioning, providing clearer insights into complex cognitive and emotional processes. These tools enable neuropsychologists to evaluate cognitive impairments more accurately and objectively, facilitating data-driven decisions grounded in scientific evidence. As these technologies continue to evolve, their potential to enhance our understanding of the brain and influence decision-making in clinical and legal contexts is bound to expand.

This section examines how emerging technologies are shaping the future of neuropsychopathological evaluations, as well as the ethical, practical, and legal challenges that accompany their use. From the application of neuroimaging to the implementation of AI-driven algorithms in legal decision-making, this section will explore the transformative impact of technology on neuropsychology and the critical questions that arise as these tools become increasingly integrated into the field. Furthermore, it will highlight the need for ethical guidelines and regulations to ensure these innovations are used responsibly, balancing their potential with the human-centered approach that neuropsychology requires.

Emerging Technologies in Neuropsychology

Neuroimaging technologies are among the most groundbreaking developments in neuropsychopathology. They provide a noninvasive way to visualize the structure and function of the brain, revolutionizing the way neuropsychologists study cognitive and emotional processes. Neuroimaging enables clinicians to observe brain activity in real time, track changes in brain structures, and pinpoint specific neural regions involved in various cognitive functions, including memory, attention, language, and executive control. These technologies have been instrumental in understanding how different brain areas interact and contribute to behavior. Additionally, neuroimaging has opened the door to more precise diagnoses of cognitive disorders, such as Alzheimer's disease, autism, and traumatic brain injury, by providing objective, visual evidence of neurological damage or dysfunction. As a result, neuroimaging enhances our understanding of the brain, allowing neuropsychologists to create more targeted and effective treatment plans for individuals with cognitive impairments.

In the clinical context, neuroimaging has become an indispensable tool for diagnosing neurological and psychiatric conditions. For example, fMRI can identify changes in brain activity associated with depression, anxiety, schizophrenia, or other mood disorders. At the same time, structural imaging techniques like MRI and CT scans can reveal brain damage caused by traumatic brain injury, stroke, or neurodegenerative diseases such as Alzheimer's disease. The ability to visualize the brain's structure and function helps neuropsychologists understand the neurobiological basis of cognitive impairments, offering more precise and objective diagnoses.

In forensic neuropsychopathology, neuroimaging has profound implications, particularly in custody disputes, divorce proceedings, and criminal evaluations. For example, neuroimaging can provide concrete evidence of neurological damage or cognitive impairments that may affect an individual's ability to function in everyday life or meet the requirements of effective parenting. In custody cases, where one parent may question the other's cognitive fitness to care for a child, neuroimaging data can offer clear evidence of conditions like brain injury, emotional dysregulation, or other neurological impairments that may impair a parent's judgment or emotional control. These objective data can help courts make better-informed decisions regarding custody arrangements by providing insight into the underlying neurological causes of certain behaviors, such as impulsivity or mood instability.

Moreover, neuroimaging is helping clinicians understand how psychological stress, trauma, and mental illness affect brain function. For instance, research has shown that exposure to trauma can alter brain structures such as the hippocampus and amygdala, areas crucial for memory and emotional processing. Neuroimaging can make these changes visible, offering valuable insights into the impact of trauma on cognition and behavior. In forensic settings, where determining an individual's mental state and emotional regulation is critical, neuroimaging can provide compelling evidence of how past experiences have shaped an individual's brain function, influencing their emotional responses and decision-making abilities.

Brain-Computer Interfaces (BCIs): Bridging the Gap Between Mind and Machine

BCIs represent a new frontier in neuropsychology, allowing direct communication between the brain and external devices. BCIs are designed to read and translate neural activity into control signals that can operate machines, computers, or prosthetic devices. This technology has been primarily used in the rehabilitation of patients with neurological conditions, such as those recovering from stroke, spinal cord injuries, or degenerative diseases. For example, BCIs can enable individuals with paralysis to control robotic limbs or communicate using a computer, improving their quality of life and autonomy.

In neuropsychopathology, BCIs provide a revolutionary real-time method for monitoring and assessing cognitive and emotional states. BCIs can measure how the brain responds to various stimuli, including emotional cues, cognitive tasks, and stressors. This makes them especially valuable in forensic evaluations, where understanding a person's neural responses to emotional or cognitive challenges is crucial for assessing their fitness to parent, participate in legal decisions, or engage in therapeutic interventions. For example, BCIs could be used in a custody case to assess how a parent responds neurologically to conflict or stressful situations, offering insight into their emotional regulation and impulse control. This technology could also track neural responses over time, providing a dynamic and objective picture of how an individual's cognitive and emotional state evolves in different contexts.

BCIs also hold promise in detecting subtle cognitive impairments that may not be easily identified through traditional neuropsychopathological assessments. For instance, individuals with MCI, early-stage dementia, or specific psychiatric conditions may not show obvious signs of dysfunction in routine neuropsychological testing. Still, BCIs can capture real-time neural activity and highlight areas of the brain where deficits may exist. By providing detailed and continuous monitoring of brain activity, BCIs offer an unprecedented opportunity for neuropsychopathologists to assess cognitive and emotional functions more accurately, providing unmistakable evidence of an individual's mental and emotional state.

Artificial Intelligence (AI): Enhancing Diagnostic Accuracy and Legal Decision-Making

AI is making profound contributions to neuropsychopathology by enabling the analysis of large datasets, identifying patterns, and making predictions based on those patterns. In neuropsychopathology, machine learning algorithms process and interpret complex data from neuropsychopathological tests, neuroimaging scans, and behavioral assessments. AI can help neuropsychopathologists identify cognitive impairments that may be subtle or difficult to detect through traditional methods, thereby improving diagnostic accuracy and enabling more tailored treatment plans.

One of the most exciting developments in neuropsychopathology is the use of AI to analyze neuroimaging data. Machine learning algorithms can be trained to detect changes in brain activity and structure indicative of neurological or psychiatric conditions, allowing for earlier and more accurate diagnoses. For example, AI systems can analyze fMRI scans to identify patterns of brain activity associated with mental health conditions, such as depression, anxiety, or psychosis, or detect changes in brain structure that are indicative of neurodegenerative diseases. This ability to analyze large amounts of data in a fraction of the time it would take a human examiner can enhance the diagnostic process and ensure that individuals receive the appropriate care more quickly.

In forensic contexts, AI is also beginning to play a role in legal decision-making. AI algorithms can process historical legal data to identify patterns in case outcomes and predict potential outcomes in future cases. For instance, AI systems can analyze numerous custody cases to identify patterns related to parents' cognitive and emotional fitness, enabling legal professionals to make more informed decisions about custody arrangements. However, this raises important questions about fairness and bias in AI systems, mainly when historical legal decisions have been influenced by biases related to gender, race, or socioeconomic status. Ensuring that AI systems are transparent, unbiased, and accountable is critical for their responsible use in legal settings.

Ethical Challenges of New Technology in Forensic Settings

As emerging technologies become increasingly integrated into neuropsychological assessments and forensic evaluations, they present various ethical challenges that must be carefully considered. These challenges center around privacy, informed consent, bias, and the potential over-reliance on technology in high-stakes legal decision-making. For instance, neuroimaging data could inadvertently expose individuals to privacy violations if sensitive brain data is mishandled or misused. At the same time, BCIs may raise concerns about how much a person's cognitive processes can be accessed without their complete understanding. Furthermore, AI systems may perpetuate existing biases in legal decisions if trained on flawed or incomplete data, leading to unfair outcomes in custody cases or criminal assessments. The potential for these technologies to influence critical decisions necessitates a careful balance between innovation and the protection of individuals' rights and dignity.

Informed Consent and Privacy Concerns

Informed consent is one of the most fundamental ethical principles in clinical and forensic settings. It requires that individuals fully understand the nature, purpose, and potential risks of any assessment or intervention, including using new technologies. The increasing use of advanced neurotechnologies makes ensuring informed consent more complex. For example, individuals undergoing neuroimaging procedures may not fully understand how their brain activity will be interpreted, how the results will be used, or the potential implications of storing and analyzing their neural data. Similarly, BCIs collect real-time data on an individual's brain activity, which could potentially reveal sensitive information about their cognitive and emotional state. In forensic cases, where this data might be used to make decisions about an individual's fitness to parent or participate in legal proceedings, individuals must understand how their data will be used and who will have access to it.

Moreover, privacy concerns are magnified by the sensitive nature of the data collected through these technologies. Neuroimaging data, BCI readings, and AI-driven assessments can provide detailed insights into a person's brain function, mental health, and emotional regulation. Protecting this data from unauthorized access and ensuring that it is used solely for its intended purpose is essential for maintaining ethical standards in forensic settings. There is a need for clear regulations and guidelines to safeguard the privacy of individuals undergoing neuropsychological evaluations that involve new technologies.

Bias is another significant ethical concern associated with the use of AI and other emerging technologies in neuropsychology and legal decision-making. Machine learning algorithms and AI systems are often trained on large datasets that may reflect historical biases in the legal system, such as gender, racial, or socioeconomic bias. If AI systems are not carefully designed to account for these biases, they can perpetuate existing inequalities and unfairly influence legal outcomes. For example, in custody cases, an AI system that analyzes past legal decisions might unintentionally favor specific demographics over others based on biased patterns in the data. If implicit biases toward gender or race have influenced historical court decisions, AI could reinforce these prejudices, resulting in unjust decisions that affect the well-being of children and families. Furthermore, machine learning algorithms are not immune to the biases of their creators. If the data used to train these algorithms is incomplete or reflects societal prejudices, AI systems could make biased predictions that are difficult to detect or challenge.

This issue of bias is not limited to AI; it also extends to neuroimaging and BCI technologies. Studies have shown that demographic factors such as age, race, and gender can influence the interpretation of neuroimaging results. For example, the interpretation of fMRI scans or EEG data might be affected by the patient's age or sex, leading to misdiagnoses or misinterpretations of cognitive or emotional impairments. In forensic settings, where decisions have profound implications for individuals' rights and responsibilities, these factors can introduce a significant source of error. Neuropsychopathologists must ensure that these technologies are used relatively unbiasedly and reflect the individual being evaluated rather than relying solely on generalized algorithms that may not account for the full complexity of human cognition and behavior.

The Risk of Over-Reliance on Technology

While the introduction of advanced technologies has brought about significant improvements in neuropsychology, there is a growing concern about the potential for over-reliance on these tools. In forensic settings, where decisions made by courts can have lifelong consequences for individuals and families, neuropsychopathological evaluations must be based on a holistic understanding of the individual. Technology can provide valuable insights into brain function but should not be seen as the sole determinant in evaluating a person's cognitive or emotional state. Over-reliance on neuroimaging, BCIs, or AI could lead to overly mechanistic decisions, ignoring the broader context of the individual's life, experiences, and social environment.

For example, in a custody case, an AI system might predict a parent's ability to co-parent based on patterns from past cases. Yet, it may fail to account for unique circumstances such as the parents' personal history, the relationship with their child, or mitigating factors like support systems or therapy. Similarly, while BCIs can provide real-time data on how a person's brain responds to emotional triggers, these technologies are imperfect. They may not capture the full complexity of a person's emotional regulation in real-world contexts. Neuropsychopathologists must balance the objective data provided by these technologies with clinical judgment, context, and empathy to ensure that their evaluations reflect a comprehensive and nuanced understanding of the individual.

The risk of over-reliance is particularly concerning in legal decisions, where individuals may already be vulnerable, such as those involved in custody disputes, divorce proceedings, or criminal cases. In such high-stakes situations, the potential for technological overreach could inadvertently lead to a reductionist approach to human behavior, disregarding the emotional, social, and psychological factors that are essential to understanding a person's overall functioning. While technology can be a powerful tool for enhancing accuracy and objectivity in neuropsychopathological evaluations, it should always be viewed as a supplement to, rather than a replacement for, professional judgment.

Legal and Ethical Considerations for the Use of Technology in Forensic Evaluations

As neuropsychopathological technologies become increasingly embedded in legal proceedings, questions of legal and ethical responsibility will inevitably arise. Issues related to accountability, transparency, and the role of expert testimony will become more prominent. In cases where neuroimaging, BCIs, or AI are used to inform legal decisions, courts must ensure that these technologies are applied correctly and that their results are interpreted by qualified professionals with the necessary expertise. This raises important questions about the qualifications and responsibilities of neuropsychopathologists and other experts who rely on these technologies in forensic settings. Are they sufficiently trained to interpret the data produced by these advanced tools? How can they ensure that they are not misinterpreting results or misrepresenting the capabilities of these technologies to the court?

Furthermore, using AI and other technologies in legal decision-making raises questions about the transparency of algorithms and the interpretability of their results. Many machine learning algorithms are "black boxes," meaning humans do not easily understand their decision-making processes. This lack of transparency poses a significant challenge in forensic settings, where the stakes are high and the potential consequences of biased or incorrect decisions are profound. Courts and legal professionals must carefully consider how AI systems are developed and how their decision-making processes can be transparent, ensuring they are held to the same ethical standards as human experts.

Another key consideration is the potential for misuse of these technologies. In forensic neuropsychopathology, the pressure to use the latest technologies to provide more definitive answers may lead some professionals to rely on them without fully understanding their limitations or potential for error. This can be particularly problematic in legal contexts, where the stakes are high, and the outcome may significantly impact individuals' lives. For example, relying too heavily on neuroimaging data that might not fully capture the complexity of an individual's cognitive or emotional state could lead to flawed conclusions about their fitness to parent or engage in legal decision-making. Similarly, AI-driven predictions about a person's likelihood to engage in criminal behavior or their suitability as a parent may overlook important contextual factors that could significantly alter the outcome. Legal systems will need to establish clear guidelines for the ethical use of these technologies, ensuring that they are applied responsibly and that their limitations are acknowledged and respected.

The Role of Neuropsychologists in Navigating Technological Advances

As technology advances, the role of the neuropsychopathologist becomes increasingly critical in ensuring that these tools are used ethically and effectively in forensic settings. They must be familiar with the latest technological developments and have the expertise to interpret the data they generate within the broader context of human behavior. This requires a deep understanding of both the capabilities and the limitations of these technologies, as well as a commitment to using them in ways that prioritize the well-being and rights of individuals.

For instance, when using neuroimaging or BCIs to evaluate an individual's cognitive and emotional functioning, neuropsychopathologists must be able to integrate objective data with clinical observations, interviews, and collateral information from family members, teachers, or caregivers. This holistic approach ensures the evaluation is comprehensive and considers all relevant factors rather than relying solely on technological outputs. Similarly, when AI is used to inform legal decision-making, neuropsychologists should be involved in ensuring that the algorithms are grounded in sound scientific principles and that their application is fair, unbiased, and transparent.

Neuropsychopathologists must also advocate for ethical guidelines and regulations surrounding the use of new technologies in forensic settings. This includes advocating for greater transparency in the development and application of AI algorithms, promoting safeguards to protect privacy, and ensuring that individuals undergoing neuropsychological evaluations are fully informed about the technologies being used and their implications. The field is evolving rapidly, and as technology continues to shape our understanding of the brain, neuropsychologists must remain at the forefront of these developments, ensuring that they are used in ways that are ethically sound, scientifically valid, and just.

Integrating technology into neuropsychology has opened new possibilities for understanding the brain and assessing cognitive and emotional functioning. Neuroimaging, BCIs, and AI are already playing a significant role in clinical and forensic settings, providing valuable insights into the neurological and psychological factors that influence behavior. However, as these technologies become more embedded in legal decision-making processes, ethical and practical challenges must be carefully addressed. Concerns about privacy, informed consent, bias, and over-reliance on technology must be addressed to ensure that these tools are used responsibly and that the decisions they inform are fair, transparent, and grounded in sound scientific principles.

Neuropsychopathologists must remain vigilant in balancing technological innovation with clinical expertise, ensuring that these tools support the best interests of individuals involved in legal proceedings, particularly in high-stakes decisions such as custody arrangements, divorce settlements, and criminal assessments. With careful oversight and ethical guidance, emerging technologies can enhance the precision and fairness of neuropsychopathological evaluations, ultimately leading to more informed and just outcomes in forensic settings. This includes continuous education and training to stay current with evolving tools and methodologies, as well as active participation in interdisciplinary dialogue with legal professionals, ethicists, and technologists. By maintaining a human-centered approach, neuropsychologists can ensure that advanced technology remains grounded in compassion, context, and clinical integrity.

Conclusion

The rapid advancement of technology has ushered in a new era in neuropsychology, particularly in forensic contexts, where tools such as neuroimaging, BCIs, and AI are increasingly used to enhance legal decision-making. These innovations have vast potential to enhance the accuracy, objectivity, and depth of neuropsychopathological evaluations, particularly in high-stakes settings such as custody cases, criminal assessments, and civil evaluations. By utilizing these tools, both NP and legal professionals can gain deeper insights into brain activity, emotional regulation, and cognitive processes that were once inaccessible. However, with these advancements come a range of ethical, legal, and practical challenges that must be addressed to ensure the responsible and fair use of these technologies in forensic settings.

A primary concern in integrating these technologies into legal evaluations is the potential for bias. AI systems, particularly those based on machine learning algorithms, heavily rely on large datasets, often containing historical legal decisions that reflect societal biases related to race, gender, and socioeconomic status. If not carefully monitored, these systems may perpetuate these biases, resulting in unjust legal outcomes. In the context of NI and BCIs, there is also the risk that these technologies may misinterpret or misrepresent cognitive or emotional states, particularly when demographic variables such as race, gender, or age are not adequately accounted for. Vigilance and transparency in developing and applying these tools are crucial to preventing the reinforcement of existing inequalities in the legal system.

Moreover, the use of NI, BCIs, and AI in forensic evaluations raises significant concerns about privacy and informed consent. The sensitive data collected by these technologies—whether neural activity patterns from NI or real-time cognitive data from BCIs—raises important questions about data ownership, storage, and access. In forensic settings, where individuals may be vulnerable, transparent and comprehensive informed consent procedures must be in place, ensuring that participants fully understand the implications of participating in such assessments, including how the data will be used, who will interpret it, and the potential legal consequences of the results. Strengthened privacy protections are necessary to safeguard individuals' rights and prevent misuse of sensitive data.

Additionally, while emerging technologies provide powerful tools for enhancing NP assessments, there is a risk of overreliance on these tools. In high-stakes legal contexts, the pressure to use advanced technology for more definitive answers can overshadow the need for a holistic understanding of the individual being assessed. AI and NI can offer valuable insights but should never replace clinical judgment or a person-centered approach. Human behavior is shaped by a complex interaction of cognitive, emotional, social, and environmental factors, and these cannot always be captured by objective data alone. In forensic settings, decisions have profound consequences; a balance must be struck between utilizing technology and retaining a comprehensive, human-centered approach to NP evaluations.

Furthermore, integrating these technologies into legal decision-making raises questions about accountability, transparency, and the reliability of expert testimony. As

AI, NI, and BCIs become more embedded in forensic evaluations, it is essential to ensure that professionals interpreting these technologies have the necessary expertise and training to understand their limitations. The opacity of many AI systems—where human understanding of decision-making processes is not easily accessible—poses a significant challenge to the integrity of legal proceedings. In such cases, legal professionals must clearly explain the technology's workings, ensuring that decisions based on these tools are grounded in scientifically valid principles.

The role of neuropsychopathologists in navigating these challenges is crucial. As both technical experts and advocates for ethical standards, they must be at the forefront of ensuring these technologies are used responsibly in forensic settings. This requires staying informed about technological developments, understanding the strengths and limitations of these tools, and ensuring they are applied ethically. They should also advocate for the development of ethical guidelines and regulations governing the use of these technologies in legal contexts, ensuring that they are not only scientifically valid but also ethically sound and legally just.

As technology continues to evolve, so will the challenges and opportunities it presents for forensic neuropsychopathology. The future promises even more sophisticated tools for understanding the brain and assessing cognitive and emotional states. However, with these advancements come ethical questions about balancing innovation with the protection of individual rights and dignity. Neuropsychopathologists, legal professionals, and technologists must engage in interdisciplinary dialogue to develop frameworks that safeguard against potential harm while maximizing the benefits of these technologies.

Ultimately, integrating technology into forensic neuropsychopathology aims not to replace expert judgment but to enhance it. Emerging technologies can offer invaluable insights into neurological and psychological factors that influence behavior, but they should always be complemented by human expertise. A responsible and ethical approach to using NI, BCIs, and AI in forensic settings ensures these technologies contribute to fairer, more informed legal decisions while protecting individuals' rights and maintaining the integrity of the legal system.

As neuroimaging, BCIs, and AI continue to shape forensic NP, their integration must be approached with caution, responsibility, and ethical commitment. These technologies have immense potential to improve legal decision-making, but they must be used to prioritize fairness, transparency, and accountability. By carefully addressing challenges and ensuring ethical standards, a future can be fostered where technology enhances, rather than undermines, the pursuit of justice in forensic settings. Continued interdisciplinary collaboration among scientists, legal professionals, and ethicists will be essential to navigate the complexities these innovations introduce. Ultimately, responsible implementation will help ensure that technological advances serve the best interests of both individuals and society.

Chapter 10: End-of-Chapter Questions

Comprehension and Reflection

1. **What are the primary technologies shaping the future of neuropsychological evaluations in legal settings?**

➢ Discuss how neuroimaging, AI, and BCIs advancements influence forensic neuropsychology.

2. **How does the use of neuroimaging data impact the reliability of neuropsychological assessments in the courtroom?**

➢ Reflect on the strengths and limitations of neuroimaging as evidence in legal cases.

3. **What are the ethical concerns surrounding the use of artificial intelligence (AI) in legal neuropsychological evaluations?**

➢ Explain how the integration of AI in legal decision-making raises questions about bias, transparency, and accountability.

4. **How do brain-computer interfaces (BCIs) contribute to assessing emotional and cognitive states in legal settings?**

➢ Discuss how BCIs can be used in forensic evaluations and the ethical challenges they present.

5. **What challenges do neuropsychologists face when using emerging technologies to evaluate cognitive and emotional functions in legal cases?**

➢ Reflect on the technical and ethical hurdles that come with the application of advanced neuropsychological tools in legal contexts.

6. **How does the use of AI and neuroimaging data affect the role of human judgment in neuropsychological evaluations for legal cases?**

➢ Analyze how technology might complement or overshadow the expert opinions of neuropsychologists in the courtroom.

7. **What is the role of neuropsychologists in ensuring that technological tools are ethically applied in legal contexts?**

➢ Discuss how neuropsychologists can advocate for ethical standards when incorporating technology in legal evaluations.

8. **How can neuropsychologists balance technological advancements with traditional assessment methods in legal cases?**

➢ Explore the challenges of combining new technologies with established neuropsychological practices.

9. **How do neuropsychologists ensure informed consent when using advanced neurotechnologies like neuroimaging and BCIs?**

➢ Reflect on the complexities of obtaining valid consent when technology is involved in legal settings.

10. **What is the significance of maintaining confidentiality when using neuroimaging and other technologies in forensic assessments?**

➢ Discuss the ethical responsibility of neuropsychologists to protect patient privacy and confidentiality in legal evaluations.

Critical Thinking and Application

11. **What ethical dilemmas arise when neuropsychologists use neuroimaging data that could potentially influence a legal decision?**

➢ Analyze the potential conflicts between scientific evidence and the risk of misinterpreting or overstating findings in court.

12. **How does using AI-driven algorithms in neuropsychological evaluations affect the fairness of legal decisions?**

➢ Discuss how biases embedded in AI algorithms could skew legal outcomes and undermine fairness in the justice system.

13. **What steps can neuropsychologists take to ensure their assessments remain objective when technology is used in legal cases?**

➢ Reflect on methods to minimize biases and ensure objectivity in interpreting technological data.

14. **How do neuropsychologists address potential misinterpretations of neuroimaging findings in legal proceedings?**

➢ Explore how neuropsychologists can clarify the limitations of neuroimaging and avoid overreliance on technological results in court.

15. **How can neuropsychologists manage the pressure of advocating for one side in a legal case while maintaining scientific integrity?**

➢ Discuss how neuropsychologists can navigate the adversarial legal process and preserve the objectivity of their evaluations.

16. **What ethical considerations arise when neuropsychologists provide testimony in cases involving emerging neurotechnologies?**

➢ Explain neuropsychologists' ethical responsibilities when their expertise is sought in cases involving new technologies like AI or BCIs.

17. **How can neuropsychologists ensure that external pressures, such as legal or financial incentives, do not influence their testimony?**

➢ Discuss strategies for maintaining impartiality and avoiding conflicts of interest in forensic evaluations.

18. **How does the rapid pace of technological advancements in neuropsychology affect the ethical guidelines that govern its use in legal settings?**

➢ Reflect on how ethical standards must evolve alongside new technologies to ensure responsible use in legal contexts.

19. **What is the role of peer review and professional development in ensuring the ethical application of neuropsychological technologies in legal cases?**

➢ Discuss how ongoing education and peer consultation help neuropsychologists maintain high ethical standards.

20. **What measures can neuropsychologists take to address the potential misuse of neuroimaging and AI in criminal cases?**

➢ Explore how neuropsychologists can advocate for the appropriate use of technology to prevent harm and ensure accurate, ethical assessments in criminal justice.

Chapter 11:
Applied Forensic Neuropsychopathology and Special Topics

Mental health diagnoses, intended to serve as tools for understanding and treating psychiatric conditions, have unfortunately been subjected to misuse and manipulation throughout history. While the primary purpose of psychiatric assessments is to promote healing, support, and well-being, a troubling undercurrent exists where these diagnoses are weaponized in legal, political, and social contexts. The weaponization of mental health diagnoses represents a complex relationship between psychiatry, law, and societal power structures, where mental health conditions are not only misunderstood but also exploited to serve ulterior motives.

Throughout history, mental health diagnoses have been manipulated for various purposes. In authoritarian regimes and periods of political repression, psychiatric diagnoses were used to silence dissent, discredit individuals, and control marginalized populations. The Soviet Union's use of psychiatry to imprison political dissidents and the criminalization of mental health in Nazi Germany serve as chilling examples of how psychiatric labels can be distorted to suppress opposition and maintain power. Even in the United States, psychiatric diagnoses were historically used to undermine social justice movements, from civil rights activism to feminist advocacy. This legacy of abuse has left an indelible mark on the relationship between mental health, politics, and the law, underscoring the vulnerability of psychiatric diagnoses to manipulation.

The legal system, particularly in the context of criminal justice, is one of the most prominent arenas where mental health diagnoses have been weaponized. In forensic settings, psychiatric evaluations are often used to determine a defendant's competency to stand trial, their criminal responsibility, or the validity of an insanity defense. Unfortunately, these evaluations are not immune to external pressures or biases. The subjective nature of psychiatric diagnoses, coupled with the vulnerability of forensic professionals to influence from legal or institutional actors, creates fertile ground for the misuse of mental health assessments. Whether intentional or unintentional, psychiatric diagnoses can be manipulated to serve legal agendas, influencing the outcome of trials and determining the fate of individuals within the justice system.

An especially concerning issue arises when individuals who commit violent crimes manipulate the use of mental health conditions or psychiatric disorders to avoid the legal consequences of their actions. In some instances, defendants exploit psychiatric diagnoses as a strategy to evade criminal responsibility, particularly in cases involving competency to stand trial, the insanity defense, or criminal responsibility. This creates significant challenges in distinguishing between individuals who genuinely suffer from severe mental illnesses and those who strategically exploit their diagnoses to avoid incarceration or other legal consequences. As a result, it becomes more challenging to ensure that individuals who truly require treatment for their mental health conditions are identified and provided with the proper care, rather than being subjected to incarceration.

Beyond the courtroom, the societal implications of weaponizing mental health diagnoses are profound. The stigma surrounding mental health conditions, combined with widespread misconceptions about the nature of psychiatric disorders, often leads to discrimination and marginalization of individuals with mental health conditions. These individuals may face biased treatment in medical, legal, or social contexts, where their diagnoses are used against them to undermine their credibility, autonomy, or rights. Racial, gender, and socioeconomic disparities in psychiatric diagnosis further exacerbate this issue, creating additional barriers to fair treatment and equality.

This chapter explores the various dimensions of the weaponization of mental health diagnoses, focusing on historical abuses, contemporary challenges, and the ethical, legal, and social implications. The role of forensic psychiatry and neuropsychopathology in legal proceedings will be examined, where the integrity of psychiatric evaluations is often compromised. The discussion will also include how public awareness and advocacy can counteract the misuse of psychiatric diagnoses by reducing stigma and promoting a more informed and empathetic approach to mental health. Finally, potential reforms aimed at safeguarding the integrity of psychiatric assessments and ensuring that mental health diagnoses serve their true purpose will be outlined: to support and treat individuals rather than to manipulate or control them.

It is essential to recognize that the weaponization of mental health diagnoses is not merely a legal or medical issue—it is a human rights issue. The abuse of psychiatric diagnoses has the potential to strip individuals of their autonomy, dignity, and freedom. Through vigilance, reform, and public advocacy, the further exploitation of mental health diagnoses can be prevented, moving toward a future where they are used to heal and support individuals rather than to oppress and control them. This chapter provides a comprehensive examination of the complexities surrounding the weaponization of mental health diagnoses. It offers a roadmap for the ethical, legal, and social reforms necessary to address these abuses.

As the discussion has highlighted, the misuse and manipulation of psychiatric diagnoses, particularly in the legal realm, raise significant ethical, legal, and social concerns. One of the primary arenas where these issues manifest is within the forensic evaluation process. In this context, psychiatric and neuropsychopathological assessments play a crucial role in determining the legal standing of individuals accused of crimes, particularly regarding their competency to stand trial, their criminal responsibility, and the validity of insanity defenses. However, the complexities surrounding the application of mental health diagnoses in these high-stakes settings require a nuanced understanding of both the psychological and legal dimensions of such evaluations.

The forensic neuropsychopathological evaluation process is integral to this discussion, as it involves a detailed assessment of an individual's cognitive and psychological functioning, particularly in the context of the criminal justice system. These evaluations are intended to clarify an individual's mental state during the offense, their ability to participate in legal proceedings, and whether they can understand the consequences of their actions. However, this process is fraught with challenges, including potential biases, the risk of misinterpreting symptoms, and the pressure to align findings with legal arguments.

As the chapter continues, a deeper exploration of the forensic neuropsychopathological evaluation process will help illuminate how these evaluations are conducted, the factors that influence their outcomes, and the ethical dilemmas faced by forensic experts. This section will also highlight the delicate balance between ensuring justice for individuals who require mental health treatment and safeguarding the integrity of the legal process. Through this examination, the chapter will provide insights into how the forensic evaluation process can be improved to prevent the exploitation of mental health diagnoses while ensuring that individuals who are genuinely in need of psychiatric care are appropriately treated within the criminal justice system.

The Forensic Neuropsychopathological Evaluation Process

While the forensic neuropsychopathological evaluation process has been comprehensively explored in previous chapters, it is essential to delve deeper into how these evaluations directly impact testimony and courtroom procedures within the legal and criminal justice systems. The evaluation process plays a pivotal role in shaping legal outcomes, particularly when determining competency, criminal responsibility, or the validity of an insanity defense. The insights provided by expert evaluators influence not only the legal arguments but also the strategies employed by attorneys and the final decision made by judges and juries.

Understanding the nuances of how forensic neuropsychopathological evaluations affect testimony is critical to appreciating their full impact on the courtroom. These evaluations provide objective, scientifically grounded findings that inform legal decisions; however, how these findings are presented and interpreted in court can significantly impact the outcome of a case. As such, it is essential to explore how expert testimony is delivered, how the legal system perceives it, and the challenges forensic evaluators face in translating complex psychological data into clear and compelling testimony in the courtroom.

This area will build upon the previous discussion of the forensic evaluation process by focusing specifically on the role of testimony in legal proceedings. It will examine the strategic considerations involved in preparing for and delivering expert testimony, how evaluators maintain neutrality, and the potential influence of their findings on the trajectory of criminal cases. Through this lens, the chapter will highlight the vital relationship between mental health expertise and legal standards, ensuring that the evaluation process contributes to fair and just outcomes for all individuals involved in the criminal justice system.

A forensic neuropsychopathological evaluation begins with a legal referral that identifies the key question (or chief complaint), often related to competency, criminal responsibility, or risk. The evaluator must clearly understand the legal framework to tailor the assessment appropriately. This initial stage defines the scope of the evaluation and the data types that will be most useful. Clarifying these goals ensures the process remains legally relevant. Without this clarity, the evaluation may miss the mark and lead to conclusions that don't address the court's needs.

The next step involves gathering and reviewing collateral records, including medical, educational, and criminal histories. These records help the evaluator identify the individual's developmental, cognitive, and psychiatric background. They also assist in identifying discrepancies between self-reported symptoms and documented history. A thorough review of records builds a strong foundation for later interpretation of testing results. It also helps generate informed hypotheses before any direct contact with the individual begins. In addition, these records can highlight any pre-existing conditions or prior treatments, which may provide critical context for understanding the individual's current mental health status. By examining these historical documents, the evaluator can better anticipate potential challenges or biases in the assessment process.

After reviewing the document, the evaluator conducts a clinical interview with the individual. Informed consent is obtained (depending upon whether the evaluation is self-referred by organizations; however, consent is not required when the evaluation is court-ordered, and the limits of confidentiality are explained clearly due to the legal context. The interview explores areas such as early development, trauma history, mental health symptoms, educational performance, and current functioning. This provides a narrative framework to understand the person's background and lived experience. It also guides the selection of the most relevant neuropsychopathological tests. During the interview, the evaluator also observes the individual's communication style and emotional state, which can provide valuable insights into their psychological functioning. Additionally, any inconsistencies or contradictions in the individual's responses may indicate areas that require further exploration or clarification through testing.

Behavioral observation is an essential evaluation component throughout the interview and testing phases. The evaluator pays attention to speech patterns, eye contact, emotional responses, attention span, and general demeanor. These real-time observations provide insights that standardized tests may overlook. Inconsistencies between observed behavior and self-report can suggest malingering or deeper psychopathology. Observational data often strengthens the interpretation of test results and is referenced in the final report. Additionally, the evaluator may note any signs of cognitive or emotional distress that could affect the individual's ability to engage in the assessment process fully. These observations help to contextualize the individual's responses and ensure that the evaluation results reflect a holistic understanding of their functioning.

Formal testing follows, using standardized instruments to assess brain and psychological functioning. Cognitive domains evaluated include memory, attention, executive function, language, and processing speed. Emotional and personality assessments are conducted using structured inventories and symptom checklists. Validity testing is also included to determine the examinee's effort level and detect symptom exaggeration or feigning. These measures ensure the integrity and reliability of the evaluation data. Further, the evaluator may incorporate neuroimaging or other specialized assessments to validate the results of the cognitive and emotional tests. This multi-faceted approach helps provide a comprehensive understanding of the individual's functioning and contributes to a more accurate evaluation.

The psychometric aspect is one of the most important components of the forensic neuropsychopathological evaluative process. Psychometrics is the science of measuring mental capacities and processes through standardized testing. Ensuring that the assessments administered during the evaluation are credible and valid is critical. Forensic neuropsychopathology incorporates psychometrics into testing protocols, utilizing validated and reliable instruments that measure cognitive abilities, emotional functioning, and personality traits. These standardized tests are designed to accurately capture an individual's neuropsychological functioning while minimizing potential bias or error.

The importance of psychometrics lies in its ability to provide objective, measurable data that can be consistently and reliably interpreted. When psychometric principles are applied correctly, evaluators can make well-supported conclusions about a defendant's cognitive abilities or mental health status, which are crucial for informed legal decision-making. The evaluation may become flawed if psychometric considerations are overlooked, resulting in inaccurate diagnoses or misleading conclusions. Inaccurate assessments can have serious consequences, including unjust legal outcomes, inappropriate treatment plans, or the violation of an individual's rights. Therefore, careful adherence to psychometric principles is essential in ensuring that forensic evaluations are fair, accurate, and legally defensible.

Once testing is complete, the evaluator enters the integration phase, where all findings are analyzed collectively. This includes synthesizing test scores, interview responses, observed behavior, and records to create a comprehensive profile. The evaluator identifies patterns that support or contradict specific diagnoses or functional impairments. The primary objective is to connect psychological and neuropsychological findings to the legal question. Functional analysis is prioritized over simply listing diagnoses. By considering the full range of the individual's cognitive, emotional, and behavioral functioning, the evaluator can provide a more accurate and nuanced understanding of the individual's capacity and mental state regarding legal standards.

A comprehensive written report is then prepared and tailored to a legal audience. The report includes background information, test results, diagnostic impressions, and clearly stated forensic opinions. Technical terms are explained in accessible language to ensure clarity for attorneys and judges. The report also outlines limitations, such as questionable effort or incomplete history. Accuracy and transparency in the report enhance the evaluator's credibility in court, ensuring that the findings are understood within their proper context and are not misused to influence the outcome of the case.

If the case proceeds, the evaluator may be called to testify as an expert witness. In preparation, they review their findings and anticipate possible lines of questioning during cross-examination. The testimony must be clear, neutral, and grounded in scientific methodology. The evaluator's primary role is to inform the court rather than advocate for either side. Being concise and confident during testimony improves both comprehension and credibility. The evaluator must remain impartial, present the facts objectively, and refrain from expressing personal opinions or biases that could compromise the integrity of the evaluation. Compelling testimony ensures that the court fully understands the implications of the neuropsychopathological findings in relation to the legal issues at hand.

Testimony in court enables the expert to explain how their findings directly relate to legal standards. This might include explaining whether cognitive deficits impair a defendant's ability to understand charges or assist counsel. The expert must remain composed, objective, and focused on the science. Effective communication ensures that judges and jurors grasp the relevance of complex psychological concepts. Strong testimony can significantly influence how the court interprets a case. Further, the expert's ability to clearly articulate the connection between the neuropsychological data and legal criteria is crucial in shaping the court's decision-making process. A well-delivered testimony may also help clarify any ambiguities or misunderstandings during the trial, ensuring a fairer and more informed legal outcome.

The forensic neuropsychopathological evaluation process is systematic, detailed, and designed for legal decision-making. Each phase—referral, records review, interview, observation, testing, integration, and testimony—builds upon the last. The evaluator's role is to bridge the gap between neuroscience and psychology with the demands of the justice system. Accurate and objective evaluations contribute to fair legal outcomes. When executed skillfully, this process provides essential insight into the relationship between the brain, behavior, and the law. Carefully integrating multiple data points ensures that all factors influencing an individual's mental state are considered. As a result, the forensic neuropsychopathological evaluation can offer the court a more comprehensive understanding of the defendant's mental health, helping to guide just decisions regarding competency, criminal responsibility, and sentencing.

Having explored the meticulous process involved in forensic neuropsychopathological evaluations, it is crucial to understand how these evaluations translate into the courtroom. One of the most significant aspects of these evaluations is the testimony that follows, as it directly impacts case outcomes. Testimony is not just a formal presentation of findings; it is a pivotal moment where expert opinions help to clarify complex psychological concepts and provide the court with the necessary insights to make informed decisions. The influence of neuropsychopathological testimony can be profound, often shaping legal strategies, influencing jury perceptions, and even determining the fate of the defendant. To better illustrate the impact of such evaluations, it is essential to examine hypothetical examples that could potentially be real-world situations where neuropsychopathological testimony plays a crucial role in legal cases. These examples illustrate the diverse ways in which expert testimony can influence the interpretation of mental health issues within the criminal justice system, highlighting the far-reaching consequences it can have on case outcomes.

Examples of Neuropsychopathological Testimony and Its Impact on Case Outcomes

Forensic neuropsychopathological testimony can dramatically shape legal outcomes. It offers insights into how brain-based impairments affect intent, behavior, and decision-making. This type of expert evidence is increasingly accepted in criminal, civil, and family court proceedings. Testimony often clarifies whether a defendant possesses the cognitive or psychological capacity to be held fully responsible for their actions. These examples demonstrate the influence of expert input in shaping fair and informed verdicts. Furthermore, neuropsychopathological testimony can be pivotal in cases involving issues such as competency to stand trial, criminal responsibility, and the evaluation of potential risks to public safety. Expert testimony offers a nuanced perspective that may not be evident through traditional legal arguments, shedding light on the mental processes underlying an individual's actions.

Example One

In one criminal case, a defendant charged with assault had a documented history of TBI. A forensic expert testified that the injury significantly affected the defendant's ability to regulate impulses and emotions. The testimony linked the aggressive behavior to neurological dysfunction rather than criminal intent. Based on this explanation, the jury reduced the charge from a felony to a misdemeanor. This outcome highlighted how brain-based testimony can influence the legal interpretation of intent. Additionally, the expert testimony stressed the importance of considering the defendant's neurological state in determining culpability, ultimately contributing to a more just and informed verdict. This case serves as an example of how neuropsychopathological insights can alter perceptions of criminal responsibility and affect sentencing outcomes.

Example Two

Another case involved a man diagnosed with schizophrenia who was evaluated for fitness to stand trial. Neuropsychopathological testing revealed that his cognitive impairments prevented him from understanding the charges or participating in his defense. The expert identified deficits in reasoning and working memory, which impaired his ability to comprehend legal matters. As a result of the testimony, the judge ordered the defendant to receive treatment before the trial could proceed. This case demonstrated the role of functional assessments in determining legal competence. Furthermore, it emphasized the importance of neuropsychopathological evaluations in ensuring that individuals are not subjected to legal proceedings unless they fully understand and participate in their defense, safeguarding both justice and the defendant's rights.

Example Three

In a high-profile insanity defense case, the defendant was suffering from a degenerative neurological condition. The forensic neuropsychopathologist presented evidence showing that the disorder caused psychosis and impaired moral reasoning. Objective test results and neuroimaging supported this conclusion. The jury found the defendant not guilty by reason of insanity. This testimony was central to reframing the defendant's mental state at the time of the offense. It highlighted the significant role that neuropsychopathological evaluations play in assessing criminal responsibility and the relationship between mental illness and legal culpability. The case emphasized the importance of expert testimony in providing a nuanced understanding of how severe mental health conditions can affect an individual's actions and decision-making.

Special Considerations

Juvenile courts have also relied heavily on neuropsychopathological evaluations in recent years. In one case, a teenager who committed a violent offense was found to have a history of developmental trauma. The evaluator explained that this trauma severely impaired the adolescent's ability to regulate emotions and make decisions. The court opted for a rehabilitative rather than punitive approach. This case illustrated how expert testimony can lead to more humane and developmentally appropriate sentencing. It also demonstrated the growing recognition of the impact of early life experiences on cognitive and emotional development, influencing how the legal system addresses juvenile offenses. Such evaluations help ensure that youth offenders receive interventions that address underlying issues rather than punitive measures.

In a capital punishment case, neuropsychopathological testimony played a life-saving role. The defendant was evaluated and found to meet the criteria for intellectual disability, including limitations in adaptive functioning. The court concluded that executing the individual would violate constitutional protections. The expert's data met all necessary legal standards for intellectual disability. This case revealed how scientific evidence directly affects sentencing in the most serious legal scenarios. It also stressed the importance of ensuring that the legal system upholds protections against cruel and unusual punishment, particularly in cases where neurological or cognitive impairments are present. Such testimony can be pivotal in ensuring that defendants are not subjected to punishment disproportionate to their mental capacity.

False confessions represent another area where neuropsychopathological input can be decisive. A defendant in one case confessed to a crime under pressure but later recanted, claiming confusion. Testing showed he had memory deficits and a high level of suggestibility due to a previous brain injury. The expert explained how these impairments made him vulnerable to coercive interrogation. As a result, the court excluded the confession, and the defendant was ultimately acquitted. This case highlighted the critical role of neuropsychopathological testimony in ensuring that confessions obtained under duress or due to cognitive impairments are not used unfairly in court. It also demonstrated how expert testimony can protect against miscarriages of justice by identifying vulnerabilities that may lead to false admissions of guilt.

Neuropsychopathological experts are also vital in detecting malingering. In one courtroom, a defendant falsely claimed to be mentally ill to avoid prosecution. Validity testing showed that the symptoms presented were exaggerated and did not align with any recognized disorder. The expert testified that the claims were inconsistent with genuine pathology. This prevented the legal system from being manipulated and ensured an appropriate verdict was reached. The expert's testimony not only safeguarded the integrity of the legal process but also reinforced the importance of accurate psychological assessments in ensuring justice is served.

In a civil lawsuit concerning an alleged brain injury, the plaintiff claimed significant cognitive dysfunction. However, the neuropsychopathologist found inconsistencies during testing and noted poor effort across multiple measures. The expert concluded that while some impairment existed, it was not as severe as claimed. As a result, the court awarded a reduced but still fair settlement. This case showcased the importance of objective analysis in civil litigation. It also highlighted how neuropsychopathological evaluations help ensure that claims are substantiated by evidence, protecting both parties from potential misuse of the legal system.

Family courts also benefit from forensic neuropsychopathological insights, especially in custody evaluations. In one instance, concerns about a parent's ability to provide safe care were raised. Testing revealed executive dysfunction, impulsivity, and difficulty with planning. The court ruled in favor of supervised visitation, combined with support services. The testimony allowed the court to protect the child while maintaining parental involvement. This case demonstrated how neuropsychopathological evaluations can inform decisions that balance safety and family dynamics, ensuring that the child's best interests are prioritized. It also highlighted the role of expert testimony in shaping fair and effective outcomes in sensitive family court matters.

These examples show the broad scope and impact of forensic neuropsychopathological testimony. Whether determining competency, assessing responsibility, or guiding sentencing, expert evaluations provide courts with scientifically grounded insight. The ability to explain complex neuropsychological findings in a legal context is crucial. Such testimony supports fairness and informed decision-making when delivered with clarity and ethical responsibility. In every type of case, it helps the legal system account for human cognition and mental health realities. By bridging the gap between science and law, neuropsychopathological experts ensure that justice is served with a deeper understanding of individual behavior and mental states. This highlights the crucial role of these experts in safeguarding both the rights of individuals and the integrity of the legal process.

As the examples have demonstrated, forensic neuropsychopathological testimony can significantly impact legal outcomes by providing valuable insights into an individual's mental health and cognitive functioning. However, the true power of this testimony is realized when it is grounded in practical application, where theory meets real-world legal scenarios. Understanding the theory behind neuropsychological assessments and their relevance to the law is one thing, but translating that knowledge into actionable insights that resonate in the courtroom is another. The following section will shift to how forensic neuropsychopathologists navigate this complex relationship. The practical aspects of conducting evaluations, presenting findings, and ensuring that scientific principles are effectively communicated to legal professionals will be explored, ultimately contributing to fair and just legal processes.

Bridging Theory to Practice

Forensic neuropsychopathology represents the relationship between scientific understanding of the brain and its direct application to the legal system. Earlier chapters discussed how neuropsychopathology offers valuable insights into brain function, behavior, and mental illness; however, applying these theories in the courtroom demands a more nuanced approach. Forensic professionals utilize the foundational knowledge of how the brain influences cognition, emotion, and behavior to address legal questions regarding criminal responsibility, competency to stand trial, and sentencing. This is not simply a matter of diagnosing a condition; rather, it is about assessing how specific neurological conditions or cognitive impairments might affect an individual's behavior concerning the law. For example, a brain injury may impair impulse control or decision-making, making it relevant to the question of whether a person should be held criminally responsible for their actions.

When assessing criminal responsibility, forensic neuropsychopathologists utilize their theoretical understanding of brain structure and function to determine whether a defendant's behavior was influenced by a neurological condition that may reduce their culpability. For instance, someone with a brain injury affecting the frontal lobe may exhibit impulsive or aggressive behavior due to a lack of impulse control, which could be significant in evaluating their mental state at the time of the offense. Forensic neuropsychopathologists apply their understanding of how the brain works, particularly in emotional regulation, judgment, and decision-making, when evaluating the defendant's behavior. This knowledge directly influences legal outcomes by helping the court understand the role of brain function in criminal behavior, which can support defenses such as diminished capacity or insanity.

The competency to stand trial is another crucial area where neuropsychopathological principles come into play. Competency involves evaluating whether a defendant has the mental capacity to understand the charges against them and participate in their defense. Forensic neuropsychopathologists will apply theoretical knowledge of cognitive functions such as memory, attention, and executive function to assess whether a defendant can meaningfully engage in the legal process. Cognitive tests help assess whether the defendant can comprehend the nature of the proceedings, understand the roles of those involved, and assist in their defense. The neuropsychologist's role is to evaluate these mental functions through standardized assessments and to provide the court with an objective, scientifically grounded evaluation of the defendant's ability to stand trial.

Mental illness, a key concept explored throughout earlier chapters, has profound implications for criminal responsibility and sentencing. In theory, mental illness affects cognition, perception, and behavior in ways that can alter an individual's understanding of their actions. Forensic neuropsychopathologists will assess whether mental illness influenced a defendant's behavior at the time of the crime, particularly in cases involving the insanity defense. The neuropsychopathological evaluation looks at whether the defendant was able to understand the wrongfulness of their actions or conform their behavior to the law due to the influence of mental illness. In these cases, the theory of how specific mental health conditions (such as schizophrenia or bipolar disorder) affect cognitive and emotional functioning is directly applied to evaluate whether the individual meets the criteria for legal insanity.

Personality disorders also play a significant role in forensic neuropsychology. The theoretical understanding of personality disorders like ASPD informs the neuropsychopathological evaluation of defendants exhibiting traits such as impulsivity, aggression, and disregard for the rights of others. These disorders are often linked to brain areas responsible for emotional processing and moral decision-making. In forensic contexts, neuropsychopathologists will assess how these personality traits manifest neurologically, helping the court understand the extent to which a personality disorder may have influenced the defendant's actions. By evaluating the neuropsychological aspects of a personality disorder, the expert can offer insight into whether the disorder played a significant role in criminal behavior and how it may impact the defendant's rehabilitation or sentencing.

Translating complex neuropsychological assessments into language understandable in the legal context is one of the most challenging aspects of forensic neuropsychopathology. Yet, neuropsychopathologists are tasked with explaining technical findings, such as brain scan results or cognitive test scores, in ways that judges, attorneys, and jurors can comprehend. For example, an expert might need to explain how a brain injury affecting the prefrontal cortex, which is responsible for executive functions like planning and impulse control, could contribute to a defendant's inability to control their actions during the commission of a crime. The goal is not only to provide scientific insight but to make that insight accessible and relevant to the specific legal questions being addressed, such as whether the defendant was legally responsible for their actions at the time of the offense.

Presenting neuropsychopathological findings in court requires careful preparation and clear communication. When neuropsychopathologists testify, they must be able to explain complex concepts in layman's terms. They need to illustrate how cognitive deficits, mental illnesses, or brain injuries might have contributed to criminal behavior, while also connecting these factors to the relevant legal standards. This can involve simplifying complex scientific data without losing its precision. For example, forensic neuropsychopathologists may use visual aids or analogies to help jurors grasp complex concepts, such as how brain damage affects an individual's behavior in the context of criminal responsibility or sentencing. Translating scientific evidence into legal language is essential for helping the court make informed decisions.

The challenge of communicating complex neuropsychopathological data in court is compounded by the need for clarity and reliability. During cross-examination, opposing counsel may challenge the validity of neuropsychological findings, questioning the methods used, the accuracy of the results, or even the expert witness's qualifications. Forensic neuropsychopathologists must be prepared to defend their conclusions and demonstrate that their findings are scientifically valid and legally relevant. This may involve explaining the rigor of the testing procedures, addressing potential biases, and showing how their conclusions were derived from solid scientific principles. The ability to defend neuropsychological evidence in court is an essential aspect of bridging the gap between theoretical knowledge and its practical application in the legal system.

Finally, as neuropsychopathological science evolves, new technologies and techniques, such as advanced neuroimaging, may offer even more precise insights into brain function and behavior. These advancements could enhance the effectiveness of forensic neuropsychology in the courtroom. For example, neuroimaging technologies can offer real-time insights into brain activity, providing more direct evidence of how brain function affects behavior. However, translating these cutting-edge tools into meaningful legal evidence will remain a challenge. Forensic neuropsychopathologists will need to balance the scientific potential of these technologies with their ability to communicate these findings in a way that is both scientifically rigorous and legally applicable.

Case Law and Precedents

Forensic neuropsychopathology has played an increasingly pivotal role in shaping modern jurisprudence, particularly in criminal law, where questions of mental capacity and culpability arise. One of the earliest and most cited examples is the case of Herbert Weinstein, which occurred in the early 1990s. Weinstein, a man in his sixties with no criminal record, strangled his wife and threw her body out of a window. Neuroimaging later revealed a cyst pressing against his brain's frontal lobe, which is associated with impulse control and decision-making (Kuersten, 2016). Although Weinstein ultimately accepted a plea deal, the introduction of MRI evidence into his defense marked a turning point in the courtroom's willingness to consider brain-based explanations for criminal behavior.

Another significant case in the evolution of forensic neuropsychopathology is *People v. Goldstein* (2004), which tested the boundaries of expert psychiatric and neuropsychopathological testimony. The central issue in this case was the admissibility of expert opinion that relied on hearsay accounts to diagnose the defendant's mental state. Like Weinstein's case, the court ultimately ruled that relying on out-of-court statements without allowing cross-examination violated the defendant's Sixth Amendment rights. Though primarily a case about procedural fairness, Goldstein influenced how neuropsychopathological experts collect and present data, emphasizing the need for rigor, transparency, and direct sources of information. It reinforced that while mental health testimony can be powerful, it must meet legal standards of reliability and fairness.

A landmark case that profoundly changed the legal landscape was *United States v. Hinckley (1982)*, involving John Hinckley Jr., who attempted to assassinate President Ronald Reagan. Hinckley's defense argued that he had severe mental illness, specifically a psychotic disorder, and was, therefore, not legally responsible for his actions (Linder, 2025). The jury found him not guilty by reason of insanity, a verdict that led to public outrage and widespread legislative changes. Many jurisdictions subsequently narrowed the criteria for the insanity defense, shifting the burden of proof to the defense or eliminating the defense. This case illustrates how psychiatric and neuropsychological testimony can impact individual verdicts and broader legal reforms.

As previously discussed in this text, in *Atkins v. Virginia* (2002), the United States Supreme Court held that executing individuals with intellectual disabilities violates the Eighth Amendment's ban on cruel and unusual punishment. Neuropsychopathological assessment was central to the case, as it helped establish the defendant's significantly impaired intellectual functioning. The ruling mandated that courts must consider reliable measures of cognitive and adaptive functioning when determining eligibility for the death penalty. This case also highlighted the importance of standardized psychological testing in forensic evaluations and raised awareness about the limitations of relying solely on IQ scores. Since Atkins, neuropsychologists have played an increasingly prominent role in capital cases involving questions of intellectual disability.

The case of *State v. Brett* (1991) in Washington State involved a defendant who was sentenced to death despite significant evidence of brain dysfunction and mental illness. Expert testimony indicated that Brett had sustained neurological damage that impaired his capacity for rational thought and impulse control. While the majority upheld the death sentence, the dissenting opinion strongly emphasized the need for courts to consider the full weight of neuropsychopathological evidence in sentencing. The case revealed the inconsistencies in how different courts evaluate such evidence and highlighted the need for clearer legal standards. It also demonstrated that even when brain dysfunction is evident, courts may struggle with how it should influence judgments of culpability and punishment.

Broader questions about the admissibility of expert scientific testimony have also shaped legal precedents. *The Daubert v. Merrell Dow Pharmaceuticals* (1993) decision established a new standard for admitting expert testimony, requiring that it be both relevant and scientifically valid. For neuropsychologists, this meant that their methods, assessments, and conclusions needed to be based on reliable principles that could be tested and peer reviewed. Courts were tasked with acting as gatekeepers, ensuring that only scientifically credible evidence would be considered by juries. This ruling significantly professionalized the field, raising the bar for forensic neuropsychopathological evaluations and their presentation in legal proceedings.

The Supreme Court's decision in *Kumho Tire Co. v. Carmichael* (1999) extended the Daubert standard to include all expert testimony, not just purely scientific evidence. This expansion directly impacts forensic experts, whose work often blends empirical data with clinical judgment. Under Kumho, trial judges were required to evaluate the reliability and applicability of technical expertise, such as neuropsychopathological assessments, in the context of the specific legal issues being addressed. This decision helped to standardize the use of neuropsychopathological testimony across jurisdictions and encouraged greater methodological rigor. As a result, neuropsychopathologists must be prepared to defend their techniques and conclusions under legal scrutiny.

Miller v. Alabama (2012) is a recent case that illustrates the growing impact of developmental neuroscience on shaping legal doctrine. The Supreme Court ruled that mandatory life sentences without parole for juveniles violated the Eighth Amendment, citing research on adolescent brain development. Neuropsychopathological findings were instrumental in showing that juveniles lack fully developed capacities for judgment, impulse control, and risk assessment. This case reflected a shift in how the law interprets responsibility and rehabilitation potential in younger offenders. It also allowed courts to reconsider previously imposed life sentences on juvenile offenders, using neuropsychological evidence as a guide.

Collectively, these cases illustrate how forensic neuropsychopathology has evolved from a novel courtroom strategy to a foundational component of many legal arguments. Courts increasingly recognize that mental illness, brain injuries, and cognitive impairments can—and often do—play a meaningful role in criminal behavior. At the same time, they have imposed strict requirements for presenting such evidence, favoring empirical validation over speculation. The legal system's relationship with neuroscience is still evolving, and while some skepticism remains, the trend is moving toward a greater inclusion of neuropsychological insights. These cases have shaped individual outcomes and informed broader judicial principles on culpability and justice.

As the field of neuroscience continues to grow, future legal precedents will likely refine and expand the application of forensic neuropsychopathology. Advancements in neuroimaging, cognitive testing, and behavioral analysis will provide more nuanced insights into how brain function influences behavior. However, courts will continue to grapple with balancing scientific evidence with legal concepts such as free will, intent, and personal responsibility. The cases discussed in this chapter serve as guideposts, showing how far the integration of brain science into the legal system has come—and hinting at where it may go next. Ultimately, the ongoing dialogue between science and law will shape a more informed, compassionate, and precise approach to justice.

As forensic neuropsychopathology continues to evolve and become more integrated into legal proceedings, its application spans various legal contexts. While the general principles of neuropsychopathological evaluations and testimony are foundational, the nuances of different legal settings require tailored approaches to how this evidence is applied and interpreted. From criminal defense cases involving competency or insanity defenses to civil litigation where cognitive function is in question, forensic neuropsychopathology provides crucial insights into mental capacity, behavior, and responsibility.

This next section will examine how forensic neuropsychopathological evaluations are applied explicitly in various legal contexts. This includes criminal cases, where questions of mental illness and cognitive impairment are central to determining guilt, sentencing, and responsibility. It will also explore civil cases, such as personal injury claims, where cognitive deficits or brain injuries can affect the case outcome. Additionally, family courts increasingly rely on neuropsychopathological assessments to guide decisions in custody and parental fitness cases, highlighting the broad reach of this discipline. By examining these specific legal contexts, the complex relationship between neuropsychology and law can be better understood, offering insight into how brain function and behavior shape legal outcomes.

Forensic Neuropsychopathology in Specific Legal Contexts

One of the most critical contributions forensic neuropsychologists make in the legal system is competency evaluations. Competency to stand trial refers to a defendant's ability to understand the legal proceedings and participate meaningfully in their defense. Emerging forensic neuropsychopathologists play a pivotal role by assessing cognitive domains such as memory, attention, comprehension, reasoning, and executive functioning. They evaluate whether a defendant understands basic courtroom procedures, such as the roles of the judge, jury, and attorneys, and whether the individual can communicate effectively with their counsel. When mental illness, intellectual disability, or brain injury impairs these abilities, a forensic neuropsychopathologist may conclude that the defendant is not competent, prompting the court to postpone proceedings or order treatment.

Determining competency is a clinical and legal task requiring neuropsychopathologists to bridge the gap between objective data and legal standards. Forensic evaluations typically include reviewing the defendant's medical and psychiatric history, interviews, behavioral observations, and standardized neuropsychopathological testing. Conditions like schizophrenia, traumatic brain injury, or severe cognitive decline from dementia can significantly impair the defendant's ability to meet legal competency standards. Forensic neuropsychopathologists synthesize this information in a forensic report that offers a clear opinion on whether the defendant meets the legal threshold for competency. In many jurisdictions, this report becomes key evidence in determining whether the court proceeds with prosecution or pauses the case for restoration efforts.

In contrast to competency, which focuses on the defendant's current mental state, the insanity defense addresses the defendant's mental state at the time of the offense. This is a retrospective evaluation, meaning the expert must reconstruct the individual's mental functioning during the crime, often months or even years after the fact. The primary legal question is whether the defendant, due to mental illness or cognitive impairment, could not appreciate the wrongfulness of their actions or conform their behavior to the law. To answer this, forensic neuropsychopathologists examine the presence of psychotic disorders, neurological damage, severe mood disorders, or delusions that might have driven the behavior. The complexity of these assessments demands clinical expertise and a deep understanding of legal definitions and jurisdictional standards for insanity.

Forensic neuropsychopathologists rely on collateral information when assessing a defendant's mental state at the time of the crime. This includes police reports, witness statements, past psychiatric records, and sometimes crime scene evidence that can illuminate the defendant's behavior and mental state. Neuropsychopathological testing might still be used to identify cognitive deficits or patterns consistent with certain disorders, but much of the insanity evaluation depends on contextual and historical analysis. For instance, a person with long-standing schizophrenia who experienced command auditory hallucinations during the offense might be found legally insane if their illness rendered them incapable of understanding the nature or wrongfulness of their actions. However, neuropsychologists must carefully distinguish between genuine cognitive impairment and malingering, using validity tests and clinical judgment to avoid wrongful use of the insanity defense.

Sentencing is another area where neuropsychopathological evaluations play a significant role, especially in cases where mental illness or neurological impairment is relevant to mitigation. Courts increasingly recognize that cognitive or emotional impairments can diminish culpability or suggest a reduced ability to conform to legal norms. For example, a defendant with a history of TBI may be found guilty but receive a more lenient sentence due to documented deficits in impulse control and judgment. In such cases, neuropsychopathologists present their findings during the sentencing phase, explaining how the individual's neurological profile contributed to their behavior and what treatment options might reduce future risk. These evaluations help courts move beyond punishment and consider rehabilitation or alternative sentencing.

In cases involving juveniles, neuropsychopathological input is significant due to the developing nature of the adolescent brain. Research consistently shows that the prefrontal cortex, which governs impulse control, foresight, and decision-making, does not fully mature until the mid-twenties. As a result, forensic professionals are often called upon to assess the maturity and neurological functioning of young defendants. Their evaluations can influence whether a juvenile is tried as an adult or how much weight is given to rehabilitation versus punishment. The findings can also help courts determine the appropriate level of supervision and treatment within juvenile justice systems, ensuring that sentencing considers the principles of developmental neuroscience and individual differences.

Neuropsychopathological input is also critical during parole evaluations, particularly when assessing an offender's risk of recidivism. Risk assessments consider the presence of mental illness, cognitive deficits, and personality factors that may predispose someone to reoffend. Forensic professionals may use structured tools to assess violence risk and combine these with neurocognitive data to provide a comprehensive risk profile. For instance, an individual with poor executive functioning, impulsivity, and no insight into their mental illness may be judged as higher risk, potentially influencing the parole board's decision. Conversely, individuals demonstrating cognitive recovery, treatment compliance, and behavioral stability may be deemed lower risk and eligible for supervised release.

In parole hearings involving individuals with neurodegenerative conditions, neuropsychologists may be asked to evaluate whether the person's cognitive decline makes them less dangerous. For example, someone incarcerated for a violent offense who now has advanced dementia may no longer pose a threat to society due to loss of cognitive faculties. In these cases, experts provide objective data on memory, orientation, and decision-making capacity to support compassionate release or placement in a supervised care environment. These evaluations strike a balance between public safety and humane treatment, recognizing that neurological deterioration fundamentally alters risk and behavioral control. The input of neuropsychologists ensures that decisions are informed by medical science and legal responsibility.

Neuropsychopathological evaluations in sentencing and parole contexts also address the issue of treatment amenability. Courts often consider whether an individual's cognitive or emotional impairments can be effectively managed with therapy, medication, or structured supervision. An expert's report might include recommendations for cognitive rehabilitation, psychiatric care, or substance abuse treatment, all of which can factor into sentencing alternatives. These reports help tailor sentencing to the individual and inform post-release planning, ensuring that resources are allocated appropriately, and risks are minimized. In this way, neuropsychopathologists contribute to both the fairness and effectiveness of the criminal justice system.

Across all these legal contexts—competency, insanity, sentencing, and parole—the role of forensic neuropsychopathologists is to integrate clinical science with legal standards. Their assessments provide courts with evidence-based insights into defendants' cognitive and emotional functioning at various legal processes. Whether determining a person's ability to stand trial, evaluating mental state at the time of a crime, or helping courts craft appropriate sentencing plans, neuropsychopathologists bring scientific rigor and ethical clarity to high-stakes legal decisions. The application of neuropsychology in these domains not only advances justice but also ensures that the rights and needs of neurologically and psychiatrically impaired individuals are appropriately considered within the legal system.

Neuropsychopathological Expertise in Jury Trials

Forensic neuropsychopathologists serve a crucial role as expert witnesses in jury trials, bringing scientific understanding of the brain and behavior into the courtroom. Their primary function is to explain how neurological conditions, cognitive impairments, or psychiatric disorders may have influenced a defendant's behavior, decision-making, or mental state at a relevant point in time. They may be asked to address issues such as whether a defendant was competent to stand trial, whether a brain injury contributed to a violent act, or whether a cognitive disorder diminishes legal culpability. In these roles, neuropsychologists bridge complex scientific knowledge and the legal questions jurors must answer. Their testimony often plays a pivotal role in shaping how jurors interpret the mental capacity and responsibility of the individual on trial.

The evidence that forensic neuropsychopathologists provide includes data from standardized assessments, behavioral observations, historical records, neuroimaging results, and clinical interviews. These data points are synthesized into a comprehensive evaluation that forms the basis of their expert opinion. Forensic neuropsychopathologists may testify, for instance, that a defendant with severe frontal lobe damage cannot inhibit impulses, which could be relevant in a case involving impulsive violence. Alternatively, they might explain how dementia impairs memory and comprehension, potentially affecting an individual's ability to participate in their defense or understand the consequences of their actions.

This evidence is not just presented in technical terms—it must be translated into a form that lay jurors can understand and apply.

Presenting neuropsychopathological findings to a jury requires both scientific precision and communication skills. Experts must distill complex concepts, such as executive dysfunction, working memory deficits, or neurodevelopmental disorders, into clear, relatable explanations. They often use analogies, charts, and visual aids to help jurors grasp abstract or unfamiliar ideas. For instance, a neuropsychologist might compare damage to the prefrontal cortex to a car with no brakes: The engine (impulse) works, but the braking system (self-control) is impaired. This framing helps jurors understand how the real, observable behavioral consequences of invisible impairments can have a direct impact on questions of intent, planning, and accountability.

Expert testimony also requires neutrality and objectivity. Although forensic professionals are often retained by one side—either the defense or prosecution—their credibility rests on their impartiality. Unlike advocates, they are bound by professional ethics to present findings honestly, even when those findings do not support the retaining party's legal position. A strong expert witness can maintain scientific integrity while being clear and persuasive. Jurors are more likely to trust experts who appear balanced, careful, and transparent about the limitations of their conclusions. A well-prepared neuropsychologist may significantly influence how the jury interprets a case's psychological and cognitive dimensions.

However, presenting neuropsychopathological evidence in court poses its own challenges. One of the most significant is the presence of opposing expert witnesses who may present contradictory findings. For example, one expert might conclude that a defendant suffers from a severe cognitive impairment that influences their behavior. At the same time, another might argue that the individual is malingering or that the tests used were invalid. These battles of the experts can create confusion among jurors, who may lack the necessary background to evaluate competing scientific claims critically. As a result, the effectiveness of the testimony often hinges on the expert's clarity, coherence, and perceived objectivity.

Another challenge lies in the inherent complexity of neuropsychopathological data. Concepts like attention deficits, neurocognitive slowing, or impaired executive function do not always translate neatly into legal categories such as "intent" or "criminal responsibility." The legal system tends to favor clear-cut answers, while neuropsychopathological findings often involve degrees of impairment, probabilities, and diagnostic uncertainty. Experts must, therefore, walk a fine line—providing scientifically accurate testimony while avoiding overly technical jargon or equivocal explanations that may distract the jury or erode their trust. Courts may struggle to balance this nuanced evidence with the need for concrete legal conclusions.

Judges also play a gatekeeping role when it comes to expert testimony, and they may exclude neuropsychological evidence if it does not meet standards for scientific validity and relevance. In the United States, this is guided by rulings that require expert opinions to be grounded in reliable methodology and accepted practices within the field. If an expert uses outdated tests, lacks relevant forensic experience, or cannot clearly explain their conclusions, their testimony may be challenged or excluded. Forensic neuropsychopathologists must be prepared for both legal scrutiny and scientific rigor, especially during cross-examination.

Cross-examination presents its own set of challenges. Attorneys may attempt to undermine the credibility of the neuropsychologist by questioning their qualifications, methods, or conclusions. They may bring up discrepancies in the data, suggest alternative interpretations, or highlight instances where the expert has testified similarly in other cases. Neuropsychopathologists must, therefore, be well-versed in the strengths and limitations of their assessments and ready to defend their findings under pressure. Being able to remain calm, consistent, and evidence-based during cross-examination can significantly affect how jurors perceive the credibility of the expert and the weight of their testimony.

Jurors themselves bring biases and misconceptions to the courtroom, which can affect how they receive neuropsychological testimony. Some jurors may be skeptical of "invisible" impairments or believe that neurological conditions are used as excuses for criminal behavior. Others may be overly persuaded by scientific-sounding language or brain scan images, a phenomenon known as the "neuroimage bias." Forensic neuropsychopathologists must be aware of these dynamics and tailor their communication accordingly—neither overwhelming jurors with complexity nor oversimplifying the science. Part of the challenge is helping jurors see the real-world implications of brain dysfunction without diminishing the seriousness of the offense or the importance of accountability.

Ultimately, the impact of forensic neuropsychopathologists' expertise in jury trials depends on the ability of the expert to communicate effectively and ethically within a legal framework. Their role is not to decide guilt or innocence but to provide the jury with the tools to make an informed decision regarding mental state, cognitive functioning, and behavioral control. In doing so, they contribute to a more nuanced and just legal process that considers the full scope of human cognition and emotion. As neuroscience continues to evolve and its applications in law expand, the role of the neuropsychopathologist as an expert witness will remain central to the future of forensic practice.

Interdisciplinary Collaboration

Interdisciplinary collaboration lies at the heart of effective forensic neuropsychopathology. Because legal cases involving neuropsychopathological concerns often span medical, psychological, and legal domains, forensic neuropsychopathologists must work closely with a wide range of professionals to form a comprehensive understanding of the case. This includes attorneys, judges, psychiatrists, psychologists, social workers, and sometimes neurologists or rehabilitation specialists. Whether evaluating competency, criminal responsibility, or risk of recidivism, these cases demand input from multiple perspectives. Effective collaboration ensures that neuropsychological findings are placed in the proper legal and clinical context, ultimately enhancing the quality and credibility of the forensic process.

Collaboration with attorneys is particularly central. Defense attorneys may consult with neuropsychologists to determine whether cognitive deficits could be relevant in formulating a defense strategy. Prosecutors might also request evaluations to confirm the validity of claims related to brain dysfunction or mental illness. In either case, forensic neuropsychopathologists help attorneys understand the scope and implications of cognitive impairments, advising them on which legal issues the neuropsychopathological data may impact, such as competency to stand trial, capacity to waive Miranda rights, or the viability of an insanity defense. In pretrial strategy meetings, neuropsychologists may also guide attorneys in crafting questions for cross-examination or assist in interpreting findings from other experts.

Judges, too, play a role in this interdisciplinary dynamic. While they do not typically collaborate in the same hands-on manner as attorneys, they rely on clear and concise input from neuropsychologists to determine admissibility, sentencing, or treatment directives. Judges may review forensic reports and expert testimony to decide whether a defendant should be diverted to mental health court or referred for competency restoration. Neuropsychopathologists who communicate findings in a legally relevant, jargon-free manner contribute to the judge's understanding and the efficiency and clarity of court proceedings. This reinforces the value of experts who can bridge the divide between science and law.

In complex cases, interdisciplinary teams may be assembled to evaluate a defendant from multiple angles. These teams can include neuropsychopathologists (and neuropsychologists), psychiatrists, psychologists, medical providers, clinical researchers and scientists, case managers, probation officers, and legal counsel. Each professional brings a unique lens: Psychiatrists may focus on psychotropic medication and psychiatric diagnosis, psychologists on behavioral assessments, and neuropsychologists on cognitive functioning and brain-behavior relationships. Working together, these teams can construct a rich, multifaceted profile of the defendant's mental health, social history, and neurocognitive status. This team-based approach is prevalent in cases involving juveniles, individuals with co-occurring disorders, or defendants facing life-altering sentences.

One example of this interdisciplinary approach is seen in mental health courts, where defendants with psychiatric or neurocognitive impairments are diverted from the traditional justice system. Neuropsychopathologists often work alongside social workers and case managers to develop individualized treatment plans, assess functional capacity, and provide recommendations for cognitive rehabilitation or supportive services. These collaborative efforts focus on reducing recidivism through treatment rather than punishment. Neuropsychopathologists support more humane and effective legal outcomes by providing nuanced insights into a person's cognitive limitations and potential for recovery. Mental health courts exemplify how integrated teamwork can address public safety and therapeutic needs.

In working with psychiatrists, forensic neuropsychopathologists must distinguish between cognitive and psychiatric contributions to a defendant's behavior. For instance, in a case involving a violent offense, the psychiatrist may assess for psychosis, mood instability, or medication effects. At the same time, the neuropsychopathologist evaluates whether brain injury, executive dysfunction, or attention deficits played a role. Such collaborative assessments compare, contrast, and synthesize findings into a shared understanding. These interactions foster more comprehensive diagnoses and better-informed legal conclusions. The synergy between neuropsychological and psychiatric perspectives can be significant in cases involving dual diagnoses or questions of criminal responsibility.

Similarly, clinical psychologists and neuropsychologists often work together during forensic evaluations. While both disciplines may conduct assessments, clinical psychologists focus more heavily on emotional, personality, and behavioral factors, utilizing tools such as the MMPI or projective tests. On the other hand, neuropsychologists emphasize cognitive domains such as memory, attention, processing speed, and executive functioning through structured performance-based tasks. When both professionals are involved in the same case, their reports complement each other, offering a broader view of the individual's psychological and cognitive functioning. This integrated approach is beneficial when differentiating between disorders with overlapping symptoms, such as depression and early-onset dementia.

Risk assessment is another domain where interdisciplinary collaboration is crucial. Psychiatrists may evaluate a defendant's current mental state and history of psychiatric hospitalization. At the same time, neuropsychopathologists assess cognitive control, impulse regulation, and problem-solving skills—key predictors of future violence or reoffending. Together, their combined data contribute to actuarial or structured professional judgment tools that estimate risk. Judges and parole boards often rely on these assessments when deciding sentencing, release, or supervision. Interdisciplinary cooperation ensures that these decisions are grounded in science and tailored to the individual's clinical and cognitive profile.

Interdisciplinary teamwork extends into post-sentencing settings, including probation, parole, and rehabilitation. Neuropsychopathologists may collaborate with correctional psychologists, counselors, and caseworkers to design cognitive remediation programs, vocational training, or behavioral interventions suited to individuals with cognitive impairments. These professionals share insights on how a person's neurological condition might impact their ability to follow rules, attend therapy, or reintegrate into society. By working together, they can develop realistic, practical plans that support rehabilitation and reduce recidivism. This benefits the individual, contributes to public safety, and is a more efficient use of legal and healthcare resources.

Ultimately, the success of forensic neuropsychopathologist evaluations depends not just on individual expertise but on the strength of interdisciplinary collaboration. When professionals across various fields communicate openly and work in tandem, they create a more accurate and holistic picture of the individual at the center of the legal case. This collaborative model leads to more informed decisions, procedural fairness, and humane outcomes. As legal cases grow more complex and intersect with issues of brain health, trauma, and psychiatric care, the need for interdisciplinary cooperation will only continue to grow. Forensic neuropsychologists are uniquely positioned to lead and contribute within these collaborative frameworks, reinforcing the value of science-informed justice.

Ethical Dilemmas in Applied Forensic Neuropsychopathology

Ethical challenges are deeply embedded in the practice of forensic neuropsychopathology, where the complex interplay between brain function, psychopathology, and the law must be interpreted responsibly and accurately. One of the most pressing concerns is the risk of bias in assessments and interpretations. Forensic neuropsychopathologists are often retained by one party in a legal dispute, which can create both overt and subtle pressures to interpret findings in favor of that party. Even unintentional bias, such as confirmation bias, can skew the selection or emphasis of data. Therefore, practitioners must use empirically supported methodologies to commit to impartiality at all stages of evaluation.

The interpretation of neuropsychopathological findings introduces its ethical complexity. Brain-based behavioral impairments, psychiatric symptoms, and cognitive deficits can be nuanced and multifactorial, often defying simple conclusions. When these findings are applied in high-stakes legal contexts, such as determining criminal responsibility or assessing the risk of future violence, the potential for misinterpretation increases significantly. Forensic neuropsychopathologists must ensure that their conclusions are not overstated or simplified for legal purposes. Clear articulation of diagnostic limitations, the probabilistic nature of findings, and alternative explanations is critical to upholding ethical standards in written reports and expert testimony.

To safeguard objectivity, forensic neuropsychopathologists must maintain rigorous documentation practices. This includes transparent test selection, adherence to standardized scoring, and detailed justification for diagnostic impressions. Validity testing is crucial for detecting exaggeration, malingering, or suboptimal effort. These measures protect the integrity of the evaluation and the rights of the individual being assessed. Ethical practice also involves seeking peer consultation in complex or ambiguous cases, helping to identify unconscious bias or methodological errors before findings are submitted in court.

Confidentiality is another foundational ethical concern, and it is uniquely challenged in the context of forensic neuropsychopathology. Unlike therapeutic relationships, forensic assessments are conducted for the benefit of the court, not the individual. From the outset, examinees must be informed that the evaluation is not confidential in the traditional sense and that the information disclosed may be used in legal proceedings. Informed consent procedures should explicitly outline these boundaries, including the intended recipients of the report and the legal implications of the findings. Ensuring that individuals understand this distinction is a core ethical obligation of the forensic neuropsychopathologist.

Despite these disclosures, ethical dilemmas arise when sensitive or unexpected information emerges during the evaluation process. For example, if a defendant reveals a desire to harm others, describes undisclosed criminal activity, or exhibits symptoms of a neurological condition with profound implications, the practitioner must decide how much to disclose, to whom, and under what circumstances. Legal jurisdictions differ, but generally, the duty to protect the public and the integrity of the legal process outweighs the obligation to maintain privacy. Nevertheless, forensic neuropsychopathologists must approach such decisions with care, disclosing only what is necessary and in line with both legal standards and professional ethics.

Ethical tensions also emerge when the neuropsychopathologist's work is selectively cited or misused by legal professionals. Attorneys may highlight portions of a report that support their argument while ignoring qualifying statements or contextual data. Forensic neuropsychopathologists are ethically bound to correct such misrepresentations, even when doing so contradicts the interests of the party that retained them. This may include clarifying testimony in court, providing written statements, or reasserting the full context of their findings. The priority must always be accuracy, objectivity, and the responsible use of science in legal settings.

It is also critical for forensic neuropsychopathologists to remain within the bounds of their expertise. While they may provide expert opinions about brain function, psychiatric symptoms, and their relationship to behavior, they must avoid making ultimate legal determinations, such as a finding of guilt or insanity. These are legal decisions, not clinical ones. Ethical practice requires forensic neuropsychopathologists to be clear about the scope of their role and resist pressure to offer conclusions outside their professional domain. This clarity protects the integrity of the legal process and avoids the appearance of overreach.

Cultural and contextual bias present another serious ethical issue in forensic neuropsychopathology. Standardized assessment tools may not account for the cultural, linguistic, or educational background of the individual being evaluated, increasing the risk of misdiagnosis or unjust legal outcomes. Practitioners must be aware of these limitations and adjust their evaluations accordingly. This might involve using culturally adapted instruments, employing interpreters, or explicitly noting limitations in the report. Ethical forensic neuropsychopathology requires sensitivity to the diverse populations it serves and an ongoing commitment to fairness in assessment and interpretation.

Ethical practice also involves maintaining independence from external pressures, whether financial or professional. Forensic neuropsychopathologists must avoid dual relationships, refrain from accepting contingent fees, and disclose any potential conflicts of interest. Their role is to provide unbiased, scientifically sound evaluations rather than advocating for one side or guaranteeing a particular outcome. Upholding these boundaries enhances credibility and supports the broader justice mission within forensic contexts. Independence and impartiality are the cornerstones of ethical forensic work, particularly when the stakes involve liberty, public safety, or mental health treatment.

Ultimately, ethical dilemmas in forensic neuropsychopathology necessitate practitioners to navigate a complex landscape of scientific rigor, legal obligations, and human impact. Whether addressing bias in interpretation, balancing confidentiality, or responding to legal misrepresentation, the forensic neuropsychopathologist must act with integrity, transparency, and professionalism. By adhering to the ethical standards established by organizations such as the American Psychological Association, the National Academy of Neuropsychology, and specialty boards, practitioners protect the individuals they assess and reinforce the legitimacy and trustworthiness of forensic mental health services.

Direction of Applied Forensic Neuropsychopathology

The future of applied forensic neuropsychopathology is poised for profound transformations driven by innovations in neuroscience, artificial intelligence, and data analytics. One of the most anticipated developments is the integration of advanced neurotechnologies—particularly neuroimaging techniques like fMRI, DTI, and real-time EEG-based monitoring—into forensic evaluations. These tools offer increasingly detailed and dynamic views of brain activity and connectivity, potentially enhancing the precision with which neuropsychopathological conditions are identified and linked to specific behaviors relevant to legal contexts. Forensic experts may one day use such scans daily to detect structural abnormalities and understand the neural underpinnings of impulsivity, aggression, or impaired decision-making.

Brain-machine interfaces (BMIs) and **neural decoding** technologies also hint at a future where internal mental states may be more directly assessed. Although still largely experimental, BMIs could theoretically provide objective markers of pain, emotional reactivity, or even intent—concepts currently relying on subjective reporting and interpretation. While these possibilities are ethically and legally complex, they suggest a trajectory in which forensic neuropsychopathology may gain new tools for assessing truthfulness, criminal intent, or mental competence. The challenge will be to ensure that such technologies are used responsibly and interpreted within appropriate clinical and ethical frameworks, rather than being treated as definitive "mind-reading" tools.

As these technologies evolve, so must the standards for their admissibility and reliability in legal settings. Courts must grapple with whether and how to incorporate neuroimaging and other high-tech methods into proceedings, particularly given historical concerns about the misuse or overvaluation of scientific evidence. Forensic neuropsychopathologists of the future will be expected to interpret these tools with scientific literacy and legal awareness, clarifying for judges and juries what the data can—and cannot—reliably reveal. As neuroscience moves closer to the courtroom, interdisciplinary collaboration will be more critical than ever, requiring ongoing dialogue between scientists, clinicians, ethicists, and legal professionals.

Beyond neurotechnology, there is significant potential for improving core forensic evaluation methods. Traditional neuropsychological assessments, although effective, have limitations, including cultural bias, providing static snapshots of performance, and relying on subjective behavioral observations. Emerging digital assessment tools offer a more dynamic and context-sensitive approach, including tablet-based cognitive testing, wearable monitoring devices, and AI-assisted behavioral analysis. These innovations could provide real-time or ecologically valid data about how individuals function daily, enhancing the courtroom's understanding of a person's capabilities and impairments.

AI and machine learning are expected to play a transformative role in analyzing and interpreting forensic neuropsychopathological data. Algorithms trained on large datasets could help identify patterns in cognitive performance, mental health symptoms, or brain scans that are too subtle or complex for traditional clinical interpretation. While human oversight will remain essential, AI could enhance diagnostic accuracy, reduce evaluator bias, and flag inconsistencies in performance that might otherwise be missed. These systems could also standardize parts of the evaluation process, making forensic assessments more consistent and defensible in court proceedings.

In addition to improving assessment tools, future forensic neuropsychopathology will likely benefit from advances in longitudinal and predictive modeling. Rather than relying on one-time evaluations, clinicians may increasingly draw upon longitudinal data, tracking how an individual's cognitive and psychological functioning changes over time, especially in correctional or rehabilitative settings. This would be particularly useful in cases involving parole, juvenile justice, or progressive conditions like dementia, where cognitive decline or improvement can significantly affect legal decisions. Predictive models based on neurocognitive and psychiatric profiles could also inform risk assessments for recidivism, violence, or treatment response. However, such tools will require careful validation to avoid reinforcing systemic biases.

Virtual reality (VR) and **augmented reality (AR)** technologies are emerging as innovative tools for forensic evaluation and rehabilitation. These platforms can simulate real-world environments and test behavior under controlled, repeatable conditions. For instance, VR-based assessments might simulate courtroom settings to evaluate trial competency or present ethically designed social scenarios to assess impulse control, moral judgment, or empathy. These immersive technologies offer an opportunity to study behavior in an engaging and ecologically valid manner, thereby bridging the gap between lab-based testing and real-world functioning.

The future will also demand that forensic neuropsychopathology becomes more culturally responsive and inclusive. As neuroscience becomes more global, it is essential to ensure that new tools, norms, and interpretive frameworks are validated across diverse populations. Researchers and clinicians must reduce cultural, linguistic, and socioeconomic biases in test development, data interpretation, and courtroom communication. The rise of global forensic practice—across borders and jurisdictions—means that ethical standards, legal precedents, and technological tools must evolve in tandem with sensitivity to the vast array of human experiences and neurodiversity.

Ethical considerations will remain at the forefront as the field continues to progress. With greater access to neural data and predictive technologies comes a greater responsibility to protect individual rights, prevent misuse, and ensure informed consent. The boundary between therapeutic and forensic use of neurodata will need constant scrutiny. Who owns the data from a brain scan conducted in a forensic context? How do we prevent coercive uses of neurotechnology in legal interrogation or sentencing? These are not hypothetical questions but pressing ethical frontiers that forensic neuropsychopathologists will be called upon to navigate.

In the coming decades, applied forensic neuropsychopathology will likely become even more influential in shaping how courts understand mental illness, brain dysfunction, and human behavior. Combining scientific advancement, technological integration, and deeper legal collaboration will push the field toward a more nuanced and humane justice model. As tools become more precise and our understanding of brain-behavior relationships more sophisticated, forensic neuropsychopathologists will play a pivotal role in bridging neuroscience and the law, not merely explaining past behavior but helping legal systems make informed, equitable decisions about the future.

Weaponizing Mental Health and the Legal System

The weaponization of mental health conditions is not a modern phenomenon; it has its roots that trace back to antiquity. From the ancient practices of linking mental illness to divine punishment or moral failure to the more formalized practices in the age of asylums and psychiatric institutions, mental health diagnoses have often been used to marginalize those who fall outside of accepted social, political, or moral norms. In the 20th century, political regimes like those in Nazi Germany and the Soviet Union exploited psychiatric diagnoses to justify political repression, while in the United States, civil rights activists and non-conforming individuals were sometimes institutionalized or diagnosed with mental illness as a tool of social control. These historical instances highlight the complex relationship between psychiatry, power, and control, making clear the capacity for mental health diagnoses to be manipulated in ways that perpetuate social injustice.

The concept of "weaponizing" mental health and psychiatric disorders in criminal justice refers to the strategic use of mental health conditions to excuse or mitigate criminal responsibility. The role of mental illness in legal defense has significantly shifted, with concerns over the abuse of mental health diagnoses to avoid criminal responsibility. As mental health defenses have grown more common, there has been a growing debate about whether they are being used appropriately or as a loophole to evade punishment for violent crimes. This issue is complex, as it interacts with mental illness stigma, legal standards, forensic practices, and law enforcement procedures. This discussion will explore the historical and contemporary contexts of mental health defenses, highlight modern cases where psychiatric disorders have been used in court, and analyze the challenges this trend poses to the justice system.

The ability to weaponize psychiatric conditions raises crucial questions about the ethical use of mental health diagnoses, particularly within the legal system. Forensic psychiatry is particularly vulnerable to misuse. Involuntary commitment, competency determinations, and mental health defenses in criminal cases all present opportunities for the legal system to be influenced by distorted or manipulated psychiatric evaluations. In these settings, the stakes of a misused diagnosis can be significant, potentially leading to wrongful convictions, unfair acquittals, or the unjust confinement of individuals based on inaccurate or fabricated mental health assessments.

Forensic neuropsychopathology plays a central role in addressing these challenges. As the field seeks to objectively assess how neurocognitive and psychopathological conditions impact behavior and competency, it faces the dual responsibility of maintaining scientific integrity while navigating the potential for exploitation in high-stakes legal cases. The pressure to conform to external agendas—whether from the defense, prosecution, or other interested parties—presents significant ethical dilemmas for clinicians in the forensic field. These dilemmas highlight the importance of establishing safeguards to protect the integrity of psychiatric evaluations and ensure they are used ethically and appropriately.

Moreover, the weaponization of mental health has wide-ranging social implications. It exacerbates existing biases, including those based on race, gender, and socioeconomic status. Individuals from marginalized communities, particularly people of color and women, are disproportionately impacted by the misapplication of psychiatric diagnoses. For example, studies have shown that African American men are more likely to be misdiagnosed with schizophrenia. At the same time, women's mood disorders, such as depression and bipolar disorder, are often underdiagnosed or dismissed. These systemic biases deepen the harm caused by weaponized mental health diagnoses, leading to further stigmatization, discrimination, and the perpetuation of inequality.

Given the significant consequences of weaponizing mental health, it is critical to consider solutions that address the root causes of these abuses. This includes strengthening forensic training to emphasize the importance of ethical evaluations, the need for independent second opinions, and the value of trauma-informed approaches. Additionally, there is a pressing need for legal reforms that establish stronger safeguards for psychiatric evaluations in high-stakes cases, such as requiring independent reviews and more stringent evidentiary standards. Public education campaigns are essential in demystifying mental health, reducing stigma, and ensuring that psychiatric diagnoses are used as tools for care rather than control.

Ultimately, the question of how to prevent the weaponization of mental health diagnoses is not just a matter of ethical psychiatry or legal integrity; it is a matter of human rights. Ensuring that mental health is not used as a tool of oppression requires vigilance, education, and reform across multiple systems—legal, medical, and societal. By exploring the history, mechanisms, and implications of weaponizing mental health, this discussion aims to provide a comprehensive understanding of the issue and offer potential solutions that protect individuals' rights while ensuring the proper use of psychiatric assessments in legal contexts.

This section will delve into the historical foundations of the weaponization of mental health, examining how psychiatric diagnoses have been used as tools of control and suppression throughout history. The mechanisms by which mental health diagnoses are weaponized will then be explored, including institutional and legal coercion as well as social and cultural manipulation. The section will also discuss the challenges faced in addressing this issue, particularly in terms of diagnostic ambiguity, ethical dilemmas for clinicians, and the sociopolitical biases that shape psychiatric evaluations. Finally, the implications for forensic neuropsychopathology will be addressed, emphasizing the importance of ethical practice in forensic evaluations and exploring potential reforms to safeguard against the misuse of psychiatric diagnoses. This discussion will highlight the need for reform and resilience, fostering a system that upholds the integrity of mental health care and the legal system.

Throughout history, mental health has often been manipulated for political, social, and religious purposes. From ancient civilizations to the modern era, psychiatric diagnoses have been used not only to treat illness but to control, isolate, and eliminate those who deviate from societal norms. The weaponization of mental health serves as a historical pattern through which individuals, particularly those marginalized, were silenced or punished. This manipulation of mental health is seen in various historical contexts, from ancient and medieval times through to the rise of psychiatric institutions and the political abuses in the 20th century.

In ancient Greece and Rome, "madness" was closely tied to spiritual or supernatural beliefs. Mental illnesses were often attributed to the wrath of gods or demonic possession, and those who exhibited erratic behavior could face execution or exile. While some philosophers, such as Hippocrates, attempted to explain mental illness in naturalistic terms, suggesting that imbalances in bodily fluids could lead to madness, these ideas were not universally accepted. Instead, madness was often seen as a moral failing or divine punishment. As a result, individuals with mental health issues could easily be ostracized, imprisoned, or even put to death. Some societies did establish rudimentary forms of care for the mentally ill. Still, these were typically isolating and poorly managed, reinforcing the notion of "madness" that required separation from society.

The Middle Ages saw a resurgence of religious and superstitious interpretations of mental illness, particularly within the Christian Church, which dominated Europe during this time. Madness was often understood as a spiritual failing, with those exhibiting atypical behavior believed to be under the influence of the devil. During the Inquisition and witch trials of the 15th and 16th centuries, people, especially women, were accused of witchcraft or heresy, and many were labeled as "mad." Heretical beliefs and behavior that deviated from accepted religious practices were often equated with mental illness, leading to imprisonment, torture, and execution. The infamous *Malleus Maleficarum* (*The Hammer of Witches*), published in 1486, further reinforced the connection between madness and demonic possession. Women were vulnerable to such diagnoses, with conditions like hysteria being frequently used to pathologize those who were seen as overly emotional, sexually assertive, or noncompliant with patriarchal norms.

The rise of psychiatric institutions in the 18th and 19th centuries marked a shift towards medicalizing mental illness, particularly in Europe and the United States. The Enlightenment ushered in a new era of rationality and scientific thinking, and asylums were established to house the mentally ill. However, this development did not necessarily lead to more humane treatment. New diagnoses such as hysteria, melancholia, and moral insanity became prevalent, and these were often weaponized against marginalized groups. These diagnoses were often vague and subjective, making them ripe for manipulation. Women, the poor, and political dissidents were disproportionately affected by such diagnoses, which were used to justify their institutionalization and social exclusion. "Moral insanity," a concept developed by the physician James Cowles Prichard in the early 19th century, suggested that individuals could be irrational or immoral due to defects in their moral faculties. This diagnosis allowed psychiatrists to justify the confinement of individuals whose behavior deviated from social expectations, effectively silencing political dissidents or social activists without recourse.

Bethlem Royal Hospital, also known as Bedlam, exemplifies the darker side of these early psychiatric institutions. Established in 1247 in London, Bedlam became notorious for its inhumane treatment of the mentally ill. While some patients received care, many others were displayed as spectacles to the public, who paid to view the "insane" patients. This turned human suffering into entertainment and further dehumanized those affected by mental illness. In many cases, asylums served not as places of healing but as tools of social control, removing individuals deemed undesirable from society and locking them away, not for treatment, but for their exclusion from public life.

The 20th century saw the weaponization of psychiatry escalate to new extremes. Totalitarian regimes, particularly in Nazi Germany and the Soviet Union, manipulated psychiatric diagnoses to eliminate threats to the state. In Nazi Germany, the T4 Euthanasia Program targeted individuals with mental disabilities and psychiatric conditions under the guise of "racial hygiene." This program led to the systematic extermination of over 70,000 people with mental illness, including those with schizophrenia, intellectual disabilities, and other conditions. Psychiatric professionals in Nazi Germany played a key role in legitimizing these atrocities, highlighting the danger of medical authority being co-opted for political purposes. Similarly, in the Soviet Union, the diagnosis of "sluggish schizophrenia" became a tool for silencing political dissidents. This fabricated diagnosis was applied to individuals who opposed Soviet policies, and the vague nature of the condition made it possible to label almost anyone exhibiting nonconformity as mentally ill. Dissidents diagnosed with sluggish schizophrenia were often sent to psychiatric hospitals, where they were subjected to brutal treatments, such as electroconvulsive therapy and psychotropic drugs, to incapacitate or permanently damage them.

In the United States, psychiatry was similarly weaponized against civil rights activists and other nonconforming individuals. During the civil rights movement, anti-war protests, and women's rights movements, individuals who challenged the status quo were sometimes labeled mentally ill. Diagnoses such as schizophrenia or hysteria were used to marginalize and discredit those who sought social change. This use of psychiatry as a tool of social control disproportionately affected marginalized populations who were often subjected to psychiatric diagnoses that reinforced their exclusion from society.

The history of psychiatric weaponization is deeply intertwined with broader political, social, and cultural struggles. Throughout history, psychiatry has been used not just for healing but as a tool to suppress dissent, reinforce existing power structures, and justify violence against marginalized groups. The tragic history of psychiatric abuse serves as a cautionary tale, highlighting the importance of ensuring that psychiatric practices remain rooted in scientific principles, ethical guidelines, and respect for human dignity. As society continues to advance in its understanding of mental health, vigilance is necessary to ensure that psychiatry is never again used as a weapon for social control or political oppression.

Mechanisms of Weaponization

The weaponization of mental health is a deeply troubling phenomenon that has evolved to serve a variety of political, social, and personal agendas. This manipulation takes many forms, ranging from institutional and legal coercion to social and cultural control and even misapplication in forensic settings. Across history, the psychiatric system has been used to silence dissent, control marginalized groups, and destabilize individuals by diagnosing them with mental illnesses that are either exaggerated or entirely fabricated. The methods of weaponization are as varied as they are harmful, but they all rely on the ability to distort mental health diagnoses into instruments of power. By understanding the key mechanisms behind this misuse, we can better grasp the extent to which mental health can be weaponized and the profound impact it has on individuals and societies.

Institutional and legal coercion is one of the most significant ways in which mental health diagnoses are weaponized. These tactics revolve around the power to control an individual's freedom and autonomy, often without due process or any meaningful checks and balances. Through **involuntary commitment**, conservatorships, guardianships, and competency determinations, authorities can exploit psychiatric diagnoses to strip individuals of their rights and liberty, using mental illness as a justification for control. These mechanisms disproportionately impact marginalized populations, including racial minorities and individuals with disabilities, who are more likely to face biased assessments and systemic neglect. The lack of consistent oversight and accountability in these legal processes further enables the misuse of mental health labels for institutional convenience or personal gain.

Involuntary commitment is one of the most direct ways in which mental health is weaponized within the legal system. It refers to the legal process in which individuals are placed in psychiatric institutions against their will, often without their consent or sufficient justification. The process for determining whether someone should be involuntarily committed can vary widely depending on jurisdiction, but in many cases, it is subjective and prone to manipulation. A person might be committed because they are deemed mentally unstable or dangerous, but what constitutes "dangerousness" can be ambiguous. For example, a political dissident or someone advocating for a minority cause might be deemed mentally unstable or a threat despite exhibiting no actual dangerous behavior. In other instances, individuals with controversial beliefs or those who challenge the status quo might be labeled as mentally ill, subjected to involuntary commitment, and removed from the public sphere as a result. This process can often be prolonged, with little or no access to legal recourse, allowing authorities to use psychiatric institutions as tools of social control rather than healing.

Conservatorships and **guardianships** provide another mechanism for weaponizing mental health diagnoses. These legal tools enable a third party, such as a family member or a legal guardian, to make decisions on behalf of another individual, including their financial matters, healthcare, and relationships. While conservatorships are generally intended to protect individuals who are mentally incapable of managing their affairs, they can easily be misused to strip people of their autonomy. This was tragically exemplified in the case of Britney Spears, where her father placed her under a conservatorship despite her having the capacity to make decisions about her personal life and career. Spears' case highlighted how conservatorships, when based on a psychiatric diagnosis, can be abused to control an individual's wealth, mobility, and overall life trajectory.

Such tools can be hazardous when they are applied to high-profile individuals, political figures, or marginalized people who may have a mental health condition that is overstated or misused to justify control.

Competency to stand trial is another area in which psychiatric diagnoses can be weaponized. In criminal proceedings, determining an individual's competency to stand trial ensures that the defendant understands the charges against them and can participate in their defense. However, this evaluation can be manipulated by both prosecutors and defense attorneys to achieve their desired outcomes. A defense attorney might argue that their client is mentally unfit to stand trial, using the diagnosis of mental illness to avoid criminal liability or to have the individual sent to a psychiatric facility rather than a prison. On the other hand, a prosecutor might argue that an individual is competent to stand trial despite having a clear mental illness to ensure that the person is criminally prosecuted. This distortion of the competency evaluation process undermines the fairness of the justice system, as it introduces biases based on the agendas of those involved and can result in defendants escaping justice or being unfairly punished.

Beyond legal and institutional contexts, mental health diagnoses can also be weaponized through social and cultural manipulation. In these cases, psychiatric labels are used to control, marginalize, and silence individuals whose behavior or opinions deviate from societal norms. Two key mechanisms within this realm are gaslighting and stigma-based marginalization, both of which use mental health diagnoses as tools for social and political control. This manipulation often serves to reinforce existing power structures by framing dissent or difference as a psychological disorder rather than a legitimate expression of identity, belief, or resistance. The pervasive use of psychiatric labels in this way further entrenches societal biases and reinforces the marginalization of those already vulnerable to discrimination and exploitation.

Gaslighting and **pathologizing** emotion are forms of psychological manipulation that involve convincing someone to doubt their perception of reality or their emotional responses. This can be achieved by labeling their emotional expression as evidence of mental instability. For instance, if a person challenges an unjust law, questions a societal norm, or protests political oppression, they may be labeled as "unstable," "hysterical," or "delusional." Their emotional reactions—whether frustration, anger, or sadness—are pathologized, and instead of being viewed as rational responses to injustice or adversity, these emotions are framed as symptoms of mental illness. This form of gaslighting serves to undermine the legitimacy of their emotions and marginalize their voice, making it harder for them to be heard or taken seriously. In this way, mental illness becomes a tool to silence dissent and stifle social movements, as people are conditioned to discredit those whose emotional expressions are seen as irrational or mentally unwell.

Stigma-based marginalization takes another approach by using psychiatric diagnoses to dehumanize individuals and make it easier for society to exclude them. Those with mental health conditions such as schizophrenia, bipolar disorder, or depression often face intense stigma, with their conditions portrayed as dangerous, unpredictable, or weak. These labels create barriers for individuals seeking employment, housing, or social connection, as they are often perceived as less competent because of their diagnosis. The stigma surrounding mental illness can lead to systemic discrimination and social exclusion, making it difficult for those affected to participate in society fully. The marginalization that results from this stigma exacerbates existing inequalities, particularly for those who are already vulnerable or marginalized based on race, gender, socioeconomic status, or other factors. In these cases, the weaponization of mental health diagnoses ensures that certain groups are consistently disempowered and excluded from mainstream society.

Finally, the forensic misapplication of psychiatric diagnoses is another powerful mechanism through which mental health can be weaponized. In the criminal justice system, psychiatric evaluations can be manipulated to either evade criminal responsibility or undermine an individual's credibility in legal proceedings. Two key forms of forensic misapplication are false insanity pleas and malicious allegations of mental illness. These tactics can distort the course of justice, allowing individuals to avoid accountability or, conversely, discrediting truthful testimonies and victimizing the mentally ill. Such misuse not only erodes public trust in psychiatric expertise but also contributes to the broader stigmatization of mental health conditions.

False insanity pleas are an especially controversial aspect of forensic psychiatry, where defense attorneys may exaggerate or fabricate symptoms of mental illness to avoid criminal liability. The insanity defense is intended to protect individuals who, due to severe mental illness, are unable to understand the nature of their actions or distinguish between right and wrong. However, in some high-profile cases, defense teams have falsely or exaggeratedly used the insanity defense as a strategy to reduce or eliminate criminal punishment. This misuse of the defense not only undermines the credibility of legitimate insanity defenses but also perpetuates negative stereotypes about mental illness in the public consciousness. The public's perception of the insanity defense can be skewed, making it more difficult for legitimate cases to be taken seriously and ultimately weakening the trust in psychiatric assessments within the justice system.

Malicious allegations of mental illness also play a significant role in the forensic misapplication of mental health diagnoses. In family law disputes, such as divorce or child custody battles, one party may falsely accuse the other of being mentally unstable to gain an advantage in the case. These malicious allegations can be incredibly damaging, not only because they attack the person's character and credibility, but also because they can directly influence legal decisions, such as the custody of children. A diagnosis of mental illness, even if unfounded, can be used to discredit the accused party and sway a judge's decision in favor of the accuser. This form of exploitation is particularly harmful because it capitalizes on the existing stigma and misconceptions about mental health, which can make it difficult for the accused to defend themselves effectively.

The weaponization of mental health is a grave issue with far-reaching consequences. From institutional and legal coercion to social and cultural manipulation and forensic misapplication, the mechanisms through which mental health is weaponized reflect the broader power dynamics at play in society. By exploiting psychiatric diagnoses for control, suppression, and exclusion, these mechanisms undermine the dignity of individuals and perpetuate inequalities. As we continue to advance our understanding of mental health, we must recognize the potential for psychiatric diagnoses to be misused and take steps to safeguard against such exploitation. Only by ensuring that mental health remains a tool for healing, not oppression, can we prevent these dangerous forms of weaponization from continuing to harm vulnerable individuals and communities.

The weaponization of mental health conditions is not merely a theoretical concern; it is a reality that has profound implications for individuals, families, communities, and society at large. It represents a fundamental violation of ethical principles central to human dignity, psychiatric practice, and the functioning of legal systems. When mental health is used as a tool for control, punishment, or social exclusion, the consequences go far beyond the immediate harm to the individual involved. The broader impacts extend to the very foundations of human rights, the trust placed in mental health professionals, and the integrity of the justice system. As we explore why the weaponization of mental health matters, it becomes clear that this issue cuts across multiple sectors, exacerbating existing inequalities and distorting the mechanisms that are supposed to protect and support vulnerable individuals.

Human Rights Violations

One of the most immediate and severe consequences of weaponizing mental health diagnoses is the violation of fundamental human rights. Autonomy, dignity, and bodily integrity are core principles that must be safeguarded in any society. When mental health diagnoses are used to manipulate or control an individual, these rights are routinely infringed upon. The practice of involuntary commitment, where individuals are confined to psychiatric hospitals against their will, often without adequate legal representation or procedural safeguards, exemplifies the violation of personal autonomy. The right to make decisions about one's life, including freedom of movement, is stripped away. In some cases, individuals may be detained for extended periods under the guise of treatment, when confinement serves as a means of silencing dissent, controlling behavior, or punishing those deemed inconvenient to the state or society.

Involuntary hospitalization is just one example of how the system can be abused to violate fundamental freedoms. Another deeply concerning practice is the use of forced medication, where individuals are administered drugs against their will. These drugs, especially psychotropic medications, can have significant side effects, including physical harm and severe emotional distress. Forced medication is sometimes used not for therapeutic reasons but as a means of controlling individuals who are non-compliant, belligerent, or otherwise seen as a nuisance. This violates the core ethical principle of "do no harm," as patients are subjected to medical treatments without their informed consent, often under conditions where they are already in a vulnerable position.

However, it is important to clarify that involuntary hospitalization and medication can, in some cases, be necessary and ethically justified. When individuals with severe mental illness are unable to make informed decisions due to psychosis or other impairments, and when they pose a significant risk to themselves or others, temporary intervention may be required to ensure safety and stability. In such instances, trained advocates, legal guardians, or court-appointed representatives must act in the best interest of the individual, ensuring that decisions are made with transparency, oversight, and compassion. Suppose no support system exists, and the individual is left untreated and homeless. In that case, society has a moral and public health obligation to intervene, not to punish, but to provide care that is truly restorative and protective of both the individual and the community.

Additionally, further research and critical review are necessary to address the complexities and controversies surrounding involuntary hospitalization and forced treatment. While these interventions may be essential in some circumstances, current practices often lack consistency, transparency, and sufficient oversight. There is an urgent need to develop comprehensive policies that ensure individuals are committed in ways that are humane, ethical, and legally sound. These policies should emphasize patient rights, procedural safeguards, and accountability for institutions and professionals involved in the process.

Moreover, there must be an open and ongoing discussion about why involuntary hospitalization is sometimes necessary—particularly in cases involving severe mental illness and impaired decision-making. However, these interventions must never be carried out under illegal, deceptive, or unethical conditions. Reform efforts should focus on creating a system that balances the protection of public safety with individual dignity, ensuring that treatment is based on medical necessity and not used as a tool for control or coercion. This includes implementing clear guidelines for assessment, legal representation, and periodic review to prevent prolonged or unwarranted confinement. Stakeholders, including mental health professionals, legal experts, patient advocates, and policymakers, must collaborate to design safeguards that prioritize human rights while addressing genuine public health concerns.

Social isolation is another powerful tool used in the weaponization of mental health. When individuals are institutionalized or subjected to long-term psychiatric care, they may be removed from their support systems, including family, friends, and communities. This isolation exacerbates feelings of alienation and helplessness, making it even harder for individuals to regain their agency and voice. The long-term impact of such isolation can be devastating, leading to worsening mental health symptoms, a decreased sense of self-worth, and the erosion of social connections that are critical for recovery and reintegration into society. Over time, individuals subjected to these forms of control may come to believe that they are, in fact, mentally unwell, further cementing their social exclusion and sense of powerlessness.

These human rights violations are not isolated incidents; they are part of a broader pattern of discrimination and oppression that disproportionately affects marginalized groups, including people of color, the poor, women, and political dissidents. When mental health is weaponized in such ways, it can exacerbate existing social and racial inequalities, leading to systemic abuses that continue to affect generations of vulnerable individuals. This highlights the need for comprehensive reforms within the mental health system to ensure that psychiatric care is used ethically and humanely, with strong safeguards to protect against exploitation and abuse.

While social isolation is often criticized for its damaging long-term consequences, it is important to acknowledge that temporary isolation may sometimes be necessary in cases where an individual poses a significant danger to themselves or others due to the severity of their mental condition. In such situations, removing the individual from external stimuli and societal pressures can provide a controlled environment that stabilizes acute symptoms, supports cognitive recovery, and facilitates the initiation of therapeutic interventions. However, this form of separation must be approached with caution and care. Prolonged or unregulated isolation can exacerbate mental health deterioration, leading to increased disorientation, emotional distress, and social withdrawal. Therefore, there must be clear, evidence-based guidelines that define when, how, and for how long isolation can be ethically used. Oversight mechanisms and regular evaluations are essential to ensure that such measures are clinically justified, proportionate, and respectful of human dignity and rights.

The Impact of Media on the Perception of Mental Illness and Violent Crime

Media portrayals have long played a central role in shaping public perceptions of mental illness, particularly when it comes to violent crime. High-profile cases involving individuals who claim mental illness as part of their defense often receive extensive media attention. In many instances, these portrayals sensationalize the link between mental disorders and violent behavior. For instance, when an individual with a psychiatric diagnosis is involved in a violent crime, media outlets often focus disproportionately on the defendant's mental health history, emphasizing the role of their psychiatric condition in the crime. This kind of coverage tends to reinforce the stereotype that people with mental health conditions are more prone to violence, a narrative that is not only misleading but also harmful.

Research, however, consistently demonstrates that individuals with mental health disorders are far more likely to be victims of violence rather than perpetrators. Studies show that people with psychiatric conditions are at increased risk of being attacked, exploited, or subjected to discrimination, and their involvement in violent crime is often the result of complex factors such as social marginalization, substance abuse, or untreated mental health issues. Despite this, the media's focus on violent offenders who invoke mental illness exacerbates the stigma surrounding psychiatric conditions, making it harder for individuals with mental disorders to seek help without fear of judgment or discrimination.

The media's tendency to sensationalize high-profile criminal cases has also led to widespread misconceptions about specific psychiatric disorders, particularly schizophrenia. When crimes involving individuals with schizophrenia or other psychotic disorders are reported, the media often portrays the condition as inherently linked to violent behavior. This portrayal is not only misleading but dangerously oversimplifies the relationship between mental illness and criminality. Research indicates that most individuals with schizophrenia and other severe mental health conditions are not violent. People with schizophrenia are more likely to suffer from isolation, poverty, and social exclusion, all of which increase their vulnerability to victimization.

Moreover, these portrayals overlook the fact that many violent offenders do not have any diagnosable psychiatric conditions. The media's focus on mental illness as a key factor in violent crime often ignores the broader social, economic, and environmental factors that contribute to criminal behavior. Issues like childhood trauma, poverty, substance abuse, and lack of access to education and healthcare play far more significant roles in shaping violent behavior than mental illness alone. Furthermore, the structural inequalities and systemic failures that often fuel violence, such as inadequate mental health services, social isolation, and discrimination, are frequently downplayed or overlooked in media narratives. This narrow focus not only distorts public understanding but also detracts from meaningful discussions on how to address the root causes of violence in society.

This persistent and distorted connection between mental illness and violence has profound consequences, not only for public perceptions of mental health but also for the treatment and rights of individuals living with psychiatric conditions. The stigma perpetuated by the media can discourage individuals from seeking necessary treatment out of fear that they will be labeled as dangerous or unpredictable. Additionally, it can fuel discriminatory practices in both the legal system and in society at large, leading to biases in the way individuals with mental health conditions are treated, particularly in cases where they are accused of violent crimes.

To counter this damaging narrative, it is essential to promote a more accurate and compassionate understanding of mental illness. This includes acknowledging the complexity of mental health issues, recognizing the social factors that influence criminal behavior, and educating the public about the realities of living with mental disorders. By challenging the stereotype that links mental illness to violence, media outlets can play a key role in reducing stigma and fostering a more nuanced and empathetic approach to both mental health and criminal justice.

Law Enforcement's Role and Interaction with Individuals with Mental Health Issues

In recent years, law enforcement agencies across the United States have encountered an increasingly complex challenge in responding to individuals with mental health issues. With the rise in mental health crises coupled with limited access to proper community-based care, police officers often find themselves as the first responders in situations involving psychiatric emergencies. This trend has highlighted a critical gap in the criminal justice system, where officers may not always be equipped to handle the nuances of mental health crises effectively. As a result, confrontations between law enforcement and individuals with mental disorders can sometimes escalate, leading to unfortunate outcomes, including injury or death.

Traditionally, law enforcement officers have been trained to address various emergencies. Still, mental health-related situations require specialized skills and knowledge that are not typically part of standard police training. This lack of preparation creates a mismatch between the demands of a mental health crisis and the officer's ability to respond in a way that prioritizes safety and de-escalation. As mental health crises become more frequent, there is an urgent need for reforms in law enforcement training and policy to ensure that officers are equipped to manage these situations with empathy, understanding, and the skills necessary to prevent harm. In response to these challenges, training initiatives and mental health courts have emerged, aiming to improve police interactions with individuals in crisis and reduce the over-incarceration of people with mental health disorders. This evolving dynamic reflects the growing recognition that mental health issues must be addressed with the same level of expertise and compassion as any other emergency.

Understanding the complex relationship between law enforcement and mental health is crucial for ensuring a more just and humane criminal justice system. As mental health-related calls increasingly fall to police officers, the need for informed, compassionate responses has become more urgent. The following discussion will explore key issues in law enforcement's interaction with individuals experiencing mental health crises, including the challenges posed by inadequate training, the impact of specialized interventions like CIT, and the potential of mental health courts to offer alternatives to incarceration.

Law enforcement agencies across the United States are facing an increasingly complex and urgent challenge in responding to individuals with mental health issues. With rising rates of mental illness and a lack of adequate resources to address these concerns in the community, police officers often find themselves as the first responders to psychiatric crises. This has led to critical gaps in how mental health crises are handled within the criminal justice system, with tragic outcomes in many instances. As police are thrust into situations where mental health expertise is needed, there is growing recognition of the necessity for law enforcement personnel to be equipped with specialized training and tools to respond appropriately to individuals with mental disorders.

Traditionally, law enforcement officers have been expected to address various emergencies; however, their primary training is not geared toward addressing mental health situations. This mismatch between police training and the needs of individuals with psychiatric conditions can result in heightened tension, misunderstandings, and, in some cases, violence or fatalities. A lack of awareness about mental health disorders, as well as how they manifest in crises, can lead to inappropriate responses that escalate rather than de-escalate interactions.

Lack of Training and Preparedness

One of the central issues in the interaction between law enforcement and individuals with mental health disorders is the lack of adequate training for officers. Most police officers receive minimal training in recognizing the signs of mental illness and how to respond to individuals in crisis. This leaves many officers unequipped to de-escalate situations where psychiatric disorders are present effectively. In some instances, officers may misinterpret behaviors associated with mental illness, such as agitation, disorganized speech, or confusion, as aggression or hostility, which can lead to tragic outcomes. The inability to distinguish between an individual experiencing a mental health crisis and someone posing a threat to public safety may result in unnecessary use of force, including deadly encounters.

Research on police shootings and fatalities involving individuals with mental health disorders consistently shows that when officers are not trained to handle psychiatric crises, the likelihood of violence escalates. In some cases, such as the shooting of mentally ill individuals, officers may mistakenly perceive an individual's erratic behavior as a threat, leading to the unnecessary use of deadly force. The outcomes are devastating, not only for the individuals involved but also for the police officers, who may be left with long-term psychological trauma after making split-second decisions in a crisis.

Crisis Intervention Training (CIT)

In response to these concerns, many police departments have implemented Crisis Intervention Teams (CIT), a model designed to provide specialized training for officers who respond to mental health crises. CIT programs are designed to help officers recognize mental health issues, identify individuals in crisis, and de-escalate situations without resorting to force. Officers participating in CIT programs undergo training that includes learning how to interact with individuals who are experiencing conditions like schizophrenia, bipolar disorder, or severe depression. Additionally, CIT programs emphasize the importance of patience, active listening, and communication, helping officers engage with individuals in crisis without exacerbating their distress.

Evidence from cities that have implemented CIT programs shows promising results. Research has found that CIT programs reduce the number of arrests made during mental health crises, lower the incidence of injuries to both officers and individuals in crisis, and decrease the number of fatalities in interactions between police and people with mental health issues. Furthermore, CIT-trained officers are more likely to divert individuals in crisis into appropriate mental health care rather than into the criminal justice system, which helps ensure that people get the treatment they need rather than being incarcerated. These outcomes not only benefit the individuals directly involved but also contribute to broader public safety and reduce the burden on overcrowded jails and emergency departments.

The success of CIT programs highlights the importance of specialized training in improving outcomes in encounters with individuals who have mental health disorders. CIT also has the potential to create a more compassionate and supportive system for individuals in psychiatric distress while promoting better public safety outcomes. This training is critical not just for preventing violent outcomes but also for reducing the stigma surrounding mental health that often arises from poorly managed police interactions. By equipping officers with the tools to recognize and appropriately respond to psychiatric symptoms, CIT fosters trust between law enforcement and the communities they serve.

The Role of Mental Health Courts

Another response to the challenges posed by mental illness within the criminal justice system is the establishment of mental health courts. These specialized courts are designed to address the specific needs of individuals who have committed offenses due to untreated mental health disorders. Rather than focusing solely on punishment, mental health courts prioritize treatment, rehabilitation, and community-based care for individuals with mental health issues. The goal is to provide an alternative to traditional incarceration, which may not be suitable or effective for individuals with psychiatric conditions.

Mental health courts are an innovative tool that has been shown to reduce recidivism among individuals with mental health disorders by ensuring that they receive appropriate treatment and support. Rather than simply punishing individuals for their criminal behavior, mental health courts work to address the root causes of that behavior, such as untreated psychiatric conditions. This can include connecting individuals with mental health services, providing counseling and medication management, and offering social services to facilitate reintegration into society. Research shows that individuals who participate in mental health court programs are more likely to stay out of jail, comply with treatment protocols, and experience improved mental health outcomes.

Mental health courts have also been found to reduce the over-incarceration of people with mental health disorders, who are often incarcerated inappropriately because of their psychiatric conditions. The focus on treatment and rehabilitation, rather than punishment, can help prevent individuals from being trapped in a cycle of criminal justice involvement that is often exacerbated by untreated mental illness. Mental health courts have, therefore, become a critical component of reform efforts aimed at reducing the number of people with mental health disorders in the criminal justice system.

Barriers to Effective Law Enforcement-Mental Health Collaboration

While programs like CIT and mental health courts have shown positive results, significant challenges must be overcome to ensure better collaboration between law enforcement and mental health services. One of the key challenges is the lack of access to mental health care for individuals before they enter the criminal justice system. Many people with mental health disorders do not receive adequate or timely care, leading to preventable crises that ultimately bring them into contact with the police.

Another barrier is the shortage of mental health professionals who can be part of police responses to mental health crises. In many areas, police officers are left to handle psychiatric crises on their own, without immediate access to mental health professionals who could provide guidance and support. This lack of resources contributes to the criminalization of mental illness, as individuals who would benefit from treatment are often arrested and incarcerated instead. The gap in mental health support services places undue pressure on law enforcement agencies, which are not equipped to serve as frontline mental health responders.

There is a growing call for greater collaboration between law enforcement agencies, mental health services, and community organizations to address these challenges. By investing in early intervention strategies, improving access to mental health care, and creating more specialized programs, such as CIT and mental health courts, the criminal justice system can begin to shift its focus from punishment to rehabilitation and treatment. Such systemic reforms could reduce the likelihood of individuals with mental health disorders being incarcerated while also improving public safety and outcomes for individuals in crisis.

The increasing understanding of mental health and law enforcement calls for a fundamental shift in how police officers interact with individuals experiencing psychiatric crises. Law enforcement agencies need to adopt specialized training to ensure officers can handle mental health emergencies with empathy and de-escalation techniques. Additionally, mental health courts represent a promising solution to address the needs of individuals with mental health disorders in the criminal justice system, focusing on treatment and rehabilitation instead of incarceration. These reforms, while promising, must be supported by continued investment in mental health care, greater collaboration between law enforcement and mental health professionals, and a broader commitment to reducing the stigma surrounding mental illness. Only through these concerted efforts can the criminal justice system effectively address the challenges posed by mental illness and work toward a more equitable, humane, and just society.

As law enforcement and mental health systems work to address the challenges of responding to individuals in crisis, another growing concern intersects with the criminal justice system: the overuse of mental health defenses in legal proceedings. While mental health issues undeniably play a significant role in criminal behavior, the increasing reliance on psychiatric conditions as a defense in court has raised concerns about potential misuse. This issue is particularly pertinent when individuals with premeditated or violent intentions attempt to use mental illness as a shield for their actions.

The complexities of mental illness in the criminal justice system extend beyond interactions with law enforcement and into the courtroom, where the legal system must balance the rights and treatment of individuals with mental health disorders against the need to hold individuals accountable for their actions. As more defendants claim mental illness as an excuse for violent crimes, growing worries emerge that the overuse of mental health defenses could erode personal responsibility, potentially leading to unjust legal outcomes and reinforcing stigmas against those with legitimate psychiatric conditions. This overuse may also create a perception that mental illness is being exploited as a convenient excuse, overshadowing the very real and significant struggles faced by individuals with genuine mental health issues. Furthermore, the increasing reliance on such defenses could weaken public trust in the criminal justice system's ability to reasonably distinguish between legitimate cases and those driven by ulterior motives.

The growing prevalence of mental health concerns in criminal cases demands a nuanced approach to justice. As this issue is explored, it is crucial to examine the implications of mental health defenses in the courtroom, the legal reforms being proposed to address the misuse of such defenses, and the broader impact on the integrity of the criminal justice system. This conversation ties directly to the broader discourse on the relationship between mental health and law enforcement, as both systems grapple with how to fairly and effectively address the needs of individuals with psychiatric conditions while ensuring that justice is served.

The Problem of Overuse of Mental Health Defenses in the Legal System

In recent years, the increasing reliance on mental health defenses in criminal cases has sparked significant debate and concern within the legal community. While mental health conditions can undeniably influence behavior and decision-making, the overuse or perceived abuse of psychiatric defenses threatens to undermine the fundamental principles of personal responsibility and accountability in the criminal justice system. The invocation of mental illness as a defense for violent behavior has raised questions about how much responsibility should be attributed to an individual when their actions appear to be driven, in part, by psychiatric conditions. Critics argue that, in some instances, mental health defenses are used to explain away violent or malicious conduct, thereby eroding the idea that individuals should be held accountable for their actions. This issue is particularly poignant when crimes are premeditated or carried out with clear intent. Yet, a mental health defense is invoked to suggest that the defendant was incapable of understanding or controlling their actions due to psychiatric impairment.

The use of mental health defenses has prompted concerns about the fairness and effectiveness of the criminal justice system. When individuals claim that their actions were a result of mental illness, it can sometimes be difficult to distinguish between those who genuinely lack criminal responsibility and those who may be using mental illness as a convenient excuse for violent behavior. This blurring of lines complicates the legal process and, in some cases, may lead to outcomes that are seen as unjust. For example, a defendant who intentionally commits a crime but successfully argues that their mental illness impaired their judgment might avoid traditional forms of punishment, such as incarceration, and instead be sent to a psychiatric facility for treatment. While this can be a just outcome in cases where mental illness genuinely impairs the defendant's ability to understand or control their actions, it raises ethical questions about whether such defenses are overused or manipulated to reduce culpability.

In addition to concerns about fairness in individual cases, the overuse of mental health defenses has broader societal implications. The public perception of mental illness is often shaped by high-profile cases where violent defendants successfully use psychiatric conditions as a defense. Media outlets, which tend to sensationalize these cases, may create a distorted image of individuals with mental health conditions, associating them with violent crime. This can contribute to the stigmatization of people living with mental illnesses, reinforcing stereotypes that they are inherently dangerous or unpredictable. Moreover, when psychiatric conditions are repeatedly linked to criminal behavior, it becomes more challenging to differentiate between those who have genuine psychiatric needs and those who are simply using mental illness to avoid responsibility for harmful behavior. The result is a more fragmented and, in some cases, more discriminatory view of mental health in the criminal justice system.

Another aspect of this problem is the potential negative impact on those with legitimate psychiatric conditions. Over time, the overuse of mental health defenses can contribute to a "slippery slope" effect in the public's perception of mental illness. As psychiatric disorders become increasingly associated with criminality, individuals who genuinely need mental health care may face greater societal resistance to seeking treatment. Mental illness could become viewed less as a medical issue and more as a potential cover for criminal behavior. This dynamic can result in increased marginalization and stigmatization, further isolating those who are already vulnerable and in need of support. As a result, the focus of the criminal justice system could shift from rehabilitation and treatment to a more punitive, exclusionary approach that harms individuals with legitimate mental health conditions.

Legal Reforms and Future Directions

As the debate over the overuse of mental health defenses continues, several legal systems around the world have taken steps to reform the criteria under which mental health defenses can be invoked in criminal trials. The overarching goal of these reforms is to balance the need for protecting individuals with genuine mental health issues and ensuring that those who engage in violent criminal behavior, regardless of mental illness, are held accountable for their actions. Legal reforms must address the complexities of mental illness and criminal responsibility while simultaneously ensuring that offenders who exploit mental health defenses are not able to escape punishment through dubious or exaggerated claims of psychiatric impairment.

One significant area of reform is the introduction of more rigorous evaluations to assess the legitimacy of mental illness claims in criminal cases. Determining whether an individual's psychiatric condition was severe enough to impair their ability to understand the nature of their actions or distinguish right from wrong is a nuanced process. Many forensic psychologists and psychiatrists are tasked with evaluating the mental state of defendants at the time of the crime. However, these evaluations can be subjective, and there is always the risk of overdiagnosis, misdiagnosis, or incomplete assessment. To improve the accuracy and reliability of mental health defenses, reforms may involve strengthening the criteria used by forensic professionals to determine whether an individual truly meets the threshold for an insanity defense or diminished capacity. This may include standardized tools, comprehensive mental health histories, and more rigorous oversight of expert testimony to ensure fairness and reduce potential bias.

Another reform measure may involve improving training for law enforcement and legal professionals to better understand the complex nature of mental illness and its relationship with criminal behavior. Police officers, attorneys, judges, and jurors frequently encounter individuals with mental health issues during criminal proceedings. Still, many may not have sufficient knowledge or understanding of how psychiatric conditions affect behavior. Providing law enforcement officers and legal professionals with ongoing education in mental health awareness and crisis intervention could go a long way in preventing misunderstandings or misinterpretations of behavior. Law enforcement officers, for example, who are trained in recognizing signs of mental illness and de-escalating crises, are less likely to respond to mentally ill individuals with force, reducing the potential for unnecessary violence or fatalities. This could also extend to the legal process, ensuring that judges and jurors are better equipped to differentiate between genuine cases of mental illness and those where mental health is being used as a defense to avoid accountability.

Alternative sentencing strategies are another potential area of reform in the handling of offenders with mental health disorders. Traditional punitive measures such as incarceration are not always the most effective response for individuals whose criminal behavior is linked to untreated or poorly managed psychiatric conditions. In some cases, the criminal justice system may fail to address the underlying causes of criminal behavior, such as trauma, substance abuse, or untreated mental illness. Instead of focusing solely on punishment, the legal system could implement more rehabilitation-oriented approaches, such as treatment programs, community-based mental health services, and inpatient psychiatric care.

Mental health courts, which have already been established in some jurisdictions, are one example of such an approach. These courts prioritize treatment over incarceration, offering individuals with mental health disorders access to therapy, medication management, and social services, which can help prevent recidivism and improve mental health outcomes. Reforms that encourage rehabilitation over punishment could help reduce the over-incarceration of individuals with mental health issues, who are often caught in cycles of criminal justice involvement due to untreated psychiatric conditions.

Striking a Balance Between Protection and Accountability

The challenge of overusing mental health defenses ultimately lies in finding the right balance between protecting individuals with genuine mental health issues and holding individuals accountable for violent behavior. Mental illness can certainly impair an individual's capacity for understanding or controlling their actions. Still, it should not automatically absolve a person of criminal responsibility, particularly in cases where the behavior was premeditated or malicious. Legal systems must recognize that mental illness is not an automatic excuse for criminal conduct; rather, it should be one factor among many that are considered in determining criminal responsibility.

At the same time, legal reforms should prioritize ensuring that people with legitimate mental health conditions are not unjustly penalized for behavior that was influenced by their psychiatric impairments. Forensic evaluations, improved training for law enforcement and legal professionals, and alternative sentencing options can help ensure that individuals with genuine psychiatric disorders are treated with fairness and provided with the appropriate care. By adopting these reforms, the legal system can begin to address the growing concern that mental health defenses are being misused and ensure that justice is served in a manner that is both fair and compassionate.

The issue of mental health defenses in criminal cases presents a multifaceted challenge that requires careful attention to both legal and psychiatric considerations. While it is essential to ensure that individuals with legitimate mental health issues are not unfairly punished, it is equally important to prevent the misuse of mental health defenses to evade responsibility for violent or malicious behavior. Legal reforms that improve evaluation standards, increase training for legal and law enforcement professionals, and focus on rehabilitation rather than solely punitive measures can help address these concerns. Moving forward, the legal system must find a balance between protecting individuals with mental health issues and ensuring that those who misuse mental illness as a defense are held accountable for their actions. This nuanced approach will help improve the fairness of the criminal justice system and provide a more just outcome for both individuals with mental health conditions and the broader society.

Erosion of Trust in Psychiatry

Another critical concern is the erosion of public trust in the psychiatric profession. Psychiatry, when practiced ethically, is a crucial part of the healthcare system, offering treatment and support to individuals who struggle with mental health conditions. However, the weaponization of psychiatry has led to a growing skepticism and distrust of the profession. When psychiatric diagnoses are used not to help but to harm or control individuals, the legitimacy of the entire field comes into question. This shift undermines the credibility of mental health professionals and the therapeutic efficacy of psychiatric interventions.

As public awareness of the misuse of psychiatric diagnoses grows, many individuals begin to perceive mental health professionals as potential agents of state power or coercion rather than healers. This fear is compounded by high-profile cases in which psychiatric diagnoses were weaponized to punish or control individuals, whether in political or social contexts. When people see the mental health system as complicit in injustice, they may be less likely to seek treatment, even when it is necessary for their well-being. This retreat from the psychiatric system creates a vicious cycle: Individuals with legitimate mental health concerns avoid care due to fear of stigmatization or misuse, and their untreated conditions may worsen, leading to more profound problems down the line.

Moreover, the erosion of trust in psychiatry has broader societal implications. As skepticism about psychiatric diagnoses grows, there is a risk that genuine efforts to address mental health issues will be undermined. Public support for mental health funding, services, and initiatives may decline if mental health professionals are seen as unreliable or biased. This can result in a reduced availability of resources for those who genuinely need help, contributing to the underfunding of mental health services and the marginalization of mental health care within the broader healthcare system.

Additionally, the fear that one's mental health may be unfairly used against them in a legal or political context can deter individuals from seeking the care they need. People may hesitate to speak openly with mental health professionals about their struggles, knowing that their words could be misinterpreted or used as evidence of instability in other areas of their lives, such as employment or legal proceedings. This creates a chilling effect that not only harms the individuals involved but also contributes to a broader cultural climate of stigma and secrecy surrounding mental health.

Legal System Integrity

The weaponization of mental health diagnoses also threatens the integrity of the legal system. The justice system relies on fairness, impartiality, and due process to ensure that individuals are treated justly and that their rights are respected, protected, and upheld. Expert testimony, including psychiatric evaluations, is crucial in determining criminal responsibility, competency to stand trial, and other key legal issues. When mental health diagnoses are weaponized, they undermine these fundamental principles by introducing bias, manipulation, and injustice into legal proceedings. This misuse can lead to wrongful outcomes, such as unjust sentencing or the discrediting of legitimate mental health conditions, ultimately eroding public trust in legal institutions.

The use of psychiatric evaluations for strategic or punitive purposes in the criminal justice system creates a dangerous precedent. For example, a defense attorney may argue that their client is not criminally responsible due to mental illness, even if the client is fully aware of their actions and their consequences. This abuse of the insanity defense can distort the course of justice, allowing guilty individuals to escape responsibility for their actions. On the flip side, an individual with a legitimate mental health condition may be declared fit to stand trial despite evidence that they are unable to comprehend the proceedings or participate in their defense fully. This can result in unjust convictions and sentences for those who should have received psychiatric treatment rather than punishment.

The weaponization of mental health diagnoses is not limited to the criminal justice system. It also extends to civil and family law, where psychiatric evaluations are sometimes used to manipulate legal outcomes. In divorce or custody battles, one party may falsely accuse the other of being mentally unstable to gain an advantage in legal proceedings. These malicious allegations can have devastating consequences for the accused party and any children or family members involved in the case. When the legal system becomes a forum for exploiting mental health diagnoses for personal gain, the entire system's credibility is called into question.

Additionally, the role of the expert witness is central to ensuring that justice is served. When psychiatric evaluations are used to manipulate legal outcomes, they compromise the objectivity of expert testimony. The expert's role should be to provide an impartial, evidence-based opinion that helps the court reach a fair decision. When this role is distorted to serve the interests of one party, it undermines the integrity of the justice system and leads to a breakdown in trust between the public and the legal system. Maintaining professional ethics and adhering to established guidelines is essential for preserving the credibility and reliability of forensic mental health assessments.

The long-term effects of this breakdown in trust are profound. If people believe that the legal system is rigged or that psychiatric evaluations are unreliable or biased, they may be less likely to trust the outcomes of legal proceedings. This diminishes the justice system's effectiveness and erodes public confidence in its ability to deliver fair and just results. Moreover, it makes it more difficult to address real injustices, as individuals may be unwilling to report abuse or seek legal redress if they feel the system is inherently flawed. Over time, this distrust can undermine the legitimacy of legal institutions and weaken societal cohesion.

The weaponization of mental health is a critical issue with far-reaching consequences that extend beyond individual cases and affect society. Whether through human rights violations, the erosion of trust in psychiatry, or the compromise of legal system integrity, the consequences of misusing psychiatric diagnoses are profound and damaging. We must recognize the deep harm caused by the misuse of mental health conditions and work toward ensuring that mental health is used as a tool for healing, not oppression. Protecting the rights of individuals, restoring trust in the psychiatric profession, and safeguarding the integrity of legal systems are all essential steps in preventing the weaponization of mental health. Only by addressing these issues head-on can we ensure that mental health diagnoses serve their intended purpose: to improve lives, not to control or exploit vulnerable individuals.

Addressing the weaponization of mental health diagnoses presents a myriad of challenges that intersect with complex clinical, ethical, sociopolitical, and cultural factors. These challenges not only complicate the process of ensuring that psychiatric evaluations are used appropriately but also raise profound questions about the nature of mental health care in the context of power dynamics, coercion, and societal norms. The risks of weaponizing psychiatric diagnoses are far-reaching, as they can be used to control, marginalize, or stigmatize individuals, particularly those in vulnerable positions. The following section explores the multifaceted challenges involved in combating the weaponization of mental health, focusing on diagnostic ambiguity, ethical dilemmas faced by clinicians, and the sociopolitical and cultural biases that shape the application of mental health diagnoses.

Diagnostic Ambiguity

One of the most fundamental challenges in addressing the weaponization of mental health lies in psychiatric diagnoses themselves. Psychiatry is inherently subjective, relying heavily on behavioral observation and self-reported symptoms rather than objective, measurable biological markers. While diagnostic systems such as the *DSM-5* (Diagnostic and Statistical Manual of Mental Disorders) and *ICD-10* (International Classification of Diseases) offer structured criteria for diagnosing various mental health conditions, these systems are not always precise and are subject to interpretation. As a result, psychiatric evaluations are open to potential misuse and manipulation by those with an interest in influencing the diagnosis.

For example, a diagnosis of bipolar disorder can be made based on the presence of elevated mood and impulsivity. However, these symptoms may appear in other conditions as well, such as borderline personality disorder, ADHD, or even severe forms of depression. This diagnostic overlap makes it easier for psychiatric diagnoses to be misapplied, as behaviors may be interpreted differently depending on the clinician's approach or the context in which the diagnosis is made. Furthermore, many psychiatric conditions do not present with a clear and distinct set of symptoms; they often exist on a spectrum, with symptoms varying in intensity and frequency. This leaves room for subjective interpretation, potentially leading to wrongful diagnoses or to the distortion of symptoms to fit a predetermined narrative, particularly when an individual's mental health is used as a weapon in legal or institutional settings.

For instance, a person with a mood disorder might be misdiagnosed with schizophrenia, which can be used to justify involuntary commitment or other forms of restrictive treatment. Misdiagnosis is particularly problematic when a diagnosis can lead to severe legal or social consequences. In cases where mental health is weaponized, it becomes easy to assign a "dangerous" label to someone vulnerable or to justify the denial of their rights based on the mistaken belief that they are unfit for society. Such errors not only harm the individual but also perpetuate systemic biases that disproportionately affect marginalized communities, reinforcing cycles of stigma and exclusion.

Ambiguity in symptom presentation is also a concern, particularly in cases where individuals do not fit neatly into the parameters of a single disorder. For example, a person who demonstrates signs of both depression and anxiety may not fit into one clear diagnostic category, but instead could be diagnosed with comorbid conditions, each with different treatment implications. This lack of clarity in psychiatric evaluation allows individuals to be subjected to potentially harmful psychiatric treatments, coercion, or institutionalization without clear justification. Misunderstanding or misuse of diagnoses in this way is especially troubling in forensic or legal contexts, where a person's mental state is under scrutiny to determine whether they are fit for trial, capable of making decisions, or responsible for their actions.

Furthermore, the lack of definitive biomarkers for many psychiatric conditions means that clinical judgment plays a large role in diagnosis. A diagnosis may ultimately be based on the patient's reported symptoms and behavior rather than hard, objective evidence. This subjectivity opens the door for potential biases to influence decision-making and can be used to justify the confinement or treatment of individuals for reasons unrelated to their actual mental health needs. Consequently, the reliability of psychiatric diagnoses can be compromised, underscoring the need for cautious, evidence-based evaluations and safeguards against misuse.

Ethical Dilemmas for Clinicians

The ethical dilemmas faced by forensic psychiatrists, psychologists, and other mental health professionals involved in legal and institutional evaluations are profound and critical to understanding the risks of weaponizing mental health diagnoses. Clinicians, especially those working within the criminal justice system or psychiatric institutions, are often placed in situations where external pressures, conflicts of interest, and competing priorities compromise their impartiality. These pressures can lead to biased assessments that serve institutional or legal agendas rather than the pursuit of truth and justice. Ensuring transparency and accountability in these evaluations is essential to uphold the integrity of both clinical practice and the legal process.

One of the most significant ethical challenges is the dual agency conflict faced by forensic clinicians. Forensic psychiatrists and psychologists are often asked to perform evaluations that will impact legal or institutional outcomes, such as determining whether a defendant is competent to stand trial, whether an individual is fit for release, or whether someone should be institutionalized. In these cases, the clinician's role is supposed to be impartial, objective, and focused on the individual's well-being. However, forensic clinicians frequently face external pressures from attorneys, courts, law enforcement, or even the institution requesting the evaluation. These external parties may have a vested interest in the evaluation's outcome and may push for conclusions that align with their objectives.

For instance, defense attorneys might pressure a psychiatrist to diagnose a defendant with a serious mental illness to avoid criminal responsibility or reduce their sentence. Instead, prosecutors or law enforcement officials may encourage a clinician to emphasize symptoms of violence or danger to justify continued detention or institutionalization. Clinicians may also face institutional pressures to provide evaluations that support the status quo, particularly in systems where a person's release may be seen as an inconvenience or a threat to institutional resources. This pressure to conform to institutional or legal agendas undermines the fundamental ethical obligation of clinicians to provide honest, unbiased evaluations. When forensic clinicians yield to these pressures, it compromises the integrity of the entire evaluation process, potentially leading to wrongful conclusions that have serious consequences for the individual involved.

Another significant ethical issue in forensic and institutional settings is the challenge of obtaining informed consent and avoiding coercion. Individuals who are incarcerated, institutionalized, or otherwise under state control are often not able to give truly informed consent to psychiatric evaluations or treatment. In many cases, individuals may feel pressured or coerced into participating in evaluations because they fear punishment, retaliation, or the loss of privileges if they refuse to participate. This can be especially problematic in institutionalized settings where power dynamics are skewed, and individuals have limited autonomy. When individuals are not free to make decisions about their care or evaluations, it raises questions about the ethical validity of any findings.

Even when a clinician seeks informed consent, the complex power structures at play often make it difficult for individuals to genuinely understand their rights. For example, an incarcerated individual may not fully comprehend the legal implications of undergoing a psychiatric evaluation or the potential consequences of the diagnosis provided. Similarly, people in psychiatric institutions may feel coerced into agreeing to evaluations or treatments, believing that refusing could lead to worse conditions or loss of freedom. These ethical concerns are particularly critical when evaluating individuals for high-stakes purposes, such as determining their competency to stand trial or assessing their risk of reoffending. Clinicians must navigate these challenges carefully to ensure that evaluations remain ethical and that patients are not exploited for the benefit of external parties.

Sociopolitical and Cultural Bias

The weaponization of mental health is deeply intertwined with broader sociopolitical and cultural biases. The way mental health diagnoses are applied often reflects societal values, stereotypes, and power structures. Racial, gender, and socioeconomic biases all play significant roles in determining who gets diagnosed, how that diagnosis is applied, and how individuals are treated within the psychiatric system. These biases not only affect the quality of care that individuals receive but also shape the likelihood of their being subjected to psychiatric abuse or coercion.

For example, racial biases in psychiatric diagnosis have long been documented. African American men are disproportionately diagnosed with schizophrenia compared to other racial groups, often with little regard for the context of their behavior or the cultural factors at play. This bias is particularly problematic because the diagnosis of schizophrenia can be used to justify institutionalization, forced medication, and other forms of coercion. In many cases, the overdiagnosis of schizophrenia in African American men is tied to cultural stereotypes about black men being violent or mentally unstable. This creates a situation where individuals from marginalized racial groups are more likely to be seen as dangerous or deviant, which increases their risk of being subjected to psychiatric treatment that is not only unwarranted but also harmful.

Similarly, gender bias plays a significant role in psychiatric diagnosis, with women often being underdiagnosed for certain mood disorders, such as depression or bipolar disorder, while being overdiagnosed with personality disorders, such as borderline personality disorder or hysteria. This pattern reflects societal stereotypes about women's emotional expression and behavior. Women who display assertiveness or challenge societal norms are often pathologized as mentally ill. For example, women who resist traditional gender roles or demonstrate high levels of emotional expression might be more likely to be diagnosed with borderline personality disorder, which has historically been associated with instability and irrationality. These gendered assumptions about behavior can have far-reaching consequences for women, as they may be treated as mentally ill rather than being addressed in their legitimate emotional struggles or needs.

Socioeconomic bias is also a pervasive issue in psychiatric diagnosis. People from low-income backgrounds are often disproportionately diagnosed with disorders that reflect societal assumptions about poverty and instability. Conditions like antisocial personality disorder or conduct disorder are often overrepresented in populations living in poverty. These diagnoses can be used to justify social exclusion or punitive measures, reinforcing the stigma associated with being poor. Additionally, people from disadvantaged backgrounds are more likely to experience barriers to accessing adequate mental health care, which can lead to misdiagnoses or a lack of proper treatment. For instance, someone from a lower socioeconomic status may be more likely to be institutionalized. At the same time, those with greater resources may receive outpatient care or access to mental health professionals who are better equipped to address complex needs.

Moreover, the intersectionality of race, gender, and class can exacerbate these biases. A Black woman from a low-income background may face multiple layers of discrimination within the psychiatric system, including the overdiagnosis of dangerousness, underdiagnosis of mood disorders, and dismissal of her emotional experiences as symptoms of mental illness. These intersecting factors increase the likelihood of being subjected to psychiatric abuse or exploitation, further entrenching the marginalization of specific populations. This systemic inequity not only undermines the fairness of psychiatric evaluations but also perpetuates social injustice within legal and institutional frameworks.

The challenges in addressing the weaponization of mental health are extensive and complex. From the diagnostic ambiguity inherent in psychiatry to the ethical dilemmas faced by clinicians and the deep-seated sociopolitical and cultural biases that permeate the mental health system, these challenges create significant barriers to ensuring that mental health care is applied fairly and responsibly. The risks of weaponization are especially pronounced in legal and institutional contexts, where psychiatric diagnoses can be used to control, punish, or exclude vulnerable individuals. To mitigate these risks, it is crucial to address the structural issues that allow for the exploitation of mental health diagnoses. This requires greater oversight, more transparency, and a commitment to ensuring that mental health services are used in ways that prioritize individuals' dignity, autonomy, and rights over societal or institutional control.

Implications for Forensic Neuropsychopathology

Forensic neuropsychopathology is a highly specialized and pivotal branch of forensic psychology that intersects the study of brain-based behavior disorders with the legal system. This subfield aims to examine how neurocognitive and psychopathological conditions shape an individual's behavior, competency, and responsibility within the legal context. Professionals in this field conduct detailed assessments to understand how various cognitive or psychological conditions might influence behavior, decision-making abilities, and one's capacity to engage with legal processes such as standing trial or making rational choices about one's defense.

However, the critical role that forensic neuropsychologists play is complicated when mental health diagnoses are weaponized, either to manipulate legal outcomes or exploit psychiatric diagnoses for personal or strategic gain. The process of weaponizing mental health can distort the truth, lead to unjust legal outcomes, and place forensic neuropsychologists in a difficult position where their assessments are under greater scrutiny. This section delves into the critical implications of weaponizing mental health diagnoses within forensic neuropsychopathology, examining the importance of evaluative integrity, the challenges of strategic manipulation, and the essential safeguards that practitioners must maintain to protect against unethical practices.

Defining the Discipline

Forensic neuropsychopathology is a subfield of forensic psychology that combines knowledge of neuropsychology, psychiatry, and the law to assess individuals' neurocognitive and psychopathological functioning within the context of legal proceedings. In forensic neuropsychopathology, professionals aim to understand how disorders of the brain and mind influence behavior, particularly in situations that involve legal responsibility, mental competency, and accountability. The goal of forensic neuropsychopathology is to provide scientifically based, objective evaluations that assess the extent to which an individual's mental health or cognitive impairments may affect their ability to understand the nature of their legal case, participate effectively in their defense, or be held responsible for their actions.

Within the legal system, forensic neuropsychologists are often tasked with determining if a defendant is competent to stand trial, whether they were of sound mind at the time of an offense, and whether they are suitable for rehabilitation or treatment. They rely on comprehensive assessments, which may include cognitive tests to measure memory, executive functioning, and emotional regulation, as well as psychiatric evaluations to explore mood disorders, psychotic symptoms, and personality traits. While forensic professionals must be objective and impartial in their assessments, their role becomes more complicated when mental health conditions are intentionally manipulated or weaponized to gain a legal advantage, such as avoiding conviction, reducing sentences, or shifting blame.

The challenge for forensic neuropsychopathology lies in its dual responsibility: It must provide accurate assessments grounded in science and clinical experience while recognizing that individuals may try to exploit the mental health evaluation process for personal gain. This dynamic can complicate assessments, requiring professionals to balance scientific rigor with awareness of the potential for manipulation or strategic exaggeration. Given that psychiatric conditions themselves can be ambiguous and sometimes subjective, forensic neuropsychologists must be prepared to critically assess and differentiate between legitimate disorders and exaggerated or fabricated claims.

Evaluative Integrity vs. Strategic Weaponization

A core challenge in forensic neuropsychopathology is preserving evaluative integrity when mental health diagnoses are weaponized. Weaponizing a mental health diagnosis involves exaggerating or fabricating psychiatric symptoms to achieve a favorable legal outcome. This may involve an individual feigning or exaggerating cognitive impairments, emotional instability, or mental illness to avoid criminal liability or manipulate the outcome of legal proceedings. Forensic neuropsychologists must exercise extreme caution in these cases to distinguish between actual mental health conditions and symptoms that are intentionally fabricated or exaggerated for tactical purposes.

Malingering, the act of feigning or exaggerating mental health symptoms for secondary gain, is one of the most common forms of strategic weaponization in forensic settings. It can involve an individual pretending to be mentally ill to escape criminal responsibility, gain access to more lenient sentences, or receive favorable treatment in legal proceedings. Detecting malingering is critical for forensic neuropsychologists, who rely on standardized psychological testing and clinical expertise to evaluate whether a person's reported symptoms are consistent with legitimate psychiatric conditions or whether they are being exaggerated for manipulative purposes. While forensic neuropsychologists use structured interviews and psychological instruments, both of which are designed to detect malingering, these tools are not infallible. Individuals may still successfully manipulate their symptoms, and detecting malingering requires careful clinical judgment and assessment.

Moreover, malingering is often a spectrum, where an individual might exaggerate their symptoms to a level that aligns with a genuine disorder but does not fully meet the diagnostic criteria. For instance, a defendant might report severe cognitive deficits or extreme emotional instability to make it appear as though they are unable to control their actions, even though their symptoms are exaggerated or inconsistent with the underlying psychiatric condition.

Forensic professionals must thoroughly assess the individual's claims and symptoms against established diagnostic criteria to determine whether the presentation is consistent with a legitimate disorder or if it has been artificially amplified to support a particular legal strategy.

Strategic weaponization is not always about outright malingering. In some cases, it may involve subtle exaggerations or misinterpretations of symptoms, where individuals present themselves in a way that emphasizes mental health issues without necessarily fabricating them. This type of manipulation may be harder to detect, but it still has the potential to skew the legal outcome. For example, a defendant might highlight specific symptoms of a mental disorder to portray themselves as unable to understand the legal consequences of their actions or incapable of participating in their defense. Forensic neuropsychologists must apply their expertise to assess the overall picture of the individual's mental health, considering the nuances of symptom presentation, historical information, and the individual's functional capabilities.

Red Flags and Protective Measures

Given the challenges posed by the weaponization of mental health diagnoses, forensic neuropsychopathologists must use a variety of protective measures to ensure the integrity of their evaluations and prevent the manipulation of the process. These protective measures are essential for identifying when mental health diagnoses are being used strategically rather than reflecting an actual psychological condition. Forensic neuropsychopathologists must employ rigorous standards in their evaluations, using multiple data sources and testing instruments to provide a comprehensive, reliable, and consistent assessment.

One of the most important safeguards is the collateral information obtained from sources outside the individual, such as medical records, educational history, employment records, criminal history, and reports from family members or others familiar with the person's history. Collateral information is critical in evaluating the consistency of the individual's claims. If an individual reports severe cognitive or emotional impairment that are inconsistent with their medical or criminal history, it may suggest that the symptoms are exaggerated. For instance, if a person claims to have experienced significant cognitive decline, but their past performance in educational or work settings contradicts this claim, it raises a red flag. Additionally, obtaining information from family members, therapists, or other close contacts can help corroborate or challenge the person's reported symptoms, providing a broader perspective on their mental health.

Cross-validation of claims is another important strategy used to ensure the accuracy of forensic evaluations. This involves using standardized testing instruments and structured interviews to assess the individual's cognitive, emotional, and psychiatric functioning. These assessments should cover multiple domains, including attention, memory, executive functioning, emotional regulation, and personality. When results from various instruments align and support the individual's reported symptoms, it strengthens the validity of the evaluation. Instead, discrepancies across different tests or interviews could suggest that the person is exaggerating their symptoms, providing inconsistent information, or potentially malingering. Cross-validation helps to ensure that the evaluation process is thorough and that no single test or data source is relied upon in isolation.

Functional neuroimaging may also be used as an adjunctive tool in forensic neuropsychology to provide objective evidence of brain activity and structure. Neuroimaging can help clinicians identify potential brain abnormalities that correlate with specific cognitive or psychological disorders. However, neuroimaging is not without its limitations, and it is still a controversial tool in forensic settings. While functional neuroimaging provides some insights into brain function, it does not always directly correlate with observed behavior, and its application in forensic contexts remains a topic of debate. Moreover, neuroimaging is costly and requires specialized expertise, which is not feasible in every case. Nonetheless, it remains a potentially valuable tool for corroborating findings from neuropsychological tests and offering an objective basis for understanding an individual's cognitive and emotional state.

Ultimately, ethical guardrails are crucial for maintaining the integrity of forensic neuropsychology. Practitioners in this field are bound by the ethical guidelines established by professional organizations such as the American Psychological Association, the American Academy of Psychiatry and the Law, and the National Academy of Neuropsychology. These ethical standards emphasize the importance of impartiality, transparency, and respect for individual rights during the evaluation process. Forensic neuropsychologists must adhere to these ethical principles to avoid becoming complicit in the manipulation or distortion of mental health assessments for legal purposes. By maintaining ethical standards, forensic neuropsychologists help ensure that their evaluations contribute to a fair and just legal process.

The implications of weaponizing mental health diagnoses within the field of forensic neuropsychopathology are vast and complex. Forensic neuropsychologists must navigate a delicate balance between providing objective assessments of cognitive and psychological conditions while recognizing the potential for strategic manipulation. The threat of malingering and exaggerated symptom presentation requires forensic neuropsychopathologists to adopt rigorous evaluation practices, including the use of collateral information, cross-validation of claims, and advanced neuroimaging techniques. They can help ensure that their work supports fairness in legal proceedings and contributes to a more just legal system by adhering to ethical standards and maintaining a commitment to impartiality and integrity. Despite the challenges posed by weaponized mental health diagnoses, forensic neuropsychologists play an essential role in safeguarding the integrity of legal processes and promoting justice by ensuring that mental health evaluations are accurate, honest, and free from manipulation.

Moving Forward: Reform and Resilience

The weaponization of mental health diagnoses is a complex and pressing issue that has serious consequences for both individuals and the legal system. To address this problem effectively, adopting a multifaceted approach that involves reforming forensic training, instituting robust legal safeguards, and promoting public education is essential. Such reforms will not only ensure the integrity of psychiatric evaluations but also help reduce the potential for mental health to be used as a tool of manipulation in legal proceedings. By strengthening the resilience of the systems that rely on mental health assessments, we can ensure that individuals are treated fairly and equitably, that the integrity of the legal system is preserved, and that the potential for exploitation is minimized.

Strengthening Forensic Training

A critical first step in addressing the weaponization of mental health diagnoses is strengthening forensic training for professionals involved in the legal and psychiatric evaluation processes. Forensic neuropsychopathologists, psychiatrists, psychologists, and other mental health professionals must be equipped with the knowledge, skills, and tools to carry out thorough and unbiased assessments. A key area that requires greater emphasis is the critical evaluation of malingering. Malingering refers to the deliberate exaggeration or fabrication of psychiatric symptoms for personal gain, such as evading criminal responsibility or reducing legal consequences. Recognizing malingering is a challenging but essential skill for forensic neuropsychopathologists, as individuals may attempt to manipulate their diagnoses in subtle ways. Professionals must be trained to detect discrepancies in reported symptoms, inconsistencies across different testing methods, and patterns that suggest an individual might be intentionally feigning or amplifying symptoms for strategic reasons.

Forensic neuropsychopathologists must also be proficient in bias recognition to prevent their own personal, cultural, or societal biases from influencing their assessments. Research has shown that factors such as race, gender, and socioeconomic status can significantly affect diagnostic outcomes, sometimes leading to the overdiagnosis or underdiagnosis of certain conditions in specific groups. For example, studies have found that African American men are more likely to be diagnosed with schizophrenia than white individuals, regardless of the actual symptoms they present. Similarly, women are often underdiagnosed with mood disorders like depression despite presenting with apparent symptoms. By training forensic evaluators to recognize these biases and mitigate their impact, we can improve the accuracy and fairness of psychiatric assessments in legal contexts.

A comprehensive approach to training should also integrate trauma-informed care, which is crucial for understanding how trauma impacts mental health. Many individuals involved in the legal system have experienced significant trauma, including physical or sexual abuse, childhood neglect, or exposure to violence. Trauma can have long-lasting effects on a person's emotional, cognitive, and psychological functioning, and it can sometimes mimic or overlap with certain psychiatric disorders. Forensic professionals who are trained in trauma-informed care are better equipped to recognize the symptoms of trauma and avoid misinterpreting them as mental illness. In addition, trauma-informed care emphasizes creating a safe, respectful environment for individuals undergoing evaluation, helping them feel more comfortable and open during the assessment process. This approach can also help prevent the misuse of mental health diagnoses by promoting a deeper understanding of the person's background and experiences rather than simply labeling them based on surface-level symptoms.

Finally, fostering interdisciplinary collaboration is essential for enhancing forensic training. No single professional or discipline can fully address the complexity of mental health diagnoses in legal settings. Collaboration among clinical professionals, medical providers, researchers, and scientists. By sharing knowledge, perspectives, and expertise, interdisciplinary teams can provide a more holistic and objective assessment of an individual's mental health, which will help prevent the weaponization of diagnoses for legal or personal gain. This collaboration is essential when evaluating high-stakes cases, such as those involving the insanity defense or competency to stand trial, where the consequences of a misdiagnosis can be severe and life-altering.

Public Education

Public education plays a pivotal role in addressing the weaponization of mental health diagnoses. By providing information about mental health conditions, the public can better understand the complexities of psychiatric disorders and reduce the stigma that often surrounds them. Destigmatizing mental health is crucial because when mental health issues are viewed as shameful or morally weak, they become easier targets for manipulation in legal and political arenas. Educating the public on the realities of mental illness—how it affects individuals differently, how it can be diagnosed, and how it should be treated—can help promote a more compassionate, informed view of psychiatric conditions. This education should include a focus on the fact that mental health diagnoses are not always straightforward and can be misused if not properly understood.

Additionally, highlighting historical abuses of mental health diagnoses in legal contexts can serve as an important tool for fostering vigilance and accountability. In many cases, psychiatric conditions have been weaponized for political, social, or personal gain.

Throughout history, there have been numerous instances where individuals have been labeled as mentally ill to justify their detention, persecution, or exclusion from society. For example, political dissidents and social reformers have been unjustly diagnosed with conditions like "sluggish schizophrenia" in the Soviet Union or "hysteria" during the Victorian era purely because their ideas were seen as subversive. By educating the public about these abuses, society can develop a stronger sense of responsibility to prevent such manipulation from occurring in the future. The more people understand how mental health diagnoses have been exploited in the past, the more likely they are to advocate for fairness and accountability in psychiatric evaluations moving forward.

To effectively combat the weaponization of mental health diagnoses, a comprehensive, multi-pronged approach is necessary—one that includes strengthening forensic training, instituting legal safeguards, and fostering public education. Enhancing forensic training ensures that professionals possess the knowledge and skills necessary to detect malingering, recognize potential biases, and apply trauma-informed approaches in assessments. Legal safeguards, such as requiring independent second opinions and enforcing stricter evidentiary standards, can prevent the misuse of psychiatric diagnoses in high-stakes cases. Public education campaigns can reduce stigma, promote understanding of mental health, and highlight historical abuses, thereby ensuring that mental health diagnoses are used ethically and responsibly in legal contexts. With these reforms in place, we can protect individuals' rights, maintain the integrity of the legal system, and ensure that mental health diagnoses serve their true purpose—

providing therapeutic support and understanding rather than being manipulated for strategic advantage.

Legal Safeguards

To address the misuse of psychiatric diagnoses in legal contexts, establishing comprehensive legal safeguards is critical. The manipulation or weaponization of mental health assessments can undermine the fairness of legal proceedings, potentially leading to unjust outcomes. The integrity of the legal system relies on ensuring that psychiatric evaluations are appropriately conducted, without influence from external pressures, and are applied ethically in court. This can be achieved through independent evaluations and rigorous judicial oversight. These safeguards help maintain the objectivity of the legal system and prevent the potential for psychiatric diagnoses to be used for exploitative or coercive purposes.

Independent evaluations form a cornerstone of these legal safeguards. In many cases where a person's mental health is a central issue, such as in criminal cases involving the insanity defense, determining competency to stand trial, or evaluating the validity of involuntary commitment, the psychiatric evaluation must be performed by professionals who have no stake in the case. This is especially important in situations where there may be significant external pressure, such as from attorneys seeking to influence the case's outcome, public opinion, or institutional interests. For example, legal teams may try to manipulate psychiatric assessments to gain a strategic advantage, whether by exaggerating a defendant's mental illness to invoke an insanity defense or by attempting to avoid responsibility for criminal actions by claiming diminished capacity. Independent evaluations are crucial in preventing such manipulations. Mental health professionals not involved in the case can assess the individual's condition with neutrality, ensuring that the diagnosis accurately reflects the individual's mental health and is not swayed by external pressures.

Furthermore, the independence of these evaluations ensures that the findings are based on a thorough and unbiased examination. Mental health professionals involved in the evaluation process should be selected based on their expertise and qualifications rather than their affiliation with any party in the case. This neutrality helps ensure that the psychiatric assessment is grounded in fact and clinical expertise rather than being influenced by any agenda. This becomes particularly vital in cases where a person's freedom, reputation, or life could be at stake. Independent evaluations help prevent the risk of misdiagnoses or distorted interpretations of a person's mental state that could have harmful consequences.

Alongside independent evaluations, judicial oversight plays a significant role in safeguarding the integrity of psychiatric evaluations in legal proceedings. While mental health professionals are responsible for providing their expertise, it is ultimately the court's responsibility to evaluate whether psychiatric evidence is appropriately applied within the context of the law. Judges must not simply accept psychiatric diagnoses at face value; instead, they must critically assess whether the evaluation process was conducted according to recognized guidelines, whether the evaluator followed ethical standards, and whether the diagnosis is both relevant and reliable. For example, in criminal cases, a judge must evaluate whether the mental health assessment genuinely supports the claim of insanity or whether the diagnosis has been exaggerated or misapplied to avoid legal consequences.

Judicial oversight is significant when dealing with high-stakes decisions, such as whether to institutionalize an individual against their will or whether to apply an insanity defense in a criminal trial. If the judge does not critically examine the psychiatric evidence, it could result in severe consequences, such as unjust imprisonment, involuntary commitment, or the dismissal of valid legal claims. Therefore, the judge must consider the context in which the diagnosis is being used, the evaluator's methods, and whether the diagnosis aligns with the individual's actual behavior and state of mind. Forensic psychiatric evaluations are complex and require careful interpretation; thus, judicial scrutiny ensures that these assessments are used correctly within the legal system.

Legal safeguards such as independent evaluations and judicial oversight are essential to prevent the misuse of psychiatric diagnoses. These safeguards ensure that mental health assessments are conducted fairly, objectively, and used appropriately within the legal context. By ensuring that evaluations are conducted impartially and that the court critically examines their results, the legal system can maintain its integrity and ensure that individuals are not unfairly impacted by misapplied or manipulated psychiatric diagnoses.

Public Awareness and Advocacy

In addition to the legal safeguards that can protect individuals in the courtroom, public awareness and advocacy efforts are equally essential in combating the misuse of psychiatric diagnoses. Over the years, there has been significant stigma surrounding mental health, and this stigma has often contributed to the exploitation of psychiatric diagnoses in legal, social, and political contexts. By fostering a better understanding of mental health issues and reducing stigma, society can reduce the likelihood of psychiatric conditions being used as tools of manipulation, coercion, or control. Public education, along with active advocacy for the rights of individuals with psychiatric disorders, plays a vital role in addressing these challenges.

One of the most effective methods for combating the misuse of psychiatric diagnoses is through education campaigns that help to demystify mental health. Often, individuals with mental health conditions are marginalized and stigmatized because people lack understanding of what these conditions entail. Many psychiatric diagnoses have been historically misunderstood or misrepresented, particularly in the media, leading to negative stereotypes about individuals with mental health disorders. For instance, psychiatric conditions are often portrayed in a sensationalized or exaggerated way, which can contribute to a widespread misconception that individuals with mental health issues are violent, unstable, or dangerous. These misconceptions can lead to discrimination and make it easier for diagnoses to be weaponized, either to discredit individuals or to remove them from positions of power or influence.

Education campaigns that focus on mental health can help to break down these stereotypes by offering accurate, evidence-based information about psychiatric conditions. When the public has a better understanding of mental health, it becomes more difficult for mental illness to be used as a tool for control or manipulation. Public education should emphasize that mental health conditions, like physical illnesses, are medical conditions that require proper treatment and care. Highlighting the complexity and diversity of mental health issues can encourage greater empathy and understanding, reducing the potential for psychiatric diagnoses to be used as a weapon against individuals.

An important aspect of public awareness campaigns is addressing the historical misuse of psychiatric diagnoses. Throughout history, individuals with mental health conditions have often been treated as objects of ridicule or suspicion. In some cases, psychiatric diagnoses were used to justify the confinement of individuals who posed a challenge to political or social norms. For instance, in the Soviet Union, political dissidents were often diagnosed with mental illnesses such as schizophrenia to discredit them and remove them from public life. Similarly, in the United States during the McCarthy era, political activists and civil rights leaders were sometimes diagnosed with psychiatric conditions to undermine their credibility and silence their activism. By raising public awareness about these historical abuses, society can better understand the potential dangers of using psychiatric diagnoses for political or personal gain. This knowledge encourages vigilance and accountability, ensuring that mental health assessments are used appropriately in the present day.

In addition to public education, advocacy for the rights of individuals with psychiatric conditions is also crucial in protecting individuals from the potential weaponization of mental health diagnoses. People with mental health conditions often face significant barriers in society, including discrimination, lack of access to proper care, and stigmatization. Advocacy organizations that focus on mental health rights work to ensure that these individuals are treated with dignity and respect and that their rights are upheld in legal, medical, and social settings. These organizations can provide legal assistance and resources for individuals who feel that they have been wrongfully diagnosed or subjected to inappropriate psychiatric treatment.

Furthermore, mental health advocacy organizations play a significant role in challenging the biases that exist in mental health diagnosis. It is well-documented that certain groups, particularly racial and ethnic minorities, are more likely to be misdiagnosed or overdiagnosed with certain psychiatric conditions. For example, African American men are disproportionately diagnosed with schizophrenia, while mood disorders such as depression and bipolar disorder may be underdiagnosed in women. These disparities can lead to unfair treatment, and the diagnoses may be used to marginalize or control individuals. Advocacy groups work to promote more equitable diagnostic standards and ensure that mental health evaluations are free from racial, gender, or socioeconomic bias. By advocating for these changes, these organizations help ensure that psychiatric diagnoses are used fairly and unbiasedly.

Public awareness and advocacy are essential components of efforts to combat the weaponization of psychiatric diagnoses. Education campaigns that challenge stigma and provide accurate information about mental health help to foster a more empathetic and informed public. By highlighting the historical misuse of psychiatric diagnoses, society can remain vigilant against future abuses. At the same time, advocacy for the rights of individuals with mental health disorders ensures that these individuals are protected from discrimination, misdiagnosis, and exploitation. Through these efforts, society can move toward a future in which mental health diagnoses are used to support and care for individuals rather than being used as a means of control or manipulation. Together, public education and advocacy can create a more just and equitable society for people living with mental health conditions, safeguarding their rights and dignity while ensuring that psychiatric assessments are applied ethically and responsibly.

The weaponization of mental health diagnoses represents one of the most complex and troubling relationships between psychiatry, law, and society. From historical abuses in ancient civilizations to the more recent manipulation of psychiatric evaluations in high-stakes legal settings, the misuse of mental health assessments has been a tool for oppression, political control, and social marginalization. The enduring impact of these practices reveals a critical need for a multifaceted approach to safeguard against the manipulation of psychiatric diagnoses, ensuring that mental health conditions are used as tools of healing and support rather than instruments of power and control.

As it has been explored throughout this chapter, the weaponization of mental health is not a new phenomenon but one that has deep roots in history. From the demonization of "madness" in ancient and medieval societies to the more organized and institutionalized abuses seen in the 18th and 19th centuries, psychiatric diagnoses have been deployed to control the marginalized, silence dissent, and justify inhumane practices. In the 20th century, totalitarian regimes such as Nazi Germany and the Soviet Union highlighted the dangerous potential of psychiatry when used as a tool of political repression. These historical examples highlight the vulnerability of psychiatric diagnoses to exploitation, particularly when intersecting with social, political, and economic power structures.

The modern era has continued this pattern, particularly within the legal system. In forensic contexts, psychiatric evaluations can be manipulated to alter the trajectory of a criminal case, influence decisions on competency to stand trial, or determine the legitimacy of mental health defenses. Forensic neuropsychopathology plays a pivotal role in these evaluations, where the need for scientific objectivity and ethical integrity is paramount. However, as highlighted in the discussion of evaluative integrity, clinicians are often pressured to conform to external agendas, whether from legal actors or institutional interests. This creates significant ethical dilemmas, especially when dealing with the complexity and subjectivity of mental health diagnoses.

The implications of weaponizing mental health extend far beyond the legal system. Such practices have profound societal consequences, particularly for marginalized groups. Racial, gender, and socioeconomic biases continue to shape who gets diagnosed and how that diagnosis is applied. African American men, for example, are disproportionately diagnosed with schizophrenia, while women's mental health needs are often underdiagnosed or misinterpreted. These systemic biases perpetuate injustice and discrimination, further exacerbating the harm caused by weaponized psychiatric diagnoses.

Addressing the weaponization of mental health requires systemic reform across multiple domains. First and foremost, strengthening forensic training is essential. Clinicians must be equipped with the tools to critically evaluate malingering, recognize biases, and apply trauma-informed approaches in their assessments. This training should also encourage interdisciplinary collaboration, particularly with attorneys, neuroscientists, and human rights advocates, to ensure that mental health evaluations are applied within the broader context of justice and human dignity. At the legal level, independent second opinions and stricter evidentiary standards are necessary to prevent the exploitation of psychiatric diagnoses for punitive or strategic purposes. Courts should maintain robust oversight over the use of mental health diagnoses, ensuring that psychiatric evaluations are used appropriately and ethically in legal proceedings.

Equally important is public education and advocacy. The stigma surrounding mental health is one of the primary drivers of its weaponization. Through education campaigns that demystify mental health conditions, society can reduce the likelihood that mental health will be used as a tool of exclusion or control. Public awareness of historical abuses, such as the use of psychiatric diagnoses to silence political opposition, can foster vigilance and accountability in the present. Advocacy for the rights of individuals with mental health conditions is also critical in challenging the systemic discrimination and biases that continue to shape psychiatric diagnoses.

Ultimately, the weaponization of mental health diagnoses is not merely a technical issue for forensic psychiatrists or legal professionals to address but a deeply human rights issue. The abuse of psychiatric diagnoses has the potential to strip individuals of their autonomy, freedom, and dignity. A commitment to preventing these abuses requires safeguarding the integrity of psychiatric evaluations and ensuring that mental health functions as a means of support and care rather than oppression and control. Clear oversight mechanisms, legal accountability, and advocacy are essential to uphold ethical standards. Without such protections, the mental health system risks becoming a tool of systemic injustice rather than a source of healing.

Moving forward, advocacy for reforms should prioritize ethical practice in mental health assessments, ensure impartiality and independence in forensic evaluations, and foster a society that values mental health as an aspect of overall well-being. The resilience of our legal and medical systems depends on our ability to adapt, evolve, and correct the historical misuses of psychiatric diagnoses. By strengthening the safeguards that protect individuals from exploitation, providing education that combats stigma, and advocating for the rights of those with psychiatric conditions, we can create a future where mental health is treated with the respect, care, and dignity it deserves. The fight against the weaponization of mental health diagnoses is ongoing, but it requires collective effort across legal, medical, and societal spheres. Through vigilance, reform, and an unwavering commitment to human rights, we can ensure that psychiatric diagnoses remain a tool of healing rather than a mechanism for control, ensuring justice, equity, and dignity for all individuals, regardless of their mental health status.

Conclusion

The weaponization of mental health diagnoses stands as a significant and troubling challenge at the connection of psychiatry, law, and society. From historical instances of political repression to modern-day legal manipulation, psychiatric evaluations have been distorted and exploited for various purposes, undermining the integrity of both the mental health field and the justice system. This manipulation has profound consequences, not only for the individuals directly impacted but for society at large. The misuse of psychiatric diagnoses for personal, political, or legal gain has the potential to strip individuals of their rights, dignity, and autonomy, further perpetuating discrimination, bias, and injustice.

The examples explored throughout this chapter, ranging from the use of psychiatric labels to discredit political dissidents in totalitarian regimes to the more subtle ways in which diagnoses are manipulated in the criminal justice system, highlight the vulnerability of mental health assessments to exploitation. In forensic contexts, the subjective nature of psychiatric evaluations—coupled with pressures from external forces, whether legal, institutional, or political—opens the door to the potential abuse of diagnostic tools. Similarly, societal attitudes toward mental health, shaped by stigma, misinformation, and historical prejudice, can make individuals more susceptible to discriminatory practices, including the weaponization of their mental health conditions.

However, this chapter has also highlighted avenues for meaningful reform and action. Strengthening forensic training, emphasizing the need for unbiased, trauma-informed, and comprehensive evaluations, is crucial in preventing the manipulation of psychiatric diagnoses. Equally important is the role of legal safeguards, including independent second opinions and stricter evidentiary standards, to ensure that psychiatric evaluations are used appropriately and ethically in legal contexts. Judicial oversight must be vigilant to ensure that mental health diagnoses are not applied as a tool for strategic advantage or coercion in high-stakes legal cases.

Moreover, public awareness and advocacy play a critical role in combating the weaponization of mental health diagnoses. Education campaigns that demystify mental health conditions and challenge the stigma surrounding them can foster greater empathy and understanding. This, in turn, can reduce the likelihood of psychiatric diagnoses being used as instruments of control or marginalization. By shedding light on the historical abuses of psychiatric diagnoses, society can remain vigilant and work collectively to prevent future exploitation. Advocacy efforts aimed at securing the rights of individuals with mental health conditions are also vital in challenging systemic biases and promoting equitable diagnostic practices.

Ultimately, the weaponization of mental health diagnoses is not simply a technical issue within forensic psychiatry or legal practice but a profound human rights concern. It emphasizes the importance of preserving the integrity of psychiatric assessments and ensuring that mental health diagnoses are applied in ways that support and care for individuals rather than exploiting or marginalizing them. As society moves forward, a multifaceted approach that includes reforms in training, legal safeguards, and public education is essential to address the misuse of psychiatric diagnoses and safeguard against future abuses.

Through collective effort, it is possible to create a society in which mental health diagnoses are used as intended: to provide understanding, support, and healing rather than as instruments of power and control. Only by continuing to confront these challenges and advocating for fairness, integrity, and human dignity in psychiatric evaluations can we ensure that mental health conditions are treated with the respect they deserve, both in the courtroom and in society at large. The work to address the weaponization of mental health diagnoses is ongoing. Still, with sustained vigilance, reform, and advocacy, progress can be made toward a more just and equitable future for all individuals, regardless of their mental health status.

Chapter 11: End-of-Chapter Questions

Comprehension and Reflection

1. **What are the primary ethical concerns surrounding the use of psychiatric diagnoses in legal settings?**

- Reflect on how these concerns influence decisions related to competence to stand trial, insanity defenses, and involuntary commitment.

2. **How can forensic psychiatrists ensure that external pressures do not influence their evaluations in legal cases?**

- Discuss the importance of maintaining objectivity and independence in forensic evaluations and the role of professional ethics in preserving this objectivity.

3. **What role does judicial oversight play in the application of psychiatric diagnoses in criminal trials?**

- Analyze the significance of judicial scrutiny in preventing the misuse of psychiatric evaluations in legal contexts.

4. **How does the public perception of mental illness affect the potential weaponization of psychiatric diagnoses?**

- Reflect on the impact of stigma and misconceptions about mental health on legal and social outcomes for individuals with psychiatric conditions.

5. **How does the history of psychiatric diagnoses being misused politically inform our understanding of their potential weaponization in the modern era?**

- Discuss the historical abuses of psychiatric diagnoses and how they shape contemporary legal practices.

6. **In what ways can independent psychiatric evaluations protect individuals from being unjustly labeled or incarcerated?**

- Reflect on the importance of impartial evaluations and their role in ensuring fairness in legal proceedings.

7. **How does the intersectionality of race, gender, and socioeconomic status impact the diagnosis and treatment of mental health conditions?**

- Explore how biases in mental health diagnoses can exacerbate discrimination within the legal system.

8. **Why is public education on mental health crucial in preventing the misuse of psychiatric diagnoses in the legal system?**

- Discuss how educating the public about mental health can reduce stigma and mitigate the potential for the exploitation of psychiatric diagnoses.

9. **How do advocacy organizations help protect the rights of individuals with psychiatric conditions in legal settings?**

- Reflect on the role of advocacy groups in ensuring that individuals with mental health disorders are treated with dignity and respect.

10. **What challenges do forensic psychiatrists face when diagnosing individuals with mental health conditions for legal purposes?**

- Analyze the difficulties associated with applying psychiatric diagnoses in legal contexts and how these challenges can impact individuals' rights.

Critical Thinking and Application

11. **How can forensic psychiatrists ensure that their assessments are objective when external pressures, such as legal strategies, come into play?**

➢ Discuss strategies that psychiatrists can use to maintain impartiality and integrity in their evaluations.

12. **How do forensic psychiatric evaluations influence the fairness of legal decisions in criminal cases?**

➢ Explore how psychiatric evaluations can affect the outcome of criminal trials, especially in cases involving insanity defenses or competency determinations.

13. **What steps can judges take to prevent the misuse of psychiatric diagnoses in criminal trials?**

➢ Discuss how judicial oversight and careful consideration of psychiatric evaluations can help ensure fair legal proceedings.

14. **How does the potential for misdiagnosis in mental health assessments impact individuals' rights and legal outcomes?**

➢ Reflect on the consequences of inaccurate psychiatric diagnoses and how they can affect an individual's freedom and legal standing.

15. **How can forensic psychiatrists address biases in their assessments of individuals from different racial, gender, or socioeconomic backgrounds?**

➢ Discuss methods to minimize bias in psychiatric evaluations to ensure more equitable legal outcomes.

16. **What ethical dilemmas arise when a psychiatric diagnosis is used to influence legal decisions, such as sentencing or parole?**

➢ Explore the ethical considerations that arise when a diagnosis is used as a factor in determining legal outcomes.

17. **How does the use of psychiatric diagnoses in legal cases affect the perception of mental health in society?**

➢ Analyze the broader social implications of psychiatric diagnoses being used in the legal system, particularly in terms of stigmatization and discrimination.

18. **How can forensic psychiatrists balance their professional duty to provide accurate assessments with the demands of the legal system?**

➢ Reflect on the ethical challenges faced by forensic psychiatrists in maintaining professional standards while navigating legal pressures.

19. **How can public awareness campaigns about mental health reduce the potential for psychiatric diagnoses to be weaponized?**

➢ Discuss the role of public education in reducing stigma and preventing the exploitation of psychiatric diagnoses.

20. **What role does advocacy for mental health rights play in safeguarding individuals from being unfairly diagnosed or incarcerated due to psychiatric conditions?**

➢ Explore how advocacy efforts can support individuals in maintaining their legal and human rights within the context of mental health diagnoses.

Afterword

Forensic neuropsychopathology is an indispensable interdisciplinary and multidisciplinary field that merges insights from neuroscience, neurology, neuropsychology, neurophysiology, psychology, psychiatry, and law. As explored throughout this textbook, it plays a pivotal role in understanding the complex relationship between brain function, behavior, and legal considerations. This field's growing significance lies in its ability to bridge the gap between scientific knowledge and legal practice, helping ensure that criminal justice decisions are informed by an accurate understanding of neurological impairments and their impact on behavior. Forensic neuropsychopathology also provides essential tools for evaluating mental state, competency, and risk assessment in both criminal and civil contexts. Comprehensive evaluations contribute to more informed legal decisions, promoting fairness and accuracy in adjudicating cases involving neurological and psychological disorders.

The complexity of forensic neuropsychopathology cannot be overstated. By addressing critical issues such as criminal responsibility, competency to stand trial, and the application of defenses like insanity, this field enables a deeper understanding of how brain dysfunction, whether from injury, mental illness, neurodevelopmental conditions, or neurocognitive disorders, affects criminal behavior. Advances in neuroimaging, neuropsychopathological testing, and molecular neuroscience have further enhanced the ability to assess and interpret these impacts, offering scientific rigor and objectivity essential for making informed legal decisions. As a result, forensic neuropsychopathology provides valuable insights into the nuances of criminal intent and mental state, which are crucial for determining appropriate legal outcomes. The continued integration of emerging technologies and research in this field holds the potential to refine legal practices, ensuring that justice is both scientifically grounded and ethically sound.

This textbook has highlighted key concepts and methods central to the field. One of the most significant takeaways is the realization that criminal behavior is not always the result of a deliberate choice but is often influenced by underlying neurological and psychological factors. Forensic neuropsychopathology provides the tools to understand how brain injuries or mental disorders can alter cognitive functioning, emotional regulation, and decision-making. These insights have profound implications, not only for legal proceedings but also for how society approaches justice and the rehabilitation of individuals. The field challenges traditional views of behavior as solely the result of moral agency and choice, emphasizing the need for a more nuanced and individualized understanding of human actions within the legal system.

Forensic neuropsychopathologists and psychologists are integral to ensuring fairness in legal decisions. Through comprehensive neuropsychopathological evaluations, expert testimony, and ethical application of neuroimaging and assessments, forensic neuropsychopathology helps clarify whether individuals are mentally fit to stand trial, whether their mental state at the time of an offense affects their criminal responsibility, and whether mitigating factors should be considered during sentencing. The field also contributes to ethical discussions surrounding the use of neuroscience, neuropsychology, and neurology in legal proceedings, ensuring that neuropsychological evidence is valid, reliable, and properly applied. Moreover, forensic neuropsychopathologists play a key role in advocating for the appropriate treatment and rehabilitation of individuals with neurological disorders rather than purely punitive measures. Their expertise ensures that the legal system considers the complexities of brain function and behavior, promoting justice that reflects scientific understanding and human dignity.

However, while this field has made significant strides, there is much more to explore and understand. One of the core messages of this textbook is the ongoing need for further research, particularly in areas such as neuroplasticity, the impact of early brain development on behavior, and the relationship between genetic factors and brain function concerning criminal activity. New advancements in neuroimaging and molecular neuroscience continue to offer exciting possibilities, and these innovations will only deepen the understanding of how neurological conditions influence criminal behavior. As research progresses, it will be essential to address the ethical and legal implications of these advancements, ensuring that they are applied in a manner that respects individual rights and freedoms. Continued collaboration among scientists, clinicians, and legal professionals will be crucial in bridging knowledge gaps and refining the role of neuroscience in the criminal justice system.

While significant progress has been made in understanding neuroplasticity and molecular neuroscience, particularly through literature reviews, systematic reviews, and meta-analyses, experimental and clinical trials are essential for further advancing the field. These methods play a crucial role in providing empirical evidence that can substantiate or challenge existing theories, thereby helping to refine our understanding of the underlying mechanisms of brain function and its impact on behavior. Literature reviews and meta-analyses aggregate existing research, offering comprehensive insights into trends and gaps. Still, they cannot replace the need for experimental trials to establish causality and test hypotheses in real-world settings.

Clinical trials allow researchers to directly observe the effects of interventions or treatments on individuals with neurological conditions, which is essential for translating laboratory findings into practical applications. Without such trials, the field risks stagnating in theoretical discussions without the robust, evidence-based data required to shape effective legal and therapeutic practices. Thus, conducting experimental and clinical research is critical for testing the potential of new technologies, refining neuropsychopathological evaluations, and ultimately bridging the gap between scientific discovery and its application within the criminal justice system.

For those seeking to apply this knowledge in real-world contexts, forensic neuropsychopathology offers immense potential in shaping more just and equitable legal practices. Beyond the courtroom, this field can inform public policy and contribute to the advancement of criminal justice reform. As research evolves, it could lead to greater emphasis on rehabilitation over punitive measures for individuals whose criminal behavior is linked to neurological impairments. Identifying and treating the underlying neurological causes of criminal behavior can significantly reduce recidivism, improving long-term outcomes for offenders and enhancing public safety. Ultimately, forensic neuropsychopathology holds the promise of a more holistic approach to justice, where the focus shifts from punishment to understanding and addressing the root causes of criminal behavior.

The future of forensic neuropsychopathology is also a future of continuous learning. As legal professionals, clinicians, and researchers, it is crucial to stay informed about ongoing studies and advancements in the field. Continuing education, participation in interdisciplinary collaborations, and exploration of emerging technologies will all be key to staying at the forefront of this dynamic field. Moreover, fostering a culture of critical thinking and ethical reflection within the field will ensure that applying neuropsychological insights in legal contexts remains responsible and just. By embracing these opportunities for growth and innovation, professionals in forensic neuropsychopathology can contribute to a more informed, fair, and effective legal system.

Forensic neuropsychopathology is not only a scientific endeavor but a profoundly human one, as it helps ensure that legal decisions are made with a thorough understanding of the brain's role in shaping behavior. This field serves as a critical reminder that justice must be informed by science, compassion, and an understanding of the complexities inherent in the human condition. As the legal system continues to evolve, integrating neuropsychological insights will remain essential in promoting fair and informed decision-making, guiding the future of criminal justice and rehabilitation. By emphasizing the relationship between brain function and behavior, forensic neuropsychopathology encourages a more nuanced perspective on criminal responsibility and mental health. This approach supports more equitable outcomes for individuals involved in the justice system. It fosters a broader societal understanding of the importance of mental health and neurological well-being in shaping human actions.

For those interested in continuing to explore this field, numerous avenues for further study are available. Pursuing advanced degrees in neuropsychology, participating in clinical or forensic case analysis, or engaging in policy advocacy for criminal justice reform are just a few ways to deepen expertise and contribute to this evolving field. The continued integration of neuropsychology into legal proceedings represents a step toward a more just, informed, and compassionate approach to the criminal justice system. Additionally, attending interdisciplinary conferences, collaborating with legal professionals, and researching emerging topics such as neuroethics and neurotechnology can provide valuable insights and foster innovation. As the field grows, those contributing to its development will be crucial in shaping the future relationship between neuroscience and law.

The importance of advanced initiatives such as advanced forensic neuropsychopathological evaluations, neuroimaging, and neurotechnology cannot be overstated. These are the gateways through which the field will continue to evolve and expand. Ongoing collaboration with leading experts, clinicians, healthcare providers, and legal teams is crucial to further defining and solidifying forensic neuropsychopathology, ensuring that it remains at the cutting edge of scientific research and its application within the criminal justice system. As these initiatives progress, they will enhance the accuracy and precision of assessments, providing a more comprehensive understanding of how neurological factors influence behavior. Ultimately, integrating these advanced tools will ensure that forensic neuropsychopathology continues contributing to more scientifically informed legal decisions, shaping the future of law and neuroscience. Thank you sincerely for taking the time to engage with my work. I genuinely hope that within these pages, you discovered something not only thought-provoking but transformative—an insight that will stand the test of time in science and law. May it inspire future understanding, spark new conversations, and continue to resonate for years to come.

References

- Aaronson, A. L., Bordelon, S. D., Brakel, S. J., Morrison, H. (2021). A review of the role of chronic traumatic encephalopathy in criminal court. *Journal of American Psychiatry Law, 49*(1), 60-64. https://doi.org/10.29158/jaapl.200054-20

- Abdelhamid, G. S. M., Bassiouni, M. G. A., & Gomez-Benito, J. (2021). Assessing cognitive abilities using the WAIS-IV: An item response theory approach. *International Journal of Environmental Res Public Health, 18*(13), 6835. https://doi.org/10.3390/ijerph18136835

- Abojedi, A., & Daoud, F. S. (2012). Validity and reliability of computerized MMPI-2 profile among a clinical sample of psychological disorders in Jordan. *Journal of the Association of Arab Universities for Basic and Applied Sciences, 1*(15).

- Abrams, Z. (2022). What neuroscience tells us about the teenage brain. *American Psychological Association.* https://www.apa.org/monitor/2022/07/feature-neuroscience-teen-brain

- Abramsky, S. (2004, August 19). Memory and manipulation: The trials of Elizabeth Loftus, defender of the wrongly accused. *LA Weekly.* https://web.archive.org/web/20130106093521/http://www.laweekly.com/2004-08-19/news/memory-and-manipulation/

- Achebe, S. C., Igboanugo, N. G., & Egbo, A. F. (2024). Deficits in frontal lobes and neurotransmitters as a determinant of violent criminal behaviors among inmates in Onitsha correctional center. *University of the Niger Umunya, 1*(2). https://acjol.org/index.php/crowther/article/view/4984

- Achoru, F. (2023). Punching through life: Mike Tyson's words of wisdom. *Medium.* https://medium.com/practice-in-public/punching-through-life-mike-tysons-words-of-wisdom-1e9c9afd5875
- Ackerman, P. L. (2022). Intelligence process vs. content and academic performance: A trip through a house of mirrors. *Journal of Intelligence, 10*(4), 128. https://doi.org/10.3390/jintelligence10040128
- Aggarwal, A., & Marwaha, R. (2022). *Oppositional defiant disorder*. In Stat Pearls [Internet] Stat Pearls Publishing. https://www.ncbi.nlm.nih.gov/books/NBK557443/
- Ahmad, A., Jagdhane, N., Ademmer, K., & Choudhari, K. (2024). Carl Wernicke of the Wernicke area: A historical review. *World Neurosurgery, 185,* 225-233. https://doi.org/10.1016/j.wneu.2024.02.103
- Ahonen, M. (2018). Ancient philosophers on mental illness. *History of Psychiatry, 30*(1). https://doi.org/10.1177/0957154X18803508
- Ahonen, M. (2014): Mental disorders in ancient philosophy. *Springer.*
- Aiello, E. N., Esposito, A., Gramegna, C., Gazzinga, V., Zago, S., Difonzo, T., Appollonio, I. M., & Bolognini, N. (2022). The Frontal Assessment Battery (FAB) and its subscales: Validation and updated normative data in an Italian population

sample. *Neurological Science, 43*(2), 979-984. https://doi.org/10.1007/s10072-021-05392-y

- Al Farsi, R. S., Al Alawi, A. M., Al Hurazizi, A. R., Al Saadi, T., Al-Hamadani, N., Al Zeedy, K. & Al-Maqbali, J. S. (2023). Delirium in medically hospitalized patients: Prevalence, recognition and risk factors: A prospective cohort study. *Journal Clinical Medicine, 12*(12), 38-97. https://doi.org/10.3390/jcm12123897
- Aljadani, A., Alshammari, K., Alshammari, M., Alshammari, S., Alhuwaydi, A., AbouZed, M., Shabaan, I., Elzahab, N., Altuhayni, A., & Alghasab, N. (2024). Prevalence and predictive factors of panic disorder among adults in Saudi Arabia: A cross-sectional study. *Journal of Epidemiology and Global Health, 14,* 730-739. https://link.springer.com/article/10.1007/s44197-024-00208-6#citeas:~:text=DOI-,https%3A//doi.org/10.1007/s44197%2D024%2D00208%2D6,-Share%20this%20article
- Alareqe, N. A., Roslan, S., Nordin, M. S., Ahmad, N. A., Taresh, S. M. (2021). Psychometric properties of the Millon Clinical Multiaxial Inventory-III in an Arabic clinical sample compared with American, Italian, and Dutch cultures. *Frontiers in Psychology, 12*. https://doi.org/10.3389/fpsyg.2021.562619
- Alexander, L., Wood, C. M., & Roberts, A. C. (2022). The ventromedial prefrontal cortex and emotion regulation: Lost in translation? *Journal of Physiology, 601*(1), 37-50. https://doi.org/10.1113/JP282627
- Alexander, N. E., & Kiehl, K. A. (2014). Psychopathy: Developmental perspectives and their

implications for treatment. *Restor Neurol Neuroscience, 32*(1), 103-117.

- Allely, C. S. (2020). The contributory role of psychopathology and inhibitory control in the case of mass shooter James Holmes. *Aggression and Violent Behavior, 51*, 101382. https://doi.org/10.1016/j.avb.2020.101382
- Almomani, F., Avi-Izhak, T., Demeter, N., Josman, N., & Al-momani, M. O. (2018). Construct validity and internal consistency reliability of the Lowenstein occupational therapy cognitive assessment (LOTCA). *BMC Psychiatry, 18,* 184. https://doi.org/10.1186/s12888-018-1776-x
- Alexander, W. H., Brown, J. W. (2018). Frontal cortex function as derived from hierarchical predictive coding. *Science Reports, 8*(3843). https://doi.org/10.1038/s41598-018-21407-9
- American Academy of Sleep Medicine. (2025). *In memoriam: Sleep pioneer and AASM founding President Dr. William C. Dement*. https://aasm.org/in-memoriam-sleep-pioneer-founding-president-william-bill-dement/
- American Association on Intellectual and Developmental Disabilities. (2025). *Defining criteria for intellectual disability*. https://www.aaidd.org/intellectual-disability/definition
- American Board of Forensic Psychology. (2024). *About*. https://abfp.com/about/

- American Psychological Association. (2020a). *Neuropsychology*. https://dictionary.apa.org/neuropsychology
- American Psychology-Law Society. (2024). *History of AP-LS*. https://ap-ls.org/about/history
- American Psychological Association. (1986). *Ford v. Wainwright*. https://www.apa.org/about/offices/ogc/amicus/ford
- American Psychological Association. (2020b). *Forensic neuropsychology*. https://dictionary.apa.org/forensic-neuropsychology
- American Psychological Association. (2020c). *Psychopathology*. https://dictionary.apa.org/psychopathology
- Anderson, C. (2018). Cruz biological mother's past a factor in school shooting. *The Associated Press*. https://www.jacksonville.com/story/news/crime/2018/09/05/cruz-biological-mother-s-past/10839405007/
- Anderson, N., & Ozakinci, G. (2018). Effectiveness of psychological interventions to improve quality of life in people with long-term conditions: Rapid systematic review of randomized controlled trials. *BMC Psychology, 6,* 11. https://doi.org/10.1186/s40359-018-0225-4
- Angum, F., Khan, T., Kaler, J., Siddiqui, L., & Hussain, A. (2020). The prevalence of autoimmune disorders in women: A narrative review. *Cureus, 12*(5), 8094.
- Anis, L., Letourneau, N., Benzies, K., Ewashen, C., & Hart, M. J. (2020). Effect of the child health parent training program on parent-child interaction quality

and child development. *Canadian Journal of Nursing Research, 52*(2), 157-168. https://doi.org/10.1016/b978-0-12-802973-2.00004-5https://doi.org/10.1177/0844562119899004

- Appelbaum, P. S. (2019). In search of a new paradigm for research on violence and schizophrenia. *The American Journal of Psychiatry.* https://doi.org/10.1176/appi.ajp.2019.19070678

- Appelbaum, P. S. (2012). Law and psychiatry: Treatment of incompetent dangerous criminal defendants: Parsing the law. *Psychiatry Service, 63*(7), 630-2. https://doi.org/10.1176/appi.ps.201200630

- Apte, M., & Kumar, A. (2023). Correlation of mutated gene and signaling pathways in ASD. *IBRO Neuroscience Report, 14,* 384-392. https://doi.org/10.1016/j.ibneur.2023.03.011

- Areh, I., Verkampt, F., & Allan, A. (2021). Critical review of the use of the Rorschach in European courts. *Psychiatry Psychology Law, 29*(2), 183-205. https://doi.org/10.1080/13218719.2021.1894260

- Arias, B. (2024). *Clinical integration of neuropsychological test results: WAIS-IV index scores*. CRC Press.

- Arias, J. A., Williams, C., Raghvani, R., Ahajani, M., Baez, S., Belzung, C., Booji, L., Busatto, G., Chiarella, J., Fu, C. H. Y., Ibanez, A., Liddell, B. J., Lowe, L., Pennix, B. W. J. H., Rosa, P., & Kemp, A. H. (2020). The neuroscience of sadness: A multidisciplinary synthesis and collaborative review.

Neuroscience & Behavioral Review, 111, 199-228. https://doi.org/10.1016/j.neubiorev.2020.01.006

- Arroyo-Ferrer, A., de Norena D., Serrano, J. I., Rios-Lago, M., Romero, J. P. (2021). Cognitive rehabilitation in a case of traumatic brain injury using EEG-based neurofeedback in comparison to conventional methods. *Journal Integr. Neuroscience, 20*(2), 449-457. https://doi.org/10.31083/j.jin2002047
- Asby, D., Boche, D., Allan, S., Love, S., & Miners, J. S. (2021). Systemic infection exacerbates cerebrovascular dysfunction in Alzheimer's disease. *Brain, 144*(6), 1869-1883. https://doi.org/10.1093/brain/awab094
- Asken, B. M., & Rabinovici, G. D. (2021). Identifying degenerative effects of repetitive head trauma with neuroimaging: A clinically-oriented review. *BMC: Acta Neuropathologica Communications, 9*(96). https://doi.org/10.1186/s40478-021-01197-4
- Associated Press. (2013). Newtown police file released. *Politico.* https://www.politico.com/story/2013/12/newtown-shooting-police-file-101561
- Associated Press. (2021). *Timeline of serial killer John Wayne Gacy's life, case.* https://apnews.com/article/chicago-2a5842ef8ee46f8d43799bc50f390ad8
- Ayyagari, R., Goldschmidt, D., Mu, F., Caroff, S. N., & Carroll, B. (2022). An experimental study to assess the professional and social consequences of tardive

dyskinesia. *Clinical Psychopharmacological Neuroscience, 20*(1). 154-166.

- Baily, S. P. (2010, May 12). Psychologist resigns from NARTH after gay prostitute's claims. *Christianity Today*. https://www.christianitytoday.com/2010/05/psychologist-resigns-from-narth-after-gay-prostitutes-claim/
- Bains, N., & Abdijadid, S. (2023). Major Depressive Disorder. *National Library of Medicine: National Center for Biotechnology Information*. https://www.ncbi.nlm.nih.gov/books/NBK559078/
- Balir, R. J., R. (2017). Emotion-based learning systems and the development of morality. *Cognition, 167,* 38-45. https://doi.org/10.1016/j.cognition.2017.03.013
- Ballester, B. R., Maier, M., Duff, A., Cameirao, M., & Mermudez, S. (2019). A critical time window for recovery extends beyond one-year post-stroke. *Nervous System Pathophysiology*. https://doi.org/10.1152/jn.00762.2018
- Balogh, L., Pulay, A. J., & Rethelyi, J. M. (2022). Genetics in the ADHD clinic: How can genetic testing support the current clinical practice. *Frontiers in Psychology, 13*. https://doi.org/10.3389/fpsyg.2022.751041
- Bamford, I. J., & Bamford, N. S. (2019). The striatum's role in executing rational and irrational economic behaviors. *Neuroscientist, 25*(5), 475-490. https://doi.org/10.1177/1073858418824256
- Bang, S., Fisher, P. M., Hjordt, L. V., Perfolk, A., Persson, S., Bock, C., Baandrup, O., Deen, M.,

Thomsen, C., Sestoft, D. M., & Knudsen, G. M. (2017). Violent offenders respond to provocations with high amygdala and striatal reactivity. *Social Cognition Affect Neuroscience, 12,* 802-810. https://www.scopus.com/record/display.uri?eid=2-s2.0-85021358651&origin=inward&txGid=5def0a39ee265da320d1346d83866bf1

- Barman, A., Chatterjee, A., & Bhide, R. (2016). Cognitive impairment and rehabilitation strategies after traumatic brain injury. *Indian Journal Psychology Medicine, 38*(3), 172-181. https://doi.org/10.4103/0253-7176.183086
- Bartol, C. R., & Bartol, A. M. (2018). Introduction to forensic psychology: Research and application. 5th ed.
- Barha, C. K., Nagamatsu, L. S., & Lui-Ambrose, T. (2016). Chapter 4 – basic and neuroanatomy and neurophysiology. *Handbook of Clinical Neurology, 138,* 53-68.
- Bathini, P., Dupanloup, I., Zenaro, E., Terrabuio, E., Fischer, A., Ballabani, E., Doucey, M-A., & Alberi, L. (2023). Systemic inflammation leads to microglial dysfunction, characterized by a vascular Alzheimer's disease (AD) phenotype. *Brain, Behavior, & Immunity – Health, 28,* 100-568. https://doi.org/10.1016/j.bbih.2022.100568
- Becker, K. A. (2003). *History of the Stanford-Binet Intelligence Scales: Content and psychometrics*. Riverside Publishing.
- Baily, S. P. (2010, May 12). Psychologist resigns from NARTH after gay prostitute's claims.

Christianity Today. https://www.christianitytoday.com/2010/05/psychologist-resigns-from-narth-after-gay-prostitutes-claim/

- Bell, L. (1995, July 26). Groups expel Texas psychiatrist known for murder cases. *Dallas Morning News*. https://web.archive.org/web/20090307034749/http://ccadp.org/DrDeath.htm
- Benedict, S. M. (2024). Neuropsychological testing in forensic psychology: An empirical study. *SSRN*. https://ssrn.com/abstract=4922754
- Benjamin, Jr., L. T. (2023). *A brief history of modern psychology*. Library of Congress.
- Berg, E. A. (1948). A simple objective technique for measuring flexibility in thinking. *Journal of General Psychology, 39,* 15-22.
- Berhouma, M. (2013). Beyond the pineal gland assumption: A neuroanatomical appraisal of dualism in Descartes' philosophy. *Clinical Neurology and Neurosurgery, 115*(9), 1661-1670. https://doi.org/10.1016/j.clineuro.2013.02.023
- Bernier, R. A., & Hillary, F. G. (2019). Chapter 22 – traumatic brain injury and frontal lobe plasticity. *Science Direct, 163,* 411-431. https://doi.org/10.1016/b978-012-804281-6.00022-7
- Beyer, T., Bidaut, L., Dickson, J., CKacherlriess, M., Kiessling, F., Leitgeb, R., Ma, J., Kumar, L., Theek, B., & Mawlawi, O. (2020). What scans we will read: Imaging instrumentation trends in clinical oncology. *Cancer Imaging, 20*(38). https://doi.org/10.1186/s40644-020-00312-3

➢ Bezdjian, S., Raine, A., Baker, L. A., & Lynam, D. R. (2011). Psychopathic personality in children: Genetic and environmental contributions. *Psychological Medicine, 41*(3), 589-600. https://doi.org/10.1017/S0033291710000966

➢ Bielecki, J. E., & Gupta, V. (2023). Cyclothymia disorder. *National Library of Medicine*. https://www.ncbi.nlm.nih.gov/books/NBK557877/

➢ Billstedt, E., Anckarsater, H., Wallinius, M., & Hofvander, B. (2017). Neurodevelopmental disorders in young violent offenders: Overlap and background characteristics. *Psychiatric Research, 252,* 234-241.

➢ Binder, J. R. (2017). Current Controversies on Wernicke's Area and Its Role in Language. *Current Neurology and Neuroscience Reports, 17,* 58. https://doi.org/10.1007/s11910-017-0764-8

➢ Binet, A., & Simon, T. (1916). Application of the new methods to the diagnosis of the intellectual level among normal and subnormal children in institutions and in primary school. (L'Annee Psych., 1905, 245-336). In A. Binet, T. Simon, & E. S. Kite (Trans.). *The Development of Intelligence in Children (The Binet-Simon Scale),* 91-181. Williams & Wilkins Co.

➢ Binet, A., & Simon, T. (1948). The development of Binet-Simon Scale, 1905-1908. In W. Dennis (ed). *Readings in the History of Psychology,* 412-424. https://psycnet.apa.org/doi/10.1037/11304-047

➢ Binet, A., & Simon, T. In: *The development of intelligence in children*. Kite Elizabeth, translator. Arno Press: New York. First published in 1905.

- Blair, R. J. (2016). The neurobiology of impulsive aggression. *Journal of Child Adolescent Psychopharmacology, 26*(1), 4-9. https://doi.org/10.1089/cap.2015.0088
- Blanco, C., Alegria, A. A., Petry, N. M., Grant, J., Simpson, H. B., Liu, S-M., Grant, B., & Hasin, D. (2010). Prevalence and correlates of firesetting in the US: Results from the National Epidemiologic Survey on Alcohol and Related Conditions (NESARC). *Journal of Clinical Psychiatry, 71*(9), 1218-1225. https://doi.org/10.4088/JCP.08m04812gry
- Branch, J. (2016 February 3). Ken Stable, a magnetic NFL star, was sapped of spirit CTE. *The New York Times*. https://www.nytimes.com/2016/02/04/sports/football/ken-stabler-nfl-cte-brain-disease.html
- Broca, P. (1864). In: Blake, C. C. eds. On the phenomena of hybridity in the genus homo. *Anthropological Society of London.*
- Broca, P. (1861). Remarks on the seat of the faculty of articulated language, following an observation of aphemia (loss of speech). *York University, 6,* 330-357. https://psychclassics.yorku.ca/Broca/aphemie-e.htm
- Brock, H., Rizvi, A., & Hany, M. (2024). *Obsessive-compulsive disorder*. In-Stat Pearls [Internet]. Stat Pearls Publishing. https://www.ncbi.nlm.nih.gov/books/NBK553162/
- Brofenbrenner, U. (1979). *The ecology of human development: Experiments by nature and design*. Harvard University Press.

- Brofenbrenner, U. (1974). Developmental research, public policy, and the ecology of childhood. *Child Development, 45,* 1-5.
- Bruggerman, G. F., Haitsma, I., Dirven, C. M. F., & Volovici, V. (2020). Traumatic axonal injury (TAI): Definitions, pathophysiology, and imaging – a narrative review. *Acta Neurochir (Wien), 163(1), 31-44*. https://doi.org/10.1007/s00701-020-04594-1
- Bodart, A., Inernizzi, S., Lefebvre, L., & Rossingnol, M. (2023). Physiological reactivity at rest and in response to social or emotional stimuli after a traumatic brain injury: A systematic review. *Frontiers in Psychology, 14*. https://doi.org/10.3389/fpsyg.2023.930177
- Boone, K. B., Kaufmann, P. M., Sweet, J. J., Leatherberry, D., Beattey, R. A., Victor, T. L., Boone, R. P., Spector, J. S., Hebben, N., Hanks, R. A., & James, J. (2024). Attorney demands for protected psychological test information: Is access necessary for cross-examination, or does it lead to misinformation? An inter-organizational position paper. *The Clinical Neuropsychologist, 38*(4), 889-906. https://doi.org/10.1080/13854046.2024.2323222
- Boone, K. B., Sweet, J. J., Byrd, D. A., Denney, R. L., Hanks, R. A., Kaufmann, P. M., Larrabee, G. J., Marcopulos, B. A., Paltzer, J. Y., Morgan, J. E., Mindt, M. R., Schroeder, R. W., Sim, A. H., & Suhr, J. A. (2022). Official position of the American Academy of Clinical Neuropsychology on test security. *The Clinical Neuropsychologist, 36*(3), 523-545. https://doi.org/10.1080/13854046.2021.2022214

- Boress, K., Gaasedelen, O. J., Croghan, A., Johnson, M. K., Caraher, K., Basso, M. R., & Whiteside, D. M. (2022). Validation of the Personality Assessment Inventory (PAI) scale of scales in a mixed clinical sample. *Clinical Neuropsychology, 36*(7), 1844-1859. https://doi.org/10.1080/13854046.2021.1900400

- Borstein, R. F. (2006). A Freudian construct lost and reclaimed: The psychodynamics of personality pathology. *Psychoanalytic Psychology, 23,* 339-353.

- Borstein, R. F. (2005). Reconnecting psychoanalysis to mainstream psychology: Challenges and opportunities. *Psychoanalytic Psychology, 22,* 323-340.

- Bosso, T., Vischia, F., Keller, R., Vai, D., Imperiale, D., & Vercelli, A. (2022). A case report and literature review of cognitive malingering and psychopathology. *Frontiers in Psychiatry, 13*(981475). https://doi.org/10.3389/fpsyt.2022.981475

- Boston University Chobanian & Avedisian School of Medicine. (2017). *New study of 111 deceased former NFL players finds 99 percent had CTE.* https://www.bumc.bu.edu/camed/2017/07/25/new-study-of-111-deceased-former-nfl-players-finds-99-percent-had-cte/#:~:text=New%20Study%20of%20111%20Deceased,as%20well%20as%20military%20veterans.

- Branch, C., Milner, B., & Rasmussen, T. (1964). Intracartoid sodium amytal for the lateralization of cerebral speech dominance; observations in 123 patients. *Journal of Neurosurgery, 21,* 399-405. http://doi.org/10.3171/Jns.1964.21.5.0399

- Brodey, B., Purcell, S. E., Rhea, K., Maier, P., First, M., Zweede, L., Sinsterra, M., Nunn, M. B., Austin, M-P., & Brodey, I. S. (2018). Rapid and accurate behavioral health diagnostic screening: Initial validation study of a web-based, self-report tool (the SAGE-SR). *Journal of International Res, 20*(3), e108. https://doi.org/10.2196/jmir.9428

- Broglio, S. P., McCrea, M., McAllister, T., Harezlak, J., Katz, B., Hack, D., Hainline, B., & CARE Consortium Investigators. (2017). National security on the effects of concussion in collegiate athletes and US military service academy members: The NCAA-DoD concussion assessment, research and education (CARE) consortium structure and methods. *Sports Medicine, 47*(7), 1437-1451. https://doi.org/10.1007/s40279-017-0707-1

- Brown, J. (2016). Psychiatry, psychology, and crime: Historical and current aspects. In: Huebner, B. M. (ed). *Oxford Bibliographies in Criminology: Oxford University Press*. http://doi.org/10.1093/OBO/9780195396607-0170

- Bruce, D. (1985). On the origin of the term “neuropsychology.” *Neuropsychologia, 23*(6), 813-814. https://psycnet.apa.org/doi/10.1016/0028-3932(85)90088-0

- Bruijnen, C. J. W., Boukje, A. G. D., Walvoort, S. J. W., Manon, J. J., Harmen, B., Cor, A. J., DeJong, C. A. J., & Kessels, R. P. C. (2020). Psychometric properties of the Montreal Cognitive Assessment (MoCA) in healthy participants aged 18-70. *International Journal of Psychiatry in Clinical*

Practice, 293-300. https://doi.org/10.1080/13651501.2020.1746348

- Buckholtz, J. W., Treadway, M. T., Cowan, R. L., Woodward, N. D., Benning, S. D., Li, R., Ansari, M. S., Baldwin, R. M., Schwartzman, A. N., Shelby, E. S., Smith, C. E., Cole, D., Kessler, R. M., & Zald, D. H. (2010). Mesolimbic dopamine reward system hypersensitivity in individuals with psychopathic traits. *National Neuroscience,* 13(4), 419-421. https://doi.org/10.1038/nn.2510

- Buhrig, A. (2012). Sane or insane? *DW.* https://www.dw.com/en/guilty-of-mass-murder-but-is-breivik-sane/a-15878549

- Bulut, O., Cormier, D. C., Aquilina, A. M., & Bulut, H. C. (2021). Age and sex invariance of the Woodcock-Johnson IV Test of Cognitive Abilities: Evidence from psychometric network modeling. *Journal of Intelligence, 9*(3), 35. https://doi.org/10.3390/jintelligence9030035

- Butcher, J. N., Butcher, G. A., Greene, R. L., & Nelson, L. D. (2015). Using the MMPI-2 in forensic assessment. *American Psychological Association.* https://www.apa.org/pubs/books/Using-The-MMPI-2-In-Forensic-Assessment-Intro-Sample.pdf

- Butler, L. S., Martinez, A. R., Sugimoto, D., Wyatt, C. W., Milian, E. K., Ulman, S., Erdman, A., Loewen, A., Hayden, K., DeVerna, A., & Tulchin-Francis, K. (2022). Reliability of the expanded cutting alignment scoring tool (E-CAST) to assess trunk and limb alignment during a 45-degree side deep cut. *IJSPT, 17*(3), 456-465. https://doi.org/10.26603/001c.33045

- Bynum, W. F., & Porter, R. (2013). *Companion encyclopedia of the history of medicine*. 1st ed. https://doi.org/10.4324/9781315002514
- Cabrera, C., Torres, H., & Harcourt, S. (2020). The neurological and neuropsychological effects of child maltreatment. *Aggression and Violent Behavior, 54,* 101-408. https://doi.org/10.1016/j.avb.2020.101408
- Cadwallader, T. C., Semrau, L. A., & Callwallader, J. V. (1971). Early physiological psychology: Circa 3000. *Proceedings of the Annual Convention of the American Psychological Association, 6*(Pt. 2), 719-720.
- Callahan, L., & Pinals, D. A. (2020). Challenges to reforming the competence to stand trial and competence restoration system. *Psychiatry Serv, 71*(7), 691-697.
- Campo-Arias, A., & Oviedo, H. C. (2008). Psychometric properties of a scale: Internal consistency. *Rev Salud Publica, 10*(5), 831-9. https://pubmed.ncbi.nlm.nih.gov/19360231/#:~:text=9.%20Spanish.%20doi%3A-,10.1590/s0124%2D00642008000500015,-.%20PMID%3A%2019360231.
- Cardoso, M. G. F., Faleiro, R. M., Jardin-Paula, J., Kummer, A., Caramelli, P., Teixeira, A. L., Cruz de Souza, L., & Miranda, A. S. (2019). Cognitive impairment following acute mild traumatic brain injury. *Frontiers in Psychology.* https://doi.org/10.3389/fneur.2019.00198
- Carey, L., Walsh, A., Adikari, A., Goodin, P., Alahakoon, D., De Silva, D., Ong, K-L., Nilsson, M.,

& Boyd, L. (2019). Finding the intersection of neuroplasticity, stroke recovery, and learning: Scope and contributions to stroke rehabilitation. *Neural Plasticity*. https://doi.org/10.1155/2019/5232374

- Casaletto, K. B., & Heaton, R. K. (2017). Neuropsychological assessments: Past and future. *Journal of International Neuropsychology Soc, 23*(9-10), 778-790. https://doi.org/10.1017/S1355617717001060
- Castle, D. J., & Murray, R. M. (1993). The epidemiology of late-onset schizophrenia. *Schizophrenia Bull, 19,* 691-700. https://doi.org/10.1093/schbul/19.4.691
- Cattell, J. M. (1921). *American men of science: A biographical directory*. 3rd ed. The Science Press.
- Cattell, J. M. (1943). The description of personality: Basic traits resolved into clusters. *The Journal of Abnormal and Social Psychology, 38*(4), 476-506. https://psycnet.apa.org/doi/10.1037/h0054116
- Cattell, J. M. (1993). The distribution of American men of science in 1932. *Science, 77*, 264-270. https://doi.org/10.1126/science.77.1993.264
- Cattell, J. M. (1981). An education in psychology: *James McKeen Cattell's and letter from Germany and England, 1880-1888*. 1st ed. MIT Press.
- Cattell, J. M. (1928). Early psychological laboratories. *Science, 67,* 543-548. https://doi.org/10.1126/science.67.1744.543
- Cattell, J. M. (1948). Mental tests and measurements, 1890. In W. Dennis (ed), *Readings in the history of*

psychology, 347-354. https://psycnet.apa.org/doi/10.1037/11304-040

- Cattell, J. M. (1890). Mental tests and measurements. *Oxford University Press, 15*(59), 373-381. https://www.jstor.org/stable/2247264#:~:text=https%3A//www.jstor.org/stable/2247264
- Cattell, J. M. (1917). Our psychological association and research. *Science, 45*(1160), 275-284. https://doi.org/10.1126/science.45.1160.275
- Cattell, J. M. (1886). *Psychometrics untersuchungen.* https://psychologie.lw.uni-leipzig.de/wundt/opera/cattell/psymtrik/PSYMETUI.htm
- Cattell, R. B., & Horn, J. L. (1978). A check on the theory of fluid and crystallized intelligence with the description of new subtest designs. *Journal of Educational Measurement.* https://doi.org/10.1111/j.1745-3984.1978.tb00065.x
- Cattell, R. B., & Horn, J. L. (1966). Refinement and test of the theory of fluid and crystallized general intelligence. *Journal of Educational Psychology, 57*(5), 253-270. https://psycnet.apa.org/doi/10.1037/h0023816
- Cattell, R. B. (1961). Fluid and crystallized intelligence. In J. J. Jenkins & D. G. Paterson (eds). *Studies in Individual Differences: The Search for Intelligence,* 738-746. https://psycnet.apa.org/doi/10.1037/11491-064
- Cattell, R. B. (1963). Theory of fluid and crystallized intelligence: A critical experiment. *Journal of*

Educational Psychology, 54(1), 1-22. https://psycnet.apa.org/doi/10.1037/h0046743

- Cattell, R. B. (1967). *The theory of fluid and crystallized general intelligence checked at the 5–6-year-old level.* https://doi.org/10.1111/j.2044-8279.1967.tb01930.x
- Cattell, R., B., Cattell, A. K., & Cattell, H. E. P., (1949). 16PF Fifth Edition Questionnaire (16PF). *APA Psyc Tests.* https://psycnet.apa.org/doi/10.1037/t02933-000
- Cerri, S., Mus, L., & Blandini, F. (2019). Parkinson's disease in women and men: What's the difference? *National Library of Medicine, 9*(3), 501-515. https://doi.org/10.3233/JPD-191683
- Charatan, F., Eaton, F., & Eaton, L. (2002). Woman may face the death penalty in postnatal depression cases. *BMJ, 324*(7338), 634. https://doi.org/10.1136/bmj.324.7338.634
- Chebat, D-R., Heimler, B., Hofsetter, S., & Amedi, A. (2018). The implications of brain plasticity and task selectivity for visual rehabilitation of blind and visually impaired individuals. *The Neuroimaging of Brain Diseases,* 295-321. https://doi.org/10.1007/978-3-319-78926-2_13
- Checknita, D., Ekstrom, T. J., Comasco, E., Nilsson, K. W., Tiihonen, J., & Hodgins, S. (2018). Association of monoamine oxidase A gene first exon methylation with sexual abuse and current depression in women. *Journal of Neural Transmission, 125,* 1053-1064. https://link.springer.com/article/10.1007/s00702-018-

1875-3#citeas:~:text=DOI-,https%3A//doi.org/10.1007/s00702%2D018%2D1875%2D3,-Share%20this%20article

- Cheesman, R., Selzam, S., Ronald, A., Dale, P. S., McAdams, T. A., Eley, T. C., & Plomin, R. (2017). Childhood behavior problems show the greatest gap between DNA-based and twin heritability. *Translational Psychiatry, 7*(1284). https://www.nature.com/articles/s41398-017-0046-x#citeas:~:text=DOI-,https%3A//doi.org/10.1038/s41398%2D017%2D0046%2Dx,-Share%20this%20article
- Chen, C-S., Barnoud, C., & Schieiermann, C. (2021). Peripheral neurotransmitters in the immune system. *Current Opinion in Physiology, 19,* 73-79. https://doi.org/10.1016/j.cophys.2020.09.009
- Cheng, Y., Wu, W., Wang, J., Feng, W., Wu, X., & Li, C. (2011). Reliability and validity of the Repeatable Battery for the Assessment of Neuropsychological Status in community-dwelling elderly. *Arch Med Sci, 7*(5), 850-857. https://doi.org/10.5114/aoms.2011.25561
- Chester, D. S., DeWall, C. N., Derefinko, K. J., Estus, S. Lynam, D. R., Peters, J. R., Jiang, Y. (2016). Looking for reward in all the wrong places: Dopamine receptor gene polymorphisms indirectly affect aggression through sensation-seeking. *Social Neurosicence, 11*(5), 487-494. https://doi.org/10.1080/17470919.2015.1119191
- Chouraeshkenazi, M. M. (2024). Commentary on forensic neuropsychopathological analysis on altered brain structures in combat veterans: A systematic

review. *Journal of Brain and Neurological Disorders, 7*(3). https://doi.org/10.31579/%202642-973X/122

- Chouraeshkenazi, M. M. (2023). Forensic neuropsychopathology and advanced initiatives. *Psychology Today.* https://www.psychologytoday.com/us/blog/in-the-public-interest/202312/forensic-neuropsychopathology-and-advanced-initiatives
- Chouraeshkenazi, M. M. Forensic neuropsychopathological analysis on altered brain structures in combat veterans: A systematic review. *Taylor & Francis: F1000 Research, 12,* 567. https://doi.org/10.12688/f1000research.132840.1
- Chouraeshkenazi, M. M. (2021a). A forensic neuropsychological review on difference brain structures in combat veterans. [Unpublished doctoral dissertation, California Southern University].
- Chouraeshkenazi, M. M. (2024b, October 1). How to become a forensic psychologist and help serve justice. *American Military University.* https://www.amu.apus.edu/area-of-study/arts-and-humanities/resources/how-to-become-a-forensic-psychologist/
- Chouraeshkenazi, M. M. (2021, April 21). Understanding forensic neuropsychopathology. *Psychology Today.* https://www.psychologytoday.com/us/blog/in-the-public-interest/202104/understanding-forensic-neuropsychopathology
- Chouraeshkenazi, M. M. (2021b). Violent crimes among U.S. male service members following 9/11:

How PTSD and comorbid psychopathologies impact force structure, mission readiness, and national security interests. [Master's thesis, American Military University]. Open-Source Network. https://doi.org/10.17605/osf.io/n2P68

- Chvatal, A., & Verkhratsky, A. (2018). An early history of neuroglial research: Personalities. *Neurologia, 1*(1), 245-257. https://doi.org/10.3329/neuroglia1010016
- Cicchetti, D. (1984). The emergence of developmental psychopathology. *Child Development, 55*(1), 1-7.
- Cicchetti, D. (2010). Resilience under conditions of extreme stress: A multilevel perspective. *World Psychiatry, 9*(3), 145.
- Cicchetti, D., & Rogosch, F.A. (2002). A developmental psychopathology perspective on adolescence. *Journal of Consulting and Clinical Psychology, 70*(1), 6.
- Cicchetti, D., & Rogosch, F.A. (1996). Equifinality and multifinality in developmental psychopathology. *Development and Psychopathology, 8*(4), 597-600.
- Cicchetti, D., & Rogosch, F.A. (1997). The role of self-organization in the promotion of resilience in maltreated children. *Development and Psychopathology, 9*(4), 797-815.
- Cicchetti, D., & Shields, A. (2001). Parental maltreatment and emotion dysregulation as risk factors for bullying and victimization in middle school. *Journal of Clinical Psychology, 30*(3), 349-363.

- Clarke, E. (1963). Aristotelian concepts of the form and function of the brain. *Bulletin of the History of Medicine, 37*(1), 1-14. https://www.jstor.org/stable/44446893#:~:text=https%3A//www.jstor.org/stable/44446893
- Clay, R. A. (2021). PSYPACT: 26 states have now passed laws in allowing interstate practice. *American Psychological Association.* https://www.apaservices.org/practice/legal/technology/psypact-interstate-practice-telehealth
- Cleveland Clinic. (2023 April 11). *Post-concussion syndrome.* https://my.clevelandclinic.org/health/diseases/24900-post-concussion-syndrome
- Coelho, C. M., Goncalves-Bradley, D., & Zsido, A. N. (2020). Who worries about specific phobias? A population-based study of risk factors. *Journal of Psychiatric Research, 126,* 67-72. https://doi.org/10.1016/j.jpsychires.2020.05.001
- Collins, A., & Koechlin, E. (2012). Reasoning, learning, and creativity: Frontal lobe function and human decision-making. *PLOS Biology, 10*(3). https://doi.org/10.1371/journal.pbio.1001291
- Collinson, R., Evans, S., Wheeler, M., Brechin, D., Moffitt, J., Hill, G., & Muncer, S. (2017). Confirmatory factor analysis of WAIS-IV in a clinical sample: Examining a bi-factor model. *Journal of Intelligence, 5*(1), 2. https://doi.org/10.3390/jintelligence5010002
- Constandi, M. (2013). Corrupted memory. *University of Michigan: Nature, 500*. p. 268.

https://www.law.umich.edu/special/exoneration/News%20Photos/Loftus%20Article.pdf

- Corkin, S. (1984). Lasting consequences of bilateral medial temporal lobectomy: Clinical course and experimental findings in H.M. *Seminars in Neurology, 4*(2). https://doi.org/10.1055%2Fs-2008-1041556
- Corkin, S. (2002). What's new with the amnesic patient H.M.? *Nature Reviews in Neuroscience, 3*(2), 153-160. https://doi.org/10.1038%2Fnrn726
- Corkin, S., Milner, B., Rasmussen, T. (1970). Somatosensory thresholds – contrasting effects of postcentral-gyrus and posterior parietal-lobe excisions. *Archives of Neurology, 23,* 41-58. http://doi.org/10.1001/archneur.1970.00480250045007
- Corkin, S., Milner, B., & Rasmussen, T. (1964). Effects of different cortical excisions on sensory thresholds in man. *Transaction of the American Neurological Association, 89,* 112-6. PMID: http://www.ncbi.nlm.nih.gov/pubmed/4953345
- Corkin, S., Milner, B., & Taylor, L. (1973). Bilateral sensory loss after unilateral cerebral lesion in man. *Transactions of the American Neurological Association, 98,* 118-22. PMID: http://www.ncbi.nlm.nih.gov/pubmed/4784916
- Cornwell, M., & Greenidge, D. (2020). Sixteen-factor model of personality, the. *Encyclopedia of Personality and Individual Differences,* 4962-4973. https://doi.org/10.1007/978-3-319-24612-3_1266

- Corwin, D., & Olfason, E. (1997). Videotaped discovery of a reportedly unrecallable memory of child sexual abuse: Comparison with a childhood interview videotaped 11 years before. *Child Maltreatment, 2*(2), 91-112. https://doi.org/10.1177%2F1077559597002002001
- Crawford, J. R., Sutherland, D., & Garthwaite, P. H. (2008). On the reliability and standard errors of measurement of contrast measures from the D-KEFS. *Journal of International Neuropsychological Society, 14*(6), 1069-1073. https://doi.org/10.1017/S1355617708081228
- Cross, D., Fani, N., Powers, A., & Bradley, B. (2017). Neurobiological development in the context of childhood trauma. *Clinical Psychology, 24*(2), 111-124. https://psycnet.apa.org/doi/10.1111/cpsp.12198
- Cunningham, R., Crowe, M., Stanley, J., Haitana, T., Pitama, S., Porter, R., Baxter, J., Huria, T., Mulder, R., Clark, M. T. R., & Lacey, C. (2020). Gender and mental health sever use in bipolar disorder: National cohort study. *BJ Psych Open, 6*(6), 138. https://doi.org/10.1192/bjo.2020.117
- Da Cunha-Bang, S., & Knudsen, G. M. (2021). The modulatory role of serotonin on human impulsive aggression. *Biological Psychiatry, 7,* 447-457. https://doi.org/10.1016/j.biopsych.2021.05.016
- Dahlstrom, W. G. (1985). The development of psychological testing. *Psychology Press*. 51.
- Daniel, R., & Pollmann, S. (2014). A universal role of the ventral striatum in reward-based learning: Evidence from human studies. *Neurobiol Learning*

and Memory, 10, 90-100. https://doi.org/10.1016/j.nlm.2014.05.002

- Darby, W. C., Considine, C. M., & Darbey, R. R. (2024). Forensic neurology and the role of neurologists in forensic evaluations. *The Journal of the American Academy of Psychiatry and the Law.* https://jaapl.org/content/early/2024/05/23/JAAPL.240018-24#:~:text=https%3A//doi.org/10.29158/JAAPL.240018%2D24
- Darby, A., Yaffe, G., & Kober, H. (2019). Neuroscientific evidence in the courtroom: A review. *Cognitive Research: Principles and Implications, 4*(40). https://doi.org/10.1186/s41235-019-0179-y
- "Daryl Renard Atkins, Petitioner v. Virginia." (2022). *Cornell Law School: Legal Information Institute*. https://www.law.cornell.edu/supct/html/00-8452.ZO.html
- Daryl Renard Atkins, Petitioner v. Virginia." (2022). *Cornell Law School: Legal Information Institute*. https://www.law.cornell.edu/supct/html/00-8452.ZO.html
- "Data and Statistics on Autism Spectrum Disorder." (2025). Center for Disease Control and Prevention. https://www.cdc.gov/autism/data-research/index.html
- Dautzenberg, G., Lijmer, J., & Beekman, A. (2019). Diagnostic accuracy of the Montreal Cognitive Assessment (MoCA) for cognitive screening in old age psychiatry: Determining cutoff scores in clinical practice. Avoiding spectrum bias caused by healthy

controls. *International Journal Geriatric Psychiatry, 35*(3), 261-269. https://doi.org/10.1002/gps.5227

- Dean, K., Laursen, T. M., Pedersen, C. B., Webb, R. T., Mortensen, P. B., Agerbo, E. (2018). Risk of being subjected to crime, including violent crime, after onset of mental illness. *JAMA Psychiatry, 75*(7), 689-696. https://doi:10.1001/jamapsychiatry.2018.0534
- Death Penalty Information Center. (2018), November 27). *Upholds death sentence based on false psychiatric testimony*. [Updated on 2025, March 14]. https://deathpenaltyinfo.org/texas-court-of-criminal-appeals-upholds-death-sentence-based-on-false-psychiatric-testimony
- Decety, J., Skelly, L. R., & Keihl, K. A. (2013). Brain response to empathy – eliciting scenarios involving pain in incarcerated individuals with psychopathy. *JAMA Psychiatry, 70*(6), 638-645. https://doi.org/10.1001/jamapsychiatry.2013.27
- Delis, D. C., Kramer, J. H., Kaplan, E., & Holdnack, J. A. (2004). Reliability and validity of the Delis-Kaplan Executive Function System: An update. *Journal of the International Neuropsychological Society, 10*(2), 301-3. http://dx.doi.org/10.1017/S1355617704102191
- Delsohn, S. (2014). OTL: Belcher's brain had CTE signs. *ESPN*. https://www.espn.com/espn/otl/story/_/id/11612386/jovan-belcher-brain-showed-signs-cte-doctor-says-report

➢ Deming, P., & Koenigs, M. (2020). Functional neural correlates of psychopathy: A meta-analysis of MRI data. *Translational Psychiatry, 10,* 133. https://www.nature.com/articles/s41398-020-0816-8#citeas:~:text=DOI-,https%3A//doi.org/10.1038/s41398%2D020%2D0816%2D8,-Share%20this%20article

➢ Denney, R. L. (2000). Clinical neuropsychology in the criminal forensic setting. *Journal of Head Trauma Rehabilitation, 15*(2), 804-828.

➢ Denno, D. W. (2003). Who is Andrea Yates? A short story about insanity. *Fordham Law School,* 10 Duke J. Gender L., & Pol'y. https://ir.lawnet.fordham.edu/faculty_scholarship/104/#:~:text=https%3A//ir.lawnet.fordham.edu/faculty_scholarship/104

➢ De Souza, K. Z., & Zago-Gomes, M. P. (2016). Frontal Assessment Battery: A tool for screening minimal hepatic encephalopathy? *World Journal of Hepatology, 8*(30), 1262-1268. https://doi.org/10.4254/wjh.v8.i30.1262

➢ De Vries, L. P., van de Weijer, M. P., Ligthart, L., Willemsen, G., Dolan, C. V., Boomsma, D. I., Baselmans, B. M. L., & Bartels, M. (2020). A comparison of the ASEBA Adult Selt Report (ASR) and the Brief Problem Monitor (BPM/18-59). *Behavior Genet, 50*(5), 363-373. https://doi.org/10.1007/s10519-020-10001-3

➢ Dhillon, H., Dhillon, S., & Dhillon, M. S. (2017). Current concepts in sports injury rehabilitation. *Indian Journal Orthopedic, 51*(5), 529-536. https://doi.org/10.4103/ortho.IJOrtho_226_17

- Dikmen, S. S., Corrigan, J. D., Levin, H. S., MacHamer, J., Stiers, W., & Weisskopf, M. G. (2009). *Cognitive outcome following traumatic brain injury.* https://pure.johnshopkins.edu/en/publications/cognitive-outcome-following-traumatic-brain-injury-5

- DiSabato, D., Quan, N., & Godbout, J. P. (2016). Neuroinflammation: The devil is in the details. *Journal of Neurochemistry, 139*(Suppl 2), 136-153. https://doi.org/10.1111/jnc.13607

- Diwan, S., Cohen, C. I., & Bankole, A. O. (2007). Depression in older adults with schizophrenia spectrum disorders: Prevalence and associated factors. *American Journal of Geriatric Psychiatry, 15,* 991-998. https://doi.org/10.1097/JGP.0b013e31815ae34b

- Dow, D. (2005). Executed on a technicality: Lethal injustice on American's death row. *Beacon Press,* 104-105. https://archive.org/details/executedontechni00davi/page/104/mode/2up

- Downey, C., & Crummy, A. (2022). The impact of childhood trauma on children's wellbeing and adult behavior. *European Journal of Trauma & Dissociation, 6*(1), 100-237. https://doi.org/10.1016/j.ejtd.2021.100237

- Dreisbach, V. (2015, January). Professor Michael Perlin: Power greed and the corruptible seed: Mental disability, prosecutorial misconduct, and the death penalty. *American Academy of Psychiatry and the Law Newsletter, 39*(1), 8.

https://www.aapl.org/docs/newsletter/January%202015%20Issue.pdf

- Dubois, B., Slachevsky, A., Pillon, L. B. (2000). The FAB: A frontal assessment battery at bedside. *Neurology, 55*(11), 1621-6. https://doi.org/10.1212/wnl.55.11.1621
- Dunbar, G. L. (2009). Donald G. Stein: Pioneer in the areas of neuroplasticity and recovery of function. *Journal of Undergraduate of Neuroscience Education, 7*(2), 3-5.
- Dvir, Y., Ford, J. D., Hill, M., & Frazier, J. A. (2015). Childhood maltreatment, emotional dysregulation, and psychiatric comorbidities. *Harvard Rev Psychiatry, 22*(3), 149-161. https://doi.org/10.1097/HRP.0000000000000014
- Eadie, M. J. (2003). A pathology of the animal spirits – The Clinical Neurology of Thomas Willis (1621-1675) part I – background and disorders of intrinsically normal animal spirits. *Journal of Clinical Neuroscience, 10*(1), 14-29. https://doi.org/10.1016/S0967-5868(02)00165-0
- Earl, J. (2018). Florida school shooting among 10 deadliest in modern US history. *Fox News.* https://www.foxnews.com/us/florida-school-shooting-among-10-deadliest-in-modern-us-history
- Edde, M., Leroux, G., Altena, E., & Chanraud, S. (2020). Functional brain connectivity changes across the human life span: From fetal developmental to old age. *Journal of Neuroscience Research, 99,* 236-262. https://onlinelibrary.wiley.com/doi/epdf/10.1002/jnr.24669

- Egelko, B. (2005, January 1). Arkansas judge Oks foster care. *The San Francisco Chronicle*. https://www.sfgate.com/bayarea/article/SAME-SEX-COUPLES-Arkansas-judge-OKs-foster-care-2741981.php
- Ehler, C. L., Schuckit, M. A., Hesselbrock, V., Gilder, D. A., Wills, D., & Bucholz, K. (2022). The clinical course of antisocial behaviors in men and women of three racial groups. *Journal of Psychiatry Res, 151,* 319-327. https://doi.org/10.1016/j.jpsychires.2022.04.038
- Elbogen, E. B., Deniis, P. A., Johnson, S. C. (2016). Beyond mental illness: Targeting stronger and more direct pathways to violence. *Clinical Psychological Science, 4*(5). https://doi.org/10.1177/2167702615619363
- Eling, P. (2019). History of neuropsychological assessment. *Frontiers of Neurology and Neuroscience, 44,* 164-178. http://dx.doi.org/10.1159/000494963
- Elmore, S. L. (2015). The insanity defense: Public opinion and the public's tendency to implicate mental illness in high-profile crimes (Order No. 3614955) *Alliant International University ProQuest Dissertation & Theses*. (1520021550). https://www.proquest.com/dissertations-theses/insanity-defense-public-opinion-publics-tendency/docview/1520021550/se-2
- Emmady, P. D., Schoo, C., & Tadi, P. (2022). *Major neurocognitive disorder (dementia)*. In StatPearls [Internet]. StatPearls Publishing. https://www.ncbi.nlm.nih.gov/books/NBK557444/

- Emory University. (2014). Progesterone offers no significant benefit in traumatic brain injury clinical trials. *Wayback Machine.*
- Ene, I., Wong, K K-Y., & Salali, G. D. (2022). Is it good to be bad? An evolutionary analysis of the adaptive potential of psychopathic traits. *Evolution Human Science, 4,* e7. https://doi.org/10.1017/ehs.2022.36
- Engelhardt, E. (2019). Cerebral localization of higher functions: The period between Thomas Willis and Paul Broca. *Dement Neuropsychol, 13*(2), 238-243. https://doi.org/10.1590/1980-57642018dn13-020014
- El-Shenawy, O.E. (2017). The use of traditional psychological tests in forensic assessment. *Journal of Forensic Legal & Investigative Science.* http://dx.doi.org/10.24966/FLIS-733X/100020
- Enán, A. (2016). The law in philosophy of Jean-Paul Sartre. En Sánchez, Alvaro y, Jacson Reflexoes. *contemporâneas sobre direitos humanos.* https://www.aacademica.org/enan.arrieta.burgos/5
- ESPN. (2007 September 5). *Study suggests brain damage may have affected Benoit.* https://www.espn.com/espn/news/story?id=3005520
- Essig, S. M., Mittenberg, W., Petersen, R. S., Strauman, S., & Cooper, J. T. (2001). Practices in forensic neuropsychology: Perspective of neuropsychologists and trial attorneys. *Archives of Neuropsychology, 16*(3), 271-291. https://doi.org/10.1016/S0887-6177(99)00065-7

- "Ethical Principles of Psychologists and Code of Conduct." (2003). *American Psychological Association*. https://www.apa.org/ethics/code

- Farhane-Medina, N. Z., Luque, B., & Castillo-Mayen, R. (2022). Factors associated with gender and sex differences in anxiety prevalence and comorbidity: A systematic review. *Sage Journals*. https://doi.org/10.1177/00368504221135469

- Faraone, S. V., & Larsson, H. (2018). Genetics of attention deficit hyperactivity disorder. *Molecular Psychiatry, 24*(4), 562-575. https://doi.org/10.1038/s41380-018-0070-0

- Farreras, I. G. (2019). History of mental illness. *General Psychology: Academia.*

- Fateh, A. A., Huang, W., Hassan, M., Zhuang, Y., Lin, J., Luo, Y., Yang, B., Zeng, H. (2023). Default mode network connectivity and social dysfunction in children with attention-deficit/hyperactivity disorder. *International Journal of Clinical Health Psychology, 23*(4), 100-393. https://doi.org/10.1016/j.ijchp.2023.100393

- Feindel, W. (2004). Soul made flesh: The English Civil War and the mapping of the mind. *Brain, 127*(10), 2373-2377. https://doi.org/10.1093/brain/awh304

- Fergusson, D. M., Boden, J. M., Horwood, L. J., Miller, A. L., & Kennedy, M. A. (2011). MAOA abuse exposure and antisocial behavior: a 30-year longitudinal study. *Br J Psychiatry, 198*(6), 457-463. https://doi.org/10.1192/bjp.bp.110.086991

- Filho, R. V. T. (2020). Phineas Gage's great legacy. *Derment Neuropsychologia, 14*(4), 419-421. https://doi.org/10.1590/1980-57642020dn14-040013

- Fioramonti, X., & Penicaud, L. (2018). Carbohydrates and the brain: Roles and impact. *Intechopen.* https://doi.org/10.5772/intechopen.88366

- Fischer, K. A., Torrico, T. J., & Hany, M. (2024, February 20). *Antisocial personality disorder*. InStat Pearls. Treasure Island. https://www.ncbi.nlm.nih.gov/books/NBK546673/

- Flaherty, S. C., & Sadler, L. S. (2010). A review of attachment theory in the context of adolescent parenting. *Journal Pediatric Health Care, 25*(2), 114-121. https://doi.org/10.1016/j.pedhc.2010.02.005

- Flanagan, D. P., & Dixon, S. G. (2014). The Cattell-Horn-Carroll theory of cognitive abilities. *Wiley Online Library.* https://doi.org/10.1002/9781118660584.ese0431

- Fischer, C. E., & Liberman, J. A. (2013). Getting the facts straight about gun violence and mental illness: Putting passion before fear. *Ann Intern Med, 159*(6), 423-424.

- Floyd, A. E., & Gupta, V. (2023, April 24). *Minnesota Multiphasic Personality Inventory*. In StatPearls. https://www.ncbi.nlm.nih.gov/books/NBK557525/

- Follman, M. (2024). Lessons from a mass shooter's mother. *Mother Jones.* https://www.motherjones.com/criminal-justice/2024/05/threat-assessment-mass-shooting-elliot-rodger-isla-vista-mother/

- Fonte, A., & Coutinho, B. (2021). Seasonal sensitivity and psychiatric morbidity: Study about seasonal affective disorder. *BMC Psychiatry, 21*(317). https://bmcpsychiatry.biomedcentral.com/articles/10.1186/s12888-021-03313-z#:~:text=DOI-,https%3A//doi.org/10.1186/s12888%2D021%2D03313%2Dz,-Share%20this%20article

- Fornaro, M., Clementi, N., & Fornaro, P. (2009). Medicine and psychiatry in Western culture: Ancient Greek myths and modern prejudices. *Annals of General Psychiatry, 8*(21). https://link.springer.com/article/10.1186/1744-859X-8-21#citeas:~:text=DOI-,https%3A//doi.org/10.1186/1744%2D859X%2D8%2D21,-Share%20this%20article

- Foutoulakis, K. N., Siamouli, M., Moysidou, S., Pantoula, E., Moutou, K., Panagiotidis, P., Kemeridou, M., Mavridou, E., Loli, E., Batsiari, E., Preti, A., Tondo, L., Gonda, X., Mobayed, N., Akikskal, K., Akiskal, H., Costa, P. & McCrae, R. (2014). Standardization of the NEO-PI-3 in the Greek general population. *Ann Gen Psychiatry, 13,* 36. https://doi.org/10.1186/s12991-014-0036-9

- Frampton, M. F. (1991). Aristotle's cardiocentric model of animal locomotion. *Journal of the History of Biology, 24*(2), 291-330. https://www.jstor.org/stable/4331175#:~:text=https%3A//www.jstor.org/stable/4331175

- Franzen, S., Papma, J. M., Berg, E., & Nielsen, T. R. (2021). Cross-cultural neuropsychological assessment in the European Union: A Delphi expert study. *Archives of Clinical Neuropsychology, 36*(5), 815-830. https://doi.org/10.1093/arclin/acaa083

- Frederick, R. I., Mikesell, J. W., Otto, R. K., Boone, K. B., Beattey, R. A., Jerry, J., Krauss, J., Daniel, A., & Scroppo, J. (2024). Ethical considerations for demands for evidence in forensic examinations. *American Psychological Association: Professional Psychology: Research and Practice, 55*(3), 179-196. https://psycnet.apa.org/buy/2025-01076-001#:~:text=https%3A//doi.org/10.1037/pro0000581

- Freud, S. (1953a). The interpretation of dreams. In J. Strachey (ed & trans). *The Standard Edition of the Complete Psychological Works of Sigmund, 4-5.* Hogarth (Original work published in 1900).

- Freud, S. (1953b). Three essays on the theory of sexuality. In. J. Strachey (ed & trans.). *The Standard Edition of the Complete Psychological Works of Sigmund Freud, 7,* 125-245. Hogarth. (Original work published in 1905).

- Freud, S. (1916a). *Introduction to Psychoanalysis.* Hugo Heller.

- Freud, S. (1916b). Sigmund Freud: Criminals from a sense of guilt. *Short Essay Analysis.*

- Freud, S. (1916). *Vorlesungen zur Einfurhurng in die (in German)*. Hugo Heller.

- Friedman, N. P., & Robbins, T. W. (2022). The role of the prefrontal cortex in cognitive control and executive function. *Neuropsychopharmacology, 47,* 72-89. https://doi.org/10.1038/s41386-021-01132-0

➢ "Frye Standard." (n.d.). *Cornell Law School: Legal Information Institute.* https://www.law.cornell.edu/wex/frye_standard

➢ Fu, Y., Zhao, J., Dong, Y., & Wang, X. (2020). Dry electrodes for human bioelectrical signal monitoring. *MDPI.*

➢ Furman, A. J., Prokhorenko, M., Keaser, M. L., Zhang, J., Chen, S., Mazaheri, A., & Seminowicz, D. A. (2020). Sensorimotor peak alpha frequency is a reliable biomarker of prolonged pain sensitivity. *Cerebral Cortex, 30*(12), 6069-6082. https://doi.org/10.1093/cercor/bhaa124

➢ Gajardo-Vidal, A., Lorca-Puls, D. L., Warner, H., Pshdary, B., Crinion, J. T., Leff, A., Hope, Thomas, M. H., Geva, S., Seghier, M. L., Green, D.W., Bowman, H., & Price, C. J. (2021). Damage to Broca's area does not contribute to long-term speech production outcomes after stroke. *Oxford Academic: Brain Neuroinflammation Collection, 144*(3), 817-832. https://doi.org/10.1093/brain/awaa460

➢ Galea, I. (2021). The blood-brain barrier in systemic infection and inflammation. *Cellular & Molecular Immunology, 18,* 2489-2501. https://www.nature.com/articles/s41423-021-00757-x#citeas:~:text=DOI-,https%3A//doi.org/10.1038/s41423%2D021%2D00757%2Dx,-Share%20this%20article

➢ Galetto, V., & Sacco, K. (2017). Neuroplastic changes induced by cognitive rehabilitation in traumatic brain injury: A review. *Neuroehabil Neural Repair, 31*(9), 800-813. https://doi.org/10.1177/1545968317723748

- Galima, S. V., Vogel, S. R., & Kowalski, A. W. (2020). Seasonal affective disorder: Common questions and answers. *American Family Physician, 102*(11), 668-672. https://www.aafp.org/pubs/afp/issues/2020/1201/p668.html

- Gao, C., Jiang, J., Tan, Y., & Chen, S. (2023). Microglia in neurodegenerative diseases: Mechanism and potential therapeutic targets. *Signal Transduction and Targeted Therapy, 8*(359). https://www.nature.com/articles/s41392-023-01588-0

- Garcia, C., Leahy, B., Corradi, K., & Forchetti, C. (2008). Component structure of the Repeatable Battery for the Assessment of Neuropsychological Status in dementia. *Archives of Clinical Neuropsychology, 23*(1), 63-72. https://doi.org/10.1016/j.acn.2007.08.008

- Garcia-Madruga, J. A., & Gomez-Veiga, I., & Vila, J. O. (2016). Executive functions and the improvement of thinking abilities: The intervention in reading comprehension. *Frontiers in Psychology, 7,* 58. https://doi.org/10.3389/fpsyg.2016.00058

- Garr, A. K. (2021). The role of the ventromedial prefrontal cortex in moral cognition: A value-centric hypothesis. *Philosophical Psychology,* 970-987. https://doi.org/10.1080/09515089.2023.2166820

- Garrigan, B., Adlam, A.L.R., Langdon, P. E. (2018). Moral decision-making and moral development: Toward an integrative framework. *Developmental Review, 49,* 80-100. https://doi.org/10.1016/j.dr.2018.06.001

- Garrigan, B., Adlam, A. L. R., & Langdon, P. E. (2016). The neural correlates of moral decision-making: A systematic review and meta-analysis of moral evaluations and response decision judgments. *Brain and Cognition, 106,* 88-97. https://doi.org/10.1016/j.bandc.2016.07.007
- Gavett, B. E., Stern, R. A., & McKee, A. C. (2011). Chronic traumatic encephalopathy: A potential late effect of sport-related concussive and subconcussive head trauma. *Clinical Sports Medicine, 30*(1), 179-88. https://doi.org/10.1016/j.csm.2010.09.007
- Geddes, J. F., Vowles, G. H., Nicoll, J. A., & Revesz, T. (1999). Neural cytoskeletal changes are an early consequence of repetitive head injury. *Acta Neuropathology, 98*(2), 171-8. https://doi.org/10.1007/s004010051066
- Gelegen, V., & Tamam, L. (2018). Prevalence and clinical correlates of intermittent explosive disorder in Turkish psychiatric outpatients. *Comprehensive Psychiatry, 83,* 64-70. https://doi.org/10.1016/j.comppsych.2018.03.003
- General Hospital Psychiatry. (2020). Delusional disorder. *ScienceDirect.* https://www.sciencedirect.com/topics/medicine-and-dentistry/delusional-disorder
- Genovese, A., & Butler, M. G. (2023). The Autism Spectrum: Behavioral, psychiatric, and genetic associations. *Genes (Basel), 14*(3), 677. https://doi.org/10.3390/genes14030677
- Georgiev, D. D., Georgieva, I., Gong, Z., Nanjappan, V., & Georgiev, G. V. (2021). Virtual reality for

neurorehabilitation and cognitive enhancement. *Brain Science, 11*(2), 221. https://doi.org/10.3390/brainsci11020221

- Ghiasi, N., Azhar, Y., & Singh, J. (2023). Psychiatric illness and criminality. In StatPearls [Internet]. *National Library of Medicine.* https://www.ncbi.nlm.nih.gov/books/NBK537064/
- Gilandas, A. J., & Touyz, S. W. (1983). Forensic neuropsychology: A selective introduction. *Journal of Forensic Science, 28*(3), 713-723. https://doi.org/10.1520/JFS11567J
- Gillett, G. (2018). From Aristotle to cognitive neuroscience. *Library of Congress.*
- Gilmore, J. H., Knickmeyer, R. C., & Wei, G. (2018). Imaging structure and functional brain development in early childhood. *Nature Reviews Neuroscience, 19,* 123-137. https://doi.org/10.1038/nrn.2018.1
- Giza, C. C., & Hovda, D. A. (2014). The new neurometabolic cascade of concussion. *Neurosurgery, 4*(4), 24-33. https://doi.org/10.1227/neu.0000000000000505
- Gloor, P., Jasper, H., & Milner, B. (1956). Higher functions of the nervous system. *Annual Review of Physiology, 18,* 359-86. http://doi.org/10.1146/annurev.ph.18.030156.002043
- Goh, W. Y., Chan, D., Ali, N. B., Chew, A. P., Chuo, A., Chan, M., & Lim, W. S. (2019). Frontal Assessment Battery in early cognitive impairment: Psychometric property and factor structure. *The Journal of Nutrition, Health and Aging, 23*(10), 966-972. https://doi.org/10.1007/s12603-019-1248-0

- Gonzalez, R., Kallis, C., & Coid, J.W. (2016). *Chapter 5 – neurodevelopmental disorders and violence: Improving risk management for violence in mental health services: A multimethod approach*. In: StatPearls [Internet] StatPearls Publishing. https://www.ncbi.nlm.nih.gov/books/NBK396481/
- Gonazalo, J. R. L., & Gonzalo, F. I. (2021). Brain dynamics: The brain activity to the dynamic conditions of nervous excitability. *Universidad Complutense Madrid, 1.*
- Graham, N. S. N., & Sharp, D. J. (2019). Understanding neurodegeneration after traumatic brain injury: From mechanism to clinical trials in dementia. *Journal of Neurology, Neurosurgery, & Psychiatry, 90*(11). https://jnnp.bmj.com/content/90/11/1221
- Grant, D. A., & Berg, E. A. (2014). *Wisconsin Card Sorting Test*. https://doi.org/10.1037%2Ft31298-000
- Gray, K. M. (2013). Atypical Autism. In Volkmar, F. R. (ed). *Encyclopedia of Autism Spectrum Disorders,* 304-309.
- Green, R. R., Jacobson, D. A., Waggoner, J. W., & Armistead, P. (2017). Neuropsychology in the military. *Handbook of Military Psychology,* 137-154. http://dx.doi.org/10.1007/978-3-319-66192-6_10
- Green, C. D. (2017). The principles of psychology: William James (1890). *York University: Classics in the History of Psychology*. http://psychclassics.yorku.ca/James/Principles/prin4.htm

- Greenberg, E., Tung, E. S., Gauvin, C., Osiecki, L., Yang, K. G., Curley, E., Essa, A., et al. (2017). Prevalence and predictors of hair pulling disorder and excoriation disorder in Tourette Syndrome. *Europe Child Adolescence Psychiatry, 27*(5), 569-579. https://doi.org/10.1007/s00787-017-1074-z

- Gregory, H. (2020). Making a murderer: Media renderings of brain injury and Aaron Hernandez as a medical and sporting subject. *Soc Sci Med, 244,* 112-598. https://doi.org/10.1016/j.socscimed.2019.112598

- Grimm, O., Kranz, T. M., & Reif, A. (2020). Genetics of ADHD: What should the clinician know? *Current Psychiatry Rep, 22*(4). https://doi.org/10.1007/s11920-020-1141-x

- Grisso, T., & Kavanaugh, A. K. (2016). Prospects for developmental evidence in juvenile sentencing based on *Miller v. Alabama. American Psychological Association: Psychology, Public Policy, & Law, 22*(3), 235-249.

- Grisson, T. (1986). *Evaluating competencies: Forensic assessments and instruments*. Plenum.

- Grisson, T. (2003). *Evaluating competencies: Forensic assessments and instruments. 2nd ed.* Kluwer/Plenum.

- Groshow, R., Terry, D. P., Iverson, G. L., DiGregorio, H., Dairi, I., et al. (2024). Perceived chronic traumatic encephalopathy and suicidality in former professional football players. *JAMA Neurology, 81*(11), 1130-1139. https://jamanetwork.com/journals/jamaneurology/fullarticle/2824064#:~:text=11)%3A1130%2D1139.-

,doi%3A10.1001/jamaneurol.2024.3083,-editorial%20comment%20icon

- Grove, W. M., Eckert, E. D., Heston, L., Bouchard, T. J., Segal, N., Lykken, D. Y. (1990). Heritability of substance abuse and antisocial behavior: A study of monozygotic twins reared apart. *Biological Psychiatry, 27,* 1293-1304.
- Gruevska, J. (2022). Analysis and/or interpretation in neurophysiology? A transatlantic discussion between F.J.J Buytendijk and K. S. Lashley, 1929-1932, *55,* 321-347. https://doi.org/10.1007/s10739-022-09680-x
- Gowensmith, W. M. (2019). Resolution or resignation: The role of forensic mental health professionals amidst the competency services crisis. *Psychology Public Policy Law, 25,* 1-14. https://psycnet.apa.org/doi/10.1037/law0000190
- The Guardian. (2025). *New images show Aaron Hernandez suffered from an extreme case of CTE.* https://www.theguardian.com/sport/2017/nov/09/aaron-hernandez-cte-brain-damage-photos
- Guest, P. C. (2016). Psychiatric disorders as "whole body" diseases. *Biomarkers and Mental Illness.* https://doi.org/10.1007/978-3-319-46088-8_1
- Guilmette, D., Faust, K., & Arkes, H. R. (1990). A national survey of psychologists who offer neuropsychological services. *Archives of Clinical Neuropsychology, 5,* 373-392.
- Guinea, S. F. (2001). Forensic neuropsychology: Principle issues and applications. *Rev Neurology, 32*(8), 783-7.

- Guina, J., Hernandez, C., Witherell, J., Cowan, A., Dixon, D., King, I., & Gentile, J.P. (2022). Neurodevelopmental disorders, criminality, and criminal responsibility. *The Journal of the American Academy of Psychiatry and the Law*. https://jaapl.org/content/early/2022/07/20/JAAPL.210103-21#:~:text=https%3A//doi.org/10.29158/JAAPL.210103%2D21

- Gurven, M., von Rueden, C., Massenkoff, M., Kaplan, H., Vie, M. L. (2012). How universal is the big five? Testing the five-factor mode of personality variation among Forager-Farmer in the Bolivian Amazon. *Journal of Personality Social Psychology, 104*(2), 354-370. https://doi.org/10.1037/a0030841

- Guskiewicz, K. M., Marshall, S. W., Bailes, J., McCrea, M., Harding, H. P., Matthews, A., Mihalik, J. R., & Cantu, R. C. (2007). Recurrent concussion and risk of depression in retired professional football players. *Medical Science Sports Exercise, 39*(6), 903-9. https://doi.org/10.1249/mss.0b013e3180383da5

- Hagaiescu, S. M. (2021). The connection between traumatic brain injury (TBI) and Attention Deficit/Hyperactivity Disorder, therapeutic approaches. *Scientific Research, 12*(8). https://doi.org/10.4236/psych.2021.128081

- Hainsworth, A. H., Markus, H. S., & Schneider, J. A. (2023). Cerebral small vessel disease, hypertension, and vascular contributions to cognitive impairment and dementia. *Cerebral Small Vessel Disease, Hypertension, and Vascular Contributions to Cognitive Impairment and Dementia, 81*(1).

https://doi.org/10.1161/HYPERTENSIONAHA.123.19943

➢ Hajar, R. (2012). The air of history: Early medicine to Galen (Part I). *Heart Views, 13*(3), 120-128. https://doi.org/10.4103/1995-705X.102164

➢ Hakamata, Y., Suzuki, Y., Kobashikawa, H., & Hori, H. (2022). Neurobiology of early life adversity: A systematic review of meta-analyses towards an integrative account of its neurobiological trajectories to mental disorders. *Frontiers in Neuroendocrinology, 65,* 100-994. https://doi.org/10.1016/j.yfrne.2022.100994

➢ Halameh, D. R., Salama, H. Z., LeUnes, E., Feitosa, D., Ansari, Y., Sachwani-Daswani, G. R., & Moisi, M. D. (2024). The role of neuropsychology in traumatic brain injury: Comprehensive literature review. *World Neurosurgery, 183,* 128-143. https://www.sciencedirect.com/science/article/pii/S1878875023017928

➢ Halle, C., Tzani-Pepelasi, C., Ntaniella-Roumpini, P., & Fumagalli, A. (2020). The link between mental health, crime, and violence. *New Ideas in Psychology, 58,* 100-779. https://doi.org/10.1016/j.newideapsych.2020.100779

➢ Halameh, D. R., Husameddin, Z. S., LeUnes, E., Feitosa, D., Ansari, Y., Sachwani-Daswani, G. R., & Moisi, M. D. (2024). The role of neuropsychology in traumatic brain injury: Comprehensive literature review. *World Neurosurgery, 184,* 128-143. https://doi.org/10.1016/j.wneu.2023.12.069

- Hanna, J., Goldschmidt, D., & Flower, K. (2015). 97 of 91 tested ex-NFL players had brain disease linked to head trauma. *CNN Health.* https://www.cnn.com/2015/09/18/health/nfl-brain-study-cte/index.html

- Hany, M., Rehman, B., Rizvi, A., & Chapman, J. (2024 February 23). *Schizophrenia.* In: StatPearls Publishing. https://www.ncbi.nlm.nih.gov/books/NBK539864/

- Harb, F., Liuzzi, M. T., Huggins, A. A., Webb, E. K., Fitzgerald, J. M., Krukowski, J. L., deRoon-Cassin, T. A., & Larson, C. L. (2024). Childhood maltreatment and amygdala-mediated anxiety and posttraumatic stress following adult trauma. *Biological Psychiatry Global Open Science, 4*(4), 100-312. https://doi.org/10.1016/j.bpsgos.2024.100312

- Hare, R. D. (2003). *The Hare Psychopathy Checklist-Revisited.* Multi-Health System.

- Harenbrock, J., Holling, H., Reid, G., & Koychev, I. (2023). A meta-analysis of the relationship between sleep and β-amyloid biomarkers in Alzheimer's disease. *Biomarkers in Neuropsychiatry, 9,* 100068. https://doi.org/10.1016/j.bionps.2023.100068

- Harms, M. B., & Pollak, S. D. (2023). Prefrontal cortex: Emotion regulation. *Science Direct.* https://www.sciencedirect.com/topics/medicine-and-dentistry/prefrontal-cortex

- Hartlage, L. C., & Stern, B. H. (2010). Historical influences in forensic neuropsychology. In A. M. Horton, Jr., & L. C. Hartlage. (eds). *Handbook of*

Forensic Neuropsychology. 2nd ed. 33-55. Springer Publishing Company.

- Harvard University. (n.d.). *Hugo Münsterberg 1813-1916*. https://psychology.fas.harvard.edu/people/hugo-m%C3%BCnsterberg
- Harvard University. (2025). *Karl Lashley (1890-1958): The representation of processing in the mammalian cerebral cortex*. https://psychology.fas.harvard.edu/people/karl-lashley
- Hatfield, G. (2008). *Rene Descartes. Stanford Encyclopedia of Philosophy*. https://plato.stanford.edu/entries/descartes/
- Hathaway, W. R., & Newton, B. W. (2023, May 29). *Neuroanatomy, prefrontal cortex*. In StatsPearls. Treasure Island. https://www.ncbi.nlm.nih.gov/books/NBK499919/
- Heilbronner, R. (2010). A status report on the practice of forensic neuropsychology. *The Clinical Neuropsychologist, 18*(2), 312-326. https://doi.org/10.1080/13854040490501574
- Heins, I. M., Troost, P. W., Lindeboom, R., Benninga, M. A., Zwaan, M., van Goudoever, J. B., & Lindauer, R. J. L. (2014). Accuracy of the MacArthur Competence Assessment Tool for Clinical Research (MacCAT-CR) for measuring children's competence to consent to clinical research. *JAMA Pediatrics, 168*(12), 1147-1153. https://jamanetwork.com/journals/jamapediatrics/fulla

rticle/1911002#:~:text=12)%3A1147%2D1153.-,doi%3A10.1001/jamapediatrics.2014.1694,-Abstract

- Herzog, J., & Schmahl, C. (2018). Adverse childhood experiences and the consequences on neurobiological, psychosocial, and somatic conditions across the lifespan. *Frontiers in Psychiatry, 9,* 420. https://doi.org/10.3389/fpsyt.2018.00420
- Heston, L. L. (1966). Psychiatric disorders in foster home reared children of schizophrenics. *British Journal of Psychiatry, 112,* 819-225.
- Hierons, R. (1962). Some priority questions arising from Thomas Willis' work. *Sage Journals.*
- Higley, J. D., Suomi, S. J., Linnoila, M. (1992). A longitudinal assessment of CSF monoamine metabolite and plasma cortisol concentrations in young rhesus monkeys. *Biological Psychiatry, 32,* 127-145.
- Hilal, M. L., Moreau, M. M., Racca, C., Pinherio, V. L., Piguel, N. H., Santoni, M. J., Carvalho, S. D. C., & Blanc, J-M. (2017). Activity-dependent neuroplasticity induced by an enriched environment reverses cognitive deficits in Scribble-deficient mice. *Cerebral Cortex, 1*(27), 5635-5651. https://doi.org/10.1093/cercor/bhw333
- Himelfarb, I. (2019). A primer on standardized testing: History, measurement, classical test theory, item response theory, and equating. *Journal of Chiropractor Education 6, 32*(2), 151-163. https://doi.org/10.7899/JCE-18-22
- Himsl, K. M., Reynolds, B. W., Nitch, S. R., Kinnery, D. I., Lee, K. N., & Britt, III., W. G. (2021). Let's

lower the floor: Clinical utility of the D-KEFS TMT with a forensic psychiatric inpatient population. *Applied Neuropsychology: Adult, 30*(6), 740-748.

- Hiser, J., & Koenigs, M. (2018). The multifaceted role of the ventromedial prefrontal cortex in emotion, decision-making, social cognition, and psychopathology. *Biol Psychiatry, 83*(8), 638-647. https://doi.org/10.1016/j.biopsych.2017.10.030
- Ho, J., Jain, A., & Abbeel, P. (2020). Denoising diffusion probabilistic models. *ACM Digital Library, 574,* 6840-6851.
- Hobart, M. P., Goldberg, R., Bartko, J. J., & Gold, J. M. (1999). Repeatable Battery for the Assessment of Neuropsychological Status as a screening test in schizophrenia, II: convergent/discriminant validity and diagnostic group comparisons. *The American Journal of Psychiatry, 156*(12). https://doi.org/10.1176/ajp.156.12.1951
- Hodgins, S., De Brito, S. A., Chhabra, P., & Cote, G. (2010). Anxiety disorders among offenders with antisocial personality disorders: A distinct subtype? *Canadian Journal of Psychiatry, 55*(12), 784-791. https://journals.sagepub.com/doi/pdf/10.1177/070674371005501206?download=true#:~:text=Historically%2C%20it%20was%20thought%20that,lead%20to%20persistent%20violent%20behaviour.
- Hodo, T. W., Prudente de Aquino, M. T., Shimamoto, A., & Shanker, A. (2020). Critical neurotransmitters in the neuroimmune network. *Frontier in Immunology, 11*. https://doi.org/10.3389/fimmu.2020.01869

- Hogan, R. (2006). *Personality and the fate of organizations*. 1st ed. Psychology Press.
- Hoge, S. K. (2016). Competence to stand trial. An overview. *Indian Journal of Psychiatry, 58*(2), 187-190. https://doi.org/10.4103/0019-5545.196830
- Hom, J. (2003). Forensic neuropsychology: Are we there yet? *Archives of Clinical Neuropsychology, 18*(8), 827-845. https://doi.org/10.1016/S0887-6177(03)00076-3
- Homack, S., Lee, D., & Riccio, C. A. (2005). Test review: Delis-Kaplan executive function system. *Journal of Clinical and Experimental Neuropsychology, 27*(5), 599-609. http://dx.doi.org/10.1080/13803390490918444
- Horn, J. L., & Cattell, R. B. (1967). A difference in fluid and crystallized intelligence. *Acta Psychologica, 26*. 107-129. https://doi.org/10.1016/0001-6918(67)90011-X
- Hostetler, N., Tavares, T. P., Ritchie, M. B., Oliver, L. D., Chen, V. V., Greening, S., Finger, E. C., & Mitchell, D. G. V. (2024). Prefrontal cortex structural and developmental associations with callous-unemotional traits and aggression. *Scientific Reports, 14*. https://www.nature.com/articles/s41598-024-54481-3#citeas:~:text=DOI-,https%3A//doi.org/10.1038/s41598%2D024%2D54481%2D3,-Share%20this%20article
- "Howard v. Arkansas – Decision." (2015). *American Civil Liberties Union.*
- Howlett, J. R., Nelson, L. D., & Stein, M. B. (2021). Mental health consequences of traumatic brain injury.

Biological Psychiatry, 91(5), 413-420. https://doi.org/10.1016/j.biopsych.2021.09.024

- Hsieh, N., Lui, H., Lai, W-H. (2021). Elevated risk of cognitive impairment among older sexual minorities: Do health conditions, health behaviors, and social connections matter? *Gerontologist, 61*(3), 352-362. https://doi.org/10.1093/geront/gnaa136
- Huard, P., & Pozzi, S. (1961). Paul Broca (1824-1880). *JSTOR: d'histoire Des Sciences et de Leurs Applications, 14*(1), 47-86. http://www.jstor.org/stable/23905004
- Husain, W., Haddad, A. J., Husain, M. A., Ghazzawi, H., Trabelsi, K., Ammar, A., Saif, Z., Pakpour, A., & Jahrami, H. (2025). Reliability generalization meta-analysis of the internal consistency of the Big Five Inventory (BFI) by comparing BFI (44 items) and BFI-2 (60 items) versions controlling for age, sex, language. *BMC Psychology, 13*(20). https://bmcpsychology.biomedcentral.com/articles/10.1186/s40359-024-02271-x#citeas:~:text=DOI-,https%3A//doi.org/10.1186/s40359%2D024%2D02271%2Dx,-Share%20this%20article
- Hussey, J., & Allen, D. N. (2017). Halstead-Reitan neuropsychological battery. *Encyclopedia of Clinical Neuropsychology,* 1-6. https://link.springer.com/referenceworkentry/10.1007/978-3-319-56782-2_189-3
- Ibrahim, K., Elibott, J. A., Ventola, P., He, G., Pelphrey, K. A., McCarthy, G., & Sukhodolsky, D. G. (2019). Reduced amygdala-prefrontal functional connectivity in children with autism spectrum disorder and co-occurring disruptive behavior.

Biology, Psychiatry Cognitive Neuroscience Neuroimaging, 4, 1031-1041. https://www.scopus.com/record/display.uri?eid=2-s2.0-85063995051&origin=inward&txGid=ca95d78ec465db6154f13914e3b11f17

- Im, S-Y., Jeong, J., Jin, G., Yeom, J., Jekal, J., Lee, S-I., Cho, J. A., Lee, S., Lee, Y., Kim, D-H., Bae, M., Heo, J., Moon, C., & Lee, C-H. (2019). MAOA variants differ in oscillatory EEG & ECG activities in response to aggression-inducing stimuli. *Science Reports, 9,* 2680. https://www.nature.com/articles/s41598-019-39103-7#citeas:~:text=DOI-,https%3A//doi.org/10.1038/s41598%2D019%2D39103%2D7,-Share%20this%20article
- Ingram, P. B., Armistead-Jehle, P., Herring, T. T., & Morris, C. S. (2023). Cross-validation of the Personality Assessment Inventory (PAI) cognitive bias of scales (CB-SOS) over-reporting indicators in a military sample. *Military Psychology, 36*(2), 192-202. https://doi.org/10.1080/08995605.2022.2160151
- Irfan, N., Nair, A., Bhaskaran, J., Akter, M., & Watts, T. (2022). Review of the current knowledge of Reactive Attachment Disorder. In Stat Pearls [Internet] Stat Pearls Publishing. https://pmc.ncbi.nlm.nih.gov/articles/PMC9736782/
- Jain, A., & Mitra, P. (2023 February 20) *Bipolar disorder*. In StatPearls [Internet]. https://www.ncbi.nlm.nih.gov/books/NBK558998/
- Jain, L., & Torrico, T. J. (2024). *Paranoid Personality Disorder*. In Stat Pearls [Internet] Stat

Pearls Publishing. https://www.ncbi.nlm.nih.gov/books/NBK606107/

- Jammula, V., Rogers, J. L., Vera, E., Christ, A., Leeper, H. E., Acquaye, A., Briceno, N., Choi, A., Grajkowska, E., Levin, J. E., Lindsley, M., Reyes, J., Roche, K. N., Timmer, M., Boris, L., Burton, E., Lollo, N., Panzer, M., Smith-Cohn, M. A., Penas-Prado, M., Pillai, V., Theeler, B. J., Wu, J., Gilbert, M. R. & Armstrong, T. S. (2022). The Montreal Cognitive Assessment (MoCA) in neuro-oncology: A pilot study of feasibility and utility in telehealth and in-person clinical assessments. *Neuro-Oncology Practice, 9*(5), 429-440. https://doi.org/10.1093/nop/npac038
- Janak, P. H., Tye, K. M. (2015). From circuits to behavior in the amygdala. *Nature, 517*(7534), 284-292. https://doi.org/10.1038/nature14188
- Jauhar, S., Johnstone, M., & McKenna, P. J. (2022). Schizophrenia. *Lancet, 399*(10323), 473-486. https://doi.org/10.1016/s0140-6736(21)01730-x
- Jawbri, K. H., & Sharma, S. (2021). Physiology, cerebral cortex functions. In: StatPearls. *National Center for Biotechnology Information.* https://www.ncbi.nlm.nih.gov/books/NBK538496/
- Jiang, C., Xue, G., Yao, S., Zhang, X., Chen, W., Cheng, K., Zhang, Y., Li, Z., Zhao, G., Zheng, X., & Bai, H. (2023). Psychometric properties of the post-traumatic stress disorder checklist for DSM-5 (PCL-5) in Chinese stroke patients. *BMC Psychiatry, 23,* 16. https://doi.org/10.1186/s12888-022-04493-y

- Jicol, C., Lloyd-Esenkaya, T., Proulx, M. J., Lange-Smith, S., Scheller, M., O'Neill, E., & Petrini, K. (2020). Efficiency of sensory substitution devices alone and in combination with self-motion for spatial navigation in sighted and visually impaired. *Frontiers in Psychology*. https://doi.org/10.3389/fpsyg.2020.01443
- Jin, H., Li, M., Jeong, E., Castro-Martinez, F., & Zuker, C. S. (2024). A body-brain circuit that regulates inflammatory responses. *Nature, 630*, 695-703. https://www.nature.com/articles/s41586-024-07469-y#citeas:~:text=DOI-,https%3A//doi.org/10.1038/s41586%2D024%2D07469%2Dy,-Share%20this%20article
- Johns Hopkins Medicine. (2025). *Brain anatomy and how the brain works*. https://www.hopkinsmedicine.org/health/conditions-and-diseases/anatomy-of-the-brain#:~:text=Weighing%20about%203%20pounds%20in,including%20neurons%20and%20glial%20cells.
- Jones-Gotman, M., & Milner, B. (1978). Right, temporal-lobe contribution to image-mediated verbal learning. *Neuropsychologia, 16,* 61-71. http://doi.org/10.1016/0028-3932(78)90043-X
- Jones-Gotman, M., & Milner, B. (1977). Design fluency: The invention of nonsense drawings after focal cortical lesions. *Neuropsychologia, 15,* 653-74. http://doi.org/10.1016/0028-3932(77)90070-7
- Jongsma, H. E., Turner, C., Kirkbride, J. B. (2019). International incidence of psychotic disorders: A systematic review and meta-analysis. *Lancet, 4*(5),

e229-e244. https://doi.org/10.1016/s2468-2667(19)30056-8

- Jovanović, G. (2021). How psychology repressed its founding father, William Wundt. *Hu Arenas, 4*. 32-47. https://doi.org/10.1007/s42087-021-00186-2

- Jurick, S. M., Eglit, G. M. L., Delis, D. C., Bondi, M. W., & Jak, A. J. (2022). D-KEFS trail-making test as an embedded performance validity measure. *Journal of Clinical and Experimental Neuropsychology, 44*(1), 62-72. https://doi.org/10.1080/13803395.2022.2073334

- Kandola, A., Hendrikse, J., Lucassen, P. J., Yucel, M. (2016). Aerobic exercise as a tool to improve hippocampal plasticity and function in humans: Practical implications for mental health treatment. *Sec Brain Health and Clinical Neuroscience, 10*. https://doi.org/10.3389/fnhum.2016.00373

- Kanen, J. W., Arntz, F. E., Yellowlees, R., Cardinal, R. N., Price, A., Christmas, D. M., Apergis-Schoute, A. M., Sahakian, B. J., & Robbins, T. W. (2021). Serotonin depletion amplifies distinct human social emotions as a function of individual differences in personality. *Translational Psychiatry, 11*(81). https://www.nature.com/articles/s41398-020-00880-9#citeas:~:text=DOI-,https%3A//doi.org/10.1038/s41398%2D020%2D00880%2D9,-Share%20this%20article

- Kania, B. F., Wronska, D., & Zieba, D. (2017). Introduction to neural plasticity mechanism. *Journal of Behavioral and Brain Science, 7*(2). https://doi.org/10.4236/jbbs.2017.72005

- Kanser, R. J., Rapport, L. J., Hanks, R. A., & Patrick, S. D. (2021). Utility of WAIS-IV digit span indices as measures of performance validity in moderate to severe traumatic brain injury. *The Clinical Neuropsychologist, 36*(7), 1950-1963. https://doi.org/10.1080/13854046.2021.1921277

- Kaplan, R., & Saccuzzo, D. (2017). *Psychological testing: Principles, applications, and issues*. 9th ed. Cengage Learning.

- Kciuk, M., Kruczkowska, W., Galeziewska, J., Wanke, K., Kaluzinska-Kolat, Z., Aleksandrowicz, M., & Kontek, R., (2024). Alzheimer's disease as Type 3 diabetes: Understanding the link and implications. *International Journal of Molecular Sciences, 25*(22), 11955. https://doi.org/10.3390/ijms252211955

- Kendler, K. S. (2020). Philippe Pinel and the foundations of modern psychiatric nosology. *Psychol Med., 50*(16), 2667-2672. https://doi.org/10.1017/s0033291720004183

- Kentner, A. C., Lambert, K. G., Hannan, A. J., & Donaldson, S. T. (2017). Editorial: Environmental enrichment: Enhancing neural plasticity, resilience, and repair. *Frontiers in Behavioral Neuroscience, 13,* 75. https://doi.org/10.3389/fnbeh.2019.00075

- Kerage, D., Sloan, E. K., Mattarollo, S. R., McCombe, P. A. (2019). Interaction of neurotransmitters and neurochemicals with lymphocytes. *Journal of Neuroimmunology, 332,* 99-111. https://doi.org/10.1016/j.jneuroim.2019.04.006

- Kiehl, K. A., Smith, A. M., Hare, R. D., Mendrek, A., Forster, B. B., Brink, J., & Liddle, P. F. (2001). Limbic abnormalities in affective processing by criminal psychopaths as revealed by functional magnetic resonance imaging. *Biological Psychiatry, 50*(9), 677-684. https://doi.org/10.1016/s0006-3223(01)01222-7

- Kiehl, K. A., Smith, A. M., Mendrek, A., Forster, B. B., Brink, J., & Liddle, P. F. (2001). Limbic abnormalities in affective processing by criminal psychopaths as revealed by functional magnetic resonance imaging. *Biology Psychiatry, 50*(9), 677-84. https://doi.org/10.1016/s0006-3223(01)01222-7

- Kim, J. G., Gregory, E., Landau, B., McCloskey, M., Turk-Browne, N. B., Kaster, S. (2020). Function of ventral visual cortex after bilateral media temporal damage. *Progress in Neurology, 191,* 101-819. https://doi.org/10.1016/j.pneurobio.2020.101819

- Kim, J-S., Kim, O-L., Seo, W-S., Ko, B-H., & Bai, D-S. (2009). Memory dysfunctions after mild and moderate traumatic brain injury: Comparison between patients with and without frontal lobe injury. *National Library of Medicine: National Center for Biotechnology Information.* https://doi.org/10.3340/jkns.2009.46.5.459

- King, S., & Mason, B. In. Carducci, B. J., Nave, C., Mio, J. S., & Riggio, R. E. (eds). (2020). *Myers Briggs Type Indicator, in Wiley-Blackwell encyclopedia and individual differences*. Vol II. Wiley Blackwell.

- Kittleson, A. R., Woodward, N. D., Heckers, S., & Sheffield, J. M. (2024). The insula: Leveraging cellular and systems level research to better understand its roles in health and schizophrenia. *Neuroscience & Biobehavioral Reviews, 160,* 105-643. https://doi.org/10.1016/j.neubiorev.2024.105643

- Knoll IV., James, L., & Annas, G. D. (2016). Mass shootings and mental illness. In L. H. God & R. I. Simon (Eds). *Gun Violence and Mental Illness,* American Psychiatric Association, pp. 81-104.
- Koenen, K. C., et al. (2017). Posttraumatic stress disorder in the world mental health surveys. In Stat Pearls [Internet]. Stat Pearls Publishing. https://pmc.ncbi.nlm.nih.gov/articles/PMC6034513/
- Koenigs, M. (2012). The role of prefrontal cortex in psychopathy. *Rev Neuroscience, 23*(3), 253-262. https://doi.org/10.1515/revneuro-2012-0036
- Kolb, B., & Milner, B. (1981). Observations on spontaneous facial expression after focal cerebral excisions and after intracarotid injection of sodium amytal. *Neuropsychologia, 19,* 505-14. http://doi.org/10.1016/0028-3932(81)90017-8
- Kolb, B., Milner, B., & Taylor, L. (1983). Perception of faces by patients with localized cortical excisions. *Canadian Journal of Psychology, 37,* 8-18. http://doi.org/10.1037/H0080697
- Kolb, B., & Milner, B. (1981). Performance of complex arm and facial movements after focal brain lesions. *Neuropsychologia, 19,* 491-503. http://doi.org/10.1016/0028-3932(81)90016-6
- Kolb, B. (2022). Brenda Milner: Pioneer of the study of the human frontal lobes. *Frontiers in Human*

Neuroscience, 15. https://doi.org/10.3389/fnhum.2021.786167

- Kolk, S. M., & Rakic, P. (2021). Development of prefrontal cortex. *Neuropsychopharmacology, 47,* 41-57. https://doi.org/10.1038/s41386-021-01137-9
- Kolla, N. J., & Bortolato, M. (2020). The role of monoamine oxidase A in the neurobiology of aggressive, antisocial, and violent behavior: A tale of mice and men. *Prog Neurobiology, 194,* 101-875. https://doi.org/10.1016/j.pneurobio.2020.101875
- Koolschijn, M., Jankovic, M., & Bogaerts, S. (2023). The impact of childhood maltreatment on aggression, criminal risk factors, and treatment trajectors in forensic psychiatric patients. *Frontiers in Psychiatry, 14,* 1128020. https://doi.org/10.3389/fpsyt.2023.1128020
- Kopp, B., Lange, F., & Steinke, A. (2019). The reliability of the Wisconsin Card Sorting Test in clinical practice. *Assessment, 28*(1), 248-263. https://doi.org/10.1177/1073191119866257
- Kopp, B., Rosser, N., Tabeling, S., Sturenburg, H. J., de Haan, B., Karnath, H-O., & Wessel, K. (2013). *Performance* on the Frontal Assessment Battery is sensitive to frontal lobe damage in stroke patients. *BMC Neurology, 13*(179). https://bmcneurol.biomedcentral.com/articles/10.1186/1471-2377-13-179#citeas:~:text=DOI-,https%3A//doi.org/10.1186/1471%2D2377%2D13%2D179,-Share%20this%20article
- Kumar, K. S., Samuelkameleshkumar, S., Viswanathan, A., & Macaden, A. S. (2017).

Cognitive rehabilitation for adults with traumatic brain injury to improve occupational outcomes. *Cochrane Database Syst Rev, (6)*. https://doi.org/10.1002/14651858.CD007935.pub2

- Labrakakis, C. (2023). The role of the insular cortex in pain. *International Journal of Molecular Sciences, 24*(6), 5736. https://doi.org/10.3390/ijms24065736
- LaDuke, C., DeMatteo, D., Kilbrun, K., & Swirsky-Sacchetti, T. (2012). Clinical neuropsychology in forensic contexts: Practitioners' experience, training, and practice. *Professional Psychology: Research and Practice, 43*(5), 503-509. https://psycnet.apa.org/doi/10.1037/a0028161
- La Fontaine, E. T. (2002). A dangerous preoccupation with future danger: Why expert predictions of future dangerousness in capital cases are unconstitutional. *Boston College, 44,* 207. https://lira.bc.edu/files/pdf?fileid=d06ab302-9fc0-493b-9173-1965286ef878
- Lapham, G. T., Matson, T. E., & Bobb, J. F. (2023). Prevalence of Cannabis Use and Adults in a US State Where Recreational Cannabis. *JAMA Network Open, 6*(8), e2328934. https://jamanetwork.com/journals/jamanetworkopen/fullarticle/2808874#google_vignette
- The LA Times. (2013). *'Night Stalker': What do you remember about him?* https://www.latimes.com/local/lanow/la-me-ln-night-stalker-what-do-you-remember-20130607-story.html

- Leer, A. (2012). Norway readies for its trial of the century. *BBC News.* https://www.bbc.com/news/world-europe-17710355
- Legal Information Institute. (2023). *The American Law Institute's Model Penal Code § 4.01.*

  https://www.law.cornell.edu/wex/model_penal_code_insanity_defense
- Legal Information Institute. (2002). Atkins v. United States. *Cornell Law School.* https://www.law.cornell.edu/supct/html/00-8452.ZS.html
- Legal Information Institute. (n.d.g.). Carrie Jafee, special administrator of Ricky Allen, Sr., deceased, petitioner v. Mary Lu. Redmond et al. *Cornell Law School.* https://www.law.cornell.edu/supct/html/95-266.ZO.html
- Legal Information Institute. (n.d.h.). Daubert et ux., individually and as guardians and litem for Daubert et al., v. Merrell Down Pharmaceuticals, Inc. *Cornell Law School.* https://www.law.cornell.edu/supct/html/92-102.ZS.html
- Legal Information Institute. (n.d.b.). Durham v. United States. *Cornell Law School.* https://casetext.com/case/durham-v-united-states/case-summaries
- Legal Information Institute. (n.d.c.). Frye standard. *Cornell Law School.* https://www.law.cornell.edu/wex/frye_standard
- Legal Information Institute. (n.d.a.). Glen Burton AKE, Petitioner v. Oklahoma. *Cornell Law School.*

https://www.law.cornell.edu/supremecourt/text/470/68

- Legal Information Institute. (n.d.k.). Insanity defense. *Cornell Law School.* https://www.law.cornell.edu/wex/insanity_defense#:~:text=In%201972%2C%20in%20an%20attempt,the%20requirements%20of%20the%20law.%22
- Legal Information Institute. (n.d.i.). Miller v. Alabama (2012). *Cornell Law School.* https://www.law.cornell.edu/supremecourt/text/10-9646
- Legal Information Institute. (n.d.e.). M'Naghten rule. *Cornell Law School.* https://www.law.cornell.edu/wex/m%27naghten_rule
- Legal Information Institute. (n.d.j.). Roper v. Simmons (2005). *Cornell Law School.* https://www.law.cornell.edu/supct/html/03-633.ZS.html
- Legal Information Institute. (n.d.d.). United States v. Hinckley, a recent successful use of the insanity defense. *Cornell Law School.* https://www.law.cornell.edu/background/unabom/hinckley.html
- Lei, L. K. S., Lam, B. Y. H., Chan, C. H., Zou, Z. (2022). Stability of Montreal Cognitive Assessment in individuals with mild cognitive impairment: Potential influence of practice effect. *Journal of Alzheimer's Disease, 87*(3). https://doi.org/10.3233/JAD-220003
- Lennox, J. G. In: Hynek Bartos, King, C. G. eds. (2020). Chapter 10 – why animals must keep their

cool: Aristotle on the need for respiration (and other forms of cooling). *Cambridge University Press*, 217-242. https://doi.org/10.1017/9781108651714.013

- Larrabee, G. J. (2012). Forensic neuropsychology: A scientific approach. *Oxford University Press.*
- Lepore, J. (2015). On evidence: Proving Frye as a matter of law, science, and history. *The Yale Law Journal.* https://www.yalelawjournal.org/essay/on-evidence-proving-frye-as-a-matter-of-law-science-and-history
- Levitt, P. (n.d.). Toxic stress and its impact on early learning and health: Building a formula for human capital development. *Purdue University.* https://www.purdue.edu/hhs/hdfs/fii/wp-content/uploads/2015/07/s_wifis32c02.pdf
- Li, S-T., Chien, W-C., Chung, C-H., & Tzeng, N-S. (2024). Increased risk of acute stress disorder and post-traumatic stress disorder in children and adolescents with autism spectrum disorder: A nation-wide cohort in Taiwan. In Stat Pearls [Internet] Stat Pearls Publishing. https://pmc.ncbi.nlm.nih.gov/articles/PMC10864464/
- Library of Congress. (n.d.). *Eighth Amendment: Cruel and unusual punishment.* https://constitution.congress.gov/browse/amendment-8/
- Lindsey, R. (1985). Dan White, the killer of the San Francisco mayor, a suicide. *The New York Times.* https://www.nytimes.com/1985/10/22/us/dan-white-killer-of-san-francisco-mayor-a-suicide.html

- Liu, X., Cheng, R., Chen, L, Gong, J., Luo, T., Lv, F. (2021). Altered neurovascular coupling in subcortical ischemic vascular disease. *Frontiers in Aging Neuroscience, 13*. https://doi.org/10.3389/fnagi.2021.598365

- Livingston, R. B. (1966). Brain mechanisms in conditioning and learning. *Neurosciences Research Program Bulletin, 4*(3), 349-354.

- Lockhurst, G. J. (2005). Descartes and the pineal gland. *Stanford Encyclopedia of Philosophy*. https://plato.stanford.edu/entries/pineal-gland/

- Lopez, M., Ruiz, M. O., Rovnaghi, C. R., Tam, G. K-Y., Hiscox, J., Gotlib, I. H., Barr, D. A., Carrion, V. G., & Anand, K. J. S. (2021). The social ecology of childhood and early life adversity. *Pediatric Res, 89*(2), 353-367. https://doi.org/10.1038/s41390-020-01264-x

- Lopez-Munoz, F., & Marin, F., & Alamo, C. (2016). History of the pineal gland as a neuroendocrine organ and the discovery of melatonin. *Melatonin, Neuroprotective Agents, and Antidepressants Therapy,* 1-23. https://link.springer.com/chapter/10.1007/978-81-322-2803-5_1#citeas:~:text=DOI-,https%3A//doi.org/10.1007/978%2D81%2D322%2D2803%2D5_1,-Published

- Lowe, R. (2022). The origins of intelligence testing, 1860-1920. *British Journal of Educational Studies, 70*(6), 737-752. https://doi.org/10.1080/00071005.2021.2008866

- Lu, Y., & Temple, J. R. (2019). Dangerous weapons or dangerous people? The temporal associations between gun violence and mental health. *Preventative Medicine, 121,* 1-6. https://doi.org/10.1016/j.ypmed.2019.01.008

- Luriogi, A. J. & Carabell, P. (2024). Psychopathy: A primer for correction professionals. *U.S. Courts, 88*(1). https://www.uscourts.gov/sites/default/files/2024-12/88_1_4.pdf

- MacDonald, H. J., Kleppe, R., Szigetvari, P. D., & Haavik, J. (2024). The dopamine hypothesis for ADHD: An evaluation of evidence accumulated from human studies and animal models. *Frontiers in Psychiatry, 15*. https://doi.org/10.3389/fpsyt.2024.1492126

- Mandler, G. (2011). *A history of modern experimental psychology: From James and Wundt to cognitive science*. MIT Press.

- Marcopulos, B. A., Kaufmann, P., & Patel, A. C. (2024). Forensic neuropsychological assessment. *Behavioral Sciences & the Law.* https://doi.org/10.1002/bsl.2656

- Marder, S. R., & Cannon, T. D. (2019). Schizophrenia. *New England Journal of Medicine, 381*(18), 1753-1761. https://doi.org/10.1056/nejmra1808803

- Maresca, G., Buono, V. L., Anselmo, A., Cardile, D., Formica, C., Latella, D., Quartertone, A., & Corallo, F. (2023). Traumatic brain injury and related antisocial behavioral outcomes: A systematic review.

Medicina (Kaunas), 59(8), 1377. https://doi.org/10.3390/medicina59081377

- Marek, R. J., Block, A. R., & Ben-Porath. (2022). Reliability and validity of Minnesota Multiphasic Personality Inventory – 3 (MMPI-3) scale scores among patients seeking spine surgery. *Psychological Assessment, 34*(4), 379-389.
- Marjani, B., Bey, K., Boberg, J., & Burton, C. (2021). Genetics of obsessive-compulsive disorder. *Psychological Medicine, 51*(13), 2247-2259. https://doi.org/10.1017/S0033291721001744
- Martell, D. A. (1992). Forensic neuropsychology and the criminal law. *American Psychological Association, 16*(3), 313-336.
- Martensen, R. L. (2004). *The brain takes shape: An early history*. Oxford University Press.
- Marzani, G., & Price, A. (2021). Bipolar disorder: Evaluation and treatment. *American Family Physician, 103*(4), 227-239. https://www.aafp.org/pubs/afp/issues/2021/0215/p227.html
- Mateos-Aparicio, P., Rodriguez-Moreno, A. (2019). The impact of studying brain plasticity. *Frontiers in Cellular Neuroscience*. https://doi.org/10.3389/fncel.2019.00066
- Mathes, B. M., Morabito, D. M., & Schmidt, N. B. (2019). Epidemiological and clinical gender differences in OCD. *Current Psychiatry Rep, 21*(5), 36. https://doi.org/10.1007/s11920-019-1015-2

- May, T., Foris, L. A., & Donnally, C. J. (2023). *Second impact syndrome*. In: StatPearls Publishing. https://www.ncbi.nlm.nih.gov/books/NBK448119/

- Mayo Clinic Staff. (2024 October 30). Persistent post-concussive symptoms (post-concussion syndrome). *Mayo Clinic*. https://www.mayoclinic.org/diseases-conditions/post-concussion-syndrome/symptoms-causes/syc-20353352

- McAllister, T., & McCrea, M. (2017). Long-term and neuropsychiatric consequences of repetitive concussion and head-impact exposure. *Journal Athletic Training, 52*(3), 309-317. https://doi.org/10.4085/1062-6050-52.1.14

- McCarthy, J.M., Alexander, R.T., & Chaplin, E. (2023). *Chapter 1 from section 1 – an overview: Definition, epidemiology, and policy issues: Forensic aspects of neurodevelopmental disorders: A clinician's guide*. Cambridge University Press.

- McCrory, P., Meeuwise, W., Johnston, K., Dvorak, J., Aubry, M., Molloy, M., & Cantu, R. (2009). Consensus statement on concussion in sport: The 3rd international conference on concussion in sport held in Zurich, November 2008. *Journal of Athletic Training, 44*(4), 434-48. https://doi.org/10.4085/1062-6050-44.4.434

- McDermott, R., Tingley, D., Cowden, J., Frazzetto, G., & Johnson, D. D. P. (2009). Monoamine oxidase A gene (MAOA) predicts behavioral aggression following provocation. *Proc National Academic Sci USA, 106*(7), 2118-2123. https://doi.org/10.1073/pnas.0808376106

- McIntyre, R. S., & Calabrese, J. R. (2019). Bipolar depression: The clinical characteristics and unmet needs of a complex disorder. *Current Medical Research and Opinion, 35*(11), 1993-2005. https://doi.org/10.1080/03007995.2019.1636017
- McKay, C., Casey, J. E., Wertheimer, J., & Fichtenberg, N. L. (2007). Reliability and validity of the RBANS in a traumatic brain injured sample. *Archives of Clinical Neuropsychology, 22*(1), 91-98. https://doi.org/10.1016/j.acn.2006.11.003
- McKee, A. C., Stern, R. A., Nowinski, C. J., Stein, T. D., Alvarez, V. E., Daneshvar, D. H., Lee, H-S., Wojtowicz, S. M., Hall, G., Baugh, C. M., Riley, D. O., Kubilus, C. A., Cormier, K. A., Jacobs, M. A., Martin, B. R., Abraham, C. R., Ikezu, T., Reichard, R. R., Wolozin, B. L., Budson, A. E., Goldstein, L. E., Kowall, N. W., & Cantu, R. C. (2013). The spectrum of disease in chronic traumatic encephalopathy. *Brain, 136*(Pt 1), 43-64. https://doi.org/10.1093/brain/aws307
- McLaughlin, E. C., & Park, M. (2018). Social paints picture of racist 'professional school shooter.' *CNN News*. https://www.cnn.com/2018/02/14/us/nikolas-cruz-florida-shooting-suspect/index.html
- McLaughlin, K. A., & Lambert, H. K. (2017). Child trauma exposure and psychopathology. *Cur Opin Psychology, 14,* 29-34. https://doi.org/10.1016/j.copsyc.2016.10.004
- McLellan, A. T. (2017). Substance misuse and Substantice Use Disorders: Why do they matter in healthcare? *Trans-Am Clin Climatol Assoc, 128,* 112-

130. PMID:
https://pubmed.ncbi.nlm.nih.gov/28790493/

- McLellan, F. (2006). Mental health and justice: The case of Andrea Yates. *Lancet, 368*(9551), P1951-P1954. https://doi.org/10.1016/S0140-6736(06)69789-4
- McMahon, P., & Alanez, T. (2018, March 7). Nikolas Cruz was indicted on 17 counts of murder and 17 counts of attempted murder. *Sun-Sentinal.* https://www.sun-sentinel.com/2018/03/07/nikolas-cruz-indicted-on-17-counts-of-murder-and-17-counts-of-attempted-murder/
- Mednick, S. A., Gabrielli, W. F., & Hutchins, B. (1984). Genetic influence in criminal convictions: Evidence from an adoption court. *Science, 224,* 891-894.
- Melton, G., Petrila, J., Poythree, N., & Slobogin, C. (1987). *Psychological evaluations for the courts: A handbook for mental health professionals and lawyers*. Guilford.
- Melton, G., Petrila, J., Poythress, N., & Slobogin, C. (1997). *Psychological evaluations for the courts: A handbook for mental health professionals and lawyers*. 2nd ed. Guilford.
- Melton, G., Petrila, J., Poythress, N., & Slobogin, C. (1997). *Psychological evaluations for the courts: A handbook for mental health professionals and lawyers*. 3rd ed. Guilford. Merkley, T. L., Esopenko, C., Zizak, V. S., Bilder, R. M., Strutt, A. M., Tate, D. F., & Irmia, A. (2022). Challenges and Opportunities for Harmonizing Cross-Cultural Neuropsychological

Data. *American Psychological Association.* https://psycnet.apa.org/manuscript/2022-60047-001.pdf

- Mercandante, A. A., & Tadi, P. (2020). *Neuroanatomy, gray matter*. In StatPearls Publishing. https://ncbi.nlm.gov/books/NBK553239
- Mercer, L., Cookson, A., Simpson-Adkins, G., & van Vuuren, J. (2023). Prevalence of adverse childhood experiences and associations with personal and professional factors in health and social care works: A systematic review. *Psychological Trauma: Theory, Research, Practice, and Policy, 15*(Supp 2), S231-S245. https://psycnet.apa.org/fulltext/2023-68180-001.html#:~:text=https%3A//doi.org/10.1037/tra0001506
- Mesfin, F. B., Gupta, N., Shapshak, A. H., & Taylor, R. S. (2023, June 12). *Diffuse axonal injury*. In: StatPearls Publishing. https://www.ncbi.nlm.nih.gov/books/NBK448102/
- Merzenich, M. M., Van Vleet, T. M., & Nahum, M. (2014). Brain plasticity-based therapeutics. *Frontiers in Human Neuroscience, 8,* 385. https://doi.org/10.3389/fnhum.2014.00385
- Metzle, J. M., Piemonte, J., McKay, T. (2021). Mental illness, mass shootings, and the future of psychiatric research into American gun violence. *Harvard Review of Psychiatry, 29*(1), pp. 81-89. https://doi.org/10.1097/HRP.0000000000000280
- Michell, J. (2011). Quantitative science and the definition of measurement in psychology. *British*

Journal of Psychology, 88(3), 355-383. https://doi.org/10.1111/j.2044-8295.1997.tb02641.x

- Milfont, T. L., & Fischer, R. (2010). Testing measurement invariance across groups: Applications in cross-cultural research. *International Journal of Psychological Research, 3,* 111-130. https://doi.org/10.21500/20112084.857
- Milner, B., Corkin, S., & Teuber, H. L. (1968). Further analysis of the hippocampal amnesic syndrome: 14-year follow-up study of H. M. *Neuropsychologia, 6,* 215-234. http://doi.org/10.1016/0028-3932(68)90021-3
- Milner, B., & Penfield, W. (1955). The effect of hippocampal lesions on recent memory. *Transactions of the American Neurological Association,* 42-8. PMID: http://www.ncbi.nlm.nih.gov/pubmed/13311995
- Milner, B., Taylor, L., & Sperry, R.W. (1968). Lateralized suppression of dichotically presented digits after the commissural section in man. *Science, 161,* 184-6. http://doi.org/10.1126/Science.161.3837.184
- Milner, B., & Taylor, L. (1972). Right-hemisphere superiority in tactile pattern recognition after cerebral commissurotomy: Evidence for nonverbal memory. *Neuropsychologia, 10,* 1-15. http://doi.org/10.1016/0028-3932(72)90038-3
- Milner, B. (1972). Disorders of learning and memory after temporal lobe lesions in man. *Clinical Neurosurgery, 19,* 421-46.

http://doi.org/10.1093/Neurosurgery/19.Cn_Suppl_1.421

- Milner, B. (1954). Intellectual function of the temporal lobes. *Psychological Bulletin, 51*. 42-62. http://doi.org/10.1037/h0054728
- Milner, B. (1968). Preface: Material-specific and generalized memory loss. *Neuropsychologia, 6,* 175-179. http://doi.org/10.1016/0028-3932(68)90017-1
- Milner, B. (1959). Perceptual and memory disturbances in human temporal lesions. *Acta Psychologica, 15,* 217-218. http://doi.org/10.1016/S0001-6918(59)80089-5
- Milner, B. (1982). Some cognitive effects of frontal lobe lesions in man. *Philosophical Transactions of the Royal Society of London. Series B, Biological Sciences,* 298, 211-26. PMID: http://www.ncbi.nlm.nih.gov/pubmed/6125972
- Milner, B. (1965). Visually-guided maze learning in man: Effects of bilateral hiccompal, bilateral frontal, and. Unilateral cerebral lesions. *Neuropsychologia, 3,* 317-338. http://doi.org/10.1016/0028-3932(65)90005-9
- Miola, A., Salvati, B., Sambataro, F., & Toffanin, T. (2020). Aripiprazole for the treatment of delusional disorders: A systematic review. *General Hospital Psychiatry, 66*, 34-43. https://doi.org/10.1016/j.genhosppsych.2020.06.012
- Mitra, P., & Jain, A. (2024). Dissociative Identity Disorder. In Stat Pearls [Internet] Stat Pearls Publishing. https://www.ncbi.nlm.nih.gov/books/NBK568768/

- Moffit, T. E. (1987). Parental mental disorder and offspring criminal behavior: An adoption study. *Psychiatry, 50,* 346-360.
- Mohammadi, M. R., Delavar, A., Hooshyari, Z., Shakiba, A., Salmanian, M., Ghandi, F., & Ahmadi, A., & Farnoody, N. (2021). Psychometric properties of the Persian version of Millon Clinical Multiaxial Inventory-IV (MCMI-IV). *Iran Journal of Psychiatry, 16*(1), 43-51. https://doi.org/10.18502/ijps.v16i1.5378
- Mohan, L., Yilani, M., & Ray, S. (2023). *Conduct Disorder*. In Stat Pearls [Internet] Stat Pearls Publishing. https://www.ncbi.nlm.nih.gov/books/NBK470238/
- Moini, J., & Piran, P. (2020). Functional and clinical neuroanatomy: A guide for healthcare professionals. *Academic Press*. https://doi.org/10.1016/c2018-0-01786-7
- Molnar, Z. (2021). On the 400th anniversary of the birth of Thomas Willis. *BRAIN, 144*(4), 1033-1037. https://doi.org/10.1093/brain/awab016
- Moreira, D., Azeredo, A., & Barbosa, F. (2019). Neurobiological findings of the psychopathic personality in adults: One century of history. *Aggression and Violent Behavior, 47,* 137-159. https://doi.org/10.1016/j.avb.2019.03.005
- Morgan, A. E., & Mc Auley, M. T. (2024). Vascular dementia: From pathobiology to emerging perspectives. *Ageing Research Reviews, 96,* 102278. https://doi.org/10.1016/j.arr.2024.102278

- Morel, K. R. (2009). Test security medicolegal cases: Proposed guidelines for attorneys utilizing neuropsychology practice. *Archives of Clinical Neuropsychology, 24*(7), 635-646. https://doi.org/10.1093/arclin/acp062
- Moriguchi, Y., & Komaki, G. (2013). Neuroimaging studies of alexithymia: Physical, affective, and social perspective. *Biopsychosocial Medicine, 7*(8). https://doi.org/10.1186/1751-0759-7-8
- Morris, N., McNeil, D. E., & Binder, R. L. (2021). Estimating annual number of competency to stand trial evaluations across the United States. *Journal of the American Academy of Psychiatry and the Law, 52*(4). https://jaapl.org/content/early/2021/08/10/JAAPL.200129-20#:~:text=https%3A//doi.org/10.29158/JAAPL.200129%2D20
- Motzkin, J. C., Newman, J. P., Kiehl, K. A., & Koenigs, M. (2011). Reduced prefrontal connectivity in psychopathy. *Journal of Neuroscience, 31*(48), 17348-57. https://doi.org/10.1523/jneurosci.4215-11.2011
- Mulberger, A. (2017). Mental association: Testing individual differences before Binet. *Journal of History Behavioral Sciences, 53*(2), 176-198. https://doi.org/10.1002/jhbs.21850
- Munhoz, T. N., Santos, I. S., Barros, A. J. D., Anselmi, L., Barros, F. C., & Matijasavich, A. (2017). Perinatal and postnatal risk factors for disruptive mood dysregulation disorder at age 11: 2004 Pelotas

birth cohort study. *Journal of Affective Disorder, 215,* 263-268. https://doi.org/10.1016/j.jad.2017.03.040

- Munkomi, S., & Puckett, Y. (2024 October 6). *Chronic traumatic encephalopathy*. In: StatPearls Publishing. https://www.ncbi.nlm.nih.gov/books/NBK541013/
- Murphy, R. J. (2023). Depersonalization/derealization disorder and neural correlates of trauma-related pathology: A critical review. *Innovative Clinical Neuroscience, 20*(1-3), 53-59. PMID: 37122581
- Münsterberg, H. (1908). On the witness stand: Essays on psychology and crime. Doubleday: New York.
- Münsterberg, H. (1922). Hugo Münsterberg, his life and work. D. Appleton, & Co.: New York.
- National Academies of Sciences, Engineering, and Medicine; Health and Medicine Division; Board on Health Care Services; Board on Health Sciences Policy; Committee on Accelerating Progress in Traumatic Brain Injury Research and Care; Matney C, Bowman K, Berwick D, editors. Traumatic Brain Injury: A Roadmap for Accelerating Progress. Washington (DC): National Academies Press (US); 2022 Feb 1. 3, Understanding Patients with Traumatic Brain Injury. Available from: https://www.ncbi.nlm.nih.gov/books/NBK580077/
- National Education Association. (2020, June 25). *History of standardized testing in the United States.* https://www.nea.org/professional-excellence/student-engagement/tools-tips/history-standardized-testing-united-states

- National Institute of Aging. (2025). *Alzheimer's disease fact sheet.* https://www.nia.nih.gov/health/alzheimers-and-dementia/alzheimers-disease-fact-sheet

- National Institute of Mental Health. *(n.d.). The teen brain: 7 things to kn*ow. https://www.nimh.nih.gov/health/publications/the-teen-brain-7-things-to-know#:~:text=The%20brain%20finishes%20developing%20and,prioritizing%2C%20and%20making%20good%20decisions.

- National Institute of Neurological Disorders and Stroke. (2020). *Brain basics: Know your brain.* https://www.ninds.nih.gov/Disorders/Patient-caregiver-Education/Know-Your-Brain

- National Institute of Mental Health. (2025) *Generalized Anxiety Disorder.* https://www.nimh.nih.gov/health/statistics/generalized-anxiety-disorder

- National Institute of Neurological Disorders and Stroke. (2025). *NINDS CDE Notice of Copyright: Woodcock-Johnson III Test of Cognitive Abilities.* https://www.commondataelements.ninds.nih.gov/report-viewer/25210/Woodcock-Johnson%20III%20Test%20of%20Cognitive%20Abilities

- Natur, N. (2014). Analysis of the validity and reliability of the Das-Naglieri CAS (CAS) – Arabic Edition. *Psychology Research, 4*(7), 525-540. https://www.davidpublisher.com/Public/uploads/Contribute/552e286a3a78c.pdf

- Neal, T. S., Slobogin, C., Saks, M. J., Faigman, D. L., & Gesinger, K. F. (2020). Psychological assessments in legal contexts: Are courts keeping "junk science" out of the courtroom? *Psychological Science in the Public Interest, 20*(3). https://doi.org/10.1177/1529100619888860

- Nejati, V., Majdi, R., Salehinejad, M. A., & Nitsche, M. A. (2021). The role of dorsolateral and ventromedial prefrontal cortex in the processing of emotional dimensions. *Scientific Reports, 11*. https://www.nature.com/articles/s41598-021-81454-7#citeas:~:text=DOI-,https%3A//doi.org/10.1038/s41598%2D021%2D81454%2D7,-Share%20this%20article

- Ng, S. Y., Lee, A. Y. W. (2019). Traumatic brain injuries: Pathophysiology and potential therapeutic targets. *Frontiers in Cellular Neuroscience, 13*. https://doi.org/10.3389/fncel.2019.00528

- Nielsen, T. R., Franzen, S., Watermeyer, T., Jiang, J., Calia, C., Kjaergaard, D., Bothe, S., & Mukdam, N. (2024). Interpreter-mediated neuropsychological assessment: Clinical considerations and recommendations from the European Consortium on Cross-Cultural Neuropsychology (ECCroN). *The Clinical Neuropsychologist, 38*(8), 1775-1805. https://doi.org/10.1080/13854046.2024.2335113

- Niileksela, C. R., Reynolds, M. R., & Kaufman, A. S. (2013). An alternative Cattell-Horn-Carroll (CHC) factor structure of the WAIS-IV: Age invariance of an alternative model for ages 70-90. *Psychological Assessment, 25,* 391-404. https://psycnet.apa.org/doi/10.1037/a0031175

➢ Nikolic, M., Pezzoli, P., Jaworski, N., & Meto, M. C. (2022). Brain responses in aggression-prone individuals: A systematic review and meta-analysis of functional magnetic resonance imaging (fMRI) studies of anger and aggression-eliciting tasks. *Progress in Neuro-Psychopharmacology and Biological Psychiatry, 119,* 110-596. https://doi.org/10.1016/j.pnpbp.2022.110596

➢ Noffsinger, S. G., & Resnick, P. J. (2017). Criminal competencies. In: Rosner and C. L. Scott, eds. *Principles and Practice of Forensic Psychiatry,* 3rd ed.

➢ Nordquist, N., & Oreland, L. (2010). Serotonin, genetic variability, behavior, and psychiatric disorders – a review. *Upsala Journal of Medicine Science, 115*(1), 2-10. https://doi.org/10.3109/03009730903573246

➢ Nouri, A. MD. (2011). Hippocrates, 'the father of medicine.' *American Association for the Advancement of Science*. https://www.aaas.org/taxonomy/term/10/hippocrates-father-medicine#:~:text=Though%20it%20has%20been%20documented,the%20vicinity%20of%20400%20B.C.).

➢ Orbach, J. (2018). *Neuropsychology after Lashley: Fifty years since the publication of brain mechanism and intelligence. Routledge, Inc.*

➢ Ouerchefani, R., Ouerchefani, N., Rejeb, M. R. B., & Gall, D.L. (2024). Pragmatic language comprehension: Role of theory of mind, executive functions, and the prefrontal cortex. *Neuropsychologia, 194,* 108-756.

https://doi.org/10.1016/j.neuropsychologia.2023.108756

- Osorio, F. L., Loureiro, S. R., Eduardo, J., Hallak, C. Machado-de-Sousa, J., Ushirohira, J. M., Baes, C. V. W., Apolinario, T. D., Donadon, M. F., Bolsoni, L. M., Guimares, T., Fracon, V. S., Silva-Rodrigues, A. P. S., Pizeta, F. A., Souza, R. M., Sanches, R. F., Santos, R. G. D., Martin-Santos, R., Crippa, J. A., S. (2019). Clinical validity and intrarater and test-retest reliability of the Structured Clinical Interview for DSM-5 Clinician Version (SCID-5-CV). *Psychiatry Clinical Neuroscience, 73*(12), 754-760. https://pubmed.ncbi.nlm.nih.gov/31490607/
- Ozonoff, S. (1995). Reliability and validity of the Wisconsin card Sorting Test in studies of autism. *Neuropsychology, 9*(4), 491-500. https://psycnet.apa.org/doi/10.1037/0894-4105.9.4.491
- Pachet, A. K. (2007). Construct validity of the Repeatable Battery of Neuropsychological Status (RBANS) with acquired brain patients. *Clinical Neuropsychology, 21*(2), 286-93. https://doi.org/10.1080/13854040500376823
- Panlilio, L. V., & Justinova, Z. (2018). Preclinical studies of cannabinoid reward, treatments for cannabis use disorder, and addiction-related effects of cannabinoid exposure. *Neuropsychopharmacology, 43,* 116-141. https://doi.org/10.1038/npp.2017.193
- Parker, K. N., Donovan, M. H., Smith, K., & Haeussein, L. J. N. (2021). Traumatic injury to the developing brain: Emerging relationship to early life

stress. *Frontiers in Neurology, 12,* 708800. https://doi.org/10.3389/fneur.2021.708800

- Patel, R. K., Aslam, S. P., & Rose, G. R. (2024). Persistent depressive disorder. *National Library of Medicine*. https://www.ncbi.nlm.nih.gov/books/NBK541052/
- Paulino, M., Edens, J. F., Moniz, M., Moura, O., Rijo, D., & Simoes, M. R. (2024). Personality Assessment Inventory (PAI) in forensic and correctional settings: A comprehensive review. *Journal of Forensic and Legal Medicine, 103,* 102-661. https://doi.org/10.1016/j.jflm.2024.102661
- Payne, W. N., De Jesus, O., & Payne, A. N. (2023 May 22). *Contrecoup brain injury*. In: StatPearls Publishing. https://www.ncbi.nlm.nih.gov/books/NBK536965/
- Pemment, J. (2013). The neurobiology of antisocial personality disorder: The quest for rehabilitation and treatment. *Aggression and Violent Behavior, 18*(1), 79-82. https://doi.org/10.1016/j.avb.2012.10.004
- Penas-Lledo, E. M. & Llerena, A. (2014). CYP2D6 variation, behavior and psychopathology: Implication for pharmacogenomics-guided clinical trials. *Br J Clinical Pharmacology, 77*(4), 673-683. https://doi.org/10.1111/bcp.12227
- Penfield, W., & Miler, B. (1958). Memory deficit produced by bilateral lesions in the hippocampal zone. *AMA Archives of Neurology and Psychiatry, 79,* 475-97. http://doi.org/10.1001/archneurpsyc.1958.02340050003001

- Perkins, A. (2019). *Toxic stress in children. Nursing, 17*(2), 42-49. https://doi.org/01.NME.0000553087.55714.d4

- Permenter, C. M., Fernandez-de Thomas, R. J., & Sherman, A. L. (2023). *Postconcussive syndrome*. In: StatPearls Publishing. https://www.ncbi.nlm.nih.gov/books/NBK534786/

- Pessoa, L., & Hof, P. R. (2015). From Paul Broca's great limbic lobe to the limbic system. *Journal of Comprehensive Neurology, 523*(17), 2495-2500. https://doi.org/10.1002/cne.23840

- Petit, D., Gutierrez Fernandez, S., Zoltwska, K. M., Enzlein, T., Ryan, N. S., O'Connor, A., Szaruga, M., Hill, E., Vandenberghe, R>, Fox, N. C., & Chavez-Gutierrez, L. (2022). Ab profiles generated by Alzheimer's disease-causing PSEN1 variants determine the pathogenicity of the mutation and predict age at disease onset. *Molecular Psychiatry, 27, 2821-2832*. https://www.nature.com/articles/s41380-022-01518-6

- Petricides, M., & Milner, B. (1982). Deficits on subject-ordered tasks after frontal and temporal lobe lesions in man. *Neuropsychologia, 20,* 249-62. http://doi.org/10.1016/0028-3932(82)90100-2

- Pflugshaupt, T., Bauer, D., Frey, J., Vanbelligen, T., Kaufman, B. C., Bohlhalter, S., & Nyffeler, T. (2020). The right anterior temporal lobe critically contributes to magnitude knowledge. *Brain Communications, 2*(2). https://doi.org/10.1093/braincomms/fcaa257

- Pilkington, E. (2011). The NFL star and the brain injuries that destroyed him. *The Guardian.* https://www.theguardian.com/science/2011/jul/19/nfl-star-brain-injuries-destroyed
- Pillmann, F. (2003). Carl Wernicke (1848-1905). *Journal of Neurology, 250,* 1390-1391. DOI 10.1007/s00415-003-0250-x
- Pirau, L., & Lui, F. (2023, July 17). *Frontal lobe syndrome*. In StatPearls. Treasure Island. https://www.ncbi.nlm.nih.gov/books/NBK532981/
- Plante, T. G. (2013). Abnormal psychology across the ages: History and conceptualizations. [3 volumes].
- Pona, A., Marek, R. J., Panigrahi, E., & Ben-Porath, Y. S. (2022). Examination of the reliability and validity of the Minnesota Multiphasic Personality Inventory-3 (MMPI-3) in a preoperative bariatric surgery sample. *Journal Clinical Psychology Medical Settings, 5,* 1-14. https://doi.org/10.1007/s10880-022-09908-2
- Pope, K., Luna, B., Thomas, C. R. (2012). Developmental neuroscience and the courts: How science is influencing the disposition of juvenile offenders. *Journal of Academy Child Adolescent Psychiatry, 51*(4), 341-342. https://doi.org/10.1016/j.jaac.2012.01.003
- Potter, P., & Wright, J. P. (2000). *Psyche and soma: Physicians and metaphysicians on the mind-body problem from antiquity to enlightenment*. Clarendon Press/Oxford University Press.
- "Psychiatrist Probes Parkland School Shooter's Mind During Jailhouse Interview." (2022, October 5).

YouTube.
https://www.youtube.com/watch?v=lVMcVs0Ty1E

- Puderbaugh, M., & Emmady, P. D. (Updated 2023, May 1). *Neuroplasticity*. In: StatPearls. https://www.ncbi.nlm.nih.gov/books/NBK557811/
- Putnam, S. H., & DeLuca, J. W. eds. (1990). The TCN professional practice survey. Part 1. General practices and neuropsychologists in primary employment and private practice settings. *The Clinical Neuropsychologists, 4,* 199-244.
- Qadeer, M. I., Amar, A., Mann, J. J., & Hasnain, S. (2017). Polymorphisms in dopaminergic system genes: Association with criminal behavior and self-reported aggression in violent prison inmates from Pakistan. *PLoS One, 12*(6), e0173571. https://journals.plos.org/plosone/article?id=10.1371/journal.pone.0173571
- Qin, Q., Yin, Y., Wang, Y., Lu, Y., Tang, Y., & Jia, J. (2020). Gene mutations associated with early onset familial Alzheimer's disease in China: An overview and current status. *Mole Genet Genomic Medicine, 8*(10), 1443. https://doi.org/10.1002/mgg3.1443
- Raine, A., Lencz, T., LaCasse, L., & Colletti, P. (2000). Reduced prefrontal gray matter volume and reduced autonomic activity in antisocial personality disorder. *Arch Gen Psychiatry, 57*(2), 119-127. https://doi.org/10.1001/archpsyc.57.2.119
- Raulin, A-C., Doss, S. V., Trottier, Z. A., Ikezu, T. C., & Lui, C-C. (2022). ApoE in Alzheimer's disease: Pathophysiology and therapeutic strategies. *Molecular Neurodegeneration, 17,* 72.

https://molecularneurodegeneration.biomedcentral.com/articles/10.1186/s13024-022-00574-4

- Raju, H., & Tadi, P. (2020). *Neuroanatomy, somatosensory cortex*. In StatPearls. PMID: 32310375
- Randolph, C., Tierney, M. C., Mohr, E., & Chase, T.N. (1998). The Repeatable Battery for the Assessment of Neuropsychology Status (RBANS): Preliminary clinical validity. *Journal of Clinical Exp Neuropsychology, 20,* (3), 310-9. https://doi.org/10.1076%2Fjcen.20.3.310.823
- Ranzenberger, L. R., Das, J. M., Snyder, T. (2023 November 12). *Continuing education activity*. In: StatPearls Publishing. https://www.ncbi.nlm.nih.gov/books/NBK537361/
- Rasmussen, T., & Milner, B. (1977). The role of early left-brain injury in determining lateralization of cerebral speech functions. *Annals of New York Academy of Science,* 299, 355-69. http://doi.org/10.1111/J.1749-6632.1977.Tb41921.X
- Ratcliff, G., Dila, C., Taylor, L., & Milner, B. (1980). The morphological asymmetry of the hemisphere and cerebral dominance for speech: A possible relationship. *Brain and Language, 11,* 87-98. http://doi.org/10.1016/0093-934X(80)90112-1
- Reddy, L., A., Alperin, A., & Lekwa, A. (2021). Construct validity and diagnostic utility of the Woodcock-Johnson Test of Cognitive Abilities and clinical clusters for children with attention-deficit/hyperactivity disorder: A preliminary investigation. *European Journal of Psychology and*

Educational Research, 4(1), 37-49. http://dx.doi.org/10.12973/ejper.4.1.37

- Rekers, G. A., & Lovaas, O. I. (1974). Behavioral treatment of deviant sex-rle behaviors in a male child. *Journal App Behav Anal., 7*(2), 173-190. https://doi.org/10.1901/jaba.1974.7-173
- Reis, P. A., & Castro-Faria-Neto, H. C. (2022). Systemic response to infection induces long-term cognitive decline: Neuroinflammation and oxidative stress as therapeutic targets. *Frontiers in Neuroscience, 15.* https://doi.org/10.3389/fnins.2021.742158
- Reybrouck, M., Vuust, P., & Brattico, E. (2017). Music and brain plasticity: How sounds trigger neurogenerative adaptations. *Neuroplasticity: Insights of Neural Reorganization.* https: doi.org/intechopen.74318
- Rieber, R. W., Robinson, D. K., Blumenthal, A. L., & Danziger, K. eds. (2001). William Wundt in history: The making of a scientific psychology. *Library of Congress.*
- Riverside Insights. (2025a). *Woodcock-Johnson Test of Cognitive Abilities – 4th edition.* https://riversideinsights.com/woodcock_johnson_iv
- Riverside Insights. (2025b). *Woodcock-Johnson Test of Cognitive Abilities – 5th edition.* https://riversideinsights.com/woodcock_johnson_v
- Roberts, N. P., Kitchiner, N. J., Lewis, C. E., Downes, A. J., & Bisson, J. I. (2021). Psychometric properties of the PTSD checklist for DSM-5 in a sample of trauma-exposed mental health service

users. *European Journal of Psychotraumatology, 12*(1). https://doi.org/10.1080/20008198.2020.1863578

- Rogers, R., Bender, S. D., & Hartigan, S. E. (2023). An overview of malingering and deception in neuropsychiatric cases. *Behavioral Sciences & the Law, 42*(1), 28-38. https://doi.org/10.1002/bsl.2636
- Rolls, E. T. (2019). The cingulate cortex and limbic systems for emotion, action, and memory. *Brain Structure Function, 229*(9), 3001-3018. https://doi.org/10.1007/s00429-019-01945-2
- Rolls, E. T., Cheng, W., & Feng, J. (2020). The orbitofrontal cortex: Reward, emotion, and depression. *Brain Communications, 2*(2), 196. https://doi.org/10.1093/braincomms/fcaa196
- Rosa, P. J. (2023). Editorial for special issues "psychophysiology and experimental psychology. *International Journal of Psychological Res, 16*(2), 1-3. https://doi.org/10.21500/20112084.6584
- Rosca, E. C., Cornea, A., & Simu, M. (2020). Montreal Cognitive Assessment for evaluating the cognitive impairment in patients with schizophrenia: A systematic review. *General Hospital Psychiatry, 65*, 64-73. https://doi.org/10.1016/j.genhosppsych.2020.05.011
- Rosch, P. J. (2015). Why the heart is much more than a pump. *The Neuropsychotherapist.*
- Ross, J. A., & Bockstaele, E. J. V. (2020). The locus coeruleus-norepinephrine system in stress and arousal: Unraveling historical, current, and future

perspectives. *Frontiers in Psychiatry, 11,* 601519. https://doi.org/10.3389/fpsyt.2020.601519

- Ross, N., Gilbert, R., Torres, S., Dugas, K., Jefferies, P., McDonald, S., Savage, S., & Ungar, M. (2020). Adverse childhood experiences: Assessing the impact on physical and psychosocial health in adulthood and the mitigating role of resilience. *Child Abuse & Neglect, 103,* 104-440. https://doi.org/10.1016/j.chiabu.2020.104440
- Rotter, M., Way, B., Steinbacher, M., Sawyer, D., & Smith, H. (2002). Personality disorder in prison: Aren't they all antisocial? *Psychiatry Quarterly, 73,* 337-349. https://link.springer.com/article/10.1023/A:1020468117930
- "Rule 702. Testimony by Expert Witness. (n.d.). *Cornell Law School: Legal Information Institute*. https://www.law.cornell.edu/rules/fre/rule_702
- Saeed, A., Lopez, O., Cohen, A., & Reis, S. E. (2023). Cardiovascular disease and Alzheimer's disease: The heart-brain axis. *Journal of the American Heart Association, 12*(21). https://doi.org/10.1161/JAHA.123.030780
- Sakai, K., Hosoi, Y., Harada, Y., Morikawa, K., & Kato, Y. (2024). Validity and reliability of the Japanese version of the Frontal Battery Assessment in patients with stroke. *Neurology International, 16*(5), 1086-1093. https://doi.org/10.3390/neurolint16050081
- Saladino, V., Lin, H., Zamparelli, E., & Verrostro, V. (2021). Neuroscience, empathy, and violent crime in

an incarcerated population: A narrative review. *Frontiers in Psychology, 12,* 6924212. https://doi.org/10.3389/fpsyg.2021.694212

- Salam, M. (2017). Adam Lanza threatened Sandy Hook killings years earlier, records show. *The New York Times*. https://www.nytimes.com/2017/10/26/us/adam-lanza-sandy-hook.html
- Sallam, H. N. (2010). Aristotle, the godfather of evidence-based medicine. *Fact Views Vis Obgyn, 2*(1), 11-9. PMID: 25206962; PMCID: PMC4154333.
- Sanders, A. E., Schoo, C., & Kalish, V. B. (2023). *Vascular dementia*. In: StatPearls [Internet]. StatPearls Publishing. https://www.ncbi.nlm.nih.gov/books/NBK430817/
- Sanz-Garcia, A., Garcia-Vera, M. P., & Sanz, J. (2024). Normative data, reliability, and validity of the NEO PI-R personality disorder scales. *Behavioral Psychology, 32*(1), 41-63. https://www.behavioralpsycho.com/wp-content/uploads/2024/04/02.Sanz_32-1En.pdf
- Schiavi, M. R. (2001). Teaching the "Boys": Mart Crowley in the millennial classroom. *Modern Language Studies, 31*(2), 75-90. https://doi.org/10.2307/3195338
- Scheffels, J. F., Ballasch, I., Scheichel, N., Voracek, M., Kalbe, E., & Kessler, J. (2023). The influence of age, gender, and education on neuropsychological test scores: Updated clinical norms for five widely used

cognitive assessments. *MDPI, 12*(16), 51-70. https://doi.org/10.3390/jcm12165170

- "Schizoid Personality Disorder." (2023). *ScienceDirect*. https://www.sciencedirect.com/topics/psychology/schizoid-personality-disorder
- Schleim, S. (2025). *Brain Development and the law: Neurolaw in theory and practice.* Palgrave MacMillan. https://doi.org/10.1007/978-3-031-72362-9
- Schmaltz, T. M. (2024). *The pineal gland in Cartesianism*. Routledge.
- Schneider, K. N., Sciarillo, X. A., Nudelman, J. L., Cheer, J. F., & Roesch, M. R. (2021). Anterior cingulate cortex signals attention in a social paradigm that manipulates reward and shock. *Current Biology, 30*(19), 3724-3735. https://doi.org/10.1016/j.cub.2020.07.039
- Schneider, K. J. (2019). Concussion – Part I: The need of a multifaceted assessment. *Musculoskeletal Science Practice, 42*, 140-150. https://pubmed.ncbi.nlm.nih.gov/31133539/#:~:text=DOI%3A-,10.1016/j.msksp.2019.05.007,-Abstract
- Schinittker, J., Larimore, S. H., & Lee, H. (2020). Neither mad nor bad? The classification of antisocial personality disorder among formerly incarcerated adults. *Soc Sci Med, 264,* 113-288. https://doi.org/10.1016/j.socscimed.2020.113288
- Schönpflug, W. (2001). Experimental laboratories: Biobehavioral. *International Encyclopedia of the Social & Behavioral Sciences.*

- Schrank, F. A., McGrew, K. S, Nancy, M., Wendling, B. J., & LaForte, E. M. (2014). *Woodcock-Johnson IV Test of Cognitive Abilities*. Riverside: Rolling Meadows.
- Schroeder, R. W., Martin, P. K., & Walling, A. (2019). Neuropsychological evaluations in adults. *American Family Physician, 99*(2), 101-108. https://www.aafp.org/pubs/afp/issues/2019/0115/p101.html
- Schrueders, E., Braams, B. R., Blankenstein, N. E., Peper, J. S., Guroglu, B., & Crone, E. A. (2018). Contributions of reward sensitivity to ventral striatum activity across adolescence and early adulthood. *Childhood Development, 89*(3), 797-800. https://doi.org/10.1111/cdev.13056
- Schwartz, A. (2011). Duerson's brain trauma was diagnosed. *The New York Times*. https://www.nytimes.com/2011/05/03/sports/football/03duerson.html
- Scoville, W. B., & Milner, B. (1957). Loss of recent memory after bilateral hippocampus lesions. *Journal of Neurology, Neurosurgery, and Psychiatry, 20,* 11-21. http://doi.org/10.1176/Jnp.12.1.103-A
- Seretny, M. L., Dean, R. S., Gray, J. W., & Hartlage, L. C. (1986). The practice of clinical neuropsychology in the United States. *Archives of Clinical Nueropsychology, 1,* 5-12.
- Shaffer, J. (2016). Neuroplasticity and clinical practice: Building brain power for health. *Frontiers in Psychology, 7,* 1118. https://dx.doi.org/10.3389%2Ffpsyg.2016.01118

- Shane, B. (2023). Exploring the role of forensic neuropsychology in the legal system: Assessing cognitive functioning and providing expert testimony. *Journal of Forensic Psychology, 8*(2). https://www.walshmedicalmedia.com/open-access/exploring-the-role-of-forensic-neuropsychology-in-the-legal-system-assessing-cognitive-functioning-and-providing-expert-testimony-120079.html#:~:text=10.35248/2475%2D319X.23.8.273

- Sherman, E. M. S., Slick, D. J., & Iverson, G. L. (2020). Multidimensional malingering criteria for neuropsychological assessment: A 20-year update of the malingered neuropsychological dysfunction criteria. *Archives Clinical Neuropsychology, 35*(6), 735-764. https://doi.org/10.1093/arclin/acaa019

- Shumlich, E. J., Reid, G. J., Hancock, M., & Hoaken, P. N. S. (2018). Executive dysfunction in criminal populations: Comparing forensic psychiatric patients and correctional offenders. *International Journal of Forensic Mental Health, 18*(3), 243-259. https://doi.org/10.1080/14999013.2018.1495279

- Silva, C., Moreira, P., Moreira, D., Rafael, F., Rodrigues, A., Leite, A., Lopes, S., & Moreira, D. (2024). Impact of adverse childhood experiences in young adults and adults: A systematic literature review. *Pediatric Rep, 16*(2), 461-481. https://doi.org/10.3390/pediatric16020040

- Simic, G., Tkalcic, M, Vukic, V., Mulc, D., Spanic, E., Sagud, M., Olucha-Bordonau, F. E., Vuksic, M., Hof, P. R. (2021). Understanding emotions: Origins and roles of the amygdala. *Biomolecules, 11*(6), 823. https://doi.org/10.3390/biom11060823

- Sinco, S. R., D'Amato, R. C., & Davis, S. (2008). Understanding and using the Halstead-Reitan Neuropsychological Test batteries with children and adults. In R. C. D'Amato & L. C. Hartlage (eds). *Essentials of neuropsychological assessment: Treatment planning for rehabilitation* (2nd ed), 105-125. Springer Publishing Company.
- Singh, A., Kumar, R., Singh, N. P., Yadav, R., & Kumar, A. (2021). Evaluation of cognitive functions in traumatic brain injury patients using mini-mental examination and clock drawing test. *Asian Journal of Neurosurgery, 16*(1), 99-105. DOI: 10.4103/ajns.AJNS_331_20
- Slachevsky, A., Villalpando, J. M., & Sarazin, M. (2004). Diagnosis of frontotemporal dementia and Alzheimer's disease, 1104-1107. *Archives of Neurology, 61*(7). https://jamanetwork.com/journals/jamaneurology/fullarticle/786118#:~:text=doi%3A10.1001/archneur.61.7.1104
- Smith, K. E., & Pollak, S. D. (2020). Early life stress and development: Potential mechanisms for adverse outcomes. *Journal of Neurodevelopmental Disorders, 12*(34). https://jneurodevdisorders.biomedcentral.com/articles/10.1186/s11689-020-09337-y#citeas:~:text=DOI-,https%3A//doi.org/10.1186/s11689%2D020%2D09337%2Dy,-Share%20this%20article
- Smith, I. C., Reichow, B., & Volkman, F. R. (2015). The effects of DSM-5 criteria on number of

individuals diagnosed with Autism Spectrum Disorder: A systematic review. *Journal of Autism and Developmental Disorder, 45,* 2541-2552. https://link.springer.com/article/10.1007/s10803-015-2423-8#citeas:~:text=DOI-,https%3A//doi.org/10.1007/s10803%2D015%2D2423%2D8,-Keywords

- Smith, M. L., & Milner, B. (1981). The role of the right hippocampus in the recall of spatial location. *Neuropsychologia, 19, 781-93.* http://doi.org/10.1016/0028-3932(81)90090-7

- Solmsen, F. (1961). Greek philosophy and the discovery of the nerves. *Museum Helveticum: JSTOR, 18*(4), 169-197. https://www.jstor.org/stable/24812482#:~:text=https%3A//www.jstor.org/stable/24812482

- Soloff, P. H., Abraham, K., Burgess, A., Ramaseshan, K., Chowdury, A., & Diwadkar, V. A. (2016). Impulsivity and aggression mediate regional brain responses in borderline personality disorder: An fMRI study. *Psychiatry Res, 260,* 76-85. https://doi.org/10.1016/j.pscychresns.2016.12.009

- "Specialty Guidelines for Forensic Psychology." (2011). *American Psychological Association.* https://www.apa.org/practice/guidelines/forensic-psychology

- Spiegel, D., & Scheflin, A. W. (1993). Dissociated or fabricated? Psychiatric aspects of repressed in memory in criminal and civil cases. *International Journal of Clinical and Experimental Hypnosis,* 411-432. https://doi.org/10.1080/00207149408409368

- Stanford University. (2020). *Computed tomography scan*. Computed tomography scan. https://stanfordhealthcare.org/medical-tests/c/ct-scan.html
- Steinke, A., Kopp, B., & Lange, F. (2021). The Wisconsin Card Sorting Test: Split-Half reliability estimates for a self-administered computerized variant. *Brain Science, 11*(5), 529. https://doi.org/10.3390/brainsci11050529
- Stein, R., & Swan, A. B. (2017). Evaluating the validity of Myers-Briggs Type Indicator theory: A teaching tool and window intuitive psychology. *Social and Personality Compass*. https://doi.org/10.1111/spc3.12434
- Stephan, A., Walter, S., & Wilutzky, W. (2013). Emotions beyond brain and body. *Philosophical Psychology, 27*(1), 65-81. https://doi.org/10.1080/09515089.2013.828376
- Stetler, D. A., David, C., Leavitt, K., Schriger, I., Benson, K., Bhakata, S., Wang, L C., Oben, C., Watters, M., Hagnegahdar, T., Bortolato, M. (2014). Association of low-activity MAOA allelic variants with violent crime in incarcerated offenders. *Journal of Psychiatric Research, 58,* 69-75. https://doi.org/10.1016/j.jpsychires.2014.07.006
- Steyer, R. (2001). Classical (psychometric) test theory. *ScienceDirect*. https://www.sciencedirect.com/topics/computer-science/classical-test-theory
- Stingl, J. C., Esslinger, C., Tost, H., Bilek, E., Kirsch, P., Ohmle, B., Vivani, R., Walter, H., Rietschel, M.,

& Meyer-Lindenberg-Meyer, A. (2012). Genetic variation in CYP2D6 impacts neural activation during cognitive tasks in humans. *Neuroimage, 59*(3), 2818-2823. https://doi.org/10.1016/j.neuroimage.2011.07.052

- Stinnett, T. J., Reddy, V., & Zabel, M. K. (2023, August 8).. Neuroanatomy Broca area. In: StatPearls [Internet]. https://www.ncbi.nlm.nih.gov/books/NBK526096/

- Stout, D., Toth, N., Schick, K., & Chaminade, T. (2008). Neural correlates of early stone age toolmaking: Technology, language, and cognition in human evolution. *Philosophical Transactions of the Royal Society B.* https://doi.org/10.1098/rstb.2008.0001

- Strom, N. I., Soda, T., Mathews, C. A., & Davis, L. K. (2021). A dimensional perspective on the genetics of obsessive-compulsive disorder. *Translational Psychiatry, 11,* 401. https://doi.org/10.1038/s41398-021-01519-z

- Strong, C-A. H., Tiesma, D., & Donders, J. (2011). Criterion validity of the Delis-Kaplan Executive Function (D-KEFS) fluency subtests after traumatic brain injury. *Journal of International Neuropsychological Society, 17*(2), 230-7. https://doi.org/10.1017/s1355617710001451

- Suchy, Y., & Brothers, S. L. (2022). Reliability and validity of composite scores from the timed subtests of the D-KFES battery. *Psychological Assessments, 34*(5), 483-495. https://doi.org/10.1037/pas0001081

- Suewen, A., Schroeter, A., Grandjean, J., Schlegal, F., & Rudin, M. (2019). Functional spectroscopic imaging reveals the specificity of glutamate response in the mouse brain to peripheral sensory information. *Scientific Reports, 9*. https://doi.org/10.1038/s41598-019-46477-1

- Sullivan, E. V., & Pfefferbaum, A. (2006). Diffusion tensor imaging and aging. *Neuroscience Biobehavioral, 30*(6), 749-761. https://doi PMID: 32310375.org/10.1016/j.neubiorev.2006.06.002

- Sullivan, T., & Maiken, P. T. (1983). *Killer Clown: The John Wayne Gacy murders*. Kensington Publishing.

- Sun, W., Zhang, Y., Zhou, J., & Wang, X. (2021). Altered resting-state functional connectivity in the default mode network in male juvenile violent offenders. *Brain Imaging Behavior, 16*(2), 608-616. https://doi.org/10.1007/s11682-021-00535-3

- Sushma, C., & Meghamala, S. (2016). Moral treatment: Philippe Pinel. *The International Journal of Indian Psychology, 3*(2), 8. ISBN: 978-1-329-95395-6

- Suter, S. M., Giordano, M., Nietlispach, S., Apollonio, M., & Passilong, D. (2016). Non-invasive acoustic detection of wolves. *Bioacoustics, 26*(3), 237-248. https://doi.org/10.1080/09524622.2016.1260052

- Sweet, J. J. (2022). Forensic neuropsychology: History and current status. *The Clinical Neuropsychologist, 37*(3), 459-474. https://doi.org/10.1080/13854046.2022.2078740

➢ Sweet, J. J., Boone, K. B., Denney, R. L., Hebben, N., Marcopulos, B. A., Morgan, J. E., Nelson, N. W., & Westerveld, M. (2023). Forensic neuropsychology: History and current status. *Clinical Neuropsychology, 37*(3), 459-474. https://doi.org/10.1080/13854046.2022.2078740

➢ Sweet, J. J. (1999). Forensic neuropsychology: Fundamentals and practice. *Psychology Press: Taylor & Francis Group.*

➢ Sweet, J. J., Moberg, P. J., & Westergoard, C. K. (1996). A five-year follow-up survey of practices and beliefs of clinical neuropsychologists. *The Clinical Neuropsychologists, 10,* 202-221.

➢ Szalavitz, M. (2011). The 'Sissy Boy' experiment: Why gender-related cases call for scientists' humility. *Time*. https://healthland.time.com/2011/06/08/the-sissy-boy-experiment-why-gender-related-cases-call-for-scientists-humility/

➢ Taber, K. S. (2018). The use of Cronbach's alpha when developing and reporting research instruments in science education. *Research in Science Education, 48,* 1273-1296. https://link.springer.com/article/10.1007/s11165-016-9602-2

➢ Talih, F. R. (2011). Kleptomania and potential exacerbating factors. *Innovations in Clinical Neuroscience, 8*(10), 35-39. PMID: https://pubmed.ncbi.nlm.nih.gov/22132369/

➢ Tampi, R. R., Young, J., Hoq, R., Resnick, K., & Tampi, D. J. (2019). Psychotic disorders in late life: A narrative review. *Therapy Advanced*

Psychopharmacology. https://doi.org/10.1177/2045125319882798

- Tate, A. E., Sahlin, H., Liu, S., Lu, Y., Lundstrom, S., Larsson, H., Lichtenstein, P., & Kuja-Halkola, R. (2022). Borderline personality disorder: Associations with psychiatric disorders, somatic illnesses, trauma, and adverse behaviors. *Nature, 27,* 2514-2521. https://www.nature.com/articles/s41380-022-01503-z#citeas:~:text=DOI-,https%3A//doi.org/10.1038/s41380%2D022%2D01503%2Dz,-Share%20this%20article
- Tachibana, M., Inada, T., Ichida, M., & Ozaki, N. (2021). Risk factors for inducing violence in patients with delirium. *Brain Behavior, 11*(8), e2276. https://doi.org/10.1002/brb3.2276
- Tehrani, J. A., & Mednick, S. A. (2000). Genetic factors and criminal behavior. *Federal Probation, 64*(2). https://www.uscourts.gov/sites/default/files/64_2_4_0.pdf
- Teicher, M. H., & Samson, J. A. (2016). Annual research review: Enduring neurobiological effects of childhood abuse and neglect. *Journal of Child Psychological Psychiatry, 57*(3), 241-266. https://doi.org/10.1111/jcpp.12507
- Telano, L. N., & Baker, S. (2023). *Physiology, cerebral spinal fluid*. In StatsPearl. https://www.ncbi.nlm.nih.gov/books/NBK519007/
- Teive, H. A., G., Coutinho, L., Carmargo, C. H. F., Munhoz, R. P., & Walusinski, O. (2022). Thomas Willis' legacy on the 400th anniversary of his birth.

Brazilian Academy of Neurology, 80(7), 759-762. https://www.thieme-connect.de/products/ejournals/abstract/10.1055/s-0042-1755278#:~:text=10.1055/s%2D0042%2D1755278

- Teuber, H. L., Milner, B., & Vaughan, H. G. (1968). Persistent anterograde after stab wound of the basal brain. *Neuropsychologia, 6,* 267-282. http://doi.org/10.1016/0028-3932(68)90025-0

- Theadom, A., Meehan, L., McCallum, S., & Pacheco, G. (2023). Mild traumatic brain injury increases engagement in criminal behavior 10 years later: A case-control study. *Frontiers in Psychiatry, 14.* https://doi.org/10.3389/fpsyt.2023.1154707

- Thibaut, F. (2018). The mind-body Cartesian dualism and psychiatry. *Dialogues Clinical Neuroscience, 20*(1), 3. https://doi.org/10.31887/DCNS.2018.20.1/fthibaut

- Thorman, J. (2009). Hoge shares a chilling story on post-concussion recovery. *SB Nation.* https://www.arrowheadpride.com/2009/11/29/1177823/hoge-shares-chilling-story-on-post

- Thornicroft, G. (2020). People with severe mental illness as the perpetrators and victims of violence: Time for a new public health approach. *The Lancet: Public Health, 5*(2), E72-E73.

- Tomoda, A., Nishitani, S., Takiguchi, S., Fijisawa, T. X., Sugiyama, T., & Teicher, M. H. (2024). The neurobiological effects of childhood maltreatment on brain structure, function, and attachment. *European*

Archives of Psychiatry and Clinical Neuroscience. https://doi.org/10.1007/s00406-024-01779-y

- Tsiompanou, E., & Marketos, S. G. (2013). Hippocrates: Timeless still. *Journal of the Royal Society of Medicine, 6*(7), 288-292. https://doi.org/10.1177/0141076813492945

- Torregrossa, W., Torrisi, M., De Luca, R., Casella, C., Rifici, C., Bananno, M., & Calabro, R. S. (2023). Neuropsychological assessment in patients with Traumatic Brain Injury: A comprehensive review with clinical recommendations. *Biomedicine, 11(7), 1991.* https://doi.org/10.3390/biomedicines11071991

- Touyz, S. W., & Gilandas, A. J. (1983). Forensic neuropsychology: A selective introduction. *Journal of Forensic Science, 28*(3), 713-23.

- Tractenberg, R. E. (2010). Classical and modern measurement theories, patient reports, and clinical outcomes. *Contemp Clinical Trials, 31*(1), 1-3. https://doi.org/10.1016/S1551-7144(09)00212-2

- Tremblay, P., & Brambati, S. M. (2024). A historical perspective on the neurobiology of speech and language: Form the 19th century to present. *Frontiers in Psychology, 15.* https://doi.org/10.3389/fpsyg.2024.1420133

- Tubbs, R. S., Loukas, M., Shoja, M. M., & Cohen-Gadol, A. A. (2009). Richard Lower (1631-1691): Acknowledging his notable contributions to the explorations of the nervous system. *Journal of Neurosurgery, 111*(5), 1096-1101. https://doi.org/10.3171/2008.11.JNS081329

- Tussey, C., Lacritz, M., Arrendondo, B. C., & Marcopulos, B. A. (2024). Forensic neuropsychological foundations in competency to stand trial evaluations. *Archives of Clinical Neuropsychology*. https://doi.org/10.1093/arclin/acae084

- Tuvblad, C., Bezdjian, S., Raine, A., & Baker, L. A. (2014). The heritability of psychopathic personality in 14 to 15 year old twins: A multi-rater, multi-measure approach. *Psychological Assessment, 26*(3), 704-716. https://doi.org/10.1037/a0036711

- Tyng, C. M., Amin, H. U., Saad, M. N. M., & Malik, A. S. (2017). The influences of emotion on learning and memory. *Frontiers in Psychology, 8,* 1454. https://doi.org/10.3389/fpsyg.2017.01454

- Tzouvara, V., Kupdere, P., Wilson, K., Matthews, L., Simpson, A., & Foye, U. (2023). Adverse childhood experiences, mental health, and social functioning: A scoping review of the literature. *Child Abuse & Neglect, 139,* 100-692. https://doi.org/10.1016/j.chiabu.2023.106092

- U.S. Department of Justice Civil Rights Division. (2025a). Guide to disability rights laws. https://www.ada.gov/resources/disability-rights-guide/#:~:text=about%20this%20topic.-,Americans%20with%20Disabilities%20Act%20(ADA),to%20the%20United%20States%20Congress.

- U.S. Department of Justice Civil Rights Division. (2025b). Criminal justice. https://www.ada.gov/topics/criminal-justice/

- U.S. Department of Justice Office of Justice Programs. (1986). Insanity defense reform. *Military Law Review, 114,* 183-224. https://www.ojp.gov/ncjrs/virtual-library/abstracts/insanity-defense-reform

- U.S. Department of Justice. (n.d.). *63 Standards for determining competency and for conducting a hearing.* https://www.justice.gov/archives/jm/criminal-resource-manual-63-standards-determining-competency-and-conducting-hearing#:~:text=In%20determining%20whether%20the%20defendant,understanding%20of%20the%20proceedings%20against

- University of Oxford. (2023 January 31). *Three or more concussions linked with worse brain function in later life*. https://www.ox.ac.uk/news/2023-01-31-three-or-more-concussions-linked-worse-brain-function-later-life

- University of Pennsylvania Law School. (n.d.). *Model Penal Code*. https://www.law.upenn.edu/faculty/paul-robinson/clrgcodes/MPC.html

- University of Virginia. (2025). *Dusky v. United States, 362, U.S. 402 (1960).* https://juvenilecompetency.virginia.edu/legal-precedents/dusky-v-united-states

- Uretsky, M., Nair, E., Burton, R., Cronin, S. W., Rosseau, D., Tuz-Zahra, F., Durape, S., Abdolmohammadi, B., Baucom, Z., Saltiel, N., Shah, A., Martin, B., Palmsiano, J., Cherry, J. D., Daneshvar, D., Dwyer, B., Dams-O'Connor, K., Cray, J., Goldstein, L., Huber, B., Katz, D., Kowall,

N., Cantu, R. C., Alvarez, V. E., Stern, R. A., Stein, T. D., Tripodis, Y., McKee, A. C., Alosco, M. L., & Mez, J. (2024). Chronic traumatic encephalopathy, family history of mental illness, and aggression in brain donors with repetitive head impact exposure. *Neurology, 103*(12). https://doi.org/10.1212/WNL.0000000000210056

- Van Dongen, J. D. M., Haveman, Y., Sergiou, C. S., & Choy, O. (2025). Neuro prediction of violence and criminal behavior using neuroimaging data: From innovation to considerations for future directions. *Aggression and Violent Behavior, 80,* 102008. https://doi.org/10.1016/j.avb.2024.102008
- Van Wijk, C. H. (2024). Prevalence estimate for adjustment disorders in the South African Navy. In Stat Pearls [Internet] Stat Pearls Publishing. https://pmc.ncbi.nlm.nih.gov/articles/PMC11318156/
- Varshney, M., Mahapatra, A. Krishnan, V., Gupta, R., & Deb, K. S. (2016). Violence and mental illness: What is the true story? *Journal of Epidemiology & Community Health, 70*(3). http://dx.doi.org/10.1136/jech-2015-205546
- Viljoen, J. L., Roesch, R., Zapf, P. A. (2003). Interrater reliability of the fitness interview test across 4 professional groups. *Canadian Journal of Psychiatry, 47*(10), 945-52. http://dx.doi.org/10.1177/070674370204701006
- Villarreal, V. (2015). Test review: Woodcock-Johnson IV test of achievement. *Journal of Educational Assessment, 33*(4). http://dx.doi.org/10.1177/0734282915569447

- Vinchur, A. J. (2018). Chapter 3 – measurement, individual differences, and psychological testing. *The Early Years of Industrial and Organizational Psychology,* 53-78. https://doi.org/10.1017/9781107588608.004
- Virkkunen, M., De Jong, J., Bartko, F., Goodwin, F., Linnoila, M. (1989). Relationship of psychobiological variable to recidivism in violent offenders and impulsive fire sitters. *Archives of General Psychiatry,* 600-604.
- Voss, P., Thomas, M. E., Cisneros-Franco, J. M., & de Villers-Sidani, E. (2017). Dynamic brains and the changing rules of neuroplasticity: Implications for learning and recovery. *Frontiers in Psychology.* https://doi.org/10.3389/fpsyg.2017.01657
- "What is Intellectual Disability? (2025). *American Psychiatry Association.* https://www.psychiatry.org/patients-families/intellectual-disability/what-is-intellectual-disability
- Wall, B. W., & Lee, R. (2020). Assessing competency to stand trial. *Psychiatric Times, 37*(10). https://www.psychiatrictimes.com/view/assessing-competency-to-stand-trial
- Walls, B. W., Keram, E., Pinals, D. A., & Thompson, C. H. (2018). *Journal of American Academy Psychiatry Law, 46*(3), 373. https://doi.org/10.29158/jaapl.003781-18
- Walters, A. J., Notebaert, L., Van Bockstaele, B., Meeten, F., Todd, J., & Clarke, P. J. F. (2024). Occurrence of potentially traumatic events, type, and

severity in undergraduate students. *Australian Psychologist, 60*(1), 43-53. https://doi.org/10.1080/00050067.2024.2404983+

- Walusinski, O., Boller, F., & Henderson, V. W. (2019). 192-229: Shining a light on some of the most famous 19th and 20th century neuropsychologists. *Frontiers of Neurology and Neuroscience*. https://doi.org/10.1159/000494964

- Wang, L., Li, T., Gu, R., & Feng, C. (2024). Large-scale meta-analyses and network analyses of neural substrates underlying human escalated aggression. *Neuroimage, 299,* 120-824. https://doi.org/10.1016/j.neuroimage.2024.120824

- Wang, C., Nester, C. O., Chang, K., Rabin, L. A., Ezzati, A., Lipton, R. B., & Katz, M. J. (2023). Tracking cognition with the T-MoCA in a racially/ethnically diverse older adult cohort. *Alzheimer's Association.* https://doi.org/10.1002/dad2.12410

- Wang, R., Sneider, H., & Hartman, C. A. (2022). Familial co-aggression and shared heritability between depression, anxiety, obesity, and substance use. *Translational Psychiatry, 12*(108). https://doi.org/10.1038/s41398-022-01868-3

- Wani, P. D. (2024). From sound to meaning: Navigating Wernicke's area in language processing. *Cureus, 16*(9), 69833. https://doi.org/10.7759/cureus.69833

- Wasserman, J. D., & Kaufman, A. S. (2016). A history of mental ability tests and theories. *Oxford Academic.*

https://doi.org/10.1093/oxfordhb/9780199765683.013.32

- Watkins, M. W. (2017). The reliability of multidimensional neuropsychological measures: From alpha to omega. *The Clinical Neuropsychologist, 31*(6-7), 1113-1126. https://doi.org/10.1080/13854046.2017.1317364
- Wechsler, D. (2024) Wechsler Adult Intelligence Scale – 5th Edition. *Pearson Assessments.* https://www.pearsonassessments.com/store/usassessments/en/Store/Professional-Assessments/Cognition-%26-Neuro/Wechsler-Adult-Intelligence-Scale-%7C-Fifth-Edition/p/P100071002.html
- Weiss, K. J., & Xuan, Y. (2015). You can't do that! Hugo Münsterberg and misapplied psychology. *International Journal of Law and Psychiatry, 42-43*, 1-10. https://doi.org/10.1016/j.ijlp.2015.08.001
- Werner, K. B., Few, L. R., & Bucholz, K. K. (2016). Epidemology, comorbidity, and behavioral genetics of antisocial personality disorder and psychopathy. *Psychiatry Ann, 45*(4), 195-199. https://doi.org/10.3928/00485713-20150401-08
- Wernicke, C. (1970). The aphasic symptom-complex: A psychological study on an anatomical basis. *Archives of Neurology, 22*(3), 280-282. https://jamanetwork.com/journals/jamaneurology/article-abstract/569614#:~:text=doi%3A10.1001/archneur.1970.00480210090013
- Wernicke, C. (1969). The symptom complex of aphasia. In: Cohen, R. S., Wartosky, M. W. (eds).

Proceedings of the Boston Colloquium for the philosophy of science 1966/1968. Boston studies in the philosophy of science. Vol. 4. *Springer.* https://link.springer.com/chapter/10.1007/978-94-010-3378-7_2#citeas:~:text=DOI-,https%3A//doi.org/10.1007/978%2D94%2D010%2D3378%2D7_2,-Publisher%20Name

- White, M. D. (2017). Andrea Yates: A continuing story about insanity. *Fordham Law Legal Studies Research Paper.* https://papers.ssrn.com/sol3/papers.cfm?abstract_id=2909041
- Wicherts, J. M., Borsboom, D., & Dolan, C. V. (2010). Evolution, brain size, and the national IQ of people around 3000 years B.C. *Personality and Individual Differences, 48*(2), 104-106. https://doi.org/10.1016/j.paid.2009.08.020
- Williams, W. H., Chitasbesan, P., Fazel, S., McMillan, T., Hughes, N., Parsonage, M. & Tonks, J. (2018). Traumatic brain injury: A potential cause of violent crime? *Lancet Psychiatry, 5*(10), 836-844. https://doi.org/10.1016/S2215-0366(18)30062-2
- Wodka, E. L., Loftis, C., Mostofsky, S. H., Prahme, C., Larson, J. C. G., Denckla, M. B., & Mahone, E. M. (2008). Prediction of ADHD in boys and girls using the D-KEFS. *Archives of Clinical Neuropsychology, 23*(3), 283-293. https://doi.org/10.1016/j.acn.2007.12.004
- Woo, E. (2004). David Reimer, 38; After botched surgery, he was raised as a girl in gender experiment. *Los Angeles Times.*

https://www.latimes.com/archives/la-xpm-2004-may-13-me-reimer13-story.html

- World Health Organization. (2023). *Depressive disorder (depression)*. https://www.who.int/news-room/fact-sheets/detail/depression
- Wozniak, R. H. (1992). Mind and body: Rene Descartes to William James. *National Library of Medicine.*
- Woods, G. W., Freedman, D., & Greenspan, S. (2012). Neurobehavioral assessment in forensic practice. *International Journal of Law Psychiatry, 9, 35*(0), 432-439. https://doi.org/10.1016/j.ijlp.2012.09.014
- Xia, C. (2006). Understanding the human brain: A lifetime of dedicated pursuit. Interview with Dr. Brenda Milner. *McGill Journal of Medicine, 9*(2), 165-172. PMCID: https://pubmed.ncbi.nlm.nih.gov/18523614/
- Xi, C., Zhong, M., Lei, X., Liu, Y., Ling, Y., Zhu, X., Yao, S., & Yi, J. (2018). Psychometric properties of the Chinese version of the neuroticism subscale of the NEO-PI. *Frontiers in Psychology, 9,* 1454. https://doi.org/10.3389/fpsyg.2018.01454
- Yang, Y., & Raine, A. (2009). Prefrontal structural and functional brain imaging findings in antisocial, violent, and psychopathic individuals: A meta-analysis. *Psychiatry Res, 174*(2), 81-88. https://doi.org/10.1016/j.pscychresns.2009.03.012
- Yapijakis, C. (2009). Hippocrates of Kos, the father of clinical medicine, and Asclepiades of Bithynia, the

father of molecular medicine. Review. *In Vivo, 23*(4), 507-514. https://pubmed.ncbi.nlm.nih.gov/19567383/

- Young, L., Bechara, A., Tranel, D., Damasio, H., Hauser, M., & Damasio, A. (2010). Damage to the ventromedial prefrontal cortex impairs judgment of harmful intent. *ScienceDirect, 65*(25), 845-851. https://doi.org/10.1016/j.neuron.2010.03.003
- Youngm S., Kopelman, M., & Gudjonsson, G. eds. (2009). Neuropsychology in practice: A guide to assessment and legal processes. *Oxford University Press.*
- Zewude, G. T., Mesfin, Y., Sadouki, F., Ayele, A. G., Goraw, S., Segon, T., & Hercz, M. (2024). A serial mediation model of Big 5 personality traits, emotional intelligence, and psychological capital as predictors of teachers' professional well-being. *Acta Psychologica, 250,* 104-500. https://doi.org/10.1016/j.actpsy.2024.104500
- Zhang, Y., Ming, Q-S., Yi, J-Y., Wang, X., Chai, Q-L., & Yao, S-Q. (2017). Gene-gene-environment interactions of serotonin transporter, monoamine oxidase A, and childhood maltreatment predict aggressive behavior in Chinese adolescents. *Frontiers in Behavioral Neuroscience, 11.* https://doi.org/10.3389/fnbeh.2017.00017
- Zhang, W., Xiao, D., Mao, Q., & Xia, H. (2023). Role of neuroinflammation in neurodegeneration development. *Signal Transduction and Targeted Therapy, 8*(267). https://www.nature.com/articles/s41392-023-01486-5

➢ Zhou, Q., Chew, P., Oei, A., Chu, C. M., Ong, M., & Hoo, E. (2024). Longitudinal effects of cumulative adverse childhood experiences on internalizing and externalizing problems in adolescents in out-of-home care: Emotion dysregulation as a mediator. *Adversity and Resilience Science*. https://link.springer.com/article/10.1007/s42844-024-00161-0#citeas:~:text=DOI-,https%3A//doi.org/10.1007/s42844%2D024%2D00161%2D0,-Share%20this%20article

➢ Zimbardo, P., Haney, C., Banks, W. C., & Jaffe, D. (1971). The Stanford prison experiment: A simulation study of the psychology of imprisonment. https://d1wqtxts1xzle7.cloudfront.net/52230942/Narration_of_prison_experiment-libre.pdf?1490075113=&response-content-disposition=inline%3B+filename%3DNarration_of_prison_experiment.pdf&Expires=1736378305&Signature=PYAjiDBnq4OqLboa4hfdXIGXTes-96hssTH9zl~hJ14nmhRM5F0AwS5itzNDNLbz6u57peoSU848pRQoShOD-Fub4sdqkQWYplw-zEocyfrGaxoiG~wHDIWWJ3TGi~sm~5wE~S9ZQ7m6G4-p4S226dB9pmk6nwErWOZWFE9GdoxX2-1ZJFm~5DPl45PZCF6hrR21tBc7F7auAJDh1n9rsfMOklzliN7XBo-pyT0P4tK6rDTPPuDbqYmmIrTKEoMG1dQIPMVzUukCo-5GX5VC3qFgMP03oWF1771xCXFymOMacZFpliOfjsIeU2qcLaANWu5ytNWPGCu4OvfxBuLQSg__&Key-Pair-Id=APKAJLOHF5GGSLRBV4ZA

➢ Zimmer, C. (2005). *Soul made flesh: The discovery of the brain – and how it changed the world*. Free Press.

- Zimmermann, J., Kliewer-Neumann, J., Bovenschen, I., Lang, K., Gabler, S., Nowacki, K., & Spangler, G. (2024). Predictors of the rate and course of reactive attachment disorder and disinhibited social engagement disorders in foster children during the first year of placement. *Child Abuse & Neglect, 154,* 106872. https://doi.org/10.1016/j.chiabu.2024.106872

- Zipp, F., Bittner, S., & Schafer, D. P. (2023). Cytokines as emerging regulators of central nervous system synapses. *Immunity, 56*(5), 914-925. https://doi.org/10.1016/j.immuni.2023.04.011

- Zucco, G. M., & Sartori, G. (2023). Sensory and cognitive malingering: Studies and tests. *MDPI, 5*(3), 27. https://doi.org/10.3390/sci503002

Glossary of Terms

abnormal psychology – also known as psychology, is the study of unusual behavior, cognition, and emotions that affect mental processing and can lead to mental disorders.

affective empathy – the ability to feel the emotions of others.

akinetopsia – a rare neurological condition where a person cannot perceive motion. Individuals with akinetopsia may perceive the world as a series of still images, making it challenging to track moving objects or comprehend movement in real time. It's often caused by damage to specific brain areas, like the area responsible for processing motion (usually in the visual cortex).

alcohol use disorder (AUD) – a condition characterized by an inability to control alcohol consumption despite negative consequences. It involves symptoms such as cravings, increased tolerance, withdrawal symptoms, and neglect of responsibilities, leading to significant impairment in daily life.

alternative sentencing – non-traditional forms of punishment given to offenders, such as community service, rehabilitation programs, house arrest, or electronic monitoring, instead of incarceration. It's often used for less severe crimes or to help with rehabilitation.

amnesia – a condition characterized by memory loss, which can be caused by brain injury, trauma, illness, or psychological factors. It can affect the ability to recall past events (retrograde amnesia) or form new memories (anterograde amnesia).

amygdala – a construct within the brain responsible for processing emotions such as anxiety, fear, or survival. Its most important role is identifying threats that can lead to the "fight or flight" response.

anorexia nervosa - an eating disorder marked by severe food restriction, an intense fear of gaining weight, and a distorted body image, often leading to extreme weight loss and health issues.

anterior cingulate cortex – is a brain region involved in emotional regulation, decision-making, and error protection.

anterograde amnesia – inability to form new memories, typically following brain injury or trauma.

anterior cingulate cortex - a region located in the frontal part of the cingulate cortex, involved in functions like emotional regulation, decision-making, error detection, and conflict resolution. It also plays a role in processing pain and regulating autonomic functions such as heart rate and blood pressure.

anxiety disorder – a set of psychological symptoms associated with anxiety that leads to excessive fear, which, if prolonged, can result in physical symptoms that affect daily functioning.

aphasia - a language disorder that affects a person's ability to communicate. It can impact speaking, understanding speech, reading, and writing, typically resulting from brain injury or damage, such as from a stroke.

apraxia – inability or difficulty to perform purposeful movements.

artificial intelligence (AI) - the simulation of human intelligence in machines that are programmed to think, learn, and problem-solve. It includes tasks such as understanding language, recognizing patterns, and making informed decisions.

ataxia – the loss of coordination and muscle control.

attention - the cognitive process of selectively focusing on specific information while ignoring other stimuli. It is essential for various mental functions, including perception, learning, memory, and decision-making.

attention deficit hyperactivity disorder – a neurodevelopmental disorder that profoundly affects an individual's cognitive functions and behavior, characterized by persistent patterns of inattention, hyperactivity, and impulsivity.

auditory processing – the ability to recognize, interpret, and make sense of sounds, including spoken language, by the brain, allowing individuals to understand and respond to auditory stimuli effectively.

augmented reality (AR) – a technology that overlays digital content, such as images or information, onto the real world in real-time, typically viewed through smartphones, tablets, or AR glasses.

autism spectrum disorder – a developmental disorder characterized by challenges in social interaction, communication, and repetitive behaviors. It affects individuals to varying degrees, and symptoms can range from mild to severe. ASD typically appears in early childhood and can impact daily functioning.

avoidant personality disorder – a mental health condition categorized by features of significant sensitivity to criticism, feelings of inadequacy, and social inhibition. Individuals with AVPD often avoid social interactions or new activities due to fear of rejection or disapproval, leading to isolation and difficulty forming relationships.

binge eating disorder (BED) – an eating disorder characterized by recurring episodes of eating large quantities of food in a short period, often accompanied by a sense of loss of control. Unlike bulimia, it does not involve compensatory behaviors like vomiting or excessive exercise.

bulimia nervosa – eating disorder characterized by episodes of binge eating followed by behaviors to prevent weight gain, such as vomiting, excessive exercise, or fasting. This cycle often occurs in secret and can lead to serious physical and emotional health issues.

bi-factor analysis – a statistical method used to model data where multiple latent factors contribute to observed variables, with one general factor influencing all items and specific factors accounting for subdomains. It allows for the examination of both the overall (general) ability or trait and the specific dimensions or subcomponents within the data.

bipolar disorders – mood disorders characterized by extreme mood swings, including episodes of mania or hypomania (elevated, irritable mood) and depression (low mood). These mood shifts can interfere with daily functioning and can occur in varying patterns and severity. The two main types are bipolar I and bipolar II.

body dysmorphic disorder (BDD) – a mental health condition where individuals become excessively preoccupied with perceived flaws or defects in their physical appearance, often focusing on minor or imagined imperfections.

borderline personality disorder – a mental health condition characterized by intense emotions, unstable relationships, distorted self-image, and impulsive behaviors. Individuals with BPD may experience mood swings, fear of abandonment, self-harming tendencies, and difficulty managing emotions, often leading to challenges in personal and professional life.

brain-computer interfaces (BCIs) – systems that enable direct communication between the brain and external devices, bypassing traditional input methods like keyboards or touchscreens. BCIs are used for applications in assistive technology, rehabilitation, and even enhancing cognitive or sensory functions.

brain injury – damage to the brain resulting from trauma, impact, or other external factors, which can affect cognitive, physical, and emotional functioning.

brain lesion – damage to brain tissue due to various factors such as disease, injury, stroke, or trauma, which can cause impairment based on the brain area (or region).

brain-machine interfaces (BMIs) – systems that enable direct communication between the brain and external devices, allowing brain signals to control machines or computers, often used in medical, research, and assistive technologies.

brain maturation - the process of the brain developing and becoming more efficient, involving the growth of neural connections and the refinement of skills, continuing into early adulthood.

brainstem – the lower portion of the brain that links the brain to the spinal cord, consisting of the midbrain, pons, and medulla oblongata. It is essential life-sustaining functions.

brief psychotic disorder – a mental health condition characterized by a sudden, short-term episode of psychosis, including symptoms such as delusions, hallucinations, or disorganized speech or behavior. These symptoms last at least one day but less than one month, with a full return to previous functioning.

Broca's area – a region in the frontal lobe, typically in the left hemisphere, responsible for speech production and language expression. Damage to this area can result in Broca's aphasia, where individuals have difficulty speaking but can still understand language.

Broca's aphasia – a language disorder caused by damage to Broca's area, characterized by difficulty speaking and forming words, while comprehension and awareness of speech remain largely intact.

Brown prediction formula – a statistical method used to estimate a person's score on one test based on their performance on another related test. It is commonly used to predict scores on a different form or version of a test, considering the correlation between the two tests.

catatonia – a state when a person is awake or alert; however, does not respond to others or their environments, such as a lack of physical movement or verbal communication. The person can also produce strange movements or unusual behavior.

cerebellum – the part of the brain that regulates balance, motor coordination, and complex movement tasks. It also affects cognitive functions, including language processing and memory.

cerebrum – the largest part of the brain, responsible for higher functions such as thought, memory, emotion, and voluntary muscle movement.

cerebral cortex – the brain's outer layer, responsible for key functions like memory, cognition, learning, reasoning, problem-solving, emotions, consciousness, and sensory processing.

chlorpromazine – an antipsychotic medication used primarily to treat schizophrenia.

chronic traumatic encephalopathy (CET) – a progressive brain condition caused by repeated head injuries, often seen in athletes and military personnel. It is associated with symptoms such as memory loss, mood changes, impaired judgment, and eventually dementia. CTE can only be definitively diagnosed after death through brain tissue analysis.

classical test theory (CTT) – a framework for understanding and analyzing psychological tests' reliability and validity, posits that an individual's observed score is the sum of their true score and measurement error. It focuses on test consistency and the relationship between observed and true values.

clinical neuropsychology – a subdiscipline of clinical psychology that examines the relationship between the brain and behavior.

clinical psychopharmacology – a specialized field that integrates medication, neuropsychological, and psychological therapies to treat mental health disorders.

clinical psychology – is the field that focuses on understanding, preventing, and treating behavioral issues and mental health disorders.

cognitive behavioral therapy (CBT) - a type of psychotherapy that focuses on identifying and changing negative thought patterns and behaviors. It helps individuals recognize how their thoughts influence their emotions and actions, and it provides practical strategies to manage and alter these patterns to improve mental health. CBT is commonly used to treat conditions like anxiety, depression, and stress.

cognitive decline – a gradual decrease in cognitive abilities such as memory, attention, and reasoning, often associated with aging or neurological conditions.

cognitive empathy – the ability to understand another person's emotions or perspective.

cognitive factors refer to mental processes, including attention, memory, perception, reasoning, and problem-solving, that influence how we process information, make decisions, and interact with the world.

cognitive flexibility – the ability to adapt thinking and behavior to changing situations, new information, or unexpected obstacles, allowing for efficient problem-solving and adjustment to shifting demands.

cognitive impairment – difficulties with memory, thinking, or decision-making that interfere with daily life, often caused by injury, illness, or aging.

cognitive rehabilitation therapy - a treatment aimed at improving cognitive functions such as memory, attention, problem-solving, and executive skills after brain injury or neurological conditions.

cognitive psychology - the study of mental processes such as perception, memory, reasoning, and problem-solving. It focuses on how people acquire, process, store, and use information.

competency standard – a set of skills and knowledge required to perform a specific task or job effectively.

comprehension-knowledge – the ability to understand, interpret, and apply acquired information or concepts, drawing on learned facts and the capacity to make sense of new or complex material.

competency to stand trial – an individual's ability to comprehend the court process and participate in legal court proceedings.

complex attention – the ability to focus, sustain, and shift attention while managing multiple tasks or handling distractions. It involves higher-level cognitive processes to process and respond to information effectively.

computerized adaptive testing (CAT) – a method of administering tests using computer technology, where the difficulty of questions adapts in real-time based on the test-taker's performance.

computed tomography (CT) scan – a medical imaging technique that uses X-rays and computer processing to create detailed cross-sectional images of the body's internal structures, including the brain, bones, and organs.

concussion - a mild traumatic brain injury caused by a blow or jolt to the head, leading to temporary disruption of brain function. Symptoms may include headache, confusion, dizziness, nausea, and memory problems.

concurrent validity – the relationship with a current criterion.

conduct disorders – a mental health condition characterized by behavioral and emotional difficulties, including a tendency to disregard the rights of others, difficulty following rules and authority, and the presence of aggressive behavior.

confabulation – the unintentional production of false memories or distorted recollections, often without the intention to deceive, typically occurring in individuals with memory impairments due to brain injury or neurological conditions.

confidentiality – refers to the ethical and legal responsibility to protect sensitive information from being disclosed to unauthorized individuals. In healthcare and mental health settings, it ensures that personal, medical, or psychological information shared by patients or clients is kept private and only disclosed with their consent or when required by law.

conservatorship – a legal arrangement in which a court appoints a person or organization (the conservator) to manage the personal, financial, or medical affairs of someone who is unable to do so themselves due to physical or mental limitations.

construct validity – the degree to which a test or measurement tool accurately assesses the theoretical concept or construct it intends to measure. It involves demonstrating that the test accurately reflects the underlying trait or ability rather than something else.

content validity – the extent to which a test or measurement tool covers the full range of the concept it intends to measure. It ensures that the items or questions on the test represent the entire domain of the construct.

conversion disorder – a mental health condition where a person experiences neurological symptoms, such as paralysis, blindness, or seizures, that medical tests cannot explain. These symptoms are thought to be triggered by psychological stress or trauma rather than a physical illness.

corpus callosum – a dense bundle of nerve fibers connecting the brain's left and right hemispheres.

corticospinal tract – a pathway of axons that control voluntary movement, connecting the brain to the spinal cord.

coup contrecoup – a type of brain injury where damage occurs at the site of impact (coup) and on the opposite side of the brain (contrecoup), caused by the brain moving within the skull during a sudden impact. This often results from events like car accidents or falls and can lead to widespread brain damage.

cranial ultrasonography – an imaging technique that uses high-frequency sound waves to create images of the brain, typically used in infants or young children to examine brain structure and detect conditions like hydrocephalus or brain injuries.

crime scene analysis – the process of examining and interpreting evidence found at a crime scene to reconstruct events, identify perpetrators, and understand the circumstances of a crime. It involves collecting physical evidence, documenting the scene, and applying forensic techniques.

crime scene staging – the act of altering a crime scene to mislead investigators or obscure the true nature of a crime. This can include planting evidence, changing the scene's appearance, or making the crime look like an accident or suicide.

criminal responsibility – the legal model that examines whether an individual can be held accountable for committing a crime.

criminologists – experts who study the root causes of criminal behavior.

criminology – the study of crime, criminal behavior, and the justice system.

crisis intervention teams (CITs) – specialized groups of law enforcement officers trained to respond to individuals experiencing mental health crises. The goal is to de-escalate situations, provide appropriate support, and connect individuals to mental health services rather than resorting to arrest or force.

criterion-related validity – the extent to which a test or measure predicts or correlates with an external criterion or outcome, such as future performance or behavior. It is often assessed through **concurrent validity** (the relationship with a current criterion) and predictive validity (the ability to forecast future outcomes).

Cronbach's alpha – a statistic used to assess the internal consistency of a test or scale, indicating how closely related a set of items are as a group. A higher Cronbach's alpha (typically above 0.7) suggests that the items reliably measure the same underlying construct.

cross-examination - the questioning of a witness by the opposing party in a legal trial, aimed at challenging the credibility, accuracy, or consistency of their testimony.

crystallized intelligence – accumulating knowledge, skills, and experiences over time.

CYP2D6 gene – codes for an enzyme in the liver that metabolizes many drugs, including antidepressants, antipsychotics, and pain medications. Variations in this gene can affect how quickly or slowly a person processes such drugs, influencing drug effectiveness and risk of side effects.

cyclothymic disorder – a mood disorder characterized by alternating periods of mild hypomanic symptoms (elevated or irritable mood) and depressive symptoms that do not meet the criteria for full-blown mania or major depression. These mood swings last for at least two years and can cause significant distress or impairment in functioning.

default mode network (DMN) – a group of interconnected brain regions that are typically active when a person is at rest.

delayed ejaculation - a male sexual dysfunction characterized by a persistent difficulty or inability to ejaculate during sexual activity, despite adequate stimulation, often leading to distress or relationship problems.

delayed memory – the ability to recall information after some time has passed, typically minutes to hours after initially learning or experiencing it.

delirium – a sudden, severe confusion or altered mental state, often caused by illness, infection, or medication, characterized by disorientation, inability to focus, and changes in behavior.

delusions – false beliefs that persist despite evidence against them.

dementia – a neurocognitive disorder based on a group of diseases that causes cognitive decline in mental ability (i.e., behavior, cognition, memory, mood, personality, reasoning) that impacts one's ability to perform daily activities.

dependent personality disorder – a mental health condition characterized by an excessive need to be taken care of, leading to submissive and clinging behaviors. Individuals with DPD often have difficulty making decisions independently and fear abandonment, relying heavily on others for guidance and support.

depersonalization disorder – a dissociative disorder characterized by persistent or recurrent feelings of detachment from one's own body, thoughts, or sense of self. Individuals may feel as though they are observing themselves from outside their bodies, as if they are in a dream, which can cause significant distress.

depressive disorders – mental health conditions characterized by persistent sadness, hopelessness, and a loss of interest in activities.

derealization disorder – a dissociative disorder where individuals experience a sense of detachment from their surroundings, feeling like the world around them is unreal or distorted. This can lead to feelings of confusion, disconnection, and distress, although the person remains aware that the experience is not real.

developmental psychopathology – the study of how psychological disorders change over time, focusing on the influence of genetic, environmental, and early life factors.

dialectical behavioral therapy (DBT) – a type of therapy that helps people manage intense emotions and improve relationships. It teaches skills in mindfulness, emotional regulation, and coping with distress.

diathesis-stress model – a psychological theory that suggests mental disorders develop due to the interaction between a genetic predisposition (diathesis) and environmental stressors. While the diathesis creates vulnerability, stressors trigger the onset of the disorder.

diencephalon – a region of the brain located between the brainstem and cerebrum. It consists of structures such as the thalamus, hypothalamus, epithalamus, and subthalamus.

diffuse axonal injury (DAI) – a type of brain injury caused by widespread damage to the brain's white matter, typically due to rapid acceleration or deceleration (like in a car accident). It disrupts the communication between neurons, leading to severe cognitive and physical impairments.

diffuse optical imaging (DOI) – a non-invasive imaging technique that uses near-infrared light to measure and visualize tissue properties, such as blood oxygenation and brain activity. It is often used for studying brain function and detecting abnormalities in a portable, real-time manner.

diffusion tensor imaging (DTI) – an MRI-based imaging technique that maps the movement of water molecules in the brain, particularly along the direction of white matter fibers. It is used to visualize and assess the integrity of brain networks and detect abnormalities, such as those seen in traumatic brain injury or neurodegenerative diseases.

diminished capacity – a legal defense suggesting that certain factors affect an individual's ability to form the mental state required to intend or commit a crime.

disability evaluations – assessments conducted by medical or psychological professionals to determine the extent of a person's physical or mental impairment and how it impacts their ability to perform daily activities or work. These evaluations are often used for determining eligibility for disability benefits.

dopamine – a neurotransmitter in the brain that plays a key role in reward, motivation, pleasure, movement, and mood regulation.

dopamine dysregulation – refers to an imbalance in the production, release, or function of dopamine, a neurotransmitter involved in reward, motivation, movement, and mood. This dysregulation is linked to several mental and neurological disorders, including schizophrenia, Parkinson's disease, addiction, and mood disorders.

dopamine receptor D2 gene (DRD2) – codes for the D2 dopamine receptor, which is involved in the brain's reward and pleasure pathways. Variations in the DRD2 have been linked to behaviors like addiction, schizophrenia, and mood disorders, as well as differences in reward sensitivity and motivation.

dopamine transporter gene (DAT1) – a protein that helps regulate dopamine levels in the brain by reabsorbing dopamine from the synapse. Variations in the DAT1 gene have been linked to conditions like ADHD, addiction, and mood disorders, as they can affect dopamine signaling and function.

dopaminergic system – a network of neurons in the brain that use dopamine as their primary neurotransmitter, regulating movement, reward, motivation, and various emotional and cognitive functions.

due process – fair treatment and legal procedures that must be followed before someone can be deprived of their rights or freedoms.

Durham Rule – states that a defendant is not criminally responsible if their actions were caused by a mental disease or defect, preventing them from understanding their actions or knowing they were wrong.

dysphasia – a language disorder that affects the ability to speak, understand, or process language, typically resulting from brain injury or neurological conditions.

dysarthria – a speech disorder caused by weakness or lack of coordination in the muscles responsible for speaking, leading to slurred or slow speech. It is often the result of neurological conditions affecting the nervous system.

dysthymia – now known as persistent depressive disorder (PDD); it is a chronic form of depression characterized by a low mood lasting for at least two years. It involves symptoms like sadness, fatigue, and low self-esteem, but they are less severe than those seen in major depression.

electroencephalography (EEG) – a diagnostic technique that measures and records the brain's electrical activity through electrodes placed on the scalp, often used to detect abnormalities like seizures, sleep disorders, or brain injuries.

electroconvulsive therapy (ECT) – a medical procedure that involves applying small electrical currents to the brain to trigger a brief seizure. It is primarily used to treat severe mental health conditions like depression, bipolar disorder, and schizophrenia, especially when other treatments have not been effective (e.g., treatment-resistant).

emotional regulation – the ability to monitor, manage, and modify emotional responses in order to adapt to situations, achieve goals, and maintain well-being. It involves strategies to influence which emotions arise, when they occur, and how they are expressed.

empirical validation – confirming the accuracy and validity of a theory or methodology through data analysis and observation.

epileptiform discharges – abnormal patterns of electrical activity in the brain, often seen on an EEG, that indicate epilepsy or seizure activity, even without a clinically observable seizure.

epilepsy – a neurological disorder characterized by recurrent, unprovoked seizures due to abnormal electrical activity in the brain. Seizures can vary in intensity and frequency, and the condition may be managed with medication or other treatments.

electrophysiology – the study of the electrical properties of biological cells and tissues, particularly the electrical activity of the nervous system and heart. It involves techniques such as EEG, ECG, and other measurements to understand how electrical signals influence bodily functions and to diagnose various conditions.

enuresis – the involuntary urination, typically occurring in children, beyond the age when bladder control is expected. It can happen during the day (diurnal) or night (nocturnal) and may be caused by medical, psychological, or developmental factors.

equipotentiality – a psychological theory by Karl Lashley that all brain regions are equally capable of performing tasks.

equivalent forms reliability – the consistency of test scores between two versions of the same test designed to measure the same construct. It assesses whether different forms of the test yield similar results, indicating that both versions are equally valid and reliable.

erectile dysfunction (ED) – is the inability to achieve or maintain an erection in a sufficient manner for engaging in sex or sexual activities.

excoriation disorder – also known as **skin picking disorder**, is a condition characterized by the repeated urge to pick at one's skin, leading to sores, scars, or other skin damage.

executive function – the ability to learn, reason, solve problems, adapt to new situations, and apply knowledge and skills in various contexts.

excitotoxicity – the damage or death of nerve cells caused by excessive stimulation, usually due to high levels of glutamate.

eye movement desensitization and reprocessing (EMDR) – a psychotherapy technique used to help individuals process and recover from traumatic memories. It involves guided eye movements while recalling distressing events, which is believed to help reprocess the memory and reduce its emotional impact.

factitious disorders – mental health conditions where individuals intentionally produce or exaggerate symptoms of illness or injury, often to assume the sick role and gain attention or sympathy, without external incentives like financial gain.

factor analysis – a statistical method used to identify underlying relationships between variables by grouping them into factors. It helps to simplify data by reducing the number of variables while retaining the most important information, often used to uncover latent constructs or dimensions in psychological tests or surveys.

factor analytical approach – a statistical method used to identify underlying relationships or patterns among a large set of variables. It helps reduce complex data by grouping related variables into factors, making the data structure easier to understand.

female orgasmic disorder – the difficulty or inability for women to achieve orgasm despite adequate sexual stimulation, often affecting sexual satisfaction.

female sexual interest/arousal disorder – a condition marked by a lack of sexual interest, desire, or arousal in women, causing distress or relationship difficulties. It can have psychological, hormonal, or relational causes.

fluid intelligence – logical thinking and solving novel problems independently of prior knowledge or experience.

fluid reasoning – the ability to think logically and solve novel problems without relying on prior knowledge or experience, often involving pattern recognition, abstract thinking, and adaptability.

forensic evaluations – assessments conducted by mental health or medical professionals to provide expert opinions in legal cases, often involving issues like competency to stand trial, criminal responsibility, or risk of reoffending.

forensic evidence – physical or biological materials found at a crime scene that can be used in legal investigations, such as DNA, fingerprints, blood, fibers, or weapons. This evidence helps to link suspects, victims, and crime scenes, and can be crucial in solving crimes.

forensic mental health law – legislation that addresses criminal justice and mental healthcare issues.

forensic neuropsychology – the study of brain function and behavior in the context of the law. It involves assessing individuals involved in legal cases to determine how brain injuries, disorders, or conditions may affect their cognitive abilities, behavior, or mental state. Forensic neuropsychologists often provide expert testimony in criminal, civil, or family court cases.

forensic neuropsychopathology – an interdisciplinary field that applies principles of neuropsychology to understanding and evaluating the intersection of neurological conditions, psychological functioning, and legal issues. It focuses on how changes within the brain affect cognitive performance and influence behavior within legal contexts, such as criminal responsibility, competency to stand trial, and risk assessment. This field combines neuroscience, clinical neuropsychology, psychology, forensic psychology, and the law to address complex questions about cognitive performance and emotional functioning related to legal questions and decisions.

forensic psychiatry – a branch of psychiatry that focuses on the relationship between mental health and the law. It involves evaluating and treating individuals with mental disorders in legal matters, such as criminal cases, civil disputes, and assessments of mental capacity.

forensic psychology – a field of psychology that applies psychological principles and techniques to the legal system. It involves evaluating individuals involved in legal proceedings, assessing mental health in criminal cases, providing expert testimony, and understanding the psychological aspects of criminal behavior and the law enforcement process.

forensic science – scientifically analyzing data of evidence from crime scenes.

frontal association cortex – part of the frontal lobe responsible for complex thinking, planning, decision-making, and controlling social and emotional behavior. It integrates information to guide purposeful and goal-directed actions.

frontotemporal dementia – a group of neurodegenerative disorders characterized by the progressive degeneration of the frontal and temporal lobes of the brain.

frontal lobe – the part of the brain located at the front, responsible for higher cognitive functions such as decision-making, problem-solving, planning, impulse control, and voluntary motor control. It also plays a key role in personality, emotions, and language.

functional compensation – when the brain or body adapts to damage by using other areas to perform lost functions.

functional magnetic resonance imaging (fMRI) - a type of brain imaging that measures and maps brain activity by detecting changes in blood flow, helping researchers understand brain function during various tasks or in response to stimuli.

functional neuroplasticity – the brain's ability to shift functions from damaged areas to healthy areas. It allows the brain to adapt by reorganizing how tasks are performed, often in response to injury, learning, or new experiences.

gamma-aminobutyric acid (GABA) – an inhibitory neurotransmitter in the brain that helps regulate neuronal excitability by reducing the activity of nerve cells. GABA plays a key role in promoting relaxation, reducing anxiety, and preventing overstimulation of the brain, making it crucial for maintaining a balanced mood and preventing seizures.

gaslighting – a form of psychological manipulation in which a person tries to make someone doubt their own perceptions, memories, or sanity, often to gain control or avoid responsibility.

gender dysphoria – a condition where a person experiences significant discomfort or distress due to a mismatch between their assigned gender at birth and their experienced or expressed gender. This can lead to a strong desire to transition to the gender with which they identify.

generalized anxiety disorder (GAD) – excessive, uncontrollable worry about various aspects of life, such as work, health, or social interactions. The anxiety is often disproportionate to the situation and lasts for at least six months, causing significant distress or impairment in daily functioning.

genito-pelvic pain/penetration disorder – a sexual dysfunction in women characterized by pain during intercourse, fear or anxiety about penetration, and difficulty with vaginal penetration. Physical, psychological, or relational factors can cause it.

Gf-Gc Theory – Raymond Cattell's theory that intelligence is not a unified factor but instead consists of multiple, distinguishable cognitive abilities.

giftedness – the possession of exceptional abilities or talents in one or more areas, such as intellectual, creative, artistic, or academic, that significantly exceed the average level of performance for a person's age or grade level.

glutamate – the most abundant excitatory neurotransmitter in the brain, involved in transmitting signals between nerve cells. It plays a crucial role in learning, memory, and overall brain function. However, excessive glutamate activity can contribute to neurotoxicity and conditions like stroke or neurodegenerative diseases.

guardianship – a legal arrangement where a court appoints a guardian to make decisions on behalf of someone who is unable to manage their own personal, medical, or financial affairs due to age, disability, or incapacity.

gyrus – raised ridge or bump on the brain's surface, often located between the sulci. The folds increase the brain's surface area, allowing for more neurons and enhancing cognitive function. The plural word is *gyri*.

hallucinations – sensory experiences (like seeing or hearing things) that are not present.

hemispatial neglect – a condition where individuals ignore or are unaware of one side of their environment, typically the left, due to brain damage, usually in the right hemisphere.

hemiparesis – a partial weakness or loss of strength on one side of the body, often resulting from brain injury or neurological conditions like stroke.

higher-order cognitive functions – complex mental processes that involve advanced thinking skills, such as reasoning, problem-solving, decision-making, planning, and abstract thinking, which allow individuals to engage in goal-directed behavior and adapt to novel situations.

hippocampus – a brain structure involved in memory formation, learning, and spatial navigation. It plays a key role in converting short-term memories into long-term ones.

histrionic personality disorder – a mental health condition characterized by a pattern of seeking attention and approval, often through dramatic, exaggerated, or seductive behavior. Individuals with HPD may feel uncomfortable when not the center of attention and may engage in attention-seeking actions or have rapidly shifting emotions.

humoral imbalance – refers to an abnormality in the body's fluids or chemicals, which can affect health and lead to various conditions.

hoarding disorder – a condition where individuals excessively accumulate items and struggle to discard them, leading to clutter that disrupts daily life and causes distress.

hypothalamus – a small brain region that controls vital functions like hunger, thirst, temperature, regulation, and hormone release.

hypoactivity – reduced or low brain activity or function.

hypomania – a milder form of mania found in individuals with bipolar disorder, particularly bipolar 2 disorder.

hyposomnia – excessive sleeping.

hypothalamic-pituitary-adrenal axis (HPA) – a system in the body that controls the stress response. It involves the hypothalamus, pituitary gland, and adrenal glands, which work together to release hormones such as cortisol in response to stress, thereby helping the body adapt to challenging situations.

illness anxiety disorder (IAD) – a mental health condition where individuals worry excessively about having or developing a serious illness, despite having little to no symptoms. This often leads to frequent medical check-ups and anxiety about health, even when there is no medical evidence to support the concern.

immediate memory – the ability to quickly retain and recall information for a short period, typically seconds to minutes.

impulse control – the ability to resist or delay an immediate urge, temptation, or behavior to act in a more appropriate or goal-directed way. It is a key component of **self-regulation** and is crucial for functioning in social, academic, and occupational settings.

impulsivity – the tendency to act quickly without careful thought or consideration of the consequences, often driven by immediate desires or emotions rather than rational decision-making.

independent medical evaluation (IME) – an assessment conducted by a doctor who is not involved in a person's treatment, often requested by insurance companies or legal parties to provide an unbiased opinion on a medical condition, disability, or injury.

inhibition – the ability to control or suppress impulses, behaviors, or responses that are inappropriate or undesirable, allowing for more deliberate and goal-directed actions.

insanity defense – a legal defense used to argue that a defendant was unable to understand the nature of their actions or distinguish right from wrong due to a severe mental illness at the time of committing the crime.

insula – part of the brain located deep within the cerebral cortex. It is involved in functions such as emotion, perception, self-awareness, and the processing of sensory information, including taste and internal body sensations.

intelligence – the ability to learn, reason, solve problems, adapt to new situations, and apply knowledge and skills in various contexts.

intellectual disabilities – a group of conditions characterized by limitations in intellectual functioning and adaptive behavior, which affect a person's ability to learn, problem-solve, and perform everyday tasks.

intelligence quotient (IQ) – a numerical score derived from standardized tests designed to measure human intelligence. It provides a way to compare an individual's cognitive abilities with those of the general population.

intelligence testing – standardized tests to measure a person's intellectual capabilities or general cognitive functioning. These tests aim to assess various mental abilities, such as reasoning, problem-solving, memory, comprehension, and verbal and mathematical skills.

intermittent explosive disorder – a mental health condition characterized by sudden, intense outbursts of anger or aggression that are disproportionate to the situation. These outbursts may result in physical violence, property damage, or verbal aggression and typically occur without warning.

internal consistency – the degree to which different items within a test or questionnaire intended to measure the same construct produce consistent results. It is often assessed using statistics such as Cronbach's alpha, with higher values indicating greater item consistency.

intrusive thoughts – unwanted, involuntary thoughts, images, or impulses that can be disturbing or distressing. These thoughts often conflict with a person's values or desires and can be a symptom of conditions like anxiety, OCD, or PTSD.

involuntary commitment – a legal process by which a person with severe mental illness can be hospitalized and treated without their consent if they are deemed a danger to themselves or others or are unable to care for themselves.

item response theory (IRT) – a statistical framework used to analyze and model the relationship between individual responses to test items and their underlying traits or abilities. It helps to assess the quality of individual test items and improve the precision of measurements across different ability levels.

juvenile delinquency – illegal or antisocial behavior committed by individuals under the age of 18, often involving acts like theft, vandalism, or violence, and typically handled through the juvenile justice system rather than adult courts.

kleptomania – a compulsive disorder characterized by the irresistible urge to steal items, often with little or no personal use for them. People with kleptomania typically experience tension before stealing and relief or pleasure afterward, but the behavior is not driven by financial need.

language – The system of communication involving the use of words, symbols, and gestures to convey thoughts, ideas, emotions, and information.

language comprehension – the ability to understand spoken or written language.

latent psychological traits – unobservable characteristics or qualities, such as intelligence, personality, or anxiety, that influence behavior and are inferred through measurable indicators or test items. These traits cannot be directly seen but are estimated based on patterns of responses or behaviors.

law – a system of rules and guidelines created and enforced by social or governmental institutions to regulate behavior, maintain order, protect rights, and ensure justice within a society.

limbic system – a group of brain structures that regulate emotions, memory, and behavior. It includes the hippocampus, amygdala, and hypothalamus, which play key roles in emotional responses, motivation, and memory formation.

lithium – a chemical element used primarily in medicine to treat bipolar disorder, helping to stabilize mood swings.

lobotomy – an outdated surgical procedure that involves removing parts of the brain's frontal lobe to treat severe mental illness or neurological conditions.

localization of function – the idea that specific brain areas (or regions) are responsible for mental processes and behaviors.

long-term memory – the part of the brain that stores information for an extended period, ranging from hours to a lifetime.

machine learning – a branch of artificial intelligence that involves training algorithms to learn from and make predictions or decisions based on data without being explicitly programmed for each task. It is used in various fields, from image recognition to recommendation systems.

major depressive disorder – a mood disorder marked by persistent sadness, loss of interest, and symptoms like fatigue and changes in sleep and appetite, affecting daily life.

magnetic resonance imaging. (MRI) – a medical imaging technique that uses strong magnets and radio waves to create detailed images of organs and tissues, commonly used to examine the brain, spine, joints, and soft tissues.

magnetoencephalography (MEG) – a non-invasive brain imaging technique that measures the magnetic fields produced by neural activity, allowing researchers and doctors to map brain function with high temporal accuracy.

major neurocognitive disorder (MND) – a condition characterized by a significant decline in cognitive abilities, such as memory, reasoning, and problem-solving, that severely impacts daily functioning and independence.

male hypoactive sexual desire disorder – a condition characterized by a persistent lack of sexual desire or interest in sexual activity, causing distress or interpersonal difficulties. Psychological, hormonal, or relational factors can influence it.

malingering – the intentional act of exaggerating or fabricating symptoms of illness or injury for personal gain, such as avoiding work, obtaining financial compensation, or evading responsibilities.

mania – abnormally elevated mood, energy, and activity levels seen in individuals with bipolar disorder, particularly bipolar 1 disorder.

medical record review – the process of examining a patient's medical history, including diagnoses, treatments, medications, and test results, to assess the quality of care, ensure accurate documentation, or support clinical decision-making and legal matters.

medication-induced movement disorders – conditions caused by the side effects of certain medications, particularly antipsychotics, that result in abnormal movements. These may include tremors, rigidity, involuntary muscle contractions, and restlessness. Common types include tardive dyskinesia, akathisia, and parkinsonism.

medulla oblongata – the part of the brainstem responsible for regulating vital functions such as breathing, heart rate, and blood pressure.

memory – the cognitive ability to encode, store, and retrieve information over time, allowing individuals to recall past experiences, facts, and learned skills.

mental capacity – the capacity to understand and make informed decisions about one's actions, including the ability to reason, recall information, and engage in rational thought processes necessary for legal or personal decision-making.

memory recall – the process of retrieving stored information from memory. It involves accessing and bringing to mind specific details, events, or knowledge that were previously learned or experienced.

mental health law – legal rules that govern the rights, treatment, and care of individuals with mental health conditions. It addresses issues like involuntary commitment, patient rights, and the responsibilities of healthcare providers.

mental health stigma – negative attitudes, beliefs, or discrimination directed at individuals with mental health conditions.

mental state – an individual's current condition of mind, including their thoughts, emotions, perceptions, and level of awareness, which can influence behavior and cognitive functioning.

mental tests – standardized procedures or instruments designed to assess cognitive functions, psychological traits, or emotional states. They can assess a range of mental abilities, including intelligence, memory, attention, problem-solving, personality traits, and mental health conditions.

mild neurocognitive disorder (mild NCD) – a condition marked by a noticeable but not severe decline in cognitive abilities, such as memory or thinking skills, that does not significantly interfere with daily life or independence.

mild traumatic brain injury (mTBI) – a type of brain injury that results from a blow or jolt to the head. It is typically less severe than other forms of brain injury and is often referred to as a concussion.

mind-body dualism – the idea that the mind and body are separate, distinctive entities.

misdiagnosis – occurs when a medical professional incorrectly identifies a disease or condition, leading to inappropriate treatment or no treatment at all.

Model Penal Code (MPC) – a set of criminal law guidelines created by the American Law Institute to standardize and modernize the criminal justice system in the United States. It provides a framework for defining crimes, penalties, and defenses, with the goal of promoting consistency and fairness in criminal law across different states.

monoamine oxidase A (MAOA) – an enzyme that breaks down neurotransmitters like serotonin, dopamine, and norepinephrine in the brain. It helps regulate mood and emotional responses, and abnormal levels of MAOA have been linked to conditions like depression, anxiety, and certain personality disorders.

mood disorders – a group of mental health conditions primarily characterized by disturbances in a person's emotional state. They include conditions such as depression, bipolar disorder, and cyclothymic disorder. Symptoms may include extreme feelings of sadness, irritability, or an elevated mood, which can impact daily functioning.

mood reactivity – when a person feels better based on positive events.

moral culpability – the degree to which a person is responsible for wrongdoings or harmful actions based on their intentions, knowledge, and ability to choose between right and wrong. It involves assessing whether someone is morally accountable for their actions.

moral reasoning – the cognitive process through which individuals make decisions about what is right or wrong, fair or unfair, based on ethical principles, societal norms, and personal values. It reflects how people think about moral issues, not just what they believe.

motor cortex – the brain region responsible for controlling voluntary muscle movements. It is in the frontal lobe, specifically in the precentral gyrus.

multidimensional scaling (MDS) – a statistical technique used to visualize the similarities or dissimilarities between data points in a lower-dimensional space, typically two or three dimensions. It helps to represent complex data structures, such as perceptions or preferences, by mapping them to reflect the relative distances or relationships among items.

narcissistic personality disorder – a mental health condition characterized by an inflated sense of self-importance, a need for excessive admiration, and a lack of empathy for others. Individuals with NPD may have difficulty maintaining healthy relationships and may exhibit arrogance, entitlement, and a tendency to exploit others.

near-infrared spectroscopy (NIRS) – a non-invasive imaging technique that uses near-infrared light to measure blood oxygen levels in the brain, often used to monitor brain activity and oxygenation, especially in research and clinical settings.

neuroanatomy – the study of the structure of the nervous system.

neurobiology – the study of the biology of the nervous system, focusing on how the brain, neurons, and other neural structures function, develop, and interact. It explores how these processes influence behavior, cognition, and emotions.

neurocriminology – the study of the biological and neurological factors that may contribute to criminal behavior, using brain imaging and neuroscience to understand the roots of aggression, impulsivity, and antisocial actions.

neural coding – refers to the way in which information is represented and processed by the brain through patterns of neural activity. It involves how neurons encode sensory input, thoughts, memories, and behaviors, allowing the brain to interpret and respond to various stimuli.

neural communication – the process by which nerve cells (neurons) transmit signals to one another and other body parts using electrical impulses and chemical neurotransmitters.

neurodata – refers to data collected from the brain, typically through techniques like neuroimaging, electrophysiology, or brainwave monitoring, used to analyze brain activity, structure, and function for research or clinical purposes.

neurodegeneration – the progressive deterioration of nerve cells (neurons), leading to loss of function and, eventually, the death of those cells. It is associated with Alzheimer's disease, Parkinson's disease, and Huntington's disease.

neurodegenerative diseases – a group of disorders characterized by the progressive degeneration of nerve cells in the brain, leading to a decline in cognitive, motor, and functional abilities.

neuroethics – the study of the ethical, legal, and social implications of neuroscience, including issues related to brain research, mental privacy, cognitive enhancement, and the treatment of neurological and psychiatric conditions.

neurofeedback – a non-invasive method designed to train individuals to regulate their brain activity.

neurogenetics – the study of how genes influence the development and function of the nervous system. It explores the genetic basis of neurological disorders, brain development, and individual differences in behavior and cognition.

neurohistology – the study of the microscopic structure of nervous tissue. It involves examining cells and tissues of the nervous system, such as neurons and glial cells, to understand their organization, function, and role in health and disease.

neuroimmunology – the study of the interaction between the nervous system and the immune system. It examines how immune responses impact brain function and how the brain influences immune processes, playing a crucial role in conditions such as multiple sclerosis, autoimmune disorders, and neuroinflammation.

neuroinflammation – chronic inflammation in the brain.

neuroimaging – techniques, such as MRI, CT scans, and PET scans, are used to visualize the structure and function of the brain, often for the purpose of diagnosing brain disorders or injuries.

neurology – the branch of medicine focused on the diagnosis, treatment, and management of disorders affecting the nervous system, including the brain, spinal cord, peripheral nerves, and muscles. It encompasses a wide range of conditions, including neurological diseases, brain injuries, and neurological disorders that affect cognitive, motor, and emotional functions.

neurophysiology – the study of how the nervous system functions, such as regulating behavior, cognition, emotion, and bodily functions.

neuroplasticity – the brain's ability to reorganize and form new neural connections in response to learning, experience, or injury.

neurophysiology – the study of how the nervous system functions.

neuropsychology – the study of how brain, behavior, and socioemotional relationships and functions are affected by neurological conditions.

neuropsychological assessments – a set of tests designed to evaluate an individual's cognitive, emotional, and psychological functioning concerning brain activity, helping to identify the effects of brain injury, disease, or other neurological conditions.

neurostimulation – a technique that uses electrical or magnetic impulses to stimulate nerves or brain regions, often used to treat neurological and psychiatric conditions like chronic pain, depression, or Parkinson's disease.

neural pathways – networks of neurons that transmit signals between different parts of the brain and body, enabling communication and coordination of functions.

neuroleptic malignant syndrome (NMS) – a rare but potentially life-threatening reaction to antipsychotic medications. Symptoms include high fever, muscle rigidity, altered mental status, and autonomic dysfunction (such as rapid heart rate or blood pressure changes). It requires immediate medical attention and discontinuation of the antipsychotic medication.

neurorestorative therapies – treatments aimed at repairing or restoring function to the nervous system, particularly after injury or neurodegenerative diseases.

neuroscience – the scientific study of the structure, function, development, genetics, and pathology of the nervous system, including the brain, spinal cord, and peripheral nerves. It seeks to understand how neural circuits and processes influence behavior, cognition, and emotion.

neurotransmitters – chemical messengers that transmit signals across synapses between neurons, influencing mood, behavior, and various bodily functions. Examples include dopamine, serotonin, and glutamate.

non compos mentis – a Latin term meaning "not of sound mind." It refers to a person who is legally considered incapable of managing their own affairs or understanding the consequences of their actions due to mental illness or incapacity.

norepinephrine – a neurotransmitter and hormone involved in the body's "fight or flight" response, regulating alertness, arousal, mood, and stress. It plays a key role in attention, focus, and the body's reaction to stress.

objective personality tests – standardized assessments with structured questions and fixed responses designed to measure personality traits consistently and objectively.

obsessive-compulsive disorder – a mental health condition characterized by persistent, intrusive thoughts (obsessions) and repetitive behaviors or mental acts (compulsions) performed to reduce anxiety or prevent feared outcomes.

obsessive-compulsive personality disorder (OCPD) – a condition marked by a preoccupation with order, perfectionism, and control, often affecting daily life and relationships.

occipital lobe – the part of the brain primarily responsible for processing visual information.

oppositional defiant disorder (ODD) – a behavioral disorder in children and adolescents characterized by a pattern of defiant, argumentative, and hostile behaviors toward authority figures. Symptoms include frequent temper tantrums, irritability, and refusal to comply with rules or requests.

orbitofrontal cortex – a region in the frontal lobe involved in decision-making, emotion regulation, and evaluating rewards and risks.

orbital prefrontal cortex – a brain region (at the front of the frontal lobes) involved in decision-making, emotional regulation, and social behavior.

orientation – the ability to be aware of and correctly identify key aspects of one's environment, such as time, place, and person (self and others).

overmedication – refers to the excessive or unnecessary use of medications, often in higher doses or for longer periods than required. This can occur when medications are prescribed too frequently, when they are used for conditions that do not necessarily require them, or when they are continued for too long.

overpathologize – to interpret or treat normal behavior, emotions, or experiences as symptoms of a mental health disorder or medical condition when they are not. This can lead to an excessive focus on diagnosing or treating something that does not require intervention.

panic disorder – an anxiety disorder characterized by recurrent and unexpected panic attacks—sudden episodes of intense fear or discomfort, accompanied by physical symptoms like rapid heartbeat, sweating, and shortness of breath.

paraphilic disorders – mental health conditions characterized by intense and persistent sexual interests in atypical objects, situations, or individuals that cause distress or harm to oneself or others. Examples include voyeurism, exhibitionism, and pedophilia. These behaviors can lead to significant impairment in daily functioning and relationships.

parietal association cortex – a region in the parietal lobe involved in integrating sensory information from different parts of the body. It plays a crucial role in spatial awareness, attention, and coordinating movements in response to sensory input.

parietal lobe – the brain region responsible for processing sensory information such as touch, temperature, and pain, as well as spatial awareness and coordination.

parkinsonism – a group of neurological symptoms, including tremors, stiffness, and slow movement, often associated with Parkinson's disease but also caused by other conditions affecting the brain's motor control.

path analysis – a statistical method used to examine the relationships between multiple variables, testing direct and indirect effects. It helps model and quantify causal connections among variables based on hypothesized paths.

pathologize – to treat or describe something as a medical or psychological condition, often by attributing abnormal or unhealthy characteristics to behaviors, traits, or experiences that may not necessarily be pathological.

pathophysiology – the study of how diseases or injuries affect normal bodily functions. It explains the physical and biological changes that occur in the body as a result of a disease, helping to understand symptoms, progression, and potential treatments.

perceptual-motor function – the ability to coordinate sensory input (such as sight and sound) with physical movement, allowing individuals to perform tasks that require both perception and motor skills, like driving or playing sports.

perceptual reasoning – the ability to interpret and analyze visual information to solve problems or make decisions.

peripartum onset – a type of depression that occurs during pregnancy or following childbirth. It is also classified as a mood disorder.

perseveration – the repetitive or uncontrollable continuation of a particular thought, behavior, or response, often seen in individuals with brain injuries or neurological conditions, even when it is no longer appropriate or relevant to the situation.

persistent postconcussive syndrome – a condition in which concussion symptoms, such as headaches, dizziness, fatigue, and difficulty concentrating, continue for weeks or months after the initial injury. It affects a minority of individuals and may interfere with daily functioning and quality of life.

PFC-amygdala connectivity – refers to the interaction between the prefrontal cortex and amygdala, where the PFC helps regulate emotional responses generated by the amygdala.

phrenology – the study of a skull's shape to evaluate personality and mental traits; now considered a pseudoscience.

physiology – the study of how living organisms function, including the processes and mechanisms that occur within the body's cells, tissues, organs, and systems.

pica – an eating disorder characterized by the persistent consumption of non-food substances, such as dirt, paper, or chalk, that are not culturally or developmentally appropriate.

planning – the cognitive process of setting goals, determining the steps needed to achieve them, and organizing resources and actions in a logical sequence to accomplish tasks or solve problems.

plea bargaining – a negotiation in which a defendant agrees to plead guilty to a lesser charge or receive a reduced sentence to avoid a trial.

polygenic risk scores (PRS) – a way of predicting an individual's genetic risk for certain traits or diseases based on the combined effect of multiple genetic variations. These scores are calculated by analyzing numerous genetic markers across a person's genome that are linked to a specific condition or trait, such as heart disease, diabetes, or mental health disorders. The higher the score, the greater the genetic risk.

pons – a part of the brainstem that connects the cerebrum to the cerebellum and medulla, playing a key role in regulating sleep, breathing, and communication between different brain regions.

positron emission tomography (PET) – an imaging test that shows how organs and tissues are functioning by detecting radioactive tracers injected into the body, often used to detect cancer, brain disorders, and heart problems.

postconcussive syndrome (PCS) – a set of symptoms that persist after a mild traumatic brain injury (concussion). These can include headaches, dizziness, fatigue, difficulty concentrating, memory problems, and mood changes lasting for weeks or months after the injury.

postpartum depression – a type of depression that occurs following childbirth, marked by sadness, fatigue, and hopelessness.

posttraumatic stress disorder (PTSD) – a mental health condition triggered by experiencing or witnessing a traumatic event, characterized by symptoms like flashbacks, nightmares, severe anxiety, and emotional numbness.

predictive validity – the ability to forecast future outcomes.

prefrontal cortex (PFC) – part of the brain responsible for behavior, executive function, and personality.

prefrontal amygdala connectivity – the pathway between the prefrontal cortex and the amygdala, a brain region involved in emotional processing.

premature ejaculation - a sexual dysfunction in men characterized by ejaculation that occurs sooner than desired, often with minimal stimulation, and causes distress or relationship issues.

premotor cortex – a region of the frontal lobe located just in front of the primary motor cortex. It helps plan and organize movements, especially those guided by external cues, and is involved in coordinating posture and movement of multiple muscle groups.

primary auditory cortex – a region of the brain located in the temporal lobe, specifically in the superior temporal gyrus. It is responsible for processing sound information, including recognizing pitch, volume, and tone.

primary motor cortex – responsible for initiating and controlling voluntary movements of the body.

primary Somatosensory Cortex – responsible for processing sensory information from the body, such as touch, temperature, pain, and proprioception (the sense of body position).

primary visual cortex – responsible for processing visual information received from the eyes.

problem solving – the process of identifying a challenge, analyzing it, and finding a solution through logical thinking, creativity, and decision-making.

processing speed – the rate at which an individual can take in, interpret, and respond to information.

projective tests – psychological assessments where individuals respond to ambiguous stimuli, revealing unconscious thoughts and feelings.

prosopagnosia – a neurological condition characterized by the inability to recognize faces. Individuals with this disorder may struggle to recognize familiar faces, despite being able to identify other objects or features. It is often referred to as "face blindness."

psychiatry – the branch of medicine focused on the diagnosis, treatment, and prevention of mental health disorders, often involving medication, therapy, and other medical interventions.

psychoanalysis – developed by Sigmund Freud, a therapy modality used to examine the unconscious mind to address psychopathological conditions.

psychoanalytical theory – the process of using psychoanalysis, which is used for treating psychopathological conditions.

psychology – the scientific study of the mind and behavior, focusing on how people think, feel, and act, individually and in groups.

psychological model – a framework that explains human behavior, emotions, and mental processes. It helps in understanding and treating mental health conditions by focusing on various aspects, such as cognition, behavior, and emotions.

psychological tests – standardized assessments designed to measure various aspects of an individual's mental processes, behaviors, and abilities, such as intelligence, personality, and emotional functioning.

psychometrics – the science of measurement in psychology.

psychomotor retardation – slowness of physical movement and speech.

psychophysical measurement – the process of quantifying the relationship between physical stimuli and the sensations and perceptions they produce in a subject. It involves systematically varying a stimulus (such as brightness, sound intensity, or weight) and recording a person's responses to determine sensory thresholds, perceptual sensitivity, or how stimuli are subjectively perceived.

psychosurgery – surgical procedures used on specific brain regions to treat psychological symptoms or severe mental illness.

psychopathology – the study of mental disorders, including their symptoms, causes, and effects on behavior and functioning. It also refers to the manifestation of abnormal or dysfunctional behaviors and thoughts.

psychopathy – a personality disorder characterized by persistent antisocial behavior, lack of empathy or remorse, superficial charm, and a tendency to manipulate others.

psychosis – a condition marked by a loss of touch with reality, including hallucinations, delusions, and disordered thinking.

pyromania – a compulsive disorder characterized by an irresistible urge to start fires. People with pyromania experience tension or excitement before setting fires and feel pleasure or relief afterward. It is not driven by financial gain or political motives, but rather by the act of fire-setting itself.

quantitative reasoning – the ability to use numerical and mathematical concepts to analyze, interpret, and solve problems, including the ability to understand data, recognize patterns, and make logical inferences based on numerical information.

rapid eye movement (REM) – a stage of sleep characterized by quick, random movements of the eyes, increased brain activity, and vivid dreams.

Rasch Model – a specific form of item response theory (IRT) used to analyze data from tests and assessments. It models the probability of a correct response to an item based on the person's ability and difficulty, aiming to produce interval-level measurements and ensuring that the item's difficulty and ability are independent of the test sample.

reactive attachment disorder (RAD) – a condition in children, characterized by difficulty forming healthy emotional bonds with caregivers, typically due to early experiences of neglect or abuse. Children with RAD may show emotional withdrawal, difficulty trusting others, and problems with social interactions.

reliability – the consistency and stability of a measure or test over time, ensuring that results are repeatable and dependable across different situations or conditions.

response inhibition – the ability to suppress or control automatic or impulsive reactions, allowing for more deliberate, thought-out responses to situations or stimuli.

retrograde amnesia – a type of memory loss where individuals are unable to recall events or information that occurred before a specific point in time, typically following brain injury or trauma.

rumination disorder – an eating disorder where a person repeatedly regurgitates, re-chews, or re-swallows food after eating, not due to a medical condition. It often occurs in infants or individuals with developmental delays and can lead to malnutrition or weight loss.

schizophrenia – a severe mental disorder characterized by distorted thinking, hallucinations, delusions, and impaired functioning, affecting perception, emotions, and behavior.

schizophreniform disorder – a psychiatric condition with symptoms similar to schizophrenia, such as hallucinations, delusions, and disorganized thinking, but lasting at least one month and less than six months. It may resolve fully or develop into schizophrenia if symptoms persist.

seasonal affective disorder (SAD) – is a type of depression that occurs during a specific time of the year, particularly the winter season, due to reduced sunlight. It can cause symptoms such as low energy, sadness, and changes in appetite.

second impact syndrome – a rare but potentially fatal condition where a person sustains a second concussion before fully recovering from the first. This can lead to rapid brain swelling, loss of consciousness, and severe neurological damage. It most commonly occurs in athletes.

selective serotonin reuptake inhibitors (SSRIs) – a class of medications commonly used to treat depression, anxiety, and other mood disorders. They work by increasing the level of serotonin in the brain, a neurotransmitter that helps regulate mood, by preventing its reabsorption (i.e., reuptake) into nerve cells. Examples include fluoxetine (Prozac) and sertraline (Zoloft).

selective memory – refers to the tendency to remember certain events, details, or information while forgetting others. It can be influenced by factors like personal significance, emotions, or cognitive biases, and is often not a conscious process.

self-regulation – the ability to manage and control one's emotions, thoughts, and behaviors in response to internal and external demands, allowing for goal-directed actions, impulse control, and adaptation to changing circumstances.

sentencing – the legal process by which a judge determines the punishment for a convicted defendant based on factors like the severity of the crime, the defendant's history, and applicable laws.

serotonin – a neurotransmitter that regulates mood, emotion, sleep, appetite, and digestion. It is often linked to feelings of well-being and happiness.

short-term memory – the capacity to temporarily store and manage a limited amount of information for brief periods, typically ranging from seconds to minutes, before it is either discarded or transferred to long-term memory.

social anxiety disorder (SAD) – an anxiety condition marked by an intense fear of social situations, where individuals worry about being judged, embarrassed, or humiliated.

sociopathy – a personality disorder characterized by a disregard for social norms, impulsivity, and a lack of empathy or remorse. Unlike psychopathy, sociopathy is often linked to environmental factors, such as trauma or abuse, and tends to involve more erratic or impulsive behaviors.

social cognition – the ability to understand and interpret social interactions, including recognizing emotions, understanding social cues, and responding appropriately in different social situations.

social isolation – the state of being disconnected from social relationships and interactions, leading to a lack of meaningful social contact. It can negatively impact mental and physical health, increasing the risk of loneliness, depression, and other health issues.

somatic symptom disorder – a mental health condition characterized by excessive focus on physical symptoms, such as pain or fatigue, that cause significant distress or disruption in daily life. The symptoms may not have a clear medical cause, but the person is preoccupied with their health concerns.

somatization – the expression of psychological distress through physical symptoms, where a person experiences and reports bodily complaints without a clear medical cause.

somatotopically – refers to the organized mapping or representation of the body within the brain or nervous system. In a somatotopic organization, specific regions of the body are represented by distinct areas in the brain, especially in the primary motor cortex and somatosensory cortex. For example, the area of the brain that controls hand movement is adjacent to the area that controls finger movement, forming a continuous map of the body's movements and sensations.

somatosensory cortex – a brain region located in the parietal lobe, responsible for processing sensory information from the body, such as touch, temperature, pain, and proprioception (sense of body position).

Spearman-Brown prediction formula – a statistical formula used to estimate the reliability or consistency of a test after changes in its length. It is particularly useful when you want to predict how the reliability of a test will change if you increase or decrease the number of items on the test.

specific phobia – an anxiety disorder characterized by an intense, irrational fear of a specific object, situation, or activity, such as heights, spiders, or flying.

structural equation modeling (SEM) – a comprehensive statistical technique used to test and estimate relationships among multiple variables, both observed and latent. SEM combines factor analysis and path analysis to model complex causal relationships, allowing researchers to evaluate direct, indirect, and total effects within a system of variables.

structural neuroplasticity – refers to the brain's ability to physically change its structure in response to learning, experience, or injury. This includes the growth of new neurons, the formation of new connections (synapses), and changes in the strength or number of existing connections.

supplementary motor area (SMA) – is a region in the frontal lobe involved in planning and coordinating complex, voluntary movements, especially those that require both sides of the body. It helps prepare and execute movements, often internally generated.

substance use disorders (SUDs) – a condition characterized by the harmful or excessive use of substances like alcohol, drugs, or medications, leading to dependency, cravings, and negative impacts on health and daily life.

substantial capacity – a legal standard used in the insanity defense, stating that a person is not criminally responsible if, due to a mental illness or defect, they lacked the substantial capacity to understand the wrongfulness of their actions or to conform their behavior to the law. It is part of the Model Penal Code test.

sulcus – a groove or furrow within the brain, typically found on its surface or other organs, that separates different regions and structures. It also divides the cerebral cortex into lobes. The plural word is *sulci*.

symptom validity tests – assessments designed to evaluate the accuracy and consistency of reported symptoms, helping to determine whether an individual is genuinely experiencing them or possibly exaggerating or feigning them.

tardive dyskinesia (TD) – a movement disorder caused by long-term use of antipsychotic medications, leading to involuntary, repetitive movements, often in the face and limbs.

tau protein – a protein that helps stabilize microtubules in neurons. When tau becomes abnormally tangled, it can disrupt cell function and lead to neurodegenerative diseases like Alzheimer's disease and other tauopathies.

teleneurology – the use of telemedicine technology to diagnose, treat, and manage neurological conditions remotely. It enables patients to consult with neurologists via video calls or other digital platforms, thereby improving access to care, particularly in underserved areas.

temporal lobe – the brain region located on the sides, responsible for processing auditory information, memory, language, and emotion. It contains structures like the hippocampus and amygdala.

test-retest reliability – the consistency of test scores when the same test is administered to the same individuals at different points in time. High test-retest reliability indicates that the test produces stable and repeatable results over time.

thalamus – a structure in the brain that acts as a relay station, transmitting sensory and motor signals to the appropriate areas of the cerebral cortex. It plays a key role in regulating consciousness, sleep, and alertness.

theory of equipotentiality – the concept that when one part of the brain is damaged, other parts can compensate for its lost function, allowing the brain to adapt and maintain its abilities.

theory of mind – the ability to attribute mental states to oneself and others.

transcranial magnetic stimulation (TMS) – a non-invasive procedure that uses magnetic fields to stimulate specific areas of the brain. It is commonly used to treat conditions like depression and is also used in research to study brain function.

trauma – a physical or emotional injury caused by a distressing event or experience, which can lead to lasting psychological or physiological effects.

traumatic brain injury (TBI) – a brain injury caused by an external force, such as a blow to the head, resulting in damage to brain tissue.

trauma-focused cognitive behavioral therapy (TF-CBT) – a form of therapy designed to help individuals, particularly children and adolescents, cope with the emotional and psychological effects of trauma. It combines cognitive-behavioral techniques with trauma-sensitive principles to address negative thoughts, feelings, and behaviors related to traumatic experiences.

trepanation – a surgical procedure where a hole is drilled into the skull, an intervention used for relieving pressure, treating brain injuries, and other medical procedures.

trichotillomania – a mental health disorder characterized by the irresistible urge to pull out one's own hair, leading to noticeable hair loss. It is considered a type of obsessive-compulsive and related disorder, and individuals may pull hair from areas such as the scalp, eyebrows, or eyelashes.

validity – the extent to which a test or measure accurately assesses its intended measure, ensuring that the results are meaningful and reflect the true characteristics being evaluated.

vascular dementia – a type of dementia caused by reduced blood flow to the brain, leading to cognitive decline. It can result from strokes or other conditions that damage blood vessels, affecting memory, thinking, and the ability to perform daily activities.

vascular diseases – conditions that affect the blood vessels, including arteries, veins, and capillaries. These diseases can lead to poor circulation, blood clots, or damage to blood vessels, and include conditions like hypertension, atherosclerosis, stroke, and peripheral artery disease.

ventral striatum – the brain region involved in reward, motivation, and reinforcing pleasurable behaviors.

ventricles – fluid-filled cavities in the brain that produce and store cerebrospinal fluid (CSF), cushion, and protect the brain and spinal cord.

ventromedial prefrontal cortex (vmPFC) – a brain region involved in decision-making, emotional regulation, and social behavior. It helps assess risks and rewards, guiding choices based on emotions and past experiences. It is also linked to self-control and moral reasoning.

verbal comprehension – the ability to understand, interpret, and use language to process information and solve problems.

verbal fluency – the ability to produce words quickly and efficiently, often measured by tasks that require generating words within a specific category or starting with a particular letter, assessing both language production and cognitive processing speed.

virtual reality (VR) – a technology that creates immersive, interactive environments using computer-generated simulations, often experienced through a headset. It is used in gaming, training, therapy, education, and research to simulate real-world or imagined experiences.

virtual reality therapy – a treatment method that uses immersive virtual environments to simulate real-life scenarios for therapeutic purposes. It is used to treat conditions such as anxiety, PTSD, phobias, and cognitive or motor impairments by providing controlled, interactive experiences.

visceral – refers to something deeply felt or instinctive, often raw, emotional, or physical. It can also relate to the internal organs of the body.

visual-spatial processing – the ability to perceive, interpret, and organize visual information about the spatial relationships between objects. It allows individuals to understand how objects are positioned in space and how they relate to one another.

volitional impairment – a condition where a person's ability to control their actions or behavior is significantly compromised, often due to mental illness or disorder, making it difficult for them to act according to their own will.

Wernicke's area – a region in the brain's left temporal lobe, primarily responsible for language comprehension. Damage to this area can result in Wernicke's aphasia, where individuals may speak fluently but struggle to understand language or produce meaningful speech.

Wernicke's aphasia – a language disorder caused by damage to Wernicke's area, characterized by fluent but meaningless speech and difficulty understanding spoken or written language. Individuals may not be aware of their language deficits.

white matter – brain tissue made up of myelinated nerve fibers that transmit signals between brain regions and the body.

working memory – the capacity to retain and manipulate information temporarily in the mind.

Legal Frameworks and Key Cases that Influence Forensic Neuropsychopathology

- *Ake v. Oklahoma* (1985)
- *Durham v. United States* (1954)
- *Frye v. United States* (1923)
- *Case of John W. Hinckley* (1981)
- *Case of Phineas Gage* (1848)
- The Durham Rule (Durham v. United States, 1954)
- *Atkins v. Virginia* (2002)
- *Roper v. Simmons* (2005)
- The McNaughten Rule (1843)
- *Jaffee v. Redmond* (1996)
- The Daubert Standard (Daubert v. Merrell Dow Pharmaceuticals, 1993)
- *Miller v. Alabama* (2012)
- Americans with Disabilities Act (ADA)
- The Eighth Amendment (Cruel and Unusual Punishment)
- The Trial of Anders Breivik (2012)
- The Trial of Jared Loughner (2012)
- The American Law Institute's Model Penal Code (MPC) § 4.01
- The Due Process Clause of the 14th Amendment

Suggested Readings and Resources for Further Study

- *APA Handbook of Neuropsychology Volume 1: Neurobehavioral Disorders and Conditions by the American Psychological Association*
- *APA Handbook of Neuropsychology Volume 2: Neuroscience and Neuromethods by the American Psychological Association*
- *Brain Development and the Law: Neurolaw in Theory and Practice* by Stephan Schleim
- *Clinical Practice of Forensic Neuropsychology* by Kyle Brauer Boone
- *Criminal Behavior: A Psychological Approach* by Curt R. Bartol and Anne M. Bartol
- *Current Perspectives in Forensic Psychology and Criminal Behavior* by Curt R. Bartol and Anne M. Bartol
- *The Memory Illusion: Remembering, Forgetting, and the Science of False Memory* by Dr. Julia Shaw
- *The Psychopath Inside: A Neuroscientist's Personal Journey into the Dark Side of the Brain* by Dr. James Fallon
- *Trials of a Forensic Psychologist: A Casebook* by Charles Patrick Ewin

www.ingramcontent.com/pod-product-compliance
Lightning Source LLC
Chambersburg PA
CBHW041929260326
41914CB00009B/1228

9781966903468